New Directions in Helping

Volume 1
RECIPIENT REACTIONS TO AID

New Directions in Helping

Volume 1

RECIPIENT REACTIONS TO AID

EDITED BY

Jeffrey D. Fisher
Department of Psychology
University of Connecticut
Storrs, Connecticut

Arie Nadler
Department of Psychology
Tel Aviv University
Ramat Aviv, Israel

Bella M. DePaulo
Department of Psychology
University of Virginia
Charlottesville, Virginia

1983

ACADEMIC PRESS

A Subsidiary of Harcourt Brace Jovanovich, Publishers

New York   London
Paris   San Diego   San Francisco   São Paulo   Sydney   Tokyo   Toronto

to Rae and Charles Blank,
Esther and Dov Grinstein,
and Joseph and Blanche Sacco

ACADEMIC PRESS, INC.
111 Fifth Avenue, New York, New York 10003

United Kingdom Edition published by
ACADEMIC PRESS, INC. (LONDON) LTD.
24/28 Oval Road, London NW1 7DX

Library of Congress Cataloging in Publication Data

Main entry under title:

New directions in helping.

   Bibliography: v. 1, p.
   Includes index.
   Contents: v. 1. Recipient reactions to aid.
1. Public welfare--United States. 2. Welfare
recipients--United States--Attitudes. 3. Social
psychology--United States. I. Fisher, Jeffrey D.
II. Nadler, Arie. III. DePaulo, Bella M.
HV95.N45 1983   361.6'0973   82-24414
ISBN 0-12-257301-3 (v.1)

PRINTED IN THE UNITED STATES OF AMERICA

83 84 85 86   9 8 7 6 5 4 3 2 1

Contents

PART I   INTRODUCTION

1. Recipient Reactions to Aid: The Parameters of the Field

JEFFREY D. FISHER

PART II   THEORETICAL PERSPECTIVES

6. Social Construction of Helping Relationships

KENNETH J. GERGEN AND MARY M. GERGEN

PART III   INDIVIDUAL DIFFERENCES

7. Recipient Self-esteem and Reactions to Help

ARIE NADLER AND OFRA MAYSELESS

8. Developmental Aspects of Recipients' Reactions to Aid

NANCY EISENBERG

PART IV   DETERMINANTS OF REACTIONS TO AID

PART V SUMMARY AND IMPLICATIONS

13. Some Thoughts about Research on Reactions to Help

LEONARD BERKOWITZ

Contributors

Numbers in parentheses indicate the pages on which the authors' contributions begin.

LEONARD BERKOWITZ (335), Department of Psychology, University of Wisconsin, Madison, Wisconsin 53706

PHILIP BRICKMAN[1] (17), Institute for Social Research, University of Michigan, Ann Arbor, Michigan 48106

PAMELA L. BROWN (223), Psychology Department, University of Virginia, Charlottesville, Virginia 22903

MARGARET S. CLARK (281), Department of Psychology, Carnegie–Mellon University, Schenley Park, Pittsburgh, Pennsylvania 15213

DAN COATES (17, 251), Department of Psychology, University of Wisconsin, Madison, Wisconsin 53706

ELLEN COHN (17), Department of Psychology, University of New Hampshire, Durham, New Hampshire 03824

BELLA M. DEPAULO (223), Department of Psychology, University of Virginia, Charlottesville, Virginia 22903

NANCY EISENBERG (189), Department of Psychology, Arizona State University, Tempe, Arizona 85281

[1] Deceased.

MARLOWE C. EMBREE[2] (251), Department of Psychology, University of Wisconsin, Madison, Wisconsin 53706

JEFFREY D. FISHER (3, 51), Department of Psychology, University of Connecticut, Storrs, Connecticut 06268

KENNETH J. GERGEN (143), Department of Psychology, Swarthmore College, Swarthmore, Pennsylvania 19801

MARY M. GERGEN (143), Department of Psychology, Swarthmore College, Swarthmore, Pennsylvania 19801

MARTIN S. GREENBERG (85), Department of Psychology, University of Pittsburgh, Pittsburgh, Pennsylvania 15260

JAMES M. GREENBERG[3] (223), Department of Psychology, University of Virginia, Charlottesville, Virginia 22901

ELAINE HATFIELD (113), Department of Psychology, University of Hawaii at Manoa, Honolulu, Hawaii 96822

JURGIS KARUZA (17), Department of Psychology, State University College at Buffalo, Buffalo, New York 14222

LOUISE H. KIDDER (17), Department of Psychology, Temple University, Philadelphia, Pennsylvania 19122

OFRA MAYSELESS (167), Department of Psychology, Tel Aviv University, Ramat Aviv, Tel Aviv, Israel 69978

STANLEY J. MORSE (305), Laboratory of Architecture and Planning, Massachusetts Institute of Technology, Cambridge, Massachusetts 02139

ARIE NADLER (51, 167), Department of Psychology, Tel Aviv University, Ramat Aviv, Tel Aviv, Israel 69978

VITA RABINOWITZ (17), Department of Psychology, Hunter College, New York, New York 10021

GARY J. RENZAGLIA (251), University Counseling Service, University of Wisconsin, Madison, Wisconsin 53706

SUSAN SPRECHER (113), Department of Sociology, University of Wisconsin, Madison, Wisconsin 53706

DAVID R. WESTCOTT (85), Department of Psychology, University of Pittsburgh, Pittsburgh, Pennsylvania 15260

SHERYLE WHITCHER-ALAGNA (51), Uniformed Services University of the Health Sciences, Department of Defense, Bethesda, Maryland 20014

---

[2] Present address: Department of Psychology, University of Wisconsin-Marathon County, Wausau, Wisconsin 54401.

[3] Present address: Catholic University of America, Washington, D.C. 20064.

Preface

A great deal of research has emerged in recent years that furthers our understanding of the reactions of recipients in helping interactions. Some of this work has been more conceptual in nature; other efforts have been more empirical. Although much of the research was done within the social psychological tradition with the explicit goal of furthering our understanding of reactions to aid, equally relevant work has been done in other areas of psychology with the initial goal of addressing other issues. It is the purpose of this book to provide reasonably comprehensive, eclectic, "state of the art" coverage of this emerging (and hopefully, converging) body of literature. We hope that this volume will stimulate interest in what we consider to be an important area of study.

To date, there has been no attempt to provide systematic coverage of work on recipient reactions to aid. There are a few extant review papers, but nothing of the present scope. One section of this book focuses on theoretical perspectives for conceptualizing reactions to help, a second on individual differences in responses to aid, and a third on various determinants of reactions to help. Each contains original work by some of the most experienced researchers in the field.

This book provides an overview of the entire field, in-depth coverage in many major areas, and a preview of important future research directions. We believe it will be of interest to social psychologists as well as to members of a number of other disciplines (e.g., clinical psychologists, social workers, counseling psychologists, educational psychologists, political scientists, and sociologists). A companion volume, *New Directions in Helping,* Volume 2: *Help-Seeking* (DePaulo, Nadler, and Fisher, in press), focuses on an area intimately related to reactions to aid. Moreover, we are editing Volume 3 in the series, subtitled *Applied Perspectives on Help-Seeking and -Receiving* (Nadler, Fisher, and DePaulo, in press), which may also be of interest to readers of the present volume.

Any volume of this type places its editors in a state of indebtedness to many people and organizations. We gratefully acknowledge the secretarial assistance of Allison Fontaine, Kathleen Buttell, and Lauren Nathan. Our work was greatly facilitated by grants from the U.S.–Israel Binational Science Foundation, the Israeli Academy of Sciences, the National Institute of Mental Health, the University of Connecticut Research Foundation and the Foundation for Child Development.

This book is dedicated to six people who generously gave us their love and support and enriched our lives: Rae and Charles Blank, Esther and Dov Grinstein, and Joseph and Blanche Sacco.

Contents of Volumes 2 and 3

PART I

Introduction

CHAPTER 1

Recipient Reactions to Aid: The Parameters of the Field

Jeffrey D. Fisher

Spurred by the Kitty Genovese incident and other sociopolitical aspects of the 1960s, the past 20 years have seen an explosion of research on helping behavior. Most of this work has tried to identify situational and personality factors that elicit prosocial acts—a focus that at first blush seems eminently reasonable. To date, a dominant theme in the prosocial behavior literature is reflected in the title of Latané and Darley's (1970) book *The Unresponsive Bystander: Why Doesn't He Help?* By contrast, a subtitle for this book could be *The Ungrateful Recipient: Why Doesn't He or She Respond More Favorably to Aid?*

Research on help-giving reflects the dominant belief in our culture that helping others is a good thing that should be encouraged. However, one can probably recall many contexts in which being helped is anything but good. In both interpersonal and international relations there are many examples of recipients "biting the hand that feeds them." Pleasant events do not usually occasion such responses. Most social psychological research has overlooked the potential costs involved in receiving help, and has assumed that the benefits warrant research aimed uncritically at promoting help-giving. In this sense, the topic of recipient reaction to aid is, as the title of this volume implies, a new direction in helping.

Work on reactions to aid is still in its infancy, yet we feel that an important body of theory and research has emerged. Thus far, a number of theoretical perspectives have been articulated for conceptualizing how recipients respond to help. Most of these perspectives are discussed in some detail in this volume. An impressive body of research—some of which is guided by these conceptualizations, some by others, and some of which is atheoretical—is also contained herein.

Why was the area of reactions to aid neglected for so long? One reason is the naive belief that helping relationships should be encouraged uniformly as a palliative for those in need, an assumption that reflects the liberal tradition in Western culture (Gergen, 1974). If one could direct sufficient resources and good intentions to the needy, surely their problems would be solved. We have found that this is not necessarily true. The fact that for many years applied work in social psychology had a bad name also contributed to our benign neglect of reactions to aid. Even so, work in this area need not be entirely applied—some of the best work has had both conceptual and applied implications. Another reason has been the strong disinterest in this phenomenon by the federal, state, and local levels of government. Although one might expect support for research from these quarters, very little has been forthcoming. A rather pessimistic possibility is that few of us—academicians, government officials, and citizens alike—care much about the plight of the recipient. Perhaps even those of us who help often do so due to ulterior motives, caring more about our own outcomes than those of the recipient.

Just because reactions to help have been understudied does not mean they are not important. Help is often a positive interpersonal act, but one with complex properties that cause recipients to respond to it either favorably or unfavorably. Because everyone plays the role of aid recipient at some time on some level, and because vast resources are apportioned to helping relationships that are often characterized by reactions that are less than satisfactory, the way in which aid-related factors affect responses to help represents an important area of investigation. Reactions to aid often comprise an intense psychological experience in which affect, cognition, and behavior are closely intertwined. Because responses to help may be significant events in social life, understanding them helps fill a meaningful gap in our understanding of human social interaction.

Research on reactions to aid may also add to our knowledge of other areas of social psychology. It can involve an impactful experimental context which is ideal to test predictions generated by theories central to the field (e.g., equity, reactance, attribution, and social comparison formulations). These tests can be made in traditional experiments, in rich laboratory settings (e.g., simulations), and in the real world (e.g., with welfare recipients, hospitalized patients, and tutees). Also, people's reactions to help cover the gamut of topics in social psychology—from aggression and attraction to reciprocity, with points in between. Furthermore, the literature on person perception, learned helplessness, attitude formation and change, sex differences, prejudice and discrimination, groups, impression management, and morality—to name but a few areas—is important in making predictions and understanding effects, and is enriched by the data obtained.

In a fundamental way, even to have a more complete understanding of help-giving, we need to know much more about responses to help. For example, reinforcement for past helping affects the likelihood of subsequent prosocial acts (e.g., Moss & Page, 1972). Recipient reactions to aid could be an important source of differential reinforcement to donors, and thus could be an important determinant of subsequent help-giving. Unfortunately, some of the same conditions that make us most apt to help (e.g., having high resources, being similar to the recipient) may elicit negative recipient reactions and negative reinforcement for our act, and may inhibit further helping (Fisher, Nadler, & Whitcher-Alagna, 1982). Other ways in which studying reactions to help informs us about help-giving abound. In continuing relationships, giving or not giving aid to another in need may constitute a positive or negative reaction to aid received from them previously. Also, fear of negative recipient reactions (e.g., damaging the beneficiary's self-esteem) may sometimes prevent us from giving help. Often, then, applying knowledge about reactions to aid can be useful in attempts to understand why help is or is not given.

In addition to its potential for enriching social psychology as traditionally conceived, work on reactions to aid can also have practical implications. Typically, help is given with some applied end in mind (e.g., to improve the recipient's performance—see the chapter by DePaulo, Brown, & Greenberg in this volume), and research on reactions to aid can help us to ensure that such ends are realized. Unfortunately, many helping interactions have been broadly institutionalized (e.g., welfare, peer tutoring, aid from computers) without adequate applied research on recipient responses. In many professions (e.g., medicine, policework) the major part of the practitioner's job involves helping. Yet, in these settings as well, research is just beginning to emerge (Nadler, Fisher, & DePaulo, in press.) This type of practical work can often serve humanitarian ends, and in some contexts (e.g., help to rape victims) a little good research could go a long way. If the needy are, in fact, needy, they need helpful and not hurtful aid.

THE BASIC PARADIGM

Past research has measured the effects of situational conditions associated with aid, and the effect of recipient characteristics on recipient responses. The organization of this book reflects this approach, with one major section devoted to the effects of various situational conditions and another focused on the effects of recipient characteristics. Situational conditions include *donor characteristics* (e.g., behaviors and attributes of the donor as perceived by the recipient), *aid characteristics* (e.g., the cost of help to the donor), and *context characteristics* of the aid transaction (e.g., recipient ability to repay the donor). *Recipient characteristics* include stable dispositions or skills, and temporary emotional or cognitive states (Gergen, 1974). Typical experiments explore the effects of varying single factors from one or at most two of these categories. More complex, interactive designs have been relatively rare, but could make a useful contribution to our understanding of donor–recipient interactions.

It should be noted that studies focus on a narrow spectrum of the potentially wide range of aid characteristics that subjects can react to. Aid can consist of money, information, goods, services, status, enhancement of self-esteem, tactile stimulation, etc., yet we have primarily studied responses to material or informational aid. The range of problems for which aid can be given is also almost unlimited. Yet most studies have dealt with reactions to aid for impersonal difficulties (e.g., intellectual tasks). Much of the aid studied has been either of trivial, low, or moderate importance to the recipient. Relatively few studies have considered reactions to help that meets very important or life-sustaining ends. However, increasing attention is now being directed to studying reactions to aid in medical and psychological settings, among others (see Nadler, *et al.,* in press).

Recipient reactions can be classified into three types: *external perceptions* (e.g., evaluations of the donor and the aid), *internal perceptions* (e.g., self-evaluations), and *behavioral responses* (e.g., reciprocity, task performance). Overall, of the broad range of potential reactions to aid, relatively few have been studied. Even within the categories that have received attention, many reactions are relatively unresearched (e.g., whether help fosters future dependency). Such responses may be important and should receive greater study in the future.

THE FINDINGS: A CAPSULE SUMMARY

There are some consistent relationships between the conditions associated with aid (i.e., donor, aid, recipient, and context characteristics), and recipient reactions. Several brief examples of the sorts of patterns which have emerged may prove useful to some readers.

Often, people seem to respond better to help when donor characteristics are positive (e.g., the donor is an ally, someone they respect) than when help is offered by those with negative qualities. The former type of benefactor tends to elicit more favorable evaluations of the donor and the aid, greater feelings of obligation, and increased reciprocity (Fisher, DePaulo, & Nadler, 1981). Also, Clark (this volume) has found that when the donor is someone with whom the recipient desires to have a communal (close) relationship, reactions to aid differ from when the donor is one with whom an exchange (businesslike) relationship is desired.

Positive reactions also occur when aid characteristics are favorable (e.g., it represents a large amount of help, is of high quality, or is appropriate to one's needs). When aid characteristics make help costly for the recipient (e.g., when it restricts important behavioral freedoms, or decreases one's rewards for successful outcomes), aid elicits more negative responses. For detailed coverage of aid characteristics which affect the recipient's rewards and costs, see Morse's chapter, as well as others in this book.

Characteristics of the recipient also affect responses to help. For example, high persistent self-esteem may predispose recipients to respond more negatively to aid. This finding is reviewed in the chapter by Nadler and Mayseless, and Eisenberg discusses developmental determinants of reactions to aid in her chapter. Finally, context characteristics surrounding the aid transaction (e.g., whether help can be reciprocated, whether the recipient can remain anonymous) determine how recipients react. For example, when help can be reciprocated, it elicits more positive reactions than when it cannot be (see the chapters by Greenberg & Westcott and Hatfield & Sprecher in this volume). How other context characteristics affect reactions to help is discussed in Morse's chapter.

From this brief summary, it is clear that aid-related conditions exert important influences on recipient reactions, which run the gamut from highly favorable to quite unfavorable. Much more detailed coverage of these relations is provided in relevant chapters.

CONCEPTUAL APPROACHES

A number of approaches have been used to conceptualize the effects of aid on those who receive it, although many studies have been atheoretical. A major section of this book is devoted to some of the primary theoretical approaches. These include equity and indebtedness theories (see

Greenberg & Westcott, this volume; Hatfield & Sprecher, this volume), and reactance, attribution, and threat to self-esteem theories (see Fisher, Nadler, & Whitcher-Alagna, this volume). Most of these perspectives have been "borrowed" from other areas of social psychology, and adapted by researchers to the present context. For introductory purposes, we will discuss each of these conceptual approaches briefly (and necessarily somewhat incompletely); for more thorough coverage, see the relevant chapters in this book. Other conceptual approaches (e.g., self-presentation [Baumeister, 1982]; learned helplessness [Wortman & Brehm, 1975]) are also becoming increasingly important. (Some implications of learned helplessness theory for reactions to aid are discussed in the chapter by Coates, Embree & Renzaglia.)

Equity theories (e.g., Adams, 1963; Blau, 1964; Gouldner, 1960; Greenberg & Westcott, this volume; Homans, 1961; Hatfield & Sprecher, this volume) suggest that the critical variable determining reactions to help is a recipient's perception of the degree of inequity between himself or herself and the donor.[1] Inequity is an aversive state, experienced when one party in a relationship has a more favorable ratio of outcomes to inputs than the other. Perceived inequity (or indebtedness) associated with help is a function both of the objective value of aid, and of other situational conditions associated with it (e.g., whether help is accidental or intentional, or whether help represents a high or low cost to the donor). For example, when a unit of help is intentional rather than accidental, or is costly for the donor to convey, perceived inequity is greater because the donor is viewed as having made more of a sacrifice (Walster, Berscheid, & Walster 1973). Recipients may alleviate uncomfortable feelings of inequity by reciprocating to the donor in equal measure—a restoration of actual equity. If this is not possible, they try to restore psychological equity, often by derogating the donor and/or the aid.

Reactance theory (Brehm, 1966; Brehm & Brehm, 1981) suggests that responses to help are determined primarily by how much recipients believe that aid restricts their freedom. People prefer to maximize their freedom of choice, and any perceived reduction of freedom arouses a motivational state (reactance) characterized by negative feelings and directed toward reestablishing the lost freedoms. For example, to the extent that help limits

---

[1]Although the concepts of inequity and indebtedness are not entirely congruent (see the chapters by Hatfield & Sprecher and by Greenberg & Westcott, both in this volume, for a discussion of their similarities and differences), their general predictions concerning reactions to help are often quite similar. Therefore, in this introductory chapter we will use the terms inequity and indebtedness interchangeably.

the recipient's present or future actions (e.g., because he or she will have to act kindly toward the benefactor), it will arouse reactance. Recipients can reduce their negative feelings by acting as though their behavior has *not* been restricted by help (e.g., by avoiding any actions based on perceived obligation toward the donor, and/or by derogating the source of the threat).

Other studies have employed *attribution theories* (Jones & Davis, 1965; Kelley, 1967) to conceptualize reactions to help. These may be used to predict when recipients will (a) make attributions of the donor's motives for giving help (theory of correspondent inference), and (b) make internal or external attributions for their own need for aid (theory of external attribution). The preconditions necessary for making attributions according to these two theories are described in detail elsewhere (e.g., Jones & Davis, 1965; Kelley, 1967). Beyond predicting when attributions will be made for a prosocial act, the theories provide no explicit conceptual links between these and other recipient responses. However, based on past research, it seems that people respond more favorably to help when they make positive attributions of donor motivation and can attribute their need-state externally (see Fisher *et al.,* this volume).

· A final set of studies have employed *threat to self-esteem* models (e.g., Fisher *et al.,* 1982; this volume; Gergen & Gergen, 1974) for prediction. These posit that the self-related consequences of aid (i.e., the effects on self- concept of receiving help) are critical in determining how one responds. They assume that aid potentially contains a mixture of self-supportive elements (e.g., instrumental value, evidence of caring and concern), as well as self-threatening ones (e.g., evidence of failure, inferiority, and dependency). Specific aspects of the helping context (i.e., the extent to which it highlights one set of elements over the other) determine whether help is primarily a supportive or a threatening experience. To the extent that it is supportive, a cluster of essentially positive responses (e.g., favorable evaluations of the donor and the aid, high acceptance of help) occur. To the extent that it is self-threatening, a cluster of essentially negative reactions (e.g., unfavorable donor and aid evaluations, high refusal of aid) are evidenced. High self-help as an alternative to continued dependency occurs when aid is threatening, whereas help that is supportive tends to foster greater long-term dependency.

Each of these models makes a contribution to understanding the phenomenon of reactions to aid. Each is probably more adequate in some contexts than in others, and there may be some formulations which have greater predictive validity than others (see the chapter by Fisher *et al.,* this volume). No formulation is entirely adequate—none can relate the broad range of potential aid contexts to the entire array of potential recipient responses.

And the fact that there are several formulations, although adding a rich conceptual backdrop, also makes predictions variable and complex.

Although the current crop of theories have served us rather well, they have not been entirely satisfactory. Those that are borrowed from other domains may not be well-enough articulated to the phenomenon of reactions to aid. As in any context in which the problem area is defined in advance of the theoretical concepts that are employed, there can be difficulties. There are also other goals for theory development. Most of the extant notions are static as opposed to dynamic. We need formulations that can conceptualize the interactive and progressive (process) characteristics of the donor–recipient relationship (e.g., how do the recipient's reactions to the donor's aid affect the donor's subsequent reactions to the recipient, and so on?). We also need theories that take helping networks into account, and we need models that allow us to transform data on help-seeking into hypotheses about reactions to aid and vice versa (e.g., when does high or low help-seeking imply favorable or unfavorable reactions to aid?) It is hoped that future work will involve further advances at the conceptual level.

RESEARCH NEEDS

The extant research forms a good foundation for the study of reactions to help. As editors, we have been impressed with the caliber of the contributions to our volumes, many of which represent substantial additions to the literature. Even now there are some aspects of help-receiving about which we know a great deal. But there is additional work to be done before a fuller understanding of the aid recipient can be achieved.

One goal of future research should be to map out the settings where consequential reactions to aid occur—to define "where the action is." What types of favorable and unfavorable responses are most common, and in what contexts are they present? To what types of everyday aid do people react most positively and negatively, and why? It is possible that we have been directing our attention to such a narrow range of aid contexts that we are missing many of the most common and perhaps most important reactions to help (e.g., reactions to aid from parents to children and vice versa; and between spouses). Finding out where the action really is would also involve studying when and how donors typically give help in various settings, what types of helping occur most often, how interested the donor really is in the recipient's well-being, and what implications all of this has for recipient reactions to help.

Other questions that could be asked involve how reactions to aid evolve over time (e.g., with developing relationships); the effects of different types of aid (e.g., affection versus money, aid given for trivial versus life-threatening needs) on various recipient reactions; and the difference between receiving help voluntarily and involuntarily (e.g., being committed to a mental institution for help versus voluntarily committing oneself, or seeking a peer tutor voluntarily versus being directed to by a teacher). The complex interactive relationships between various donor, aid, recipient, and context characteristics also need to be explored. Research could focus on crossing different donor and recipient characteristics to determine the optimal donor–recipient "fit," and on crossing different recipient characteristics with various types of aid. Aspects of some of these issues have been addressed conceptually by Brickman, Rabinowitz, Karuza, Coates, Cohn, & Kidder (1982).

Future research should also focus more on individual differences as they affect reactions to aid. The chapters by Nadler and Mayseless and by Eisenberg in this volume make a good start in this direction. It is also important for us to know more about the reasons why people develop the attitudes they do toward receiving help. Fisher et al. (this volume) suggest that internalization of Protestant ethic values in Western cultures is important in this regard. A thorough investigation of this question would involve exploring cross-cultural, developmental, and socialization-related differences.

We should also study a broader range of recipient reactions to aid. The chapter by DePaulo et al. focuses on how receiving aid affects subsequent performance, an important response that has been heretofore neglected. And Clark goes beyond studying how aid influences initial attraction to focus on aid's consequences for the quality of deep relationships. A major—though too infrequently considered—reaction to help is learned helplessness, which is discussed in the chapter by Coates et al. Other reactions that would be interesting to study include how help affects one's feelings toward the task during which help occurs, and whether recipients subsequently choose to perform or to avoid the task. Also, when do recipients respond to help by becoming socially alienated, or by engaging in dishonest practices?

To date, the modal social psychological experiment on reactions to help has been of the traditional laboratory variety. This type of research has proved very useful for understanding many aspects of the phenomena, and often it may be the best means of explicating the issues under study. Nevertheless, future work should also approach reactions to aid in settings that are as involving and "real-world-like" as possible. There are several factors that argue persuasively for this. First, receiving aid generally implies that one is experiencing some type of need-state, often occasioned by personal failure. It may be difficult to approximate the psychological state experienced under these conditions in, for example, an uninvolving role play. Also, although research suggests that reactions to help may be either positive or negative, socialization stresses primarily the positive aspects. Unless the experimental situation has sufficient impact and involvement for subjects to experience the potentially negative effects of aid, they may respond in terms of stereotyped beliefs. Laboratory experiments that attempt to simulate the richness of real-world conditions (e.g., Nadler, Fisher, & Streufert, 1974), and studies that induce experimental manipulations in the real world (e.g., Piliavin & Gross, 1977) should be more characteristic of future research. We should also rely more on social psychologically oriented evaluations of real-world helping programs (e.g., the negative income tax), public opinion data, and in-depth interviews with aid recipients.

CONCLUSION

The pages of this book will reveal that although the study of reactions to aid is relatively new, there are many well-researched and consistent effects and patterns of effects that do form the bedrock of a social psychology of the aid recipient. This data base is significant at both a conceptual and an applied level.

One consistent pattern of effects that recurs throughout the literature (and throughout this book) is that help constitutes a "mixed blessing." Although it can communicate the donor's liking and concern, and can provide instrumental elements and hence be a supportive experience for the recipient, there have now been documented a surprisingly large number of conditions under which aid is relatively more threatening than supportive. Aid can be a debilitating experience (a) when the recipient has no opportunity to save face by reciprocating; (b) when the task on which it is offered is especially meaningful to the recipient; (c) when it is unusual for people to need help; (d) when the donor is a social comparison peer or is thought to be motivated by self-serving goals; or (e) when the help is conferred in such a way as to limit the recipient's behavioral freedoms. Dispositional as well as situational factors serve to highlight the threatening aspects of receiving help. For example, recipients with high self-esteem, those who value achievements that are obtained by their own efforts, and those who are especially sensitive to covert cues that might communicate a helper's annoyance or displeasure are especially likely to react negatively to aid (Fisher et al., 1981).

What can be concluded from all this? Some readers may draw the conclusion that we must reevaluate the common assumption that helping is a uniformly positive act that should always be encouraged. We seem to be socializing people with sets of conflicting (yet strongly internalized) norms pertaining to helping relationships. On the one hand the norm of social responsibility (Berkowitz, 1972) dictates that the needy should be cared for by the more fortunate members of society. On the other, people in Western cultures are taught that independence is a virtue and that dependence is evil (e.g., Blau, 1964; Heider, 1958; Weber, 1930). This makes it difficult to be an aid recipient without experiencing some negative psychological side effects. To deal with this problem, we need to redouble our efforts to identify why and when aid leads to detrimental effects.

It seems important for future social psychological research on prosocial behavior to give more evenhanded treatment to recipient reactions to aid, as well as to conditions that facilitate help-giving. We need to determine under what conditions the helping efforts we so frequently encourage are efficient in terms of recipient reactions. If this were done, the study of reactions to help could become a vital part of the literature on helping behavior.

Before concluding, we should note that past research on reactions to aid has been dispersed over several disciplines (e.g., social psychology, social work, sociology, political science). Work in each of these has great merit, and we encourage the reader to explore beyond the confines of this book. Our own explorations have suggested that there is much for us to learn from such reading, but we also believe that the social psychological approach we take in this volume has much to recommend it to researchers in other areas.

REFERENCES

Adams, J. S. Toward an understanding of inequity. *Journal of Abnormal and Social Psychology,* 1963, **67,** 422–436.

Baumeister, R. J. A self-presentational view of social phenomena. *Psychological Bulletin,* 1982, **91,** 3–26.

Berkowitz, L. Social norms, feelings and other factors affecting helping and altruism. In L. Berkowitz (Ed.), *Advances in experimental social psychology* (Vol. 6). New York: Academic Press, 1972.

Blau, P. M. *Exchange and power in social life.* New York: Wiley, 1964.

Brehm, J. W. *A theory of psychological reactance.* New York: Academic Press, 1966.

Brehm, S. S., & Brehm, J. W. *Psychological reactance: A theory of freedom and control.* New York: Academic Press, 1981.

Brickman, P., Rabinowitz, V. C., Karuza, J., Jr., Coates, D., Cohn, E., & Kidder, L. Models of helping and coping. *American Psychologist,* 1982, **37,** 369–384.

Fisher, J. D., DePaulo, B. M., & Nadler, A. Extending altruism beyond the altruistic act: The mixed effects of aid on the help recipient. In J. P. Rushton & R. M. Sorrentino (Eds.), *Altruism and helping behavior.* New Jersey: Lawrence Erlbaum Associates, 1981.

Fisher, J. D., Nadler, A., & Whitcher-Alagna, S. Recipient reactions to aid. *Psychological Bulletin,* 1982, **91,** 27–54.

Gergen, K. J. Toward a psychology of receiving help. *Journal of Applied Social Psychology,* 1974, **44,** 187–194.

Gergen, K. J., & Gergen, M. Understanding foreign assistance through public opinion. *Yearbook of World Affairs* (Vol. 27). London: Institute of World Affairs, 1974.

Gouldner, A. W. The norm of reciprocity: A preliminary statement. *American Sociological Review,* 1960, **25,** 161–178.

Heider, F. *The psychology of interpersonal relations.* New York: Wiley, 1958.

Homans, G. C. *Social behavior: Its elementary forms.* New York: Harcourt, Brace & World, 1961.

Jones, E. E., & Davis, K. E. From acts to dispositions: The attribution process in person perception. In L. Berkowitz (Ed.), *Advances in Experimental Social Psychology* (Vol. 2). New York: Academic Press, 1965.

Kelley, H. H. Attribution theory in social psychology. In D. Levine (Ed.), *Nebraska Symposium on Motivation* (Vol. 15). Lincoln, Nebraska: University of Nebraska Press, 1967.

Latané, B., & Darley, J. *The unresponsive bystander: Why doesn't he help?* New York: Appleton-Century-Crofts, 1970.

Moss, M. K., & Page, R. A. Reinforcement and helping behavior. *Journal of Applied Social Psychology,* 1972, **2,** 360–371.

Nadler, A., Fisher, J. D., & DePaulo, B. M. (Eds.). *New directions in helping,* (Vol. 3). *Applied perspectives on help-seeking and receiving.* New York: Academic Press, in press.

Nadler, A., Fisher, J. D., & Streufert, S. The donor's dilemma: Recipient's reaction to aid from friend or foe. *Journal of Applied Social Psychology,* 1974, **4,** 275–285.

Piliavin, I. M., & Gross, A. E. The effects of separation of services and income maintenance on AFDC recipients' perceptions and use of social services: Results of a field experiment. *Social Service Review,* 1977, **9,** 389–406.

Walster, E., Berscheid, E., & Walster, G. W. New directions in equity theory. *Journal of Personality and Social Psychology,* 1973, **25,** 151–176.

Weber, M. *The Protestant ethic and the spirit of capitalism.* London: Allen & Unwin, 1930.

Wortman, C., & Brehm, J. Responses to uncontrollable outcomes: An integration of reactance theory and the learned helplessness model. In L. Berkowitz, (Ed.), *Advances in experimental social psychology* (Vol. 8). New York: Academic Press, 1975.

PART II

Theoretical Perspectives

CHAPTER 2

The Dilemmas of Helping: Making Aid Fair and Effective

Philip Brickman*
Louise H. Kidder
Dan Coates
Vita Rabinowitz
Ellen Cohn
Jurgis Karuza†

When people help others they redistribute resources by giving services, goods, money, information, or esteem (see Foa & Foa, 1974). Two questions we may ask of an effort to help are, (1) Is it fair? and (2) Is it effective? Before asking these questions about all help, we will exempt some forms

*The untimely death of Philip Brickman has left us bereft of an irreplaceable friend and mentor. His thoughts and words continue to live in our work, and we wish to acknowledge our indebtedness to him for having started us along the paths portrayed in this chapter. LHK

†Thanks to Michelle Fine and David Kipnis for helpful readings of the manuscript.

of help from these requirements. There are several forms of help, not all of which are motivated by a desire to be fair or effective.

FORMS OF HELP

Even though we can analyze the redistribution of resources that results from any act of help, not all help is motivated by an explicit desire to redistribute resources, as in the first two cases described next.

Impulsive Help

In some instances, people give help impulsively as an immediate response to another person's need, regardless of how deserved or effective the help may be. Impulsive helping is based on empathy; helpers respond to a victim's distress as though they were in the victim's place (see Ekman & Bratfish, 1965; Stotland, 1969). Bystanders at the scene of an accident who rush to the aid of a victim are responding impulsively, although they are more likely to do this if there are no other bystanders around who the person believes might help, who may seem indifferent to the situation, or who may serve as an audience before whom the person could look foolish (Latané & Darley, 1970).

Strategic Help

In other instances, people give help strategically with the hope that they will be repaid, possibly with interest. Strategic helping is based on a calculation of how likely the donor is to be repaid, either directly by the recipient or indirectly by the esteem or gratitude of other people. For instance, ambitious members of an organization will help others because the credit they accumulate by so doing furthers their own rise in the organization (see Blau, 1955; Kanter, 1977).

Normative Help

The principle underlying normative help is fairness. In instances of normative helping, donors regard the recipient as deserving and regard themselves as obliged to provide. They give so that the redistribution of resources after their help is more fair than the distribution that existed before (Brickman & Bryan, 1975, 1976). The form of help we examine in this chapter is normative help—given with the intention of redistributing resources in a fair and effective manner.

FAIRNESS AND EFFECTIVENESS: COMPETING GOALS?

Considerations of fairness and effectiveness are not entirely independent of each other. They are separate but overlapping constructs. Help is fair if it restores a balance in the distribution of resources so that people receive what they deserve. Help is effective if it enables the recipient to become more self-sustaining and less in need of future help.

The overlap between fairness and effectiveness occurs because most helpers' resources are limited rather than boundless. If we help someone and our help is ineffective, it eventually becomes unfair to continue pouring our resources into what seems like a bottomless hole. A recipient who does not benefit from our help, who needs perpetual help, requires that we devote endless resources to that person. It becomes unfair to give endlessly to one person when other people also deserve goods, time, or money. Therefore, if help is completely ineffective, it becomes unfair.

By the same reasoning, if it is not fair to help—that is, if the distribution in its present form is just and the recipient already has what he or she actually deserves—then helping is not only unfair but also ineffective. The help will not benefit that recipient as much as it might benefit someone who has less than he or she deserves. For instance, a healthy, informed woman will not show as much improvement in her condition from prenatal health care as a woman who has never received medical attention or nutritional advice. The marginal benefits are potentially greater for the person who has further to go. If the person who needs more help has been deprived through no fault of her own, then it is both more fair and more effective to help her.

In spite of the fact that fairness and effectiveness are intertwined, there is also a paradoxical conflict between them. Their combined demands create what we call the *dilemmas of helping*. The very conditions that make it fair to help someone also make is less likely that helping them will be effective. For help to be fair, we must not hold recipients responsible for their misfortune; persons deserving help are in a state of need through no fault of their own. If they were to blame for their misfortune, they would thereby "deserve what they got" and not deserve help in the form of resources from anyone else (Walster, Walster, & Berscheid, 1978). It is, therefore, most fair to help those whom we do not hold responsible for their problems.

On the other hand, we have said that our help will be most effective if it not only sustains the person but also eventually makes the person self-sustaining. The recipient then does not drain the donor and produce the "staff burnout" that human service professionals sometimes experience (see Maslach, 1976). Therefore, it is most effective to help those who will be responsible for their own maintenance. Note, this is precisely the opposite of the condition that makes helping fair.

If it is fairest to help people who are *not* responsible for their plight, but most effective to help people who *are* responsible for their fate, it appears impossible for help to be both fair and effective. The contradiction is not as resolute as this dilemma makes it seem, however, when we introduce a distinction between what a person may have been responsible for in the past and what the person can be responsible for in the future. For help to be fair, we do not hold a person responsible for the past, for the cause of the problem. For help to be effective, we hold the person responsible in the future, for the solution to the problem. We shall return to a discussion of how to resolve the contradiction between what makes help fair and what makes it effective after our discussion of each of these alone in the two sections that follow.

FAIRNESS

Evidence on the Role of Fairness

Research on the connection between justice and helping by Lerner and his colleagues (Lerner, 1975; Lerner, Miller & Holmes, 1976) has repeatedly demonstrated an almost paradoxical fact: People's commitment to a sense of justice is so strong that when they encounter a victim they cannot help (or cannot help without threatening what they feel entitled to for themselves), they will derogate and reject this unfortunate other to make his or her misfortune seem more deserved.

Fairness in helping is determined by whether or not the people needing help are seen as responsible for their own misfortune. Schopler and Matthews (1965) and Berkowitz (1969) have demonstrated that subjects who appear to need help either because of laziness or mismanagement get less help than subjects who appear to need it through an experimenter's error or an arbitrary experimental rule. The relevant property of donors is also responsibility, namely the extent to which they have accepted responsibility for others and feel an obligation to their well-being. Staub (1970, 1974) and

Berkowitz (1972) have documented that to instruct people specifically that they are responsible for someone else or that another person's success depends on them increases their willingness to help.

Unlike impulsive and strategic helping that grow out of empathy and reciprocity, helping in the service of fairness does not require recipients to be grateful. Normative help is perceived as deserved or as a matter of right, and giving such help is an obligation, not a disinterested expression of love for humanity (see Schwartz, 1972). Altruism as a personal motive, learned or inherited, is more likely to seek its outlet in the unstructured impulsive giving that characterizes rescues or donations. Fairness is a central issue for the study of normative helping. We now turn to research on when helping is perceived as fair, and how the requirements of fairness in turn work for or against our ability to provide effective help.

It is not hard to generate examples of unfair helping, as in the fable of the diligent ant versus the carefree, self-indulgent grasshopper who initially mocks the ant's providence but ultimately begs for some much-needed food. In the student world, student grasshoppers gambol and play during a term, then ask friends to lend them notes or term papers or to help them pass exams. This example actually involves questions of fairness to three people: fairness to the donor, fairness to the recipient, and fairness to other potential recipients.

Once it is established that a recipient deserves help and that a donor is obligated to give it, the dilemma of fairness is substantially solved, but sometimes help will still not be forthcoming if what is required is too costly. Help withheld on these grounds may be withheld in the service of effectiveness as well as fairness. Both help that must be given perpetually and help that is too costly drain donors of resources that other people also deserve. What is ineffective also becomes unfair when we include other needy recipients in our estimate of the fairness of a distribution.

Condition: Recipients Must Not Be Responsible

Helping in the service of fairness requires that the potential recipients be seen as deserving more than they have received, and therefore not be responsible for their misfortune. Recipients who are unfairly deprived by an error on the part of someone in authority deserve help. For example, in the Brickman and Bryan (1976) study, children were supposed to receive one token for each test booklet they filled out. In some cases, due to a clerical error by an experimental assistant, one child received 12 tokens too many for her work and another child received 12 tokens too few. The children approved of helping the child with too few chips rather than helping a different child. Similarly, a person who needed help completing an assigned task because the experimenter had initially given him the wrong materials received more help than a person who had not suffered from such a mistake. Subjects who learned that the other person needed help because he had mismanaged his work helped less (Berkowitz, 1969).

Similar results were obtained by Austin and Walster (1974) , who found that subjects approved a confederate who restored fairness despite the fact that this cost the subjects part of their own earnings. The subject and the confederate were told that they had done equally well on a task that earned them a joint total of three dollars. In some cases the confederate kept two dollars and gave only one to the subject. Subjects were less upset with this if the confederate explained that in an earlier, similar experiment she herself had been cheated by receiving an underpayment.

One obvious case in which recipients are not responsible for their state arises when the damage has been inflicted by the potential donors. Here, help may be motivated by both a sense of fairness and a sense of guilt. Carlsmith and Gross (1969) and Freedman, Wallington, and Bless (1967), among others, have shown that feeling guilty over having hurt someone else will make people more likely to help not only the victim but any passing stranger who requests it.

For helping to be fair, it is necessary that people's current low outcomes be seen as low through no fault of their own, or through external reasons rather than internal ones. Schopler and Matthews (1968) manipulated whether people believed that a subordinate's request for help on a task was a request the subordinate simply decided to make or a request the subordinate had been instructed by the experimenter to make. Subjects helped significantly more if the request was seen as externally imposed on the subordinate. Piliavin, Rodin, and Piliavin (1969) found that subway passengers were more likely to help someone who fell down when the person appeared to be physically disabled than when he appeared to be drunk. A reluctance to help drunks has been found even in hospital emergency rooms (Roth, 1972). Bryan and Davenport (cited in Berkowitz, 1975) analyzed how much money was contributed to the 100 neediest cases described during the Christmas season in the *New York Times*. More was given to people whose troubles appeared externally imposed, such as children who were victims of abuse, than to people who seemed to be the source of their own troubles, such as mental patients.

Similar effects of attribution of responsibility on helping have been reported in survey research. Staines, Tavris, and Jayaratne (1974) found that successful career women who saw chance or circumstance as the difference between their own achievement and the lesser success of other women were more likely to support the women's movement than successful women who saw skill and hard work as the major explanation of their state. Stark and Glock (1968, 1969) have shown that Christians who believed more strongly in the doctrine of free will—that people's destinies are determined by their own free choice between sin and salvation—were more likely to reject the civil rights movement because they were more likely to believe that the disadvantaged were responsible for their own state. This was true for black Christians as well as white Christians (Marx, 1967).

In these surveys, how people explain their own good fortune and how they explain other people's misfortune are usually confounded. For example, if a woman endorses the statement, "Women have only themselves to blame for not doing better in life" (Staines *et al.,* 1974), this automatically implies that successful women are responsible for their success, and that unsuccessful women are responsible for their lack of success. Two studies have attempted to separate people's attributions for their own success or failure from their attributions for other people's success or failure. Both indicate that to judge whether or not others are responsible for their misfortune is the critical element in the occurrence of helping. Lao (1970) and Gurin and Epps (1975) found that black college students who saw blacks in general as externally controlled, and who attributed black failures to discrimination, were more likely to participate in collective actions designed to help fellow blacks. This was true both for those who saw their own lives as externally controlled and for those who saw their own lives as internally controlled. The latter, however, were more likely to achieve in school—especially if they also saw failure by other blacks (not themselves) as due to external forces. Ickes, Kidd, and Berkowitz (1976) found that subjects who believed they had been rewarded on a task because of their ability (rather than by chance), whereas other students had received no payment through no fault of their own (e.g., equipment or scheduling problems), were most likely to donate money. The fact that persons deprived through no fault of their own received more help confirms our analysis of recipient responsibility.

It is hard to justify helping criminal offenders who are seen as responsible for their own state. These sentiments no doubt erode meaningful rehabilitation programs in prisons. It may be that our need to see justice done is psychologically prior to our sense of mercy and compassion, in the same sense that the God of the Old Testament, the God of justice, is psychologically prior to the God of the New Testament, the God of love. We first want our penalties to restore fairness rather than to rehabilitate or even to deter (Brickman, 1977). Requiring offenders to engage in therapeutic programs is likely to be resented, for different reasons, by both offenders and the public. Recent proposals to make such participation optional and contingent on inmates' behavior—something inmates must earn if they are interested—should increase both the perceived fairness and value of such programs.

When people are expected to help others they believe do not deserve it, the helpers find the situation frustrating and painful. Here is the report of one of our students who worked as a caseworker for the welfare department in her home town.

> Conversations with co-workers ran as follows: "Hey, that woman didn't come to the last mass redetermination and you're going to give her kids school clothes!" "Isn't that the woman who refused to use any birth control? I wouldn't give her a pregnancy allowance." In dealing with welfare clients very seldom did I feel good about helping them. For the most part I was caught up in the "deserving" aspect of helping. The longer I worked at the agency . . . the less I was able to help in a kind and gracious way.

Finally, even if recipients deserve help, other people may resent it if they receive what looks like too much help. In this case, the distribution of resources that exists after the helping may be no more fair than the distribution that existed before it, thus defeating the aim of helping as a means of restoring fairness. In one condition of the Berscheid and Walster (1967) and Berscheid, Walster, and Barclay (1968) studies, women had to choose between giving a victim many more trading stamps than she had been deprived of or not helping her at all. Subjects who could only overcompensate were less likely to help the victim than subjects who could compensate the loss exactly. Schopler (1967) found that male subjects were especially unlikely to help a partner when help could mean that the partner's outcomes equalled or exceeded their own. On a broader canvas, Welfeld (1977:133) provides this description of why groups in the American public have opposed public housing:

> In the case of good clothing or health care . . . the poor can be provided for in a way that leaves the donor in better shape (in material as well as spiritual terms) after the deed than the receiver. Even in the case of welfare, the givers are in the main better off than the recipients. In the case of housing, however, the results run far beyond egalitarianism. The programs involve a redistribution that leaves recipients better off than donors . . . . The redistributive aspects of a new housing program are so great because of the cost of a newly constructed housing unit . . . . Ordinary working people cannot be expected to sit by calmly while the poor are placed in superior housing.

Negation: We See People as Responsible

If people do not help, it may be that they usually see potential recipients as responsible for their own fate. Helping would be effectively blocked if there were a general force inducing people to see others as responsible for their own behavior and outcomes, and there appears to be just such a force. Ross (1977) reviews evidence indicating that people overestimate internal or personal causes of other people's behavior, and underestimate external or situational causes, which Ross calls the "fundamental attribution error." For example, Jones and Harris (1967) found that knowing someone had been assigned the task of making a pro-Castro speech did not prevent subjects from inferring some degree of pro-Castro sentiment on the part of the person making the speech (see also Snyder & Jones, 1974). Knowing that someone had been assigned the task of relaying an antimarijuana message, subjects still came to dislike the person when the message conflicted with their own views (Manis, Cornell, & Moore, 1974). Even psychologists are prone to overestimate the extent to which consistent internal factors or individual differences in personality influence behavior, and to underestimate the strength of situational factors (Mischel, 1969).

In a number of recent experiments, subjects have been told specifically that most or all people observed in a particular situation behave in a certain way. If people are assured that the sample observed was randomly chosen and representative of people in general, they are then likely to attribute the behavior to the situation rather than to the characteristics of the people involved (Wells & Harvey, 1977), as predicted by Kelley's (1967) model of attribution. However, without these assurances, people attribute even what they know is quite common behavior to properties of the individuals. According to Miller, Gillen, Schenker, and Radlove (1973), knowing that a majority of subjects had delivered the most painful shock to a victim in the Milgram (1963) experiment did not prevent people from making personal attributions about an individual subject who delivered the most extreme shock. Those of us who have shown the Milgram film to classes have first-hand evidence of this tendency. Nisbett and Borgida (1975) likewise found that people were just as likely to judge unfavorably someone who had not helped in an emergency when they knew that declining to help was usual as when they did not know (Darley & Latané, 1968). Similarly, the testimony by leading social psychologists such as Orne and Lifton that most people would have behaved as Patty Hearst did under the circumstances of her captivity did not stop the jury from holding her responsible.

A blind tendency to hold other people responsible for their actions and conditions may once have had survival value for the species because it would facilitate vigorous and forceful action against individuals who appeared to fail in their social obligations. Trivers (1971) and Campbell (1975) have both argued that moralistic aggression against those not contributing to the general welfare would have survival value for individuals displaying it. In addition, a blind tendency to hold others responsible for their misfortunes would reduce efforts to help the sick and the crippled. Abandoning the burden of caring for injured members may have had direct survival value for others in the group, as well as the indirect value of removing individuals prone to misfortune from the breeding pool (see Campbell, 1975; Trivers, 1971).

These interpretations shed new light on the recent powerful indictments of society for blaming victims for their plight rather than seeking out and blaming the social causes that made them victims. Social scientists, and especially psychologists, are seen as no less guilty of this than politicians or the general public (Caplan & Nelson, 1973; Ryan, 1972). A number of motives have been nominated as lying behind the search for personal causes. Drabeck and Quarantelli (1967) see blaming accidents on particular individuals as serving our need for control, creating the illusion (but only the illusion) that something is being done to prevent reoccurrence in the future. Ryan (1972) and Lerner (1975) see this tendency as working to justify our own status and in particular our unwillingness to help. These are reasonable explanations. But it may not be sufficient to neutralize these special motives if we wish to stop blaming victims. Attribution of responsibility to victims is part of a more pervasive tendency to attribute responsibility to individuals in general. Perhaps, as Walster (1966) has suggested, attribution of responsibility to a victim increases the more severe is the victim's misfortune and the more strongly we are motivated to believe that a similar misfortune could not happen to us. The evidence on this point is contradictory (see Wortman, 1976). But we do not need these studies to establish the more general proposition that people are sometimes held responsible for outcomes even when the effective causes of the behavior lie in the situation.

A Parallel Dilemma of Fairness for Donors

Although our major focus is on recipients, a parallel thesis can be developed for donors. Helping in the service of fairness also requires that potential donors be seen as having received more than they deserve, or as not responsible for their own good fortune. For example, Brickman and Bryan (1975, 1976) showed that when one child was seen as clearly overrewarded, the transfer of this excess reward to another child was seen as fair. Once people know that they themselves will be receiving a fair wage for their work, they are willing to work extra hours if they are told that an additional sum will be earned for needy others by each hour's work (Miller, 1977). Money to help the needy, however, was no incentive for subjects to work if they themselves were not first paid what they felt they deserved. Similarly, Lerner *et al.* (1976) report that people were more willing to buy goods, part of whose proceeds went to charity, if those goods were fairly priced (i.e., if customers were receiving what they believed they deserved), but not if the goods were overpriced.

Just as there are powerful forces operating on people to hold others responsible, there are powerful forces operating on them to hold themselves responsible. Much of the literature documenting the extent to which people tend to exaggerate their own responsibility for events is reviewed by Wortman (1976). In one series of experiments, Langer (1975) found that subjects in a clear situation of chance often behaved as if their outcome were to some extent under their control. This was especially true if subjects were familiar with the situation or if they had been given some choice concerning their participation. Wortman (1975) demonstrated that merely knowing beforehand what outcome they wanted made subjects in a chance situation feel that they had some control over the outcome. The entire edifice of dissonance-theory research (see Wicklund & Brehm [1976] for a review) also supports the idea that people exaggerate the degree to which they are responsible for their own outcomes. This follows quite apart from the conclusions of dissonance theory, but simply from the methods used in dissonance research. In a typical dissonance experiment, subjects in one condition are encouraged by the experimenter to believe that they are freely choosing whether or not to participate. In fact, the experimenter wants all of them to participate, and structures the situation so that all, or almost all, do. Subjects believe they have chosen freely, but experimenters and observers know that subjects have been uniformly manipulated into making a particular choice.

People who see their outcomes as contingent on their own behavior are likely to cope more effectively in a wide variety of situations (see Lefcourt, 1977; Rotter, 1966; Seligman, 1975). This means that attribution of responsibility to oneself, like attribution of responsibility to others, should have survival value. However, for attribution of responsibility to oneself there is an inhibitory force that is absent for attribution of responsibility to others. It may have survival value to blame someone else for a misfortune that was not actually their fault. But it will not have survival value to blame oneself for a misfortune that was unpredictable or unavoidable. Indeed, there is evidence that individuals will be worse off if they mistakenly attribute responsibility to themselves for outcomes that are in fact beyond their control (Bulman & Brickman, 1976; Weiss, 1971a, 1971b). We do not have to settle here the question of whether a tendency to attribute responsibility to oneself is greater or less than the tendency to attribute responsibility to others, because the literature is contradictory (see Miller & Ross, 1975). It is only necessary that we establish that there exist strong forces for the attribution of responsibility in both cases. Nonetheless, as indicated, we suspect that the forces allow stronger attributions to others than to ourselves (see Jones & Nisbett, 1971) despite people's inclination to see themselves rather than others as free and in control of a situation (Miller & Norman, 1975; Wortman, 1976). An example would clarify our hunch. Consider children who accompany their parents to a grocery store one day and impress others as either quite charming or quite ill-mannered. Naive observers would see the parents (and the children) as more responsible for the particular behavior than would the parents or observers who had children of their own. Parents know that neither charming behavior nor ill-mannered behavior is highly representative of the children or within the parents' control. Nonetheless, parents also attribute more responsibility for their children's outcomes to themselves and less to situations or circumstances than an objective or scientific analysis would warrant. They may, for example, see their own past misdeeds as partly responsible for the fate of their terminally ill children (Chodoff, Friedman, & Hamburg, 1964).

It seems especially unlikely that people will see themselves as over-rewarded or not responsible for the rewards they have received. Because they choose to be rewarded or reinforced, they see themselves as responsible for these outcomes whether they are in fact or not (Skinner, 1972). Even though lottery winners saw their outcome as more a matter of chance than did accident victims, the lottery winners were more likely to feel that they deserved their outcome (Brickman, Coates, & Janoff-Bulman, 1978). When people are forced to see themselves as having been given a greater reward than they deserve, they are inclined either to work harder or to increase their perceptions of the difficulty of the task (Adams, 1965; Gergen, Morse, & Bode, 1974) to justify their retention of this reward. This general tendency works against helping because helping in the service of fairness is easiest when donors are seen as contributing a portion of their goods that they did not deserve or as not responsible for their excess of good fortune.

The general argument of this entire section may be summarized in two central propositions for a theory of helping as fairness:

1. Recipients will be seen as deserving of help to the extent that they are not responsible for their deficit in resources.
2. Donors will be seen as obligated to help to the extent that they are not responsible for their surplus of resources.

As noted earlier, there is a special case in which these two propositions can be reduced to one: when a recipient's lack of responsibility for a deficit can be traced to a donor's transgression, either in the form of carelessness or exploitation. In the general case, however, the deservingness of the recipient cannot be established by an examination of the responsibility of the donor, and the obligation of the donor cannot be established by an examination of the deservingness of the recipient. These two propositions are quite sobering. To establish helping as fair it is necessary to work against all those forces documented by social psychological research as inducing people to attribute responsibility to persons rather than situations.

EFFECTIVENESS

Evidence on the Role of Effectiveness

Effective help leaves the recipient better-off after the help than before, and maximally effective help leaves the recipient no longer in need of help. Help which must be given permanently may leave the recipient better-off, but help that need be given only temporarily is more effective because it enables donors to turn their resources to the next person in need.

We demand that help be effective for two reasons. The first is to sustain our own feelings of competence and control. In this sense, helping behavior requires reinforcement, like all other behavior. Even an altruist who values helping for its own sake can be expected to seek the reinforcement of knowing that the recipient has benefited or that the help has been effective rather than irrelevant or harmful. The second reason we demand helping be effective is to justify the fairness of our initial decision to help. By helping, we give people access to resources that they have not explicitly earned. Though their lack of such resources may not be their fault, the gratuitous transfer of resources is still a delicate question for equity theory, no matter how it is described, because it involves giving some people outcomes that exceed their investments (Walster, Berscheid, & Walster, 1973). This residual tension can be resolved if the recipients increase their investments in the future, working harder or more effectively than they have in the past, and thus not only sustaining a new level of reward but justifying the excess reward or help that they received in the past.

The specter of help backfiring is enough to chill the best of intentions. In one famous case, Sharp (1952) traces the consequences of giving steel axes to members of a Stone Age Australian culture. The technical effects of the new axes were minimal. However, stone axes had occupied a critical symbolic role in the age, sex, clan, and intertribal relationships of the group. All of these were undermined by the new goods which the culture could neither produce nor explain. Another recently publicized example is the success of Western commercial interests in convincing African mothers to bottle-feed rather than breast-feed their infants. In a tropical climate, with little electricity for refrigeration, it is difficult to keep prepared infant formula from spoiling. The net effect of the change appears to have been an increase in illness and malnutrition.

People may also not help when they believe their help will be insufficient to undo the injustice that has been done. In a study by Berscheid and Walster (1967), women were led to believe that their own failure had caused another woman to lose two books of trading stamps that she very much needed. Subsequently, they were given an opportunity to donate trading stamps either to the person they had hurt or to a needy third party. The women helped the person they had hurt more often when they could compensate her exactly for what she had lost than when they could offer her only partial compensation. Perhaps such token help may be seen as adding insult to injury and therefore ineffective. Similar results were obtained by Berscheid, *et al.* (1968). People who believe the world is a just place (Rubin & Peplau, 1973, 1975) are especially sensitive to this effect. Miller (1977) has shown that people who believe the world is just offer less of their time when a victim is presented as only one of many victims in a similar predicament than when the victim is presented as an isolated case. In a second experiment, high believers in a just world donated more money when the need of the victims was presented as being temporary than when their suffering was presented as continuing. Only when the injustice and the need are seen as limited and temporary can help from a few concerned individuals effectively restore justice.

When people receiving help do not improve, donors may be disappointed. This expectation for future improvement constitutes a hidden liability that is not present when a person receives an award on the basis of merit. People receiving a scholarship on the basis of need are expected to show future gains, whereas people receiving a scholarship on the basis of merit are not. These ideas were tested in an experiment carried out by Philip Brickman and his co-worker Michael Andrykowski. As predicted, subjects judged the future performance of the recipient of a compensatory award as less satisfactory when the recipient did not improve, while they did not do so for the recipient of a merit award.

Medicine supplies some of the more dramatic examples of importance of anticipated effectiveness in helping. The examples are dramatic because they have been, at least until recently, covert. The ideology of medical practice specifies that help is to be given to all, regardless of personal or social characteristics. But doctors sometimes privately acknowledge that they work harder to save the life of an ordinary baby than to save the life of an infant born malformed, with no chance to lead a normal life. At the other end of the life cycle, advances in medical technology have made it possible to prolong the lives of people who are critically ill or injured. These life-sustaining devices are costly and in many instances offer no hope that the patient will improve. Sudnow (1967:101) reports the case of an alcoholic man bleeding badly from a stomach ulcer: "The intern in charge of treating the patient was asked by a nurse, 'Should we order more blood for this afternoon?' and the doctor answered, 'I can't see any sense in pumping it into him because if we can stop the bleeding, he'll turn around and start drinking again and next week he'll be back needing more blood.'" Thus, beliefs about the effectiveness of help determine whether we will help in some critical situations.

Condition: Recipients Must Be Seen Responsible

Effective help requires that recipients be seen by themselves and others as active, responsible agents. Profiting from help can be quite difficult. A person may need to endure considerable frustration and failure before visible results are achieved. An extensive literature indicates that people who have confidence in their ultimate ability to succeed (Brickman, Linsenmeier, & McCareins, 1976), or confidence that outcomes are contingent on their own behavior (Dweck & Goetz, 1977; Wortman & Brehm, 1975), are better able to discount failures and to persevere in their pursuit of success.

Two lines of evidence bear on this proposition. The first indicates that other people's belief in the recipients' capacity to improve may itself be a critical determinant of whether recipients improve. The importance of donors' beliefs on the effectiveness of their efforts to help follows from the research on teachers' expectations by Rosenthal and Jacobson (1968). Elementary school teachers were told that certain of their pupils had hidden potential and could be expected to bloom in the coming year. In fact, the pupils so designated had been randomly selected. Nonetheless, at least in the early grades, the pupils expected to improve did indeed show sharp improvement over the year. The implementation and analysis of these and related studies by Rosenthal have been harshly criticized (Barber & Silver, 1968; Elashoff & Snow, 1971); nonetheless, the effect has since been obtained in a number of different studies that are not vulnerable to the earlier criticisms (e.g., Seaver, 1973). In a laboratory setting, Beez (1968) found that teachers who thought their pupils were bright conveyed more information to them than teachers who thought their pupils were dull. Thus, not surprisingly, the allegedly bright pupils demonstrated more learning on a subsequent test.

Further evidence for the importance of attributing competence comes from the ironic fact that helping may generate more improvement in donors than in recipients. Donors are assumed to be competent and responsible both in the fact that they are asked to help and in the way they are usually treated by recipients. There is no demand that donors improve in the future, a demand that by implication casts doubt on their present status (see Miller, Brickman, & Bolen, 1975). School children who are having difficulty themselves profit from being asked to tutor younger children (Allen, 1976). For example, underachieving seventh graders improved significantly in reading after serving as tutors for third graders (Erickson & Cromack, 1972). In another study (Allen & Feldman, 1974), fifth graders who were doing poorly in reading either taught a third grader or studied alone for 2 weeks. Performance in reading at the end of this period was significantly better for the tutors than for those who studied alone. These results indicate that it was the tutoring role, and not merely the extra time spent working on the lessons, that produced the improved understanding. In both studies, the tutees did not show the same benefit from being taught as the tutors did from teaching, although other studies have found that tutees also benefit from the experience (Feldman, Devin-Sheehan, & Allen, 1976). New college professors are also commonly impressed with how much one learns from teaching a course.

The second line of evidence indicates that recipients' own belief in themselves as active causal agents determines whether the gains they make will last or disappear. Unless recipients see themselves as active causal agents, they attribute gains made following help to external causes (the helper) rather than to their own internal properties. Crediting the helper rather than themselves for the changes in turn makes it less likely that the changes will persist. Davison and Valins (1969) had two groups of subjects take a series of electrical shocks and then a second series that was actually less severe than the first one. Some subjects were told that a pill they had been given made the second shocks seem less painful. Other subjects believed the pill had been a placebo with no effect on their experience of pain. This implied that their increased ability to tolerate shock was due to qualities within themselves, rather than qualities of the pill. In a subsequent test, only subjects who attributed their apparent improvement to themselves were willing to endure significantly more shock than they had in the beginning. Miller *et al.* (1975) compared two groups of children who had been induced to keep their classrooms neat and clean. One group had been repeatedly told by their teacher that they should put their litter in the garbage can and pick up after other children. The second group had been repeatedly told that they were neat and tidy people. Only the second group, who attributed their new-found neat and tidy behavior to themselves, maintained the improvement over subsequent weeks and months. The more general argument that people persist more in their pursuit of behavior that they see as intrinsically motivated rather than behavior that they see motivated by external forces, like pay, is developed by Deci (1974) and Lepper and Green (1975).

For these reasons Alinsky (1969, 1972) recommends that radical organizers attribute gains made by organizations to their members rather than to help from outsiders. He recounts one of his early experiences in organizing the Back of the Yards neighborhood in Chicago:

> The people had no confidence in themselves or in their neighbors or in their cause. So we staged a cinch fight. One of the major problems in Back of the Yards in those days was an extraordinarily high rate of infant mortality . . . . After checking it out, I found out that all we had to do to get Infant Welfare Society medical services . . . was ask for it. However, I kept this information to myself. We called an emergency meeting, recommended we go in committee to the society's offices and demand medical services . . . . We stormed into the Infant Welfare Society downtown, identified ourselves, and began a tirade consisting of militant demands, refusing to permit them to say anything. All the time the poor woman was desperately trying to say, "Why of course you can have it. We'll start it immediately." (After finally allowing her to say yes), we stormed out of the place. All the way back to Back of the Yards you could hear the members of the committee saying, "Well, that's the way to get things done: you just tell them off and don't give them a chance to say anything. If we could get this with just the few people that we have in the organization now, just imagine what we can get when we have a big organization." (Alinsky, 1972, pp. 114–115)

Alinsky (1969, pp. 104–105) recounts another instance in which organizers could not get people to attend a meeting until the community felt that it was they, not smart outsiders, who were responsible for diagnosing their local problems and organizing the meeting.

Negation: The Label of Help Implies Recipients Are Not Responsible

The dilemma of effectiveness in helping comes from the fact that the label of help itself works against the perception of recipients as active, responsible agents. Thus, while recipients are expected to improve, an essential condition for their making and sustaining gains is removed. They are supposed to get better and urged to get better, no small burden in itself, but an essential doubt remains as to whether they will, a doubt that can undermine the most well-intentioned urgings (Miller et al., 1975). The act of extending help communicates to recipients that they need not think of themselves as responsible for their recent past or their immediate future. If they were held so responsible, the help would not be seen as fair. In being seen as not fully responsible for their own states, however, recipients are also seen as less predictable, reliable, and competent.

People who seek help are sometimes derogated in proportion to the amount of help they seek. For instance, people with identical symptoms of mental illness are rejected most if they are described as seeking help from a mental hospital, second if seeking help from a psychiatrist, third if from a physician, fourth if from the clergy, and least if they are described as seeking no help (Phillips, 1963). Thus, seeking help and seeking more serious forms of help threaten recipients' social status.

Ironically, the only case in which help is exempt from this penalty is when the person receiving help least needs it. When superiors ask for help, it is characteristically assumed that they could do the task themselves but are simply disinclined or too busy to do so (Blau, 1964). When subordinates ask for help, it is assumed that they could not do the task themselves. There is also evidence that people are most willing to accept help when they feel competent and confident in general. Subjects are more likely to ask for needed help when they have done well on a previous task than when they have done poorly (Morris & Rosen, 1973). People are also more likely to request help on a task when they expect to be able to repay that help in the future than when they do not expect to be able to repay (Castro, 1974; Greenberg & Shapiro, 1971). Feeling competent or able to repay protects recipients against the negative implications of being helped.

By assuming that people are not competent, well-intentioned helpers can leave recipients worse-off than they would have been without the help. For this reason, Skinner (1978) questions whether most of what we call helping is in fact ethical. Help supplies a needed resource but leads the person to see the production of that resource as contingent on what the helpers do rather than on his or her own behavior.

> To begin with a very simple example, we may not really help others by doing things for them. This is often the case when they are learning to do things for themselves. We watch a child tying a shoelace and grow jittery, and to escape from our jitteriness we "help" the child tie the lace. In doing so we destroy one chance to learn to tie shoes. Comenius made the point nearly four hundred years ago when he said that "the more the teacher teaches, the less the student learns . . ." By giving too much help we postpone the acquisition of effective behavior and perpetuate the need for help [Skinner, 1978: 250].

Skinner cites a report by Jensen (1973) on a program intended to help the Eskimos of Greenland.

> Thousands of construction workers were sent in to build modern houses and facilities. But the local industry, fishing, could not support these material standards, and an annual subsidy of many millions of dollars will now be needed—indefinitely—for the fifty thousand inhabitants. The goods supplied are not contingent on productive behavior, and it is not surprising that a long-established, cooperative culture has broken down . . . . It will not be enough that the teams of construction workers are now to be followed by teams of social workers [Skinner, 1978: 259].

People seen as needing help are often seen as needing to be protected from further shocks, failures, or negative events, but this in turn may cut recipients off from precisely the experiences that are important to their future improvement. Lemert (1962) and Coyne (1976) analyze the social interaction of people suffering from paranoia and depression and show how others withhold information that they feel would be upsetting to the disturbed person. Eventually, the targets of this strategy become aware of the limited and one-sided nature of the information they are getting and consequently stop trusting it. Furthermore, they learn to provoke others with more and more extreme behavior to get any information from them at all. This, of course, is interpreted as additional evidence of pathology. Cut off from feedback, the disturbed individuals are unable to change their maladaptive behavior, they feel more isolated and lost, and they find their condition worsening rather than improving.

Recipients' implied lack of competence is intensified by contrast with the image of donors as active and powerful, even omnipotent, agents. The confidence of doctors and teachers in themselves is one important element in the confidence they inspire in others, whose faith in turn generates self-assurance in the helpers. Indeed, mutual confidence in the source of help may itself be a sufficient condition for the recipient to experience initial improvement. Frank (1963) reviews much of the evidence for this placebo effect in his book on persuasion and healing.

With power attributed to helping agents and deficits attributed to recipients, credit for improvement goes to the helping agent rather than to the recipient. Kipnis (1972) demonstrated that people subject to extensive supervision are given less credit for what they achieve than people not subject to such supervision. Several studies have indicated that helpers are more apt to credit themselves for the successes of those they help, and less apt to blame themselves for failures. Johnson, Feigenbaum, and Weiby (1964) had subjects attempt to teach arithmetic concepts to students who in some cases improved and in other cases continued to perform poorly. Instructors spontaneously credited themselves for improvement and the students for lack of improvement. Beckman (1970) found similar results, as did Schopler and Layton (1972). Ross, Bierbrauer, and Polly (1974) note that these results do not necessarily represent biased or defensive attribution by the teachers, but merely their reasonable tendency to take more responsibility for an expected outcome (success or improvement) than for an unexpected one (failure or lack of improvement). For our purposes, however, the effect works equally to the disadvantage of the person being helped if it occurs as a result of rational information processing or if it occurs as a result of motivational bias.

More generally, the behavior of lower status parties is likely to be seen as produced by outside sources, whereas identical behavior by higher status parties is seen as internally motivated (Thibaut & Riecken, 1955). If receiving help lowers people's status, their subsequent acts are more likely to be seen as externally caused rather than as a consequence of their own capacities and inclinations. A powerful case in point is provided by the unintended consequences of affirmative action programs in this country. At least in academia, the institution of formal guidelines for minority hiring has had little demonstrable effect (Sowell, 1976). After documenting this, Sowell goes on to write (p. 63)

> If the "affirmative action" program were merely inane, futile, and costly, it might deserve no more attention than other government programs of the same description. But it has side effects which are negative in the short run and perhaps poisonous in the long run. While doing little or nothing to advance the position of minorities and females, it creates the impression that hard-won *achievements* of these groups are *conferred* benefits . . . . During the 1960's—*before* "affirmative action"—black incomes in the United States rose at a higher rate than white incomes. So too did the proportion of blacks in college and in skilled and professional occupations—and along with this came a faster decline in the proportion of black families below the poverty line or living in substandard housing. When people ask why blacks cannot pull themselves up the way other oppressed minorities did in the past, many white liberals and black 'spokesmen' fall right into the trap and rush in to offer sociological "explanations." But there is nothing to explain. The fact is that blacks *have* pulled themselves up—from further down, against stronger opposition—and show every indication of continuing to advance . . . . What "affirmative action" has done is to destroy the legitimacy of what had already been achieved, by making all black achievements look like questionable accomplishments or even outright gifts.

When people have been dependent on others for a long time, the process of freeing themselves from this dependence may be painful for both donors and recipients. The magical powers of parents and teachers are exaggerated by those in their care. To gain freedom and independence, it may be necessary for children to pass through a period in which they deny these powers as totally as they once accepted them (Mann, 1967).

Memmi (1965) presents a similar analysis of relationships between colonized people and colonizers. He examines benevolent colonizers who want to help the colonized gain independence. As long as such persons are physically and culturally identifiable as colonizers, they enjoy the privileges of their group no matter how sincerely they disclaim such status. Their language and actions will be "constantly out of step" because they are not the language and actions of the colonized. Help, Memmi concludes, is patronizing. The well-intentioned colonizer should "remain silent . . . . If he cannot stand this silence and make his life a perpetual compromise, he can end by leaving the colony and its privileges" (Memmi, 1965:43).

A Parallel Dilemma of Effectiveness for Donors

Donors, like recipients, are more likely to act effectively when they are seen and see themselves as responsible agents (Brickman *et al.,* 1976; Frank, 1963; Wortman & Brehm, 1975). In addition, we may note that people are simply more willing to help someone else when they feel competent. Schwartz and Ben David (1976) found that subjects who were told they had the ability to work with rats were much more likely to respond to an appeal to help catch an escaped rat than subjects told they did not have this ability. Berkowitz and Conner (1966) found that subjects were more willing to help a dependent recipient make envelopes if the subjects had succeeded on a previous jigsaw task than if they had failed or had had no previous feedback. It is not necessary for the person to have succeeded on a task that was relevant to the help requested; previous success on an irrelevant task can be just as effective in increasing helping (Kazdin & Bryan, 1971).

The negation of donors' sense of effectiveness comes not from the label of helping but, over time, from the process of trying to help. All the evidence we have reviewed previously on attributions that make it difficult for recipients of help to improve also stands as evidence of factors that ultimately make it difficult for donors to feel effective and to derive pleasure and satisfaction from their role. As Lerner and Simmons (1966) have noted, this will, in the end, cause donors to derogate recipients, even if their inability to help is neither their own nor the victim's fault. The end point of unchecked, uninterrupted efforts to help is burn-out, a loss of caring. Maslach (1976) summarizes her observations and interviews with 200 professionals, including poverty lawyers, physicians, prison personnel, social welfare workers, mental hospital staff, child-care workers, and nurses, as follows:

> Hour after hour, day after day, health and social service professionals are intimately involved with troubled human beings. What happens to people who work intensely with others, learning about their psychological, social, or physical problems? Ideally, the helpers retain objectivity and distance from the situation without losing their concern for the person they are working with. Instead, our research indicates, they are often unable to cope with this continual emotional feeling for the persons they work with and come to treat them in detached or even dehumanized ways.

Ironically, the most dedicated staff members may be most vulnerable to burn-out (Freudenberger, 1974). Alternatively, staff members highest in self-esteem may protect themselves most effectively from the sense of failure that accompanies their work by rejecting and putting more psychological distance between themselves and potential help recipients (Pines & Solomon, 1977).

The general argument of this entire section may be summarized in two central propositions for a theory of effective helping:

1. Recipients will be able to use help more effectively if they are seen as responsible for the outcomes.

2. Donors will be able to give help more effectively if they are seen as responsible for the outcomes.

Like the two propositions with which we closed our review of helping as fairness, these two propositions are quite sobering. The very label of help works against perception of recipients as responsible agents, while the long-run outcome of efforts to help work against perception of donors as responsible agents. Moreover, the conditions that make help fair are the opposite of the conditions that make it effective. It is fair to help persons who are not responsible for the problem but effective to help those who *can* be responsible for the solution. In the section that follows, we present four models of helping that represent four different positions on the question of responsibility. We arrived at these four positions by asking two questions about responsibility: (1) Is the recipient responsible for the past (or for the problem)? and (2) Is the recipient responsible for the future (or for the solution)?

FOUR MODELS OF HELPING

The distinction between past and future responsibility generates the models of helping shown in Table 1.

The compensatory model contains the conditions that should make help both fair and effective. In this model the recipient is *not* held responsible for the problem and therefore does not deserve his or her misfortune. By helping such a person we can restore equity, making it fair to spend time and resources on such aid. With the compensatory model the recipient *is* held responsible for the future, making it effective to help because the recipient can be counted upon to profit from other people's efforts and not to fall prey to misfortune again.

TABLE 1

Four Models of Helping and the Extent of Recipients' Responsibility

Recipients' responsibility for the past (problem)	Recipients' responsibility for the future (solution)	
	High	Low
High	Moral model (e.g., est)	Enlightenment model (e.g., Alcoholics Anonymous)
Low	Compensatory model (e.g., Head Start, CETA)	Medical model (e.g., hospital)

In each of the other models help is either not fair, not effective, or both. For instance, in the moral model recipients do not deserve help because they are responsible for the position they are in. Persons and organizations who adopt this model are not likely to seek or speak about help. Help from other people is uncalled for. Graduates of est (erhard seminars training) have learned the lessons of the moral model and do not describe the training as help. Instead they say they "got it" and use other terms unrelated to helping (see Rabinovitz, 1978), although they do acknowledge that other people, especially est teachers, played an important role in exhorting or encouraging them to "get it."

In the medical model, recipients have a just claim for help because they are not responsible for their suffering and do not deserve their plight. It is fair to help people in this condition but it is not maximally effective because, by assuming no responsibility for the solution, they run the risk of becoming dependent and perhaps requiring perpetual or undue amounts of help.

In the enlightenment model, recipients are responsible for their past and have received their just desserts. They are not held responsible for the future and therefore cannot cure themselves. Helping under these conditions is neither maximally fair nor effective because the recipients are guilty and there is no cure. The solution requires continued self discipline as well as group support.

Much more can be said about each of these models (see Brickman, Rabinowitz, Karuza, Coates, Cohn, & Kidder, 1982; and the chapters in this volume by Cohn and Coates). In this chapter, we focus on the compensatory model because that is the one in which help can be both fair and effective, thus resolving the dilemma. In the section that follows we discuss some of the problems that beset the compensatory model, even though it may be the fairest and (presumably) most effective of them all.

THE COMPENSATORY MODEL—CAN IT
KEEP ITS PROMISE?

Characteristics of the Model

According to the compensatory model, recipients are innocent victims of a prior injustice, injury, or deprivation and therefore are not responsible for the onset of their problem. Once they have received the needed resource and the injustice, injury, or deprivation has been eliminated, however, they are expected to remain trouble free. An assumption of this model is that help will be temporary. A consequence of this model is that recipients who have once received help as innocent victims have difficulty claiming innocent-victim status if they fail and need help again, because they are held responsible for their futures. They receive credit for their subsequent success but also blame for subsequent failure. This is a logical consequence of the compensatory model, and it makes the model fragile.

Instability and Fragility

According to the compensatory model, recipients are innocent until after they have received help, at which point they either are held responsible for their fate or they appear helpless. If help given under the compensatory model works so that recipients prosper and remain trouble free, then both the model and the help have been successful. If, however, the recipients do not prosper, one must conclude either that the help was insufficient or that the model was inappropriate. If one concludes that help was insufficient and gives more help, and the recipient still does not prosper, one is likely to relinquish the model. According to the compensatory model, help should be temporary, so when temporary help does not work the model also fails for that situation. It is, therefore, an unstable and fragile model by the nature of its assumptions. When help given under the compensatory model fails, we are likely to switch our assumptions and adopt either of two other models: the moral model, which holds recipients responsible for both their problems and the solutions, or the medical model, which holds recipients responsible for neither.

By shifting to the moral model, donors or recipients may characterize the recipients as lazy or unmotivated. By shifting to the medical model they may declare the recipients genetically or biologically inferior and therefore beyond remediation of the kind offered by compensatory programs.

The compensatory model, therefore, which enables donors and recipients to regard help as both fair and effective, requires that the help indeed be effective or else the model collapses. There are a number of instances of compensatory programs that were not effective in recent American history, however, and we examine next the factors that militate against successful compensatory help. The way compensatory programs are implemented sometimes contradicts the assumptions of the model.

Contradictions in Applications

The compensatory model is exemplified by remedial training programs for children and adults who are considered deprived of adequate skills. For instance, Head Start compensatory education for preschool children was designed to make up for deficiencies in poor children's experiences so that they could begin school on a par with classmates from wealthier families. The children were given educational games, books, field trips, and other resources that their parents could not provide.

Under the assumptions of such programs, the children were not held responsible for the fact that their parents did not have the resources to give them a head start. Once they completed the program, however, the children were expected to maintain their progress even though the resources were removed. The children's world remained unchanged, however. Their parents had no more time or money after the Head Start program than before, so the original causes of the children's needs remained untouched. The program eliminated the children's deficits, but the children returned to the same conditions from which their presumed deficits came.

The contradiction in the compensatory model is that initially we do not hold people responsible because they are victims of an unjust world, but after aid we do hold them responsible even though they return to the same unjust world. We employ a double standard, one before help is given and the other after it has been removed. How do we account for the shift?

One way to shift our assumptions from innocence to guilt or from no responsibility to responsibility is to attach great importance to individual effort and willpower: Once an individual's deficits have been removed, that person can surmount all obstacles if he or she truly wants to. It is not inconsistent, therefore, to return people to the same conditions that caused their misfortune originally if we believe that once they are personally equipped they need only the will to succeed. They should be able to pull themselves up by their new bootstraps—never mind the quicksand.

One way to remove the contradiction is to address the original causes. Once the causes have been removed, or the individual has been removed from the causes, it is no longer so contradictory or futile to hold the person responsible. Another way for the compensatory model to avoid the trap of bootstrapping in quicksand is for it to be used by an organized collectivity rather than by individuals.

The Compensatory Model and Collective Action

Taking Instead of Receiving

Instead of being recipients of gifts, some organized groups take direct action and demand rights or resources. Their actions are consistent with the compensatory model but their confrontational style leads to different consequences, both actual and psychological. Labor organizers depicted in *The Grapes of Wrath, Norma Rae,* and historical accounts of farm labor organizing (e.g., Galarza, 1970) convey the message of the compensatory model without the hidden liabilities of bootstrapping described in the previous section. What makes it different?

Collective action makes it unnecessary for the actors to assume personal, internal responsibility for subsequent failures because it focuses the group's attention on external opposition. Isolated recipients of the compensatory model are not given that option; they focus on their personal assets, and if they fail or need help again, they have no one to blame but themselves.

Collective action gives a sense of empowerment to those who participate. The sense of empowerment that people gain from participating in confrontations and taking direct action has been described by Alinsky (1971) and Mondros (1979). Mondros compared the feeling of empowerment among secretaries who belonged to WAJE (Women's Alliance for Job Equity), an organization of clerical workers, and the feelings of secretaries who were not members. WAJE members had engaged in a number of Alinsky-style actions. On National Secretaries' Day, they organized a rally at which several secretaries addressed the gathering and talked about various problems they encountered at work: being expected to perform household or wifely duties such as buying birthday presents or taking clothes to the dry cleaners, being asked to provide sexual favors, being addressed like a child, and receiving low wages. Although they planned no direct actions at the rally, they heard their personal discontents voiced and echoed by many women. Their burden of guilt or responsibility was removed as they heard that their problems were shared, were collective. The rallying cry was "raises, not roses" and the participants had a sense of their strength in numbers.

On another occasion, members of WAJE planned a hiring test-case on behalf of a secretary who quit her job because of sexual harrassment. The employer had a history of hiring young, attractive, single women to be his personal secretary. He fired them if they refused to perform sexual favors. The secretary who quit of her own accord did so only after experiencing considerable self-doubt whether she was to blame for his advances and insinuations. Was it something about the way she dressed, sat, walked, or talked that caused the problem? She brought her problem to WAJE. They had two women pose as job candidates for the vacancy. One described herself as a married woman who had many years of experience and was highly qualified for secretarial work. The other claimed to be single, listed a file clerk's job with a fictional company as her previous work experience, and met the qualifications that were rumored to be important: she was pretty, with dark eyes and dark hair. She got the job. After working in the office for a week, she resigned. Her resignation was accompanied by an "award ceremony" to which television and newspaper reporters were invited. Several secretaries from WAJE presented the employer (in absentia) with an inflatable life-size doll that had "squeeze me, I'm qualified" written across her torso.

In addition to recording the drama of the confrontations and the practical consequences of such actions, Mondros studied the sense of empowerment gained by members of such collective actions. She developed a scale with four dimensions: (1) the feeling that the person can act on the world rather than vice versa, (2) the perception of causes leading to consequences, (3) the feeling that one is a member of a group with strong group ties and a clear ideology, and (4) the willingness to confront opposition, to fight or attack an identifiable foe. Secretaries who belonged to WAJE scored significantly higher than a comparison group of secretaries on all four dimensions of empowerment (Mondros, 1979).

Redefining the Problem and Solution

Groups that organize collective action to take rather than to receive resources redefine the problem and the solution. By adopting a confrontational stance, such groups depart from compensatory programs for individuals in several ways:

1. They focus on the conflict of interest between competing parties and identify an "enemy" instead of a benevolent helper. By identifying the competition, organized groups locate the cause of their problem outside themselves. By organizing and threatening to take direct action they do assume responsibility for the solution. But if their actions do not produce the desired outcome, they do not shift into the moral or medical model and assume that the problem lies within themselves. They continue to point to the opposition and they redouble their efforts or increase their numbers for the next confrontation (see Gerlach & Hie, 1970). When organized groups give up because the opposition is stronger than they are, they can still point to the strength of the opposition rather than to their personal shortcomings as the cause of their failure.

2. Their goal is not to improve themselves personally in order to move up and out of their station in life. Unlike the recipients of compensatory education or job training who seek to move out of their present positions, labor organizations and tenants' unions seek to improve their working or living conditions because they anticipate remaining in those jobs or homes. The goal of collectivites is not to raise member's skill levels but to raise their collective consciousness, anger, and indigation.

3. They assume that the struggle will not end. Unlike the assumption of the compensatory model that help can be temporary, the assumption of

collective action is that the fight will go on. One victory is only a beginning, not the end, because the conflict of interests remains.

The compensatory model applied to individuals is fragile, and in practice it runs into contradictions. The compensatory model used by organized groups is robust. Collective efforts to put the compensatory model into action provide an alternative to bootstrapping. They go some distance in making help fair and effective.

REFERENCES

Adams, J. S. Inequity in social exchange. In L. Berkowitz (Ed.), *Advances in experimental social psychology* (Vol. 2). New York: Academic Press, 1965.

Alinsky, S. D. *Reveille for radicals.* New York: Vintage, 1969.

Alinsky, S. D. *Rules for radicals.* New York: Vintage, 1972.

Allen, V. L. *Children as teachers: Theory and research on tutoring.* New York: Academic Press, 1976.

Allen, V. L., & Feldman, R. S. Learning through tutoring: Low-achieving children as tutors. *Journal of Experimental Education,* 1974, **42**, 1–5.

Austin, W., & Walster, E. Participants' reactions to equity with the world. *Journal of Experimental Social Psychology,* 1974, **10**, 528–548.

Barber, T. X., & Silver, M. J. Fact, fiction, and the experimenter bias effect. *Psychological Bulletin,* 1968, **70**, (6, Part 2), 1–29.

Beckman, L. Effects of students' performance on teacher's and observers' attributions of causality. *Journal of Educational Psychology,* 1970, **61**, 75–82.

Beez, W. V. Influence of biased psychological reports on teacher behavior and pupil performance. *Proceedings of the 76th Annual Convention of the American Psychological Association,* 1968, 605–606.

Berkowitz, L. Resistance to improper dependency relationships. *Journal of Experimental Social Psychology,* 1969, **5**, 283–294.

Berkowitz, L. Social norms, feelings, and other factors affecting helping behavior and altruism. In L. Berkowitz (Ed.), *Advances in experimental social psychology* (Vol. 6). New York: Academic Press, 1972.

Berkowitz, L. *A survey of social psychology.* Hinsdale, Illinois: Dryden Press, 1975.

Berkowitz, L., & Conner, W. H. Success, failure, and social responsibility. *Journal of Personality and Social Psychology,* 1966, **4**, 664–669.

Berscheid, E., & Walster, E. When does a harm-doer compensate a victim? *Journal of Personality and Social Psychology,* 1967, **6**, 435–441.

Berscheid, E., Walster, E., & Barclay, A. Effect of time on tendency to compensate a victim. *Psychological Reports,* 1968, **25**, 431–436.

Blau, P. M. *The dynamics of bureaucracy.* Chicago: University of Chicago Press, 1955.

Blau, P. M. *Exchange and power in social life.* New York: Wiley, 1964.

Brickman, P. Crime and punishment in sports and society. *Journal of Social Issues,* 1977, **33**(1), 140–164.

Brickman, P., & Bryan, J. H. Moral judgment of theft, charity, and third-party transfers that increase or decrease equality. *Journal of Personality and Social Psychology,* 1975, **31**, 156–161.

Brickman, P., & Bryan, J. H. Equity versus equality as factors in children's moral judgments of theft, charity, and third-party transfers. *Journal of Personality and Social Psychology*, 1976, **34**, 757-761.

Brickman, P., Coates, D., & Janoff-Bulman, R. Lottery winners and accident victims: Is happiness relative? *Journal of Personality and Social Psychology*, 1978, **36**, 917-927.

Brickman, P., Linsenmeier, J. A. W., & McCareins, A. G. Performance enhancement by relevant success and irrelevant failure. *Journal of Personality and Social Psychology*, 1976, **33**, 149-160.

Brickman, P., Rabinowitz, V. C., Karuza, J., Coates, D., Cohn, E., & Kidder, L. H. Models of helping and coping, *American Psychologist*, 1982, **37**, (4), 368-384.

Bulman, R. J., & Brickman, P. When not all problems are soluble, does it still help to expect success? Unpublished manuscript, Northwestern University, 1976.

Campbell, D. T. On the conflicts between biological and social evolution and between psychology and moral tradition. *American Psychologist*, 1975, **30**, 1103-1126.

Caplan, N., & Nelson, S. D. On being useful: The nature and consequences of psychological research on social problems. *American Psychologist*, 1973, **28**, 199-211.

Carlsmith, J. M., & Gross, A. E. Some effects of guilt on compliance. *Journal of Personality and Social Psychology*, 1969, **11**, 232-239.

Castro, M. A. C. Reactions to receiving aid as a function of cost to donor and opportunity to aid. *Journal of Applied Social Psychology*, 1974, **4**, 194-209.

Chodoff, P., Friedman, S., & Hamburg, D. Stress defenses and coping behavior: Observations in parents of children with malignant diseases. *American Journal of Psychiatry*, 1964, **120**, 743-749.

Coyne, J. C. Toward an interactional description of depression. *Psychiatry*, 1976, **39**, 28-40.

Darley, J. M., & Latané, B. Bystander intervention in emergencies: Diffusion of responsibility. *Journal of Personality and Social Psychology*, 1968, **8**, 377-383.

Davison, G. C., & Valins, S. Maintenance of self-attributed and drug-attributed behavior change. *Journal of Personality and Social Psychology*, 1969, **11**, 25-33.

Deci, E. L. *Intrinsic motivation*. New York: Plenum Press, 1974.

Drabeck, T., & Quarantelli, E. L. Scapegoats, villains, and disasters. *Trans-Action*, 1967, **4**, 12-17.

Dweck, C. S., & Goetz, T. E. Attributions and learned helplessness. In J. H. Harvey, W. J. Ickes, & R. F. Kidd (Eds.), *New Directions in Attribution Research* (Vol. 2). Hillsdale, New Jersey: Lawrence Erlbaum, 1977.

Ekman, G., & Bratfish, O. Subjective distance and emotional involvement: A psychological mechanism. *Acta Psychologica*, 1965, **24**, 446-459.

Elashoff, J. D., & Snow, R. E. (Eds.) *Pygmalion reconsidered*. Worthington, Ohio: Charles A. Jones, 1971.

Erickson, M. R., & Cromack, T. Evaluating a tutoring program. *Journal of Experimental Education*, 1972, **41**, 27-31.

Feldman, R. S., Devin-Sheehan, L., & Allen, V. L. Children tutoring children: A critical review of research. In V. L. Allen (Ed.), *Children as teachers: Theory and research on tutoring*. New York: Academic Press, 1976.

Foa, U. G., & Foa, E. B. *Societal Structures of the Mind*, Springfield, Illinois: Thomas, 1974.

Frank, J. D. *Persuasion and healing*. New York: Schocken, 1963.

Freedman, J. L., Wallington, S. A., & Bless, E. Compliance without pressure: The effect of guilt. *Journal of Personality and Social Psychology*, 1967, **7**, 117-125.

Galarza, E. *Spiders in the House and Workers in the Field*. Notre Dame: University of Notre Dame Press, 1970.

Gergen, K. J., Morse, S. J., & Bode, K. A. Overpaid or overworked? Cognitive and behavioral reactions to inequitable rewards. *Journal of Applied Social Psychology*, 1974, **4**, 259-274.

Gerlach, L., & Hine, V. *People, Power, Change.* Indianapolis, Indiana: Bobbs Merrill, 1970.

Greenberg, M. S., & Shapiro, S. P. Indebtedness: An aversive aspect of asking for and receiving help. *Sociometry,* 1971, **34,** 290–301.

Gurin, P., & Epps, E. G. *Black consciousness, identity, and achievement.* New York: Wiley, 1975.

Ickes, W. J., Kidd, R. F., & Berkowitz, L. Attributional determinants of monetary help-giving. *Journal of Personality,* 1976, **44,** 163–176.

Jensen, B. Human reciprocity: An arctic exemplification. *American Journal of Orthopsychiatry,* 1973, 43(2).

Johnson, T. J., Feigenbaum, R., & Weiby, M. Some determinants and consequences of the teacher's perception of causation. *Journal of Educational Psychology,* 1964, **55,** 237–246.

Jones, E. E., & Harris, V. A. The attribution of attitudes. *Journal of Experimental Social Psychology,* 1967, **3,** 1–24.

Jones, E. E., & Nisbett, R. E. *The actor and the observer: Divergent perceptions of the causes of behavior.* Morristown, New Jersey: General Learning Press, 1971.

Kanter, R. M. *Men and Women of the corporation.* New York: Basic Books, 1977.

Kazdin, A. E., & Bryan, J. A. Competence and volunteering. *Journal of Experimental Social Psychology,* 1971, **7,** 87–97.

Kelley, H. H. Attribution theory in social psychology. In D. Levine (Ed.), *Nebraska Symposium on Motivation.* Lincoln, Nebraska: University of Nebraska Press, 1967.

Kipnis, D. Does power corrupt? *Journal of Personality and Social Psychology,* 1972, **24,** 33–41.

Langer, E. J. The illusion of control. *Journal of Personality and Social Psychology,* 1975, **32,** 311–328.

Lao, R. Internal-external control and competent and innovative behavior among Negro college students. *Journal of Personality and Social Psychology,* 1970, **14,** 263–270.

Latané, B., & Darley, J. M. *The unresponsive bystander: Why doesn't he help?* New York: Appleton, 1970.

Lefcourt, H. M. *Locus of control: Current trends in theory and research.* New York: Wiley, 1977.

Lemert, E. M. Paranoia and the dynamics of exclusion. *Sociometry,* 1962, **25,** 2–20.

Lepper, M. R., & Green, D. Turning play into work: Effects of adult surveillance and extrinsic rewards on children's intrinsic motivation. *Journal of Personality and Social Psychology,* 1975, **31,** 479–486.

Lerner, M. J. The justice motive in social behavior. *Journal of Social Issues,* 1975, **31,** 1–20.

Lerner, M. J., Miller, D. T., & Holmes, J. G. Deserving and the emergence of forms of justice. In L. Berkowitz & E. Walster (Eds.) *Advances in experimental social psychology* (Vol. 9). New York: Academic Press, 1976.

Lerner, M. J., & Simmons, Ch. Observers reaction to the 'innocent victim': Compassion or rejection? *Journal of Personality and Social Psychology,* 1966, **4,** 203–210.

Manis, M., Cornell, S. D., & Moore, J. C. The transmission of attitude-relevant information through a communication chain. *Journal of Personality and Social Psychology,* 1974, **30,** 91–94.

Mann, R. D., in collaboration with G. S. Gibbard & J. J. Hartman. *Interpersonal styles and group development.* New York: Wiley, 1967.

Marx, G. T. *Protest and prejudice: A study of belief in the black community.* New York: Harper, 1967.

Maslach, C. Burned-out. *Human Behavior,* September, 1976, 16–22.

Memmi, A. *The colonizer and the colonized.* Boston, Massachusetts; Beacon Press, 1967.

Milgram, S. Behavioral study of obedience. *Journal of Abnormal and Social Psychology,* 1963, **67,** 371–378.

Miller, A. G., Gillen, G., Schenker, C., & Radlove, S. Perception of obedience to authority. *Proceedings of the 81st Annual Convention of the American Psychological Association,* 1973, **8**, 127–128.

Miller, D. T. Personal deserving versus justice for others: An exploration of the justice motive. *Journal of Experimental Social Psychology,* 1977, **13**, 1–13.

Miller, D. T., & Norman, S. A. Actor-observer differences in perceptions of effective control. *Journal of Personality and Social Psychology,* 1975, **31**, 379–381.

Miller, D. T. & Ross, M. Self-serving biases in the attributions of causality: Fact or fiction? *Psychological Bulletin,* 1975, **82**, 213–225.

Miller, R. L., Brickman, P., & Bolan, D. Attribution versus persuasion as a means of modifying behavior. *Journal of Personality and Social Psychology,* 1975, **31**, 430–441.

Mischel, W. Continuity and change in personality. *American Psychologist,* 1969, **24**, 1012–1018.

Mondros, J. B. Empowerment versus dependency: The case of women office workers. Paper presented at the American Psychological Association, New York, September, 1979.

Morris, S. C., III, & Rosen, S. Effects of felt adequacy and opportunity to reciprocate on help seeking. *Journal of Experimental Social Psychology,* 1973, **9**, 265–276.

Nisbett, R. E., & Borgida, E. Attribution and the psychology of prediction. *Journal of Personality and Social Psychology,* 1975, **32**, 932–943.

Phillips, D. L. Rejection: A possible consequence of seeking help for mental disorders. *American Sociological Review,* 1963, **29**, 963–972.

Piliavin, I. M., Rodin, J., & Piliavin, J. A good Samaritanism: An underground phenomenon? *Journal of Personality and Social Psychology,* 1969, **13**, 289–299.

Pines, A., & Solomon, T. Perception of self as a mediator in the dehumanization process. *Personality and Social Psychology Bulletin,* 1977, **3**, 219–223.

Rabinowitz, V. S. *Orientations to help in four natural settings.* Unpublished doctoral dissertation, Northwestern University, Evanston, Illinois, 1978.

Rosenthal, R., & Jacobson, L. *Pygmalion in the classroom.* New York: Holt, 1968.

Ross, L. The intuitive psychologist and his shortcomings: Distortions in the attribution process. In L. Berkowitz (Ed.), *Advances in experimental social psychology* (Vol. 10). New York: Academic Press, 1977.

Ross, L., Bierbrauer, G., & Polly, S. Attribution of educational outcomes by professional and nonprofessional instructors. *Journal of Personality and Social Psychology,* 1974, **29**, 609–618.

Roth, J. A. Some contingencies of the moral evaluation and control of clientele: The case of the hospital emergency service. *American Journal of Sociology,* 1972, **77**, 839–856.

Rotter, J. B. Generalized expectancies for internal vs. external control of reinforcement. *Psychological Monographs,* 1966, **80**, No. 1 (Whole No. 287).

Rubin, Z., & Peplau, A. Belief in a just world and reactions to another's lot: A study of the national draft lottery. *Journal of Social Issues,* 1973, **29**, 73–93.

Rubin, Z., & Peplau, A. Who believes in a just world? *Journal of Social Issues,* 1975, **31**, 65–89.

Ryan, W. *Blaming the victim.* New York: Vintage, 1972.

Schopler, J. An investigation of sex differences on the influence of dependence. *Sociometry,* 1967, **30**, 50–63.

Schopler, J., & Layton, B. Determinants of the self-attribution of having influenced another person. *Journal of Personality and Social Psychology,* 1972, **22**, 326–332.

Schopler, J., & Matthews, M. W. The influence of the perceived causal locus of the partner's dependence on the use of interpersonal power. *Journal of Personality and Social Psychology,* 1968, **10**, 243–250.

Schwartz, S. H., Normative influences on altruism. In L. Berkowitz (Ed.), *Advances in Experimental Social Psychology* (Vol. 10). New York: Academic Press, 1972.

Schwartz, S. H., & Ben David, A. Responsibility and helping in an emergency: Effects of blame, ability and denial of responsibility. *Sociometry*, 1976, **39**, 406–425.

Seaver, W. B. Effects of naturally induced teacher expectancies. *Journal of Personality and Social Psychology*, 1973, **38**, 333–342.

Seligman, M. E. P. *Helplessness*. San Francisco, California: Freeman, 1975.

Sharp, L. Steel axes for Stone Age Australians. In E. H. Spicer (Ed.), *Human problems and technical change*. New York: Russell Sage, 1952.

Skinner, B. F. *Beyond freedom and dignity*. New York: Bantam, 1972.

Skinner, B. F. The ethics of helping people. In L. Wispé (Ed.), *Sympathy, altruism and helping behavior*. New York: Academic Press, 1978.

Snyder, M. L., Stephan, W., & Rosenfield, D. Attributional egotism, In J. H. Harvey, W. J. Ickes, & R. F. Kidd (Eds.), *New direction in attribution research* (Vol. 2). Hillsdale, New Jersey: Lawrence Erlbaum. In press.

Sowell, T. "Affirmative action" reconsidered. *Public Interest*, 1976, **42**, 47–65.

Staines, J., Tavris, C., & Jayaratne. The Queen bee syndrome. *Psychology Today*, January 1974, **7**, 55–60.

Stark, R., & Glock, C. Y. *American piety: The nature of religious commitment*. Los Angeles, California: University of California Press, 1968.

Stark, R., & Glock, C. Y. *By their fruits: The consequences of religious commitment*. Los Angeles, California: University of California Press, 1969.

Staub, E. A. A child in distress: The effects of focusing responsibility on children on their attempts to help. *Developmental Psychology*, 1970, **2**, 152–154.

Staub, E. A. Helping a distressed person: Social, personality, and stimulus determinants. In L. Berkowitz (Ed.), *Advances in experimental social psychology*. New York: Academic Press, 1974.

Stotland, E. Exploratory investigations of empathy. In L. Berkowitz (Ed.), *Advances in experimental social psychology* (Vol. 4). New York: Academic Press, 1969.

Sudnow, D. *Passing on: The social organization of dying*. Englewood Cliffs, New Jersey: Prentice-Hall, 1967.

Thibaut, J. W., & Riecken, H. W. Some determinants and consequences of the perception of social causality. *Journal of Personality*, 1955, **24**, 113–133.

Titmuss, R. M. *The gift relationship*. New York: Vintage, 1972.

Trivers, R. L. The evolution of reciprocal altruism. *Quarterly Review of Biology*, 1971, **46**, 35–57.

United States, President, *Economic Report of the President together with Annual Report of the Council of Economic Advisers*. Washington, D.C.: U.S. Government Printing Office, 1964.

Walster, E. Assignment of responsibility for an accident. *Journal of Personality and Social Psychology*, 1966, **3**, 73–79.

Walster, E., Berscheid, E., & Walster, G. W. New directions in equity research. *Journal of Personality and Social Psychology*, 1973, **25**, 176.

Walster, E., Walster, G. W., & Berscheid, E. *Equity: Theory and research*. Boston, Massachusetts: Allyn & Bacon, 1978.

Weiss, J. M. Effects of coping behavior in different warning signal conditions on stress pathology in rats. *Journal of Comparative and Physiological*, 1971, **77**, 1–13. (a)

Weiss, J. M. Effects of punishing the coping response (conflict) on stress pathology in rats. *Journal of Comparative and Physiological Psychology*, 1971, **77**, 14–21. (b)

Welfield, I. American housing policy: Perverse programs by prudent people *Public Interest,* Summer, 1977, No. 48, 129–144.

Wells, G. L., & Harvey, J. H. Do people use consensus information in making causal attributions? *Journal of Personality and Social Psychology,* 1977, **35,** 279–293.

Wicklund, R. A., & Brehm, J. W. *Perspectives on cognitive dissonance.* Hillsdale, New Jersey: Erlbaum, 1976.

Wortman, C. B. Some determinants of perceived control. *Journal of Personality and Social Psychology,* 1975, **31,** 282–294.

Wortman, C. B. Causal attributions of personal control. In J. H. Harvey, W. J. Ickes, & R. F. Kidd (Eds.), *New directions in attribution research* (Vol. 1). Hillsdale, New Jersey: Lawrence Erlbaum, 1976.

Wortman, C. B., & Brehm, J. W. Responses to uncontrollable outcomes: An integration of reactance theory and the learned helplessness model. In L. Berkowitz (Ed.), *Advances in experimental social psychology* (Vol. 8). New York: Academic Press, 1975.

CHAPTER 3

Four Conceptualizations of Reactions to Aid*

Jeffrey D. Fisher
Arie Nadler
Sheryle Whitcher-Alagna

A number of theoretical frameworks have been utilized by researchers to conceptualize reactions to help. These include *equity theories* (e.g., Greenberg & Westcott, this volume; Hatfield & Sprecher, this volume), *re-*

*This chapter represents an elaboration and extension of ideas presented in August, 1974 in a technical report by J. D. Fisher and A. Nadler, entitled "Recipient Reactions to Aid: Literature Review and a Conceptual Framework." That report was prepared under a grant awarded by the Office of Naval Research, and is technical Report 23, Contract No. N00014-0226-0030, NR 177-946, August 1974. Work on the present version of this manuscript was greatly facilitated by a grant from the United States–Israel Binational Science Foundation to the first two authors. Some of the research described herein was supported by a grant from the University of Connecticut Research Foundation to Jeffrey D. Fisher, and by a grant from the Israeli Academy of Sciences to Arie Nadler. The first authorship of Fisher and Nadler on the present manuscript is alphabetical. We thank Aharon Bizman, Donn Byrne, Kay Deaux, Bella DePaulo, Reuben M. Baron, Martin Greenberg, and David A. Kenny for their comments on earlier drafts of this paper.

51

actance theory (e.g., Brehm, 1966; Brehm & Brehm, 1981), *attribution theories* (e.g., Jones & Davis, 1965; Kelley, 1967), *threat to self-esteem models* (e.g., Fisher, Nadler, & Whitcher-Alagna, 1982) and other formulations (e.g., self-presentation [Baumeister, 1982]; learned helplessness [Wortman & Brehm, 1975]). Although most of these were not developed specifically to conceptualize reactions to aid, they have proved useful for helping us understand when and why people react positively or negatively to help. Each can be applied in at least some helping contexts, and each predicts one or more potential recipient responses. However, each views receiving help from a different perspective. Although allowing for a richer conceptual background, this diversity frequently leads to conflicting predictions and makes an overall theoretical integration difficult.

In this chapter, we review four of the major conceptual perspectives that have been applied to reactions to help (i.e., equity, reactance, attribution, and threat to self-esteem models), and the research done with each. The chapter is organized into four sections, corresponding to the four approaches. At the beginning of each section, we describe the theoretical assumptions and conditions basic to prediction. Then we review supportive and nonsupportive research, draw general conclusions, and offer an overall appraisal. Studies of reactions to help are placed in the section that best corresponds to the conceptual orientation taken by their authors. However, where a study has been interpreted meaningfully from more than one perspective, it is referred to in other sections as well.

EQUITY THEORIES

Equity theories (e.g., Adams, 1963; Blau, 1964; Walster, Berscheid, & Walster, 1973, 1978) and related formulations, that is reciprocity and indebtedness models (Gouldner, 1960; Greenberg, 1980) assume that we desire to maintain equity in our interpersonal relations and that inequitable relations produce distress. Individuals try to eliminate this by restoring actual equity (i.e., altering objective inputs–outcomes to yield parity), or by achieving psychological equity (i.e., cognitive distortion of inputs–outputs of self or others).

Walster's reformulation of equity theory (Hatfield & Sprecher, this volume; Walster *et al.,* 1973) and Greenberg's work on indebtedness (1980, this volume) are specific attempts to apply equity considerations to the aid recipient.[1] Both argue that in interactions in which the recipient has a more

---

[1]Although Greenberg's (1980) notion of indebtedness and Walster *et al.*'s (1973; Walster, Walster, & Berscheid, 1978) concept of inequity are not entirely congruent (see Greenberg, [1980, this volume] for a discussion of their similarities and differences), their general pre-

favorable ratio of outcomes to inputs than does the donor, inequity occurs, resulting in affective distress (e.g., feelings of indebtedness). Recipients attempt to eliminate these via behavioral or psychological means (i.e., by reciprocation or derogation of the aid and the donor). As noted by Hatfield and Sprecher (this volume) the amount of distress is positively related to the magnitude of the inequity. Some researchers (e.g., Adams, 1963, 1965) calculate inequity by including only the objective costs and rewards accruing from aid, whereas others (e.g., Greenberg, 1980; Walster *et al.,* 1973) include subjective aspects as well (e.g., the donor's motivation for helping).

Affective Consequences of Inequity

Studies corroborate the prediction that inequity is distressing. Individuals who receive "more than they deserve" experience negative affect (e.g., Adams, 1963; Adams & Rosenbaum, 1962) as do those who perceive themselves to be indebted to others (see Leventhal, Allen, & Kemelgor, 1969). The pain of inequity has also been documented in field reports on the aged (Kalish, 1967; Lipman & Sterne, 1962) that suggest that they want to avoid feelings of indebtedness and prefer to view retirement stipends as "due pay" rather than as a "dole" (Lipman & Sterne, 1962, p. 200).

Additional evidence that inequity is aversive is provided by studies on the influence of inability to reciprocate on help-seeking. When they are unable to reciprocate, individuals refrain more from seeking help or are slower to ask for it (e.g., Castro, 1974; Clark, Gotay, & Mills, 1974; DePaulo, 1978a; Greenberg & Shapiro, 1971; Morris & Rosen, 1973), more likely to break off an aid relationship after reaching a performance criterion (Greenberg & Shapiro, 1971), and less likely to seek future help (Castro, 1974) than when they can reciprocate. Receiving aid that cannot be reciprocated contradicts the deeply rooted norm of equity in social relations. So does aid that requires inequitably high repayment. Aid relationships that violate this norm may lower a recipient's self-esteem (see Gergen *et al.,* 1975; Gross & Latané, 1974; Pritchard, 1969; Walster *et al.,* 1973). (See Hatfield & Sprecher, this volume, for details of many of these studies.)

Determinants of the Intensity of Distress from Inequity

Greenberg (1980) asserts that the greater the recipient's net benefits from aid, the greater the feeling of indebtedness. Also, higher net costs to

---

dictions concerning reactions to help are similar. Therefore, we shall use the terms *inequity* and *indebtedness* interchangeably to refer to a recipient's felt obligation to repay a benefit and the negative feelings associated with that felt obligation.

the donor increase indebtedness (e.g., Gergen, Ellsworth, Maslach, & Seipel, 1975; Pruitt, 1968). If both donor costs and recipient benefits can increase indebtedness, the question arises, Which figures more heavily in determining indebtedness? Although this issue has not been definitively resolved, some research (e.g., Greenberg, Block, & Silverman, 1971; Greenberg & Saxe, 1975) suggests the recipient's rewards are more heavily weighted (see also Greenberg & Westcott, this volume).

In addition to donor costs and recipient rewards, research suggests that subjective aspects of aid affect the intensity of distress. When aid is voluntary (Goranson & Berkowitz, 1966) and deliberate (e.g., Greenberg & Frisch, 1972), it has greater value for the recipient and creates stronger feelings of inequity than when it is not voluntary and deliberate. Also, aid that is positively motivated elicits greater feelings of inequity than aid resulting from ulterior motives (e.g., Lerner & Lichtman, 1968).

Restoring Equity

To alleviate the discomfort associated with inequity, the recipient must equalize the input–output ratios of the donor and self. A direct way is through reciprocity. Wilke and Lanzetta (1970) found that subjects who had received help (which presumably created inequity) were more apt to assist the donor than those in a no-prior-aid condition. Moreover, greater inequity generates greater reciprocity. This occurs when conditions associated with aid are more favorable (e.g., when aid is voluntary [Gross & Latané, 1974]), when greater amounts of help are given (e.g., Greenberg & Frisch, 1972; Kahn & Tice, 1973; Stapleton, Nacci, & Tedeschi, 1973), and when the donor's costs rise (e.g., Gergen et al., 1975; Pruitt, 1968). Also, the magnitude of recipients rewards more strongly determines reciprocity than do donor costs (e.g., Greenberg et al., 1971).

Whether recipients engage in immediate reciprocity depends on the quality of their relationship with the donor. Immediate reciprocity is diminished when recipients expect to have many future opportunities for repayment (e.g., when help is given by friends or members of close-knit groups) (Bar-Tal, Zohar, Greenberg, & Hermon, 1977; Nadler, Fisher, & Streufert, 1974), and may be less when the recipient aspires to a "communal" rather than an "exchange" relationship with the donor (Clark & Mills, 1979). (See discussions by Greenberg & Westcott, Hatfield & Sprecher, and Clark, this volume, for different viewpoints on this issue.)

A question of interest is whether recipients can reduce inequity distress only via direct reciprocity to a benefactor, or also by doing a favor for a third party. If reciprocating to anyone eliminates the discomfort, the case for inequity as a general state of negative arousal related to feelings of incompetence and inferiority is strengthened. However, if distress is mitigated only when recipients repay the individual who helped them, the argument is corroborated that inequity involves feelings of injustice with a particular other.

In studies contrasting an opportunity to reciprocate to the donor with one to reciprocate to a third party, subjects generally engaged in more reciprocity (Goranson & Berkowitz, 1966; Gross & Latané, 1974; Shumaker & Jackson, 1979) and evaluated the donor more positively (Castro, 1974; Gross & Latané, 1974; Shumaker & Jackson, 1979) when they were allowed to reciprocate directly than when they helped a third person or when they could not reciprocate at all. However, aiding a third party can enhance the recipients' liking for the person who actually helped them (Castro, 1974; Gross & Latané, 1974). (See Greenberg & Westcott and Hatfield & Sprecher, this volume, for a discussion of the importance of donor–third party similarity in this regard.) Overall, at this point it is unclear whether inequity is a specific or more general state of obligation.

Equity theories assert that recipients may alleviate negative feelings not only by behavioral means (i.e., reciprocity) but also by altering perceptions. That individuals may cognitively redefine a situation rather than engage in actual reciprocity has received support. Overpaid workers altered perceptions of task difficulty and the level of pay they considered fair but did not increase output (Gergen, Morse, & Bode, 1974). Similar findings have been obtained by others (e.g., Lawler, Koplin, Young, & Faden, 1968; Pritchard, Dunnette, & Jorgenson, 1972), and Gergen and Gergen (1971) found recipients often redefine aid as the donor's "rightful obligation" rather than view it as a benefit that must be reciprocated.

Studies suggest that cognitive restructuring may be especially likely when direct reciprocity is not possible (cf. Greenberg & Westcott, this volume). According to Castro (1974), recipients who cannot repay a donation may blame the donor for creating the inequity that makes them feel uncomfortable. In line with this reasoning, Gergen et al. (1975) found that recipients evaluated donors who allowed opportunities for reciprocation more positively than donors who did not.

Equity and the Aid Recipient: a Summary

Equity formulations place receiving aid in the larger context of exchange relations, which allows an elaborate system of predictions and explanations. Overall, the data support the importance of these theories in understanding reactions to help. Their predictions generally have been corroborated with regard to the affective responses of the recipient (and their determinants), and the effects of inequity-indebtedness on help-seeking and other behavioral reactions.

However, an equity model is inadequate for making predictions in certain contexts because some variables likely to affect reactions to aid (e.g., donor–recipient similarity) do not arouse feelings that may be easily classified on an equity–inequity dimension. Further, an equity model focuses on predicting degrees of *negative* reactions to aid. Any helping relationship that results in greater relative outcomes for the recipient produces inequity, and except in certain instances (see Greenberg & Westcott, this volume) the most favorable response envisioned is a restoration of equity. Also, traditional equity approaches do not indicate what conditions lead a recipient to choose direct reciprocity or cognitive distortion to restore equity. There is evidence (Walster & Prestholdt, 1966) that the two modes are not used simultaneously and may be complementary, but Walster *et al.* (1973) were unable to delineate criteria of sufficient power to permit prediction. Greenberg and Westcott (this volume) suggest, however, that the *type* of indebtedness and the extent to which restructured cognitions are open to disconfirmation are important criteria.

Finally, some predictions that can be derived from equity theories are not supported. For example, it has been observed that recipients are more likely to accept large than small amounts of help (Freeman, 1977; Rosen, 1971). Although this appears reasonable in an instrumental sense, it conflicts with the prediction that one should be increasingly likely to avoid help as it leads to greater inequity. Also, equity formulations assume that aversive feelings mediate reciprocity. Some data suggest that reciprocity may be mediated by positive affect as well (see Fisher & Nadler, 1976; Greenberg, 1980).

REACTANCE THEORY

Reactance theory (Brehm, 1966; Brehm & Brehm, 1981) predicts that freedom restriction inherent in aid is a major determinant of recipient reactions. The theory stipulates that individuals desire to maintain freedom of choice. Perceived reductions in freedom result in a negative psychological state (reactance), which motivates people to restore lost freedoms. The magnitude of reactance is a positive function of the importance of the freedom to the individual and a monotonic function of the number of freedoms lost or threatened directly or by implication. Reactance results in attempts to engage in the threatened behavior (i.e., to behave as if freedom has not been lost), but may also produce modifications in perceptions and judgments, and physiological indications of stress.[2]

Applied to the help recipient, the theory suggests that when aid threatens the freedom to perform present or future actions, it will arouse reactance. Such conditions are probably directly inherent in certain types of aid (e.g., help that has stipulations on its use). However, many types of help are potentially freedom restricting due to inextricably linked, socialized beliefs about how one should respond to help and benefactors (e.g., "Don't bite the hand that feeds you"; the reciprocity norm), and beliefs about the nature of help (e.g., "You don't get something for nothing"). So, even when there is no direct threat to freedom, reactance may be experienced.

Clearly, a broad interpretation of reactance theory suggests that many aid contexts could elicit negative responses. Reactance should be greater when a range of freedoms are endangered, rather than just a few, and should increase when freedoms more important to the individual are affected. Recipients can reduce reactance by acting as though their behavior has not been restricted by help (e.g., by avoiding actions based on feelings of obligation to the donor, such as returning the aid or evaluating the giver favorably) (Brehm, 1966; Brehm & Brehm, 1981).

In support of reactance theory, aid does severely restrict freedom in certain situations (welfare settings, hospitalization, old age homes) (e.g., Briar, 1966; Goldin, Perry, Margolin & Stotsky, 1972). And as predicted, help is aversive under these circumstances. For example, if donors restrict the use of aid, recipients resent the help and the donor (e.g., Gergen & Gergen, 1971, 1974a). Also, potential recipients avoid placing themselves in situations likely to result in reactance. Gergen, Morse, and Kristeller (1973) and Rosen (1971) found that when donors give "with strings attached," less of their aid is accepted than when recipients are allowed to determine how aid will be used. Coupled with other relevant data (e.g., Brehm & Brehm, 1981), it appears that aid that causes reactance produces discomfort and is avoided if possible.

A receipt of reactance-producing aid may result in behavioral or cognitive attempts to regain freedom. Behaviorally, recipients restore freedom by acting as if aid has not been given (e.g., they tend not to reciprocate to the donor [e.g., Brehm & Cole, 1966; Schopler & Thompson, 1968]). One situation in which help frequently threatens freedom and reciprocity fails to occur, is when help is inappropriate to the setting (Schopler & Thompson, 1968). If the importance of the imperiled freedom is great, reciprocity is especially unlikely (Worchel, Andreoli, & Archer, 1976). Gergen and Ger-

---

[2]Although much research reported in this section adheres closely to Brehm's formulation of reactance theory, some makes predictions that could be derived from it but which, strictly speaking, are not pure "Brehmian" reactance.

gen (1971) concluded on the basis of survey data that when recipients have little freedom in designing international aid programs, they work "less constructively" to implement them. This also can be viewed as a failure to reciprocate.

Cognitive attempts to restore freedom include derogation of the donor and the aid. Ladieu, Hanfman, and Dembo (1947) found that disabled veterans resent help and view the helper as incompetent when aid restricts the freedom of the recipient. Similarly, Gergen and Gergen (1970) and Gergen et al. (1973) showed that aid with strings attached engenders negative evaluations of the donor and the aid. This is especially likely when aid restricts important freedoms (Worchel & Andreoli, 1974).

Although some research supports reactance predictions, there are inconsistent data. Gross and associates (see Gross, Wallston & Piliavin, 1979) explored the effect of locus of help-initiation on recipient reactions. Reactance theory predicts help offered by the donor is more freedom restricting than is aid that one is free to request when one chooses. (This assumes that performing *without* aid constitutes an important freedom; see DePaulo & Fisher, 1980.) Thus, help that can be requested, rather than help offered arbitrarily, should elicit more favorable reactions. However, more help is obtained and donors are liked better when help is offered than when it is requested. These findings have been replicated in a field study with welfare recipients (Piliavin & Gross, 1977). Although the results do not support reactance assumptions, they are not a strong test. Even though aid was offered arbitrarily recipients retained a degree of freedom because they could refuse the aid. A more stringent test would include an experimental condition with subjects given aid that cannot be refused.

Other studies also fail to support reactance predictions. Gergen et al. (1975) further question the assumption that the more restrictions on freedom, the more negative the recipient's reactions. Instead, they found an inverted-U-shaped relationship. Donors who asked for equal return of their aid (moderate freedom restriction) were liked better than those who asked for no return (low freedom restriction) or for equal return plus interest (high freedom restriction). However, the negative implications for reactance theory are tempered by two studies (Freeman, 1977; Gergen et al., 1973) in which evaluations of the donor did become more negative with increased obligation for repayment. The studies report that aid with no obligation to repay led to greater attraction than did "equal return plus interest aid." This suggests that the Gergen et al. (1975) data should be interpreted cautiously, though several characteristics of the experiments (e.g., within-subject designs, role playing) make them susceptible to demand characteristics.

Reactance theory predictions are most strongly contradicted by studies examining reciprocity to voluntary versus involuntary aid, deliberate versus nondeliberate aid, and high- versus low-cost aid. In the nonintimate relationships characteristic of this research (which was done with strangers in a laboratory setting), freedom from indebtedness to others is important (see Clark & Mills, 1979). Reactance theory predicts that aid that is voluntary, deliberate, or costly to the donor is more freedom restricting because it implies a greater demand for reciprocity and gratitude (see Greenberg & Frisch, 1972; Tesser, Gatewood, & Driver, 1968). The results were the opposite of what the theory predicts. Greater donor attraction and reciprocity occurred when aid was voluntary (e.g., Goranson & Berkowitz, 1966; Gross & Latané, 1974; Nemeth, 1970), deliberate (e.g., Garrett & Libby, 1973; Greenberg & Frisch, 1972; Leventhal, Weiss & Long, 1969), or when the donor incurred high costs in helping the recipient (Fisher & Nadler, 1976; Greenberg & Bar-Tal, 1976; Gergen et al., 1975; Pruitt, 1968).

Reactance and the Aid Recipient: a Summary

Reactance theory emphasizes an important motivational factor that may affect aid relationships. However, the data reveal mixed support for reactance-based predictions. The theory is limited as a model for predicting reactions to aid. First, it only applies when conditions associated with aid differentially restrict a recipient's perceived freedom. This excludes many situational variables that may be associated with help. Viewing reactance more broadly as a form of loss of control (see Wortman & Brehm, 1975) could allow prediction for a larger array of aid contexts, though still a restricted set. From this perspective, negative responses to aid (e.g., helplessness) might be expected in those who receive help that is noncontingent on their responses (Skinner, 1976). To date, no research has employed such an approach.

Another problem is that the theory predicts reactions only at the level of an independent variable for which threat to freedom is aroused, not at levels for which freedom is not inhibited. The theory predicts low attraction and reciprocity for "restrictive" aid, but implies nothing about reactions to "nonrestrictive" help. Aid research employing reactance theory has primarily examined reciprocity behavior and evaluations of the donor and the help, a focus partly determined by the predictive concerns of the formulation. Whether aid that limits perceived freedom lowers recipients' self-perceptions is an open question. On theoretical (e.g., Brehm, 1966) and empirical grounds (e.g., Andreas, 1969; Gergen & Gergen, 1971, 1974a), one could assume that such help would precipitate a loss in self-esteem.

ATTRIBUTION THEORIES

Attribution theories (e.g., Jones & Davis, 1965; Jones & McGillis, 1975; Kelley, 1967) view the recipient as actively attempting to make sense of the helping interaction. Those receiving help want to understand the donor's behavior and certain aspects of the situation in which dependency occurred. Specifically, recipients want to know, Why did the donor help me? (i.e., What were the donor's intentions?) and, Why did I need help? (e.g., because of incompetence or task difficulty). Research pertaining to the first question has typically employed the theory of correspondent inference (Jones & Davis, 1965; Jones & McGillis, 1975) as a conceptual perspective. The theory of external attribution (Kelley, 1967) has generally been employed in studies relating to the second question.

Theory of Correspondent Inference

Attributions of intent are made when actors are perceived to have knowledge of an action and ability to produce the effects observed (Jones & Davis, 1965; Jones & McGillis, 1975). Further, the probability of an intent attribution decreases to the extent that an action is situationally constrained. Behaviors that are strictly role prescribed or socially desirable acts are generally uninformative about the actor's personality and do not usually result in intent attributions. However, such actions may be judged to reflect personal traits when negative outcomes are endured in performing the behavior (e.g., pain is involved). These outcomes highlight the individualistic nature of the act, increasing the likelihood that it was intentional and reflects the actor's personality.

Applying this analysis to the aid recipient suggests that, in trying to discern a donor's intentions, the recipient is faced with a threefold dilemma. The donor may have acted out of true concern for the recipient's welfare, for ulterior motives, or because role requirements dictated helpfulness. According to the theory, a recipient can attribute a donor's behavior to a personality disposition only when the donor acted freely and deliberately, not because of role demands or situational constraints. Thus, no altruistic intentions are likely to be attributed to those who administer help as part of their job, unless they act independently of requirements, or incur negative outcomes (e.g., loss of free time, money) in helping.

There is support for the proposition that recipients are more likely to attribute aid to a personality disposition when it is not constrained by the setting. Enzle and Schopflocher (1978) found that subjects who received help that they believed to be spontaneous judged the donor to be more altruistic than those who received it at the experimenter's request. Further support can be derived from the finding that when help is deliberate the recipient is more likely to attribute it to personal motives than when is it situationally caused (Greenberg & Frisch, 1972).

Indirect evidence that situationally dictated help is less informative about the donor's character can also be inferred from experiments by Morse and associates (e.g., Morse, Gergen, Peele, & Van Ryneveld, 1977). They studied the effects of expected (e.g., role-prescribed) versus unexpected (e.g., not-role-prescribed) aid. Expected help did not lead to more favorable behaviors toward the donor, but unexpected help did. However, for unexpected help to have positive effects, it must be appropriate to the context (e.g., Morse *et al.*, 1977; Worchel & Andreoli, 1974).

The assertion that aid will be judged more often to reflect personal attributes, motives or intentions when negative outcomes (e.g., costs, risks) are incurred has also received support. Greenberg and Frisch (1972) and Fisher and Nadler (1976) observed that as donor costs in providing aid rise, recipients impute more care and concern to the donor. Other studies (Andreas, 1969; Tesser *et al.*, 1968) also suggest that correspondent inferences are more likely when donors give help in spite of inhibitory factors.

Although the theory specifies only the conditions that precipitate attributions, there is evidence that the aid context determines the quality of donor intent attributions. When recipient nations disagree with American foreign policy, they are more likely to make attributions of manipulative intent for the aid (Gergen & Gergen, 1974a). In an international conflict simulation, Nadler *et al.* (1974) demonstrated that aid from an enemy precipitated fewer attributions of altruistic intent than did equivalent aid from an ally. Other studies show the same pattern (e.g., Gergen & Gergen, 1974a). Similarly, negative attributions for aid are more likely when the helping relationship is bilateral than when it is multilateral (Andreas, 1969; Gergen & Gergen, 1974b).

The theory does not relate the quality of recipient attributions to other reactions to aid (e.g., attraction toward the donor, reciprocity). This relationship may be derived from studies that vary factors that affect intent attributions and measure other reactions. When recipients make positive attributions, they are generally more attracted to the donor (e.g., Gergen & Gergen, 1974b; Greenberg & Frisch, 1972; Nadler *et al.*, 1974), find aid more supportive (e.g., Fisher & Nadler, 1976; Gergen & Gergen, 1974a), accept more aid (Freeman, 1977; Rosen, 1971), engage in less self-help as an alternative to dependency (Andreas, 1969; Fisher & Nadler, 1976), and reciprocate more to the donor (e.g., Greenberg & Frisch, 1972; Lerner &

Lichtman, 1968; Schopler & Thompson, 1968). Thus, favorable intent attributions are associated with a cluster of positive reactions to aid, whereas unfavorable intent attributions are associated with negative responses.

The Theory of Correspondent Inference and the Recipient: a Summary

The theory of correspondent inference provides a valuable conceptual framework within which perceptions of donor motivation can be treated. It contributes primarily to understanding perceptions of donor intent and evaluations of the donor and the aid. Although one can infer links between attributions of donor intent and other reactions (e.g., internal perceptions and behaviors), these are not as easily predicted with the theory.

Theory of External Attribution

The theory of external attribution (e.g., Kelley, 1967) specifies when the cause for an event is attributed to the environment (external attribution) or to a personal disposition of the actor (internal attribution). Such attributions are based on information from two sources: relevant expectations individuals bring to a situation, and information contributed by the particular interaction. The theory further stipulates that there are three kinds of information—distinctiveness, consistency, and consensus—that when present in varying degrees, facilitate one causal attribution over another. Internal attributions result when a behavior is characterized by low distinctiveness, low consensus, and high consistency, whereas external attributions are made when behaviors reflect high distinctiveness, high consensus, and high consistency.

Kelley's (1967) formulation is relevant to the question, Why did I need help (i.e., internalization–externalization of the need for aid)? Recipients may conclude that their need was caused by internal–dispositional factors (e.g., one's own inadequacy) or external–situational factors (e.g., task difficulty). Research indicates that the locus of causal perception has important implications for reactions to aid. If the need for help is attributed dispositionally (i.e., to personal inadequacy) more unfavorable self-perceptions and less help-seeking occur than if it is attributed externally.

A pioneering study examined the impact of consensus information on help-seeking (Tessler & Schwartz, 1972). Tessler and Schwartz reasoned that, other things being equal, if consensus is high (i.e., many people need help on a similar task), the need for help should be attributed externally. When consensus is low, need for aid should be attributed internally. Further, if an internal attribution is made, individuals may be unwilling to expose inadequacy by seeking help. The results supported this analysis. When subjects believed only 10% of others working on a similar task needed help (low consensus information facilitating an internal attribution of need for help), less help was sought than when they believed 90% of others needed assistance. However, using the same manipulation of consensus, Nadler and Porat (1978) demonstrated that it affected help-seeking only when individuals remained anonymous. When identifiable, subjects refrained from help-seeking regardless of the consensus information.

Also suggesting that help-seeking is facilitated when people can attribute their need to the situation is a study of bereavement (Gerber, 1969). Survivors were more likely to accept professional assistance when they defined the situation as one calling for "uncustomary" sources of support. Further, Morris and Rosen (1973) found that if a situational attribution was not possible (personal inadequacy on a task was made salient), people were more reluctant to seek help than when performance was "competent." Work by Gross and associates (Broll, Gross, & Piliavin, 1974; Gross et al., 1979) also supports the relationship between external attributions and greater help-seeking. This research was originally described in the previous section on reactance and, although the data contradict reactance assumptions, they fit an attribution model.

Gross and associates found that more help was obtained (and the donor was better liked) when aid was offered to the recipient than when it had to be requested. They suggested that having to request aid may promote an internal attribution for failure, which inhibits help-seeking. Being offered help is less apt to prompt such an attribution, and facilitates help-seeking. This interpretation is corroborated because "request" subjects reported more anxiety and more negative self-ratings than those in "offer" conditions (see Gross et al., 1979). Although offered help may facilitate more favorable self-attributions, there are conditions under which it, too, may be aversive (e.g., Nadler, Fisher, & Streufert, 1976).

There is evidence that in addition to help-seeking, locus of attribution may affect reciprocity. Felt obligation to the donor is higher when the cause for dependency resides in the recipient than in the environment (e.g., Greenberg & Saxe, 1975). The assumption that more personal responsibility accrues to internally caused aid is congruent with the finding that people more often reject others whose problems are internally than externally caused (Calhoun, Pierce, Walters, & Dawes, 1974).

Finally, Kelley's theory offers principles that predict the strength of attributions. The augmentation principle states that when inhibitory factors (e.g., costs, risks, sacrifices) are encountered in performing a behavior, stronger attributions result. Applied to the aid recipient, when the penalties for seeking help are high, more confident internal attributions for needing help may occur. Such attributions may ensue when aid precludes reciprocity (e.g., Gross & Latané, 1974), when it emphasizes recipient inferiority vis-à-vis the donor (e.g., Gergen & Gergen, 1974a; Kalish, 1967; Nadler *et al.*, 1976), or when it involves a central task (e.g., Tessler & Schwartz, 1972), than when these conditions are absent.

The Theory of External Attribution and the Recipient: a Summary

The theory of external attribution is useful for predicting reactions to help. However, its range of application has only been touched upon by previous studies. A more complete delineation of the conditions that determine locus of attribution for dependency awaits further research. At this point, data suggest that aid associated with internal attributions for failure is unpleasant, and precipitates negative self- and donor evaluations, and diminished help-seeking. A more positive set of reactions is associated with external attributions for needing help.

The theory has several shortcomings. It has direct application only for recipient self- and other perceptions, though one may infer data-based links between locus of attribution and other reactions (e.g., help-seeking and reciprocity). Also, the criteria specified by Kelley for making attributions appear to be too rigid (Shaw & Constanzo, 1970). Confident external attributions seem to be made even when information from one or more of Kelley's "necessary" criteria are lacking. For example, recipients may attribute needing help to the environment whenever possible (e.g., Worchel & Andreoli, 1974). Finally, although Kelley's criteria for making attributions involve data gathered over several behavioral episodes, attributions are frequently made when the recipient first encounters the donor and the circumstances.

THREAT TO SELF-ESTEEM

A final perspective can be termed threat to self-esteem. Unlike the equity, reactance, and attribution formulations, this approach assumes explicitly that self-related consequences of aid are critical in determining recipient reactions. An underlying assumption of this approach is that aid contains a mixture of self-threatening and -supportive elements. Help may be threatening in that it implies an inferiority–superiority relationship between recipient and donor, and conflicts with values of self-reliance and independence that are stressed throughout socialization (Merton, 1968). On the other hand, help may be supportive, in that it may communicate donor caring and concern, and may provide instrumental benefits (e.g., money, advice). Based on this assumption, the approach makes two major predictions concerning reactions to help.

The first prediction is that *situational conditions* (i.e., donor characteristics, aid characteristics, and context characteristics) and *recipient characteristics* determine whether help is primarily threatening or supportive in a given setting. The second prediction is that when help is experienced as predominantly threatening, reactions are negative–defensive (e.g., lowered self-concept, negative donor and aid evaluations, low acceptance of aid, high self-help). When help is primarily supportive, reactions are positive–nondefensive (e.g., enhanced self-concept, positive donor and aid evaluations, high acceptance of aid, low self-help).

These assertions have been made frequently by aid researchers (e.g., Broll et al., 1974; Fisher & Nadler, 1976; Gergen & Gergen, 1974a, 1974b; Nadler et al., 1976). Conceptual work by Blau (1964), Coopersmith (1967), and Heider (1958), among others, has pointed to similar conclusions. And the self-related implications of aid have received attention in a large number of field studies (e.g., Lipman & Sterne, 1962; Nadler, Sheinberg, & Jaffe, 1981). Nevertheless, experimental research in social psychology has tended to ignore the recipient's internal feelings and self-cognitions. The studies we will describe are unique in their use of threat to self-esteem as a major conceptual construct.

Situational Conditions

A number of studies support the assertion that situational conditions determine the self-related consequences of aid. In one of the first studies, Fisher and Nadler (1974) demonstrated that aid from an attitudinally similar other on an intellectual task was self-threatening, whereas the same help from a dissimilar other was supportive. It was suggested that because similar individuals serve as social comparison others (see Castore & DeNinno, 1977; Festinger, 1954), their aid amplifies elements of relative inferiority and dependency inherent in receiving help. This explanation was corroborated in research by Nadler et al. (1976).

The fore-mentioned findings were extended in an experiment that may have implications for peer tutoring in the classroom. Fisher, Harrison, and Nadler (1978) found that being helped by a peer (someone with similar task-relevant experience) is more threatening than help from a nonpeer (someone with greater task-relevant experience). In addition, Weiss (1969) showed that welfare mothers interviewed by someone similar in ethnic and socio-economic background report being more "bothered" by welfare than those assigned a dissimilar interviewer.

Also in line with the threat to self-esteem approach, other situational conditions may moderate the self-consequences of aid from a similar other. Nadler and Fisher (Note 1) suggest that the locus of the donor's ability to help may have such an effect. Aid was threatening when it indicated the donor's superior knowledge (as in the Fisher & Nadler, 1974, Fisher *et al.*, 1978, and Nadler *et al.*, 1976 studies), but was supportive when the locus of the donor's ability was external. A second variable (degree of friendship) affects the self-threat in aid from a similar other. Help from similar donors who are close friends may not be threatening (Clark *et al.*, 1974; DePaulo, 1978a), especially when it is given on a noncentral task (Nadler, Fisher, & Ben-Itzak, 1983).

Another situational variable affecting the self-consequences of help is donor resources. Fisher and Nadler (1976) found that aid from one who accumulated high resources in a setting in which the recipient failed precipitated negative affect and lower situational self-esteem. Positive affect and higher situational self-esteem resulted when the donor had relatively fewer resources. Presumably, aid from an other who begins with equivalent resources but is extremely successful (in a setting in which the recipient fails) carries a strong message of relative incompetence and threat. When the donor is barely able to help (a low-resource donor), the message of relative inferiority is less salient, and such "high-cost" aid may be supportive because it conveys a message of caring and concern.[3] Whether parallel results would be obtained when resources are different at the start awaits research.

Other studies demonstrate that situational conditions determine recipient self-threat or support. Gergen and Gergen (1974a) found that aid from positively motivated donors was more supportive than help from negatively motivated ones. It may be threatening to be dependent on someone perceived to have ulterior motives (a donor who may take advantage of one), and positively motivated help may be supportive because it is viewed as reflecting true liking and concern. Gergen and Gergen (1970, 1974b) and DePaulo and associates (DePaulo, 1978a; Druian & DePaulo, 1977) found that conditions that emphasize status or ability differences, or that place the donor in a superordinate position, lead to threat. Stokes and Bickman

---

[3]The data on the effects of donor–recipient similarity and those on the effects of donor resources may seem to be in disagreement. Specifically, they appear to suggest that although overall dissimilarity decreases self-threat, resource disparity (or dissimilarity) increases self-threat. However, this conclusion would be misleading due to a number of differences in the two bodies of research. For a complete discussion of this issue, and for an integration of these two sets of studies, see Nadler and Fisher (Note 2).

(1974) and Nadler (1980) reported that having to seek help from a physically attractive individual was more threatening than dependency on an unattractive other. This may be because one risks a greater loss in esteem in admitting needing help to someone who enjoys an enviable social status. Alternatively, people may feel that attractive others will be less likely to comply with their request. Finally, when recipients expect to meet the donor, they experience more threat than when they are allowed to remain anonymous (Nadler, 1980; Nadler & Porat, 1978).

Recipient Characteristics

The threat to self-esteem perspective assumes further that recipient characteristics determine the self-consequences of help. Several recipient characteristics are associated with differential sensitivity to the threatening elements in aid. DePaulo and Fisher (1980) and Nadler, Sheinberg, and Jaffe (1981) found that recipients who were ego- involved with tasks were more threatened by aid than those with lower involvement. Also, high-need achievers, for whom autonomy and individual achievement may be central to self-concept, are more threatened by aid than are low-need achievers (Tessler & Schwartz, 1972). DePaulo and Rosenthal (1980) and DePaulo and Fisher (1981) found that recipients who are sensitive to covert nonverbal cues (e.g., negative messages donors may "leak" while overtly expressing a desire to help) are particularly susceptible to threatening implications of aid. There is also evidence (reviewed in detail by Nadler & Mayseless, this volume) that high and low self-esteem individuals are differentially sensitive to the self-threat in aid.

Corroborative Support from Other Studies

The predictions of the threat to self-esteem approach are corroborated by studies using other conceptualizations. Situational conditions such as whether aid is offered or requested (e.g., Gross *et al.,* 1979) and whether or not the recipient can reciprocate (e.g., Gross & Latané, 1974), among others, determine the self-consequences of aid. Aid that must be requested may elicit threat because it involves a public admission of inferiority, whereas an offer of aid does not. Having to accept help that one cannot reciprocate may be threatening because it conflicts with the norm that one should be equitable in social relations.

Research using other conceptualizations has also related recipient characteristics to the self-threat or support in aid. Less positive reactions among recipients with high need (those with relatively severe emotional problems) occurred in studies of psychiatric help-seeking (Calhoun, Dawes, & Lewis, 1972). And recipients with relatively high *material* need are more threatened by help than those with low need (Morse & Gergen, 1971). Morse and Gergen suggest that people with low material need may expect aid less than those with high need, so aid constitutes more of a positive disconfirmation (and hence is more supportive for them). Also, low-need individuals (because of their low need) may find the inadequate levels of aid typical of many helping programs useful rather than frustrating. Although studies suggest better reactions in low- than high-need individuals, one can envision situations in which this pattern might reverse (e.g., when help effectively meets a life threatening rather than a trivial need, especially when the problem is not the recipient's fault).

Overall, the relation specified by the threat to self-esteem approach between aid-related conditions and recipient self-threat or self-support is corroborated by many studies. There is also evidence, reviewed below, for the second assumption of this approach. Specifically, threatening aid leads to negative–defensive reactions (e.g., unfavorable donor and aid evaluations, low help-seeking and acceptance of aid, and high self-help), whereas supportive aid leads to positive–nondefensive responses (e.g., favorable donor and aid evaluations, high help-seeking and acceptance of aid, and low self-help).

Relationship between Self-Consequences of Aid and Recipient Reactions

Studies have found that when dependency is threatening, less aid is sought than when it is supportive. For example, Druian and DePaulo (1977) and DePaulo (1978b) suggest that adults are more threatened by dependency on children than on equally competent adults, and seek less help from them. And individuals (especially those with high self-esteem) are more resistant to seeking help on ego-involving than on non-ego-involving tasks (e.g., DePaulo & Fisher, 1980; Tessler & Schwartz, 1972; Wallston, 1976). Finally, Nadler (1980) and Stokes and Bickman (1974) observed that one's esteem is more threatened by dependency on physically attractive than unattractive others, and that such aid is sought less. When helping is perceived as out of role for a physically attractive other, help-seeking is depressed still further (Stokes & Bickman, 1974).

The assertions of the model are also corroborated by data on recipient efforts toward self-sufficiency. Fisher and Nadler (1976) and Nadler and Fisher (Note 1) found that when aid is threatening (i.e., help from a high-resource donor or a similar donor whose success is due to superior ability), recipients make more self-help efforts than when aid is supportive. This pattern is supported anecdotally in a study of editorials in India and Pakistan (Andreas, 1969). When American aid was perceived as emphasizing donor superiority (i.e., when it was threatening), editors called for their nation to better itself so that the humiliating dependency could be terminated. When help was supportive, self-help efforts were not stressed. Finally, after receiving threatening help, high self-esteem subjects perform especially well on a subsequent task, presumably to avoid further need for help (DePaulo, Brown, Ishii, & Fisher, 1981).

Complementing these studies is clinical research suggesting that threatening aid leads to higher self-help, whereas supportive aid leads to continued dependency. Subjects told that mental disorders were due to social learning (a threatening belief because it places the blame for the problem on the individual) engaged in high self-help behavior. Those told that mental disorders were diseases (a less-threatening belief because the cause is external) engaged in less self-help (Farina, Fisher, Getter, & Fischer, 1978; Fisher & Farina, 1979). However, it should be noted that when aid is extremely threatening, a state of debilitation rather than self-help efforts may ensue.

In addition to help-seeking and self-help, research done using other theories suggests the self-consequences of aid can be used to predict reciprocity. When aid is supportive (e.g., when it is given voluntarily, or on non-ego involving tasks) positive forms of reciprocity occur (Greenberg & Frisch, 1972; Morse, 1972). Positive reciprocity includes various behaviors motivated by favorable feelings toward the donor (e.g., reciprocating the aid, cooperating with the donor, expressing gratitude). These probably occur because the recipient has come to like the donor, feels comfortable in the dependency relationship, and, if necessary, would accept help again. When aid is threatening (e.g., when it is involuntary, or on an ego-involving task), such behaviors are less likely (Greenberg & Frisch, 1972; Morse, 1972).

In addition to positive reciprocity, negative reciprocity may also occur. These are behaviors motivated by unfavorable feelings toward the donor (e.g., sabotaging the aid program, reacting against donor attempts at social influence, returning aid immediately to negate the helping transaction). They may be viewed as means of restoring self-esteem that had been lowered by receiving aid. Negative reciprocity is high when aid is threatening and is low when aid is supportive (e.g., Morse, 1972; Nadler et al., 1974).

Finally, self-threatening and self-supportive aid lead to differential affective states, self-evaluations, and evaluations of the donor. When aid conveys information about relative inferiority and incompetence (e.g., help from a similar or highly successful donor), recipients experience more negative affect than when such information is not transmitted (e.g., Fisher & Nadler, 1976; Fisher et al., 1982). Also, threatening aid often elicits more negative donor evaluations than does supportive aid (e.g., Fisher & Nadler, 1976; Gergen & Gergen, 1974a; Gergen et al., 1973; Greenberg & Frisch, 1972). However, some data (e.g., Fisher & Nadler, 1974; Nadler et al., 1976) are equivocal, suggesting that sometimes donors receive positive evaluations regardless of the self-implications of help. Several explanations for this, all focusing on methodological problems involved in measuring recipient evaluations of benefactors, have been offered (see Greenberg, 1980). For example, social desirability and the reciprocity norm may cause positive evaluations of donors even when aid is aversive. Thus, findings should be interpreted cautiously, and more unobtrusive measures should be used (see Morse, 1972).

Threat to Self-Esteem and the Aid Recipient: a Summary

The data support the assertions of the threat to self-esteem approach, and highlight the major role the self-consequences of aid play in determining recipient responses. Unfortunately, earlier threat to self-esteem formulations have been relatively informal. Based on our review, an expanded, formalized threat to self-esteem model could prove beneficial. Another reason for such a model would be its potential breadth in predicting across aid contexts. Self-consequences are inherent in a broad array of aid situations, due to aspects of socialization and qualities of help itself. In contrast to the threat to self-esteem construct, those used in other formulations (e.g., degree of inequity, limitation of freedom) omit a large segment of aid situations from their domain.

Complementing its cross-situational breadth, a formalized threat to self-esteem model could relate a unified mediator to a wide range of reactions that may occur in a given aid context. Other theories are limited in direct applicability to one or a few responses to help. The threat to self-esteem approach is also the first to specify how responses relate to one another (i.e., it posits that positive–nondefensive reactions cluster together, as do negative–defensive ones.)

TOWARD A FORMALIZED THREAT TO SELF-ESTEEM MODEL

We will attempt to demonstrate that a formalized threat to self-esteem model could provide an accurate and parsimonious means of predicting reactions to aid across diverse contexts. We begin with an analysis of the data in past research. This yields a set of common patterns similar to those proposed by a threat to self-esteem formulation. It suggests that such a model constitutes a "best fit" to the extant data, and that the model's assumptions are borne out by research across theoretical contexts.

Analysis of Past Research

Two patterns exist in the literature on reactions to aid that strongly corroborate a threat to self-esteem model. First, a descriptive factor analysis of past research reveals two distinct clusters of recipient responses that are distinct on evaluative, affective, and behavioral levels. Cluster 1 is essentially negative–defensive and includes negative affect, negative donor and aid evaluations, low positive and high negative reciprocity, high subsequent self-help, low help-seeking, and low acceptance of aid. Cluster 2 is essentially positive–nondefensive and includes positive affect, positive donor and aid evaluations, high positive and low negative reciprocity, low subsequent self-help, high help-seeking, and high aid acceptance. Numerous studies show that reactions within a particular cluster tend to occur simultaneously and tend to exclude reactions in the other cluster (e.g., Fisher & Nadler, 1976; Gergen & Gergen, 1974a; Goranson & Berkowitz, 1966; Greenberg & Frisch, 1972; Broll et al., 1974; Gross & Latané, 1974; Morse, 1972; Stokes & Bickman, 1974).

Second, the data reveal that Cluster 1 and 2 reactions are elicited by different types of situational conditions. When the conditions associated with each cluster are grouped separately (see Table 1), it is clear that Cluster 1 reactions occur when it can be assumed aid leads to absolute or relative threat to self-esteem, and Cluster 2 reactions occur when it can be assumed aid leads to absolute or relative self-support.

Together, these two patterns corroborate the assumptions of a threat to self-esteem model and show that it may subsume the valid predictions of earlier theoretical formulations. Regardless of the formulation used originally to make predictions, when conditions associated with aid could be classified as self-threatening, a negative set of responses occurred. When conditions elicited self-support, a more positive set of reactions occurred. The threat to self-esteem mediating construct is sufficiently broad to predict across a diverse range of aid situations, and for many modes of reactions to aid.

Commonalities with Other Conceptualizations

That a threat to self-esteem model can subsume the predictions of earlier formulations can also be derived from those models themselves. Equity

TABLE 1

Some Conditions that Elicit Cluster 1 (Negative–Defensive) and Cluster 2 (Positive–Nondefensive) Responses Associated with Aid

Cluster 1 conditions	Cluster 2 conditions	Specific studies
Negative donor attributes and motivation[a]	Positive donor attributes and motivation[a]	Gergen & Gergen, 1974a
Donor–recipient social comparability[a]	Donor-recipient non-social comparability[a]	Fisher & Nadler, 1974, Nadler et al., 1976
Inability to reciprocate[a]	Ability to reciprocate[a]	Gross & Latané, 1974
Threat to autonomy[a]	Little threat to autonomy[a]	Gergen & Gergen, 1970, 1971
High donor resources or expertise[a]	Low donor resources or expertise[a]	Fisher & Nadler, 1976
Very high obligation to repay, or none	Moderate obligation to repay	Gergen et al., 1975
Aid that implies the loss of important freedoms	Aid that implies few lost freedoms	Brehm & Cole, 1966
Aid that is requested rather than offered[a]	Aid that is offered rather than requested[a]	Gross et al., 1979
Aid on a central task	Aid on a noncentral task	Morse, 1972
Involuntarily administered aid	Voluntarily administered aid	Goranson & Berkowitz, 1966
Aid that is nondeliberate	Aid that is deliberate	Greenberg & Frisch, 1972
Aid that is bilateral	Aid that is multilateral	Gergen & Gergen, 1974b
Aid that is low normative	Aid that is highly normative	Tessler & Schwartz, 1972
Aid that constitutes a negative disconfirmation of expectancies	Aid that constitutes a positive disconfirmation of expectancies	Morse & Gergen, 1971

[a]Absolute or relative self-threat were measured. However, all conditions listed can be reasonably assumed to elicit absolute or relative self-threat.

and reactance predictions are based, in essence, on the same general rationale as are predictions for a threat to self-esteem model. Implicit in the hypothesized negative consequences of inequity (for equity theory) and limitations on freedom (for reactance theory) is the assumption these conditions elicit self-concept distress because they violate socialized norms of fairness, self-reliance, and independence. According to Walster *et al.* (1973), people in inequitable relationships experience a threat to self-esteem because they are violating the ethical principal that "one should be fair and equitable in dealing with others" (Walster *et al.*, 1973, p. 155). For individuals socialized under the Protestant ethic, which specifies self-reliance and independence as the greatest good and dependency as the greatest sin

(Weber, 1930), aid that limits freedom of action (help that causes reactance) clearly threatens self-esteem.

It could be argued that attribution theories are only effective predictors of reactions to aid insofar as they identify the implications of help for recipient self-concept. The predictive domain of the theory of correspondent inference is limited to attributions of specific motives for donor behavior. The bridge to other reactions to aid is the self-threat or support inherent in such attributions. When positive donor motives are attributed (e.g., the donor is perceived to act out of kindness or generosity), aid is more supportive and results in more favorable reactions (see Gergen & Gergen, 1970, 1974a). The predictive domain of the theory of external attribution is limited to the recipient's locus of attribution for the positive or negative information inherent in aid. Again, the bridge between this and other reactions is threat to self-esteem. When locus of attribution leads to self-threat, reactions are negative; when it leads to self-support, reactions are positive (see Gergen & Gergen, 1974a).

Earlier, it was established that a threat to self-esteem model can be extracted from and is congruent with data in past research generated by various conceptual formulations. It was also shown that this formulation is in accord with critical conceptual elements of the formulations themselves. Now, we suggest that such a model would also be congruent with self-esteem theories in personality research.

Relation to Self-esteem Theories

Self-esteem formulations (e.g., Coopersmith, 1967; Wylie, 1974) suggest individuals are motivated to maintain favorable self-attitudes, and to defend the self-concept against alteration, diminution, or insult. Information that threatens feelings of self-worth causes anxiety and precipitates attempts to restore self-esteem. These may include devaluating the source of the information, blaming others for the problem, or engaging in behaviors that have enhanced self-feelings in the past (see Coopersmith, 1967, Wylie, 1974).

These assumptions find parallels in a threat to self-esteem model of reactions to aid. The model predicts that recipients who are threatened by aid experience negative affect and engage in defensive attempts to restore positive feelings about the self. These involve derogating the donor and the aid, exhibiting high negative and low positive reciprocity, engaging in self-help to prevent further aid from being necessary, and seeking little subsequent help. All of these responses reaffirm the recipient's feelings of power and control. In contrast, aid that supports the recipient's self-concept precipitates a host of different reactions. Recipients of such help (who are not concerned with restoring self-esteem) enjoy positive affect, evaluate the donor and the aid positively, and engage in high positive and low negative reciprocity. They also engage in low self-help and high help-seeking, probably because past dependency was pleasant and they expect future dependency would be the same.

A FORMALIZED THREAT
TO SELF-ESTEEM MODEL

Given the converging lines of evidence suggesting the viability of a formalized threat to self-esteem model, we propose one formally. Though many of its assertions have received experimental support, others remain to be tested. Thus, the model is subject to refinement based on future research.

Our model, like the informal threat to self-esteem approach on which it is based, assumes that (1) most aid situations contain a mixture of positive and negative self-related elements, and (2) situational conditions and recipient characteristics determine whether a particular receipt of aid is predominantly threatening or supportive. However, our model is far more explicit in its predictions and rationale. We present each of the hypotheses in a summary statement, which we then explicate. Figure 1 represents a schematic diagram of the entire model.

1. *Dependency relations have potential for self-threat and support due to (a) self-relevant messages contained in aid itself, (b) values instilled during socialization, and (c) inherent instrumental qualities of help.*

Self-relevant Messages Contained in Aid Itself Aid in and of itself often contains positive or negative self-relevant messages (due to the way it is offered, the type of help given, qualities of the helper, etc.). For example, it may be clear from how aid is given or other characteristics of the transaction that donors like, care, and are concerned about recipients and view them as worthy (a supportive message) or else disdain recipients and view them as unworthy (a threatening message). Similarly, aid may stress one's relative inferiority and dependency compared with peers (threatening information) or allow recipients to see themselves as equally adept as others (more supportive information). To the extent that such messages are primarily positive, aid will contain elements of self-support; to the extent that they are negative, aid will be threatening.

Socialized Values In modern Western culture, some values relevant to the receipt of aid are broadly socialized. These can be identified with

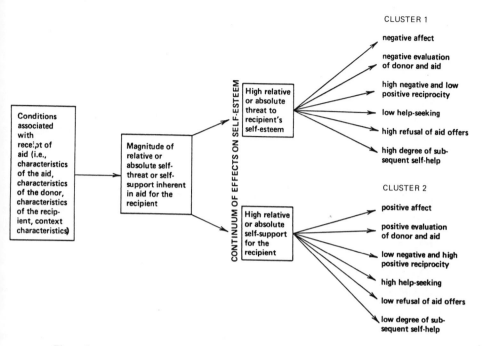

Figure 1.

great consensus. To the extent that aid conflicts with such values, it contains elements of self-threat; to the extent that it is congruent with them, it contains elements of self-support.[4]

First, there is the prevalent value that people should be independent and self-reliant (see Berkowitz & Daniels, 1963; Merton, 1968; Weber, 1930). From this perspective, aid that limits freedom of action is threatening, aid that fosters it is supportive. This value also implies an individual should be a viable entity with basic competence in certain areas (i.e., ability to care for basic needs) and expertise in some domain. Aid that signifies a failure to correspond to this ideal contains threatening elements. Aid in an area in which one is not expected to have basic or expert competence does not represent a failure to conform to this value, and may be supportive.

[4]What we are describing here is a process that affects whether an offer of aid will be experienced as self-supportive or self-threatening. The specific values described should not be assumed to hold across all cultures, but we believe the reasoning (that receipts of aid that correspond with established values relevant to dependency will elicit elements of self-support in the recipient, whereas receipts of aid that conflict with such values elicit elements of self-threat) will hold across cultures.

When aid signifies that one has lived up to this value (e.g., grants or fellowships to researchers, recognizing their expertise), it is experienced as supportive.

People are also socialized to believe they should deal fairly with others (e.g., conform to the value of equity in social exchange, and the reciprocity norm). Recipients thus aspire to maintain fair relations with donors (to restore equity after receiving aid; to deal fairly with the donor in other respects). When they cannot comply with such values, recipients experience self-threat; when they are able to comply, aid may contain supportive elements.

Finally, people believe they should be treated fairly by others. Aid that exploits or otherwise takes advantage of recipients conflicts with this value and contains threatening elements, aid that constitutes fair treatment is congruent and contains supportive elements. We more often fear that aid constitutes an unfair arrangement and experience it as threatening when it does not contain clear signs of the donor's liking and caring, or when the donor has negative characteristics (e.g., is perceived as dishonest) (Gergen & Gergen, 1971).[5]

Instrumental Qualities of Aid   The amount of aid and the efficacy of aid affect its self-consequences. To the extent that aid (i) decreases threat associated with one's current condition, and (ii) increases the probability of future success, it will contain supportive elements. Thus, aid that fully meets recipients' current needs *and* enables them to avoid future dependency (e.g., a *process* allowing recipients to care for themselves in the future) is more supportive than a "handout" that meets only current needs. However, to meet current needs, or even a portion of them, may be supportive because it makes one's problem less bothersome. In contrast, aid that is not instrumental in significantly relieving one's need state (e.g., because it is insufficient or ineffective) will be threatening because (i) one continues to bear both the failure that caused the current need state and the prospect of future problems, (ii) persisting problems often become more embarrassing, (iii) ineffective help may suggest one is being exploited, and (iv) accepting ineffective help may call into question one's judgment, status, means, or power.

[5]In addition to these value orientations, dispositional qualities (e.g., persistent self-esteem, sex typing) may also be viewed as systems of socialized values within an individual. Aid will be threatening to the extent that it is inconsistent with these, and supportive to the extent it is consistent. For example, because dependency is more inconsistent with the values of high than low self-esteem individuals, and of masculine than of feminine sex-typed people, it should be more threatening to them.

2. *Situational conditions and recipient characteristics associated with receipt of aid determine whether it is a predominantly self-supportive or self-threatening experience.*

Many, if not most instances of aid include both self-threatening and self-supportive elements. For example, aid may be supportive (e.g., provide instrumental benefits) and yet imply a threatening failure to exhibit competence when one is supposed to be an expert. Hypothesis 2a specifies that situational conditions and recipient characteristics determine the configuration of self-threatening and self-supportive elements in a receipt of aid. Specifically, these variables determine the extent to which aid is experienced: (i) as containing a favorable or unfavorable self-relevant message, (ii) as consistent or inconsistent with socialized values, and (iii) as meeting or failing to meet one's needs.

Hypothesis 2b proposes that situational conditions and recipient characteristics determine the relative weights of the self-related information deriving from the above three sources. For example, in situations of very high recipient need, the self-consequences accruing from the instrumental qualities of aid outweigh those from the other two sources. In low-need situations, the reverse would be true. Similarly, the weight associated with consistency–inconsistency with socialized values (e.g., Protestant ethic orientations) depends on how strongly these values are internalized. If they are highly internalized, the self-support from consistency, and the threat from inconsistency, will be more heavily weighted.

Finally, hypothesis 2c incorporates 2a and 2b into the following summary statement. To the extent that overall, aid-related situational conditions and recipient characteristics highlight aspects of aid that elicit self-threat relative to aspects that elicit self-support, aid is predominantly threatening. To the extent that situational conditions and recipient characteristics highlight aspects of aid that elicit self-support relative to aspects that elicit self-threat, aid is predominantly supportive.

3. *Other things being equal, whether aid is predominantly self-supportive or self-threatening determines reactions to aid.*

Other things being equal (e.g., the type of problem for which help is needed), when aid is predominantly threatening, negative reactions that are defensive in nature (Cluster 1 reactions) tend to occur. In contrast, when help is predominantly supportive, it elicits essentially positive–nondefensive reactions (Cluster 2 reactions). The hypothesized relationship between self-threat and Cluster 1 reactions, and self-support and Cluster 2 reactions has received direct experimental corroboration (e.g., Fisher & Nadler, 1976; Farina *et al.*, 1978; Fisher & Farina, 1979), and indirect support from past research, as discussed previously.

4. *Elements of self-threat and self-support are the intervening construct between aid-related situational conditions and recipient characteristics, and recipient reactions to aid.*

The assumption that elements of self-threat and self-support are the intervening construct between aid-related situational conditions and recipient characteristics, and reactions to aid follows from Hypothesis 3. Hypothesis 4 has also received direct experimental support in studies by Nadler *et al.* (1976; Nadler, Altman, & Fisher, 1979) that used Underwood's strategy for validating hypothesized intervening constructs. Briefly, Underwood (1975) suggested that a hypothesized intervening construct can be substantiated if people who differ on a relevant personality dimension respond to the manipulation in question (i) differentially, and (ii) consistently with extant theory. Using both "trait" and "state" operationalizations of self-concept, Nadler *et al.* (1976, 1979) found that individuals with high and low self-esteem responded to aid differentially and in line with a consistency formulation (Bramel, 1968). This is strong evidence for elements of self-threat and self-support as a mediator between aid-related conditions and reactions to aid.

5. *The degree to which aid is predominantly self-supportive or self-threatening determines the intensity of Cluster 1 and 2 responses.*

To the extent that aid is predominantly self-threatening, Cluster 1 responses become more numerous and/or intense.[6] To the extent aid is predominantly self-supportive, Cluster 2 responses become more numerous and/or intense. This hypothesis implies an inherent limitation on reactions to self-supportive or self-threatening aid: Cluster 1 responses are limited in intensity and/or number by the magnitude of self-threat, whereas Cluster 2 responses are similarly limited by the magnitude of self-support.

It is hypothesized that a second self-regulatory mechanism occurs, which is analogous to affect dissipation (Byrne, 1971). When evaluating the donor and the aid negatively, failing to reciprocate, etc., results in a dissipation of negative affect (and raises situational self-esteem), this reduces the impetus for subsequent Cluster 1 responses. A similar process occurs for Cluster 2 responses, that is, when allowing the donor to exert social influence, reciprocating in kind, etc., results in a dissipation of positive affect, this reduces the impetus for subsequent Cluster 2 responses. Although these assertions have never been tested directly in an aid context, they are based on findings for affect dissipation demonstrated in other interpersonal interaction situations (Byrne, 1971).

These five hypotheses summarize the major assertions of a threat to

---

[6]An exception is that when aid becomes extremely threatening, a state of debilitation will ensue under which self-help will not occur.

self-esteem model. Before concluding, we will briefly discuss the use of the model with other psychological formulations.

Interface with Other Conceptual Formulations

The threat to self-esteem model predicts when aid will be self-threatening or self-supportive, and specifies the relationship between the self-implications of help and other reactions to aid. We acknowledge that there may be situations for which the self-consequences of receiving aid are minimal, and for which other theoretical approaches would be more appropriate. Moreover, in many cases in which aid does affect the recipient's self-esteem, other conceptual approaches can help determine these effects. Any psychological theory that accurately predicts conditions under which aid will be self-supportive or self-threatening (e.g., attribution theories, social comparison theory) can be used along with the principles specified in the model to generate predictions. Once the self-related implications of a particular aid context have been established, the grouping of potential reactions in clusters allows a unified set of predictions for recipient responses.

CONCLUSION

Through a review of past research on reactions to aid and the theoretical approaches employed, we have shown that previous conceptualizations are unable to predict reactions to aid for a large number of relevant situational conditions and recipient characteristics. We believe that the threat to self-esteem model, which assumes that the consequences of receiving aid for feelings of self-worth mediate recipient reactions, offers a valuable alternative. Such a model has considerable advantages over past theoretical frameworks in breadth, parsimony, and conceptual clarity, and is well supported by data from extant research. We hope that the present articulation of the model will stimulate research to define further the variables of interest.

REFERENCE NOTES

1. Nadler, A., & Fisher, J. D. Donor-recipient similarity and recipient reactions to aid. Paper presented at the International Conference on the Development and Maintenance of Prosocial Behavior, Jablonna, Poland, June 1980.
2. Nadler, A., & Fisher, J. D. *When giving does not pay: Recipient reactions to aid as a function of donor expertise.* Unpublished manuscript, Tel-Aviv University, 1978.

REFERENCES

Adams, J. S. Toward an understanding of inequity. *Journal of Abnormal and Social Psychology,* 1963, **67**, 422–436.

Adams, J. S. Inequity in social exchange. In L. Berkowitz (Ed.), *Advances in experimental social psychology* (Vol. 2). New York: Academic Press, 1965.

Adams, J. S., & Rosenbaum, W. E. The relationship of worker productivity to cognitive dissonance about wage inequity. *Journal of Applied Psychology,* 1962, **46**, 161–164.

Andreas, C. R. To receive from kings: An examination of government-to-government aid and its unintended consequences. *Journal of Social Issues,* 1969, **25**, 167–180.

Bar-Tal, D., Zohar, Y. B., Greenberg, M. S., & Hermon, M. Reciprocity in the relationship between donor and recipient and between harm-doer and victim. *Sociometry,* 1977, **40**, 293–298.

Baumeister, R. J. A self-presentational view of social phenomena. *Psychological Bulletin,* 1982, **91**, 3–26.

Berkowitz, L., & Daniels, I. Q. Affecting the salience of the social responsibility norm: Effects of past help on the responses to dependency relationships. *Journal of Abnormal and Social Psychology,* 1963, **66**, 429–436.

Blau, P. M. *Exchange and power in social life.* New York: Wiley, 1964.

Bramel, D. Dissonance, expectation and the self. In R. Abelson, E. Aronson, T. M. Newcomb, W. J. McGuire, M. J. Rosenberg, & P. H. Tannenbaum (Eds.), *Sourcebook of cognitive consistency.* New York: Rand-McNally, 1968.

Brehm, J. W. *A theory of psychological reactance.* New York: Academic Press, 1966.

Brehm, S. S., & Brehm, J. W. *Psychological reactance: A theory of freedom and control.* New York: Academic Press, 1981.

Brehm, J. W., & Cole, A. H. Effect of a favor which reduces freedom. *Journal of Personality and Social Psychology,* 1966, **3**, 420–426.

Briar, S. Welfare from below: Recipients' view of the public welfare system. In J. Brock (Ed.), *The law of the poor.* San Francisco, California: Chandler, 1966.

Broll, L., Gross, A. E., & Piliavin, I. Effects of offered and requested help on help-seeking and reactions to being helped. *Journal of Applied Social Psychology,* 1974, **4**, 244–258.

Byrne, D. *The attraction paradigm.* New York: Academic Press, 1971.

Calhoun, L. G., Dawes, A. S., & Lewis, P. M. Correlates of attitudes toward help-seeking in outpatients. *Journal of Consulting and Clinical Psychology,* 1972, **38**, 153.

Calhoun, L. G., Pierce, J. R., Walters, S., & Dawes, A. S. Determinants of social rejection for help-seeking: Locus of causal attribution, help source, and the "Mental Illness" label. *Journal of Consulting and Clinical Psychology,* 1974, **42**, 618.

Castore, C. H., & DeNinno, J. A. Investigations in the social comparison of attitudes. In J. M. Suls & R. L. Miller (Eds.), *Social comparison processes: Theoretical and empirical approaches.* Washington, D.C.: Halstead, 1977.

Castro, M. A. Reactions to receiving aid as a function of cost to the donor and opportunity to aid. *Journal of Applied Social Psychology,* 1974, **4**, 194–209.

Clark, M. Recipient–donor relationship and reactions to benefits. In J.D. Fisher, A., Nadler, & B. DePaulo (Eds.), *New directions in helping,* (Vol. 1). New York: Academic Press, 1983.

Clark, M. S., Gotay, C. C., & Mills, J. Acceptance of help as a function of similarity of the potential helper and opportunity to repay. *Journal of Applied Social Psychology,* 1974, **4**, 224–229.

Clark, M. S., & Mills, J. Interpersonal attraction in exchange and communal relationships. *Journal of Personality & Social Psychology,* 1979, **37**, 12–24.

Coopersmith, S. *The antecedents of self-esteem.* San Francisco; California: Freeman, 1967.

DePaulo, B. M. Accepting help from teachers—when the teachers are children. *Human Relations,* 1978, **31,** 459–474. (a)

DePaulo, B. M. Help-seeking from the recipient's point of view. *JSAS Catalog of Selected Documents in Psychology,* 1978, **8,** 62. (Ms. No. 1721) (b)

DePaulo, B. M., Brown, P., Ishii, S., & Fisher, J. D. Help that works: The effects of aid on subsequent task performance. *Journal of Personality and Social Psychology,* 1981, **41,** 478–487.

DePaulo, B. M., & Fisher, J. D. The costs of asking for help. *Basic and Applied Social Psychology,* 1980, **1,** 23–35.

DePaulo, B. M., & Fisher, J. D. Too tuned out to take: The role of nonverbal sensitivity in help-seeking. *Personality and Social Psychology Bulletin,* 1981, **7,** 201–205.

DePaulo, B. M., & Rosenthal, R. Ambivalence, discrepancy, and deception in nonverbal communication. In R. Rosenthal (Ed.), *Skill in nonverbal communication.* Cambridge, Massachusetts: Oelgeschlager, Gunn & Hain, 1980.

Druian, P. R., & DePaulo, B. M. Asking a child for help. *Social Behavior & Personality,* 1977, **5,** 33–39.

Enzle, M. E., & Schopflocher, D. Instigation of attributional process by attributional questions. *Personality and Social Psychology Bulletin,* 1978, **4,** 595–599.

Farina, A., Fisher, J. D., Getter, H., & Fischer, E. Some consequences of changing people's views regarding the nature of mental illness. *Journal of Abnormal Psychology,* 1978, **87,** 272–279.

Festinger, L. A theory of social comparison processes. *Human Relations,* 1954, **1,** 117–140.

Fisher, J. D., & Farina, A. Consequences of beliefs about the nature of mental disorders. *Journal of Abnormal Psychology,* 1979, **88,** 320–327.

Fisher, J. D., Harrison, C., & Nadler, A. Exploring the generalizability of donor-recipient similarity effects. *Personality and Social Psychology Bulletin,* 1978, **4,** 627–630.

Fisher, J. D., & Nadler, A. The effect of similarity between donor and recipient on reactions to aid. *Journal of Applied Social Psychology,* 1974, **4,** 230–243.

Fisher, J. D., & Nadler, A. Effect of donor resources on recipient self-esteem and self-help. *Journal of Experimental Social Psychology,* 1976, **12,** 139–150.

Fisher, J.D., Nadler, A., & Whitcher-Alagna, S. Recipient reactions to aid. *Psychological Bulletin,* 1982, **91,** 27–54.

Freeman, H. R. Reward vs. reciprocity as related to attraction. *Journal of Applied Social Psychology,* 1977, **1,** 57–66.

Garrett, J., & Libby, W. L., Jr. Role of intentionality in mediating responses to inequity in the dyad. *Journal of Personality and Social Psychology,* 1973, **28,** 21–27.

Gerber, I. Bereavement and the acceptance of professional service. *Community Mental Health Journal,* 1969, **5,** 487–495.

Gergen, K. J., Ellsworth, P., Maslach, C., & Seipel, M. Obligation, donor resources, and reactions to aid in three nations. *Journal of Personality and Social Psychology,* 1975, **3,** 390–400.

Gergen, K. J., & Gergen, M. International assistance from a psychological perspective. *1971 Yearbook of World Affairs* (Vol. 25). London: Institute of World Affairs, 1971.

Gergen, K. J., & Gergen, M. Understanding foreign assistance through public opinion. *1974 Yearbook of World Affairs* (Vol. 27). London: Institute of World Affairs, 1974. (a)

Gergen, K. J., & Gergen, M. Foreign aid that works. *Psychology Today,* June 1974, pp. 53–58.(b)

Gergen, K. J., Morse, S. J., & Bode, K. A. Overpaid or overworked? Cognitive and behavioral reactions to inequitable rewards. *Journal of Applied Social Psychology,* 1974, **4,** 259–274.

Gergen, K. J., Morse, S. J., & Kristeller, J. L. The manner of giving: Cross-national continuities in reactions to aid. *Psychologia,* 1973, **16,** 121–131.

Gergen, M. K., & Gergen, K. J. Foreign aid: A poison gift. *Trends Magazine,* December 1970, pp. 20-24.

Goldin, G. J., Perry, S. L., Margolin, R. J., & Stotsky, B. A. *Dependency and its implications for rehabilitation* (Rev. ed.). Lexington, Massachusetts: Heath, 1972.

Goranson, R. E., & Berkowitz, L. Reciprocity and responsibility reactions to prior help. *Journal of Personality and Social Psychology,* 1966, **3,** 227-232.

Gouldner, A. W. The norm of reciprocity: A preliminary statement. *American Sociological Review,* 1960, **25,** 161-178.

Greenberg, M. S. A theory of indebtedness. In K. Gergen, M. S. Greenberg, & R. Willis (Eds.). *Social exchange: Advances in theory and research.* New York: Plenum Press, 1980.

Greenberg, M. S., & Bar-Tal, D. Indebtedness as a motive for acquisition of "helpful" information. *Representative Research in Social Psychology,* 1976, **1,** 19-27.

Greenberg, M. S., Block, M. W., & Silverman, M. A. Determinants of helping behavior: Person's rewards versus other's costs. *Journal of Personality,* 1971, **39,** 79-93.

Greenberg, M. S., & Frisch, D. M. Effect of intentionality on willingness to reciprocate a favor. *Journal of Experimental Social Psychology,* 1972, **8,** 99-111.

Greenberg, M. S., & Saxe, L. Importance of locus of help initiation and type of outcome as determinants of reactions to another's help attempt. *Social Behavior and Personality,* 1975, **3,** 101-111.

Greenberg, M. S., & Shapiro, S. P. Indebtedness: An adverse aspect of asking for and receiving help. *Sociometry,* 1971, **34,** 290-301.

Greenberg, M., & Westcott, D.R. Indebtedness as a mediator of reactions to aid. In J. D. Fisher, A. Nadler, & B. DePaulo (Eds.), *New directions in helping* (Vol. 1). New York: Academic Press, 1983.

Gross, A. E., & Latané, J. G. Receiving help, giving help, and interpersonal attraction. *Journal of Applied Social Psychology,* 1974, **4,** 210-223.

Gross, A. E., Wallston, B. S., & Piliavin, I. Reactance, attribution, equity, and the help recipient. *Journal of Applied Social Psychology,* 1979, **9,** 297-313.

Hatfield, E., & Sprecher, S. Equity theories and recipient reactions to aid. In J. D. Fisher, A. Nadler, & B. DePaulo (Eds.), *New directions in helping,* (Vol. 1). *Recipient reactions to aid.* New York: Academic Press, 1983.

Heider, F. *The psychology of interpersonal relations.* New York: Wiley, 1958.

Jones, E. E., & Davis, K. E. From acts to dispositions: The attribution process in person perception. In L. Berkowitz (Ed.), *Advances in Experimental Social Psychology* (Vol. 2). New York: Academic Press, 1965.

Jones, E. E., & McGillis, D. Correspondent inference and the attribution cube: A comparative reappraisal. In J. Harvey, W. Ickes, & R. Kidd (Eds.), *New directions in attribution theory.* Hillsdale, New Jersey: Erlbaum, 1975.

Kahn, A., & Tice, T. E. Returning a favor and retaliating harm: The effects of stated intentions and actual behavior. *Journal of Experimental Social Psychology,* 1973, **9,** 43-56.

Kalish, R. A. Of children and grandfathers: A speculative essay on dependency. *The Gerontologist,* 1967, **7,** 65-69.

Kelley, H. H. Attribution theory in social psychology. In D. Levine (Ed.), *Nebraska Symposium on Motivation* (Vol. 15). Lincoln, Nebraska: University of Nebraska Press, 1967.

Ladieu, G., Hanfman, E., & Dembo, T. Studies in adjustment to visible injuries: Evaluation of help by the injured. *Journal of Abnormal and Social Psychology,* 1947, **42,** 169-192.

Lawler, E. E., Koplin, L. A., Young, T. F., & Faden, A. Inequity reduction over time in an induced overpayment situation. *Organizational Behavior and Human Performance,* 1968, **3,** 253-268.

Lerner, M. J., & Lichtman, R. R. Effects of perceived norms on attitudes and altruistic behavior toward a dependent other. *Journal of Personality and Social Psychology,* 1968, **9,** 226–232.

Leventhal, G. S., Allen, J., & Kemelgor, B. Reducing inequity by reallocating rewards. *Psychonomic Science,* 1969, **14,** 295–296.

Leventhal, G. S., Weiss, T., & Long, G. Equity, reciprocity, and reallocating the rewards in the dyad. *Journal of Personality and Social Psychology,* 1969, **13,** 300–305.

Lipman, A., & Sterne, R. Aging in the United States: Ascription of a terminal sick role. *Sociology and Social Research,* 1962, **53,** 194–203.

Merton, R. K. Contributions to the theory of reference group behavior. In R. K. Merton (Ed.), *Social theory and social structure.* New York: Free Press, 1968.

Morris, S. C., III, & Rosen, S. Effects of felt adequacy and opportunity to reciprocate on help-seeking. *Journal of Experimental Social Psychology,* 1973, **9,** 265–276.

Morse, S. Help, likeability, and social influence, *Journal of Applied Social Psychology,* 1972, **2,** 34–46.

Morse, S., & Gergen, K. Material aid and social attraction. *Journal of Applied Social Psychology,* 1971, **1,** 150–162.

Morse, S. J., Gergen, K. J., Peele, S., & Van Ryneveld, J. Reactions to receiving expected and unexpected help from a person who violates or does not violate a norm. *Journal of Experimental Social Psychology,* 1977, **13,** 397–402.

Nadler, A. Good looks do help: Effects of helper's physical attractiveness and expectations for future interaction on help-seeking behavior. *Personality and Social Psychology Bulletin,* 1980, **6,** 378–384.

Nadler, A., Altman, A., & Fisher, J. D. Helping is not enough: Recipient's reactions to aid as a function of positive and negative self-regard. *Journal of Personality,* 1979, **47,** 615–628.

Nadler, A., Fisher, J. D., & Ben-Itzhak, S. B. With a little help from my friend: Effect of single or multiple act aid as a function of donor and task characteristics. *Journal of Personality and Social Psychology,* 1983, **44,** 310–321.

Nadler, A., Fisher, J. D., & Streufert, S. The donor's dilemma: Recipient's reaction to aid from friend or foe: *Journal of Applied Social Psychology,* 1974, **4,** 275–285.

Nadler, A., Fisher, J. D., & Streufert, S. When helping hurts: The effects of donor-recipient similarity and recipient self-esteem on reactions to aid. *Journal of Personality,* 1976, **44,** 392–409.

Nadler, A., & Porat, I. Names do not help: Effects of anonymity and locus of need attribution on help-seeking behavior. *Personality and Social Psychology Bulletin,* 1978, **4,** 624–626.

Nadler, A., Sheinberg, O., & Jaffe, Y. Seeking help from the wheelchair. In C. Spielberger & I. Saranson (Eds.), *Stress and anxiety* (Vol. 8). Washington, D.C.: Hemisphere, 1981.

Nemeth, C. Effects of free versus constrained behavior on attraction between people. *Journal of Personality and Social Psychology,* 1970, **15,** 302–311.

Piliavin, I. M., & Gross, A. E. The effects of separation of services and income maintenance on AFDC recipients' perceptions and use of social services: Results of a field experiment. *Social Service Review,* 1977, **9,** 389–406.

Pritchard, R. D. Equity theory: A review and critique. *Organizational Behavior and Human Performance,* 1969, **4,** 176–211.

Pritchard, R. D., Dunnette, M. D., & Jorgenson, D. O. Effects of perception of equity and inequity on worker performance and satisfaction. *Journal of Applied Psychology,* 1972, **56,** 75–94.

Pruitt, D. G. Reciprocity and credit building in a laboratory dyad. *Journal of Personality and Social Psychology,* 1968, **8,** 143–147.

Rosen, B. Evaluation of help by a potential recipient. *Psychonomic Science,* 1971, **23,** 269–271.

Schopler, J., & Thompson, V. D. Role of attribution processes in mediating amount of reciprocity for a favor. *Journal of Personality and Social Psychology,* 1968, **10,** 243–250.

Shaw, M. E., & Constanzo, P. R. *Theories of social psychology.* New York: McGraw-Hill, 1970.

Shumaker, S. A., & Jackson, J. S. The aversive effects of nonreciprocated benefits. *Social Psychology Quarterly,* 1979, **42,** 148–158.

Skinner, B. F. The ethics of helping people. *The Humanist,* January/February 1976, pp. 7–11.

Stapleton, R. E., Nacci, P., & Tedeschi, J. T. Interpersonal attraction and the reciprocation of benefits. *Journal of Personality and Social Psychology,* 1973, **28,** 199–205.

Stokes, S., & Bickman, L. The effect of the physical attractiveness and role of the helper on help-seeking. *Journal of Applied Social Psychology,* 1974, **4,** 286–293.

Tesser, A., Gatewood, R., & Driver, M. Some determinants of gratitude. *Journal of Personality and Social Psychology,* 1968, **9,** 233–236.

Tessler, R. C., & Schwartz, S. H. Help-seeking, self-esteem, and achievement motivation: An attributional analysis. *Journal of Personality and Social Psychology,* 1972, **21,** 318–326.

Underwood, B. J. Individual differences as a crucible in theory construction. *American Psychologist,* 1975, **30,** 128–134.

Wallston, B. S. The effects of sex-role ideology, self-esteem, and expected future interactions with an audience on male help-seeking. *Sex Roles,* 1976, **2,** 353–356.

Walster, E., Berscheid, E., & Walster, G. W. New directions in equity theory. *Journal of Personality and Social Psychology,* 1973, **25,** 151–176.

Walster, E., & Prestholdt, P. The effect of misjudging another: Overcompensation or dissonance reduction? *Journal of Experimental Social Psychology,* 1966, **2,** 85–97.

Walster, E., Walster, G. W., & Berscheid, E. *Equity: Theory and research.* Boston, Massachusetts: Allyn & Bacon, 1978.

Weber, M. *The Protestant ethic and the spirit of capitalism.* London: Allen & Unwin, 1930.

Weiss, C. H. Validity of welfare mothers' responses. *Public Opinion Quarterly,* 1969, **32,** 622–633.

Wilke, H., & Lanzetta, J. T. The obligation to help: The effects of amount of prior help on subsequent helping behavior. *Journal of Experimental Social Psychology,* 1970, **6,** 488–493.

Worchel, S., & Andreoli, V. A. Attribution of causality as a means of restoring behavioral freedom. *Journal of Personality and Social Psychology,* 1974, **29,** 237–245.

Worchel, S., Andreoli, V., & Archer, R. When is a favor a threat to freedom?: The effects of attribution and importance of freedom on reciprocity. *Journal of Personality,* 1976, **44,** 294–310.

Wortman, C., & Brehm, J. Responses to uncontrollable outcomes: An integration of reactance theory and the learned helplessness model. In L. Berkowitz (Ed.), *Advances in experimental social psychology* (Vol. 8). New York: Academic Press, 1975.

Wylie, R. C. *The self-concept.* Lincoln, Nebraska: University of Nebraska Press, 1974.

CHAPTER 4

Indebtedness as a Mediator of Reactions to Aid

Martin S. Greenberg
David R. Westcott

Common sense suggests that the receipt of aid generates positive reactions in recipients. We expect recipients to be appreciative of the help received and to harbor feelings of warmth and gratitude toward their benefactor. Such is not always the case. There is a growing body of literature that suggests that there is a negative component to the receipt of aid. Thus, a review of this literature by Fisher, DePaulo, and Nadler (1981) led them to conclude that the receipt of aid constitutes a mixed blessing. In this chapter we discuss one such source of discomfort following the receipt of aid—the feeling of *indebtedness*. As defined elsewhere (Greenberg, 1980), indebtedness represents a state of obligation to repay another. It is predicated on the existence of a norm of reciprocity, which, according to Gouldner (1960), states that "(1) people should help those who have helped them, and (2) people should not injure those who have helped them" (p. 171). Indebtedness is conceived of as a psychological state having motivational properties such that the greater the magnitude of indebtedness, the greater the arousal and, hence, the stronger the ensuing attempt to deal with or to reduce indebtedness.

In the first part of this chapter we show how indebtedness is but one of several mediators of reactions to aid. Following this, a theory of indebtedness will be outlined. Because the theory and supporting evidence have been presented elsewhere (Greenberg, 1980), no attempt is made to elaborate fully the theory. Rather, our purpose is to elaborate selectively, to refine, and to extend the earlier version of the theory. After showing how indebtedness is conceptually distinct from the related concept of inequity (see Chapter 2), we discuss three sources of variability in feelings of indebtedness: group differences, individual differences, and the nature of the prior relationship between the donor and the recipient. The chapter concludes with an examination of areas of application and directions for future research.

MEDIATORS OF REACTIONS TO AID

Indebtedness is but one of several mediators of reactions to aid. As shown in Figure 1, when a donor attempts to render aid, a variety of cognitions may be created in potential recipients. Some of these cognitions are sources of positive affect whereas others are sources of negative affect. The

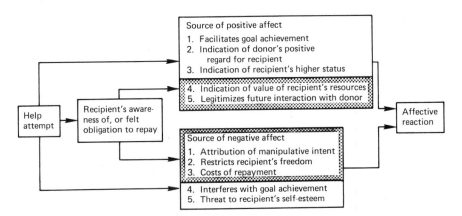

Figure 1. Sources of positive and negative affect in response to a help attempt. Shaded portions indicate the sources of positive and negative affect that can result from the awareness of or felt obligation to repay.

overall affective reaction to the help attempt represents the sum of the affect associated with each cognition with the affective consequences of each cognition presumably weighted for their importance. Several of these cognitions require no mediating awareness of an obligation to repay the donor. Let us look first at the sources of positive affect. Receipt of aid is likely to produce positive affect when the aid facilitates the achievement of goals important to recipients. Similarly, positive affect can be generated when recipients perceive the attempt to help as a sign of the donors positive regard for them, such as when recipients view the help attempt as a reflection of concern for their welfare.

The help attempt may also generate positive reactions in recipients when they perceive it as a sign of their higher status, as when the helping act consists of emptying their ashtray. Signs of deference are usually highly rewarding. For each of the above cognitions and associated affect to occur, there is no need to presuppose the existence of an obligation to repay. However, we can identify two sources of positive cognitions that do require recipients awareness that such an obligation exists. In the first instance, recipients may perceive the aid as a deliberate attempt by the donor to obligate them to reciprocate. Recipients may draw the flattering conclusion that the donor places high value on their resources. In yet another instance, the presence of an obligation to repay the donor may be welcomed by recipients because it legitimizes further interaction with the donor. Thus, Juliet would have welcomed a gift from Romeo because the obligation to repay would have provided her with a legitimate reason for further interaction with her lover. Although the obligation to reciprocate help may, on occasion, generate cognitions having positive affective meaning for recipients, it appears to be a more potent source of cognitions having negative affective meaning, as the following discussion will show.

As shown in Figure 1, recipients' awareness that people are obligated to return favors may cause them to view the donor's motives with suspicion and lead them to conclude that the donor is both manipulative and deceitful. In this case, the negative affect does not derive from the recipients' *feelings* of indebtedness, but rather from their *belief* that the donor may be trying to generate such feelings while pretending to do otherwise. In the next two cases, the negative affect derives from the recipients' feelings of indebtedness to the donor. Recipients may discover that by accepting the aid they have surrendered some of their freedom in future dealings with the donor. This loss of freedom incurred by their indebtedness may be a major source of distress to recipients (Brehm, 1966). In addition, the state of indebtedness may produce distress by calling attention to future costs that will have to be incurred in repaying the donor. Each of the above two cog-

nitions assumes the mediating presence of a feeling of obligation to reciprocate. However, as Figure 1 indicates, a help attempt can produce negative
affect even when recipients neither suspect the donor's intentions nor when
they actually feel indebted. Let us explore this further.

Although a help attempt may facilitate the recipients' attainment of
certain goals, it may also interfere with the achievement of other, more
important goals. Thus, although providing someone with an answer to a
problem may lead to its solution, recipients of such aid may resent the aid
because it prevents them from achieving the more important goal of solving
the problem themselves. The often-heard expression, "I'd rather do it myself," aptly reflects this source of frustration. In addition, recipients may
perceive the help attempt as reflecting the donor's beliefs that the recipient
is incapable of completing the task alone. Such signs of doubt and pity may
constitute a major source of threat to recipient self-esteem—a position taken
by Fisher, Nadler, and Whitcher-Alagna (1982).

What we have attempted to show in the preceding discussion is that,
from the recipient's point of view, a help attempt can be an extremely complex event. When help is received, a number of diverse cognitions may be
generated which may either increase or reduce the recipients' state of well-
being and thus influence their subsequent affective reactions. For certain
of these cognitions to occur, one need not assume the awareness of an obligation to repay the donor. However, for other cognitions generated by a
help attempt, this assumption usually must be made. In some cases, the
negative affect derives from the mere *knowledge* that the other is trying to
make them indebted, whereas in other cases the negative affect derives from
the recipients' *feeling* indebted. A question of paramount concern is, When
does a help attempt produce a state of indebtedness and when does it not?
In the following pages we will attempt to explicate the conditions under
which a help attempt leads to feelings of indebtedness and the role that
such indebtedness plays in determining recipients' subsequent reactions.

DETERMINANTS OF THE MAGNITUDE
OF INDEBTEDNESS

The extent to which recipients of help feel indebted is determined by
the combined weighting of four factors. These refer to the recipient's perception of (1) the magnitude of rewards and costs incurred by the recipient
and the donor as a result of the help attempt, (2) the locus of causality of
the donor's action, (3) the donor's motives, and (4) cues emitted by comparison others. For a discussion of the rationale underlying selection of
these four factors, see Greenberg (1980, pp. 5–11).

The Magnitude of Recipient and Donor
Rewards and Costs

The magnitude of indebtedness is in part an additive function of the recipient's net benefits from the aid attempt (i.e., perceived rewards minus perceived costs) and the donor's net costs (i.e., costs minus rewards). This relationship is expressed by the equation $I = B + C$, where I refers to the magnitude of indebtedness, B refers to the recipient's perception of net benefits received, and C refers to the recipient's perception of the donor's net costs. The value of either person's rewards and costs is a function of the perceived need of the person to whom it relates. The greater the perceived need for a resource, the greater its reward value when received and the greater its cost when given up. It is assumed that in making this calculation recipients evaluate their own rewards and costs in relation to their own needs, and that they evaluate the donor's rewards and costs in terms of their perception of the donor's needs.

There currently exists strong empirical support for the proposition linking the magnitude of indebtedness with the recipient's net benefits (e.g., Greenberg & Frisch, 1972; Pruitt, 1968; Wilke & Lanzetta, 1970). Although there has not been as much empirical research conducted on the role of the donor's net costs, the existing findings are uniformly supportive of the proposition linking such costs to the magnitude of indebtedness (Gergen, Ellsworth, Maslach, & Seipel, 1975; Gross & Somersan, 1974; Pruitt, 1968).

It should be noted that in viewing indebtedness as an additive function of the recipient's net benefits and the donor's net costs, the formulation raises the possibility that recipients can feel indebted to one who fails to provide them with benefits, but instead incurs only costs while unsuccessfully trying to render aid. However, results of several studies comparing the weights attached to the recipient's net benefits and the donor's net costs suggest that indebtedness is more a function of the recipient's net benefits than of the donor's net costs (Greenberg, Block, & Silverman, 1971; Greenberg & Saxe, 1975; Morse, Gergen, Peele, & van Ryneveld, 1977). These studies suggest that the indebtedness equation be modified to reflect differential weighting of donors' net benefits and recipients' net costs: $I = x_1 B + x_2 C$, where x_1 and x_2 are empirically determined weights. These studies further suggest that x_1 may be greater than x_2. This hypothesis requires additional testing.

The Locus of Causality of Donor Action

Another determinant of the magnitude of indebtedness is the recipient's perception of the locus of causality of the donor's help attempt. The magnitude of indebtedness is greatest when the locus of causality resides in the recipient, such as when the recipient requests or pleads for help. The magnitude is somewhat less when the locus of causality is perceived to reside in the donor, such as when the latter either offers or imposes help on the recipient. Least indebtedness is expected when the locus of causality resides in the environment, such as when the aid is perceived to derive from the donor's role obligations or luck. As Heider (1958) has observed, "We do not feel grateful to a person who helps us fortuitously, or because he was forced to do so or because he was obliged to do so. Gratitude is determined by the will, the intention of the benefactor" (p. 265).

Recent studies tend to support the importance of the locus of causality variable. Thus, recipients have been found to reciprocate more when the locus of causality resides in the donor than when it resides in the environment (e.g., Greenberg & Frisch, 1972; Gross & Latané, 1974; Nemeth, 1970), and they feel the strongest obligation to reciprocate when the locus of causality resides in themselves (Greenberg & Saxe, 1975; Muir & Weinstein, 1962).

Donor Motives for Attempting to Render Aid

That a donor chooses to help does not in itself guarantee that recipients will feel indebted. Recipients are usually concerned with the donor's motives. They frequently ask themselves questions such as, "Why is she helping me? Is she concerned about my welfare or does she have an ulterior motive?" The answers to these questions can have an important bearing on how obligated recipients feel to reciprocate. In general, the magnitude of indebtedness can be presumed to vary as a function of the extent to which donors are perceived to be more or less concerned with the recipient's welfare than their own. Thus, results from several studies show that the greater the perceived altruism underlying the donor's help attempt, the greater is the magnitude of indebtedness (Greenberg & Frisch, 1972; Lerner & Lichtman, 1968; Schopler & Thompson, 1968).

Cues Emitted by Comparison Others

Recipients sometimes experience difficulty in deciding how obligated they are to repay their benefactor. The difficulty stems from the fact that, on occasion, the previously cited determinants of the magnitude of indebtedness appear confusing or ambiguous to recipients. Recipients may ask themselves, "How valuable was the help? Did he help me because he wanted to or because he was supposed to? If he wanted to help me, what were his motives?" As in other situations in which they are confronted with an ambiguous reality, recipients tend to rely on the judgments of others for clarification (Festinger, 1954). For the recipient, these "others" may consist of *witnesses* to the help attempt, *co-recipients,* as well as the *donor.* Just as Schachter (1964) has shown that people tend to label their emotional states in terms of socially available cues, so might recipients use others to label their state of indebtedness. This proposition is yet to be rigorously tested. In the lone study examining this proposition (Greenberg, Bar-Tal, Mowrey, & Steinberg, 1982), recipients' feelings of indebtedness were influenced by the reactions of the donor. Subjects were asked to indicate how indebted they would feel if they had repaid a hypothetical donor but the donor was unaware that the subject was the source of repayment. On a 7-point scale that ranged from "still feel indebted" (7) to "no longer feel indebted" (1), more than half the responses fell between scale points 4 and 7. This would indicate that, despite having repaid the debt, the fact that the donor believed the debt still existed was sufficient to lead more than half the respondents to conclude that they were still indebted to the donor.

Four determinants of the magnitude of indebtedness have been described in this section. In its present form, the theory does not provide any precise formula for weighting the importance of each determinant. Presumably, the weight assigned is a function of each determinant's *salience* at the time when recipients assess their indebtedness. Salience, in turn, reflects the combined influence of both situational and individual difference variables. Given the current state of our knowledge, we can only speculate about what some of these situational and individual difference variables might be. Situations that may heighten the salience of the recipient's benefits or the donor's costs are likely to be those in which the recipient's or the donor's needs are extreme, such as when a person has been saved from drowning by a lifeguard. The benefit of having one's life saved presumably would carry far more weight than any of the other determinants of indebtedness, such as the realization that the lifeguard was only doing his or her duty (i.e., the help attempt was externally caused).

The factors pertaining to the locus of causality and the donor's motivation for the help attempt are likely to be most salient when recipients have a particularly strong need to understand, predict, and control their environment (Harvey & Weary, 1981; Kelley, 1972). Such occasions might arise when recipients anticipate frequent future interactions with the donor. As we have already speculated, cues emitted by comparison others are likely to be given maximum weight when recipients are confronted with an ambiguous reality for which there exists no objective means of reality testing other than to compare one's beliefs and feelings with the beliefs and feelings of relevant others (Festinger, 1954).

To be sure, individual differences also affect the salience of each determinant of the magnitude of indebtedness. For example, the level of the individual's cognitive development may affect the weight given to the benefits received, the locus of causality, and the donor's motivation for the help attempt. As Piaget (1965) has shown, individuals who have attained less mature levels of cognitive development tend to focus more on the magnitude of benefits and harm than on others' intentions and motives. Further, we would speculate that cues emitted by comparison others are likely to be salient for recipients who are field dependent (Witkin, 1949), high in need for approval (Crowne & Marlowe, 1964), and who are high self-monitors (Snyder, 1979). However, it must remain for others to explicate more fully the role of individual difference variables.

What this discussion suggests is that there may be qualitatively different types of indebtedness depending on which determinant is prepotent or salient at the time. Although the indebtedness of two individuals may be of similar or equal magnitude, the qualitative basis for the indebtedness may differ. Consider the case of two individuals helped by the same donor. The indebtedness of the first may derive primarily from the need for the aid whereas the indebtedness of the second may derive primarily from the perception of the donor's motives. This distinction has important implications for the use of cognitive restructuring as a mode of indebtedness reduction, as we show when this topic is later discussed. We propose that attempts to reduce indebtedness by cognitive restructuring, far from being random, are likely to be directed at the major or salient sources of the indebtedness.

ASSESSMENT OF THE MAGNITUDE
OF INDEBTEDNESS

How can the magnitude of indebtedness be assessed? Two sources of data are available for measuring indebtedness: (1) self-reports and (2) behavioral and cognitive attempts to reduce indebtedness. In this section we examine separately each mode of assessment, beginning with self-reports.

Self-reports

Indebtedness is assumed to be a conscious state having both a cognitive and an affective component. In most circumstances, the state can be measured by self-reports. The cognitive–affective components are reflected by

(1) a feeling of obligation to repay the donor, (2) a feeling of discomfort and uneasiness, and (3) an increased alertness and sensitivity to cues relevant to reducing the indebtedness. The affective arousal associated with indebtedness may range anywhere from intense discomfort, characterized by vigorous cognitive and behavioral efforts to reduce the indebtedness, to a rather mild, somewhat vague sense of unease. In some respects, the discomfort characteristic of indebtedness is analogous to a mild case of sunburn. It exists, barely noticed, and only becomes acutely distressful when we are slapped on the back with a reminder of what we owe the other, such as when we have missed an opportunity to repay. Perhaps Demosthenes had this thought in mind when he said, "To remind the man of the good turns you have done him is very much like a reproach."

The use of self-reports to measure the recipient's discomfort and felt obligation may not always yield reliable findings. In situations in which people need help and receive it, their immediate attention is likely to be focused more on the positive than on the negative features of the aid. Thus, immediately after being helped, recipients may not report any feelings of discomfort or distress, but instead, may cheerfully describe their desire, and perhaps obligation, to repay the donor. However, with the passage of time the aversive qualities of being indebted are likely to become more salient and thus reportable. Even in this situation, recipients may be reluctant to characterize themselves as uncomfortable lest it be construed as a sign of ingratitude. Self-reports obtained after the recipient has repaid the donor are also subject to error. Recipients may prefer to view their repayment in the most favorable way, that is, as a generous, caring act, and not one motivated by feelings of obligation and discomfort.

Although self-reports may tend to underestimate the strength of feelings of discomfort and obligation, several studies have yielded data showing that recipients of aid experience such feelings (e.g., Bar-Tal & Greenberg, 1974; Brehm & Cole, 1966; Gross & Latané, 1974; Muir & Weinstein, 1962).

The Phenomenology of Indebtedness

In order to investigate further the cognitions and feelings associated with the state of indebtedness, a questionnaire was administered to American and Israeli students (Greenberg et al., 1982). (Because the analysis is incomplete, only the data from the American sample is discussed here.) Indebtedness was defined in the questionnaire as "a person's feelings of obligation to repay another." To measure subjects' perceptions and feelings, a variety of types of items were employed, including bipolar rating scales, sentence completions, and open-ended items. A number of interesting insights emerged from the data. When asked, "What kinds of thoughts cross your mind when you are indebted to someone?" respondents said that their thoughts tended to focus on repayment and obligation. Less often cited were thoughts about the positive or negative consequences of being indebted, such as feelings of gratitude or uneasiness. Slightly less than half the responses reflected feelings of uncertainty. Respondents seemed to be preoccupied with such questions as "How can I repay her?" "Will he remind me of the debt?" "What will he expect from me?" "Will I be able to repay her?" and "When will I be able to repay her?"

Respondents clearly viewed the state as aversive, with 92% indicating that they did not "enjoy" being indebted to someone. Elsewhere in the questionnaire, we attempted to find out just what it was that subjects found aversive about the state of indebtedness. They were given a sentence completion item which read, "The worst thing about being indebted _____."
Mentioned most often were feelings of obligation and owing, being unable to repay the debt, and uncertainty about if, when, and how the debt could be repaid. What respondents seemed to be saying is that the state of indebtedness produces a feeling of a lack of completeness, a "social *Zeigarnik* effect," if you will. This theme is captured by one respondent who described her feelings about being indebted in the following way: "Owing someone something gives me an odd feeling—as if I am constantly aware that I have left something unfinished—something needs to be done." Another respondent described being indebted as "like having a big pile of papers on your desk that you have to clean up." That same person described the sense of relief associated with repayment when she wrote, "you feel like you just ate a green pepper, which means kind of refreshed and satisfied."

The questionnaire also yielded corroborative evidence concerning the sources of indebtedness. When asked to complete the sentence, "I feel most obligated to repay someone when _____", respondents focused mainly on the magnitude of the recipient's benefits, the donor's costs, and on the donor's motives. Less frequently cited were the locus of causality of the donor's action and cues emitted by comparison others. Additional insights concerning the phenomenology of indebtedness were provided when respondents were asked to describe an incident in their lives in which they felt indebted to someone. Responses were analyzed with regard to the relationship between the recipient and the donor and the nature of the help provided. In 75% of the cases, the donor was either a relative or a close friend, whereas the donor was described as a stranger in just 10% of the cases. The types of help received consisted of some form of service (e.g., "He helped me fix my car"), financial assistance, material help, and emotional support (e.g., "I was depressed and he stayed with me"). Relatives tended to provide financial help whereas close friends most often provided a service.

In summary, the questionnaire results show that indebtedness is a state with which all respondents were familiar. Moreover, the study yielded data confirming the cognitive–affective nature of the state and provided information about the kinds of situations that are most likely to generate feelings of indebtedness.

Measuring Attempts to Reduce Indebtedness

The magnitude of indebtedness can also be assessed by measuring the strength of attempts to reduce it. As stated earlier, the greater the magnitude of indebtedness, the greater the arousal and, hence, the stronger the ensuing attempts at its reduction. The two major modes of indebtedness reduction are *reciprocation* and *cognitive restructuring*. When deciding between these two modes of reduction, recipients will be motivated to choose the one that is more efficient, that is, the one that is perceived to be less costly. Let us examine each of these modes more closely.

Reciprocity Mode

Reciprocity is likely to become the preferred mode of reducing indebtedness to the extent that recipients are made aware of this option and they perceive that the opportunity to reciprocate exists. Awareness of this option may derive from the recipient's direct or indirect experience in similar situations or from cues emitted by others. Thus, verbal or nonverbal behavior by the donor, co-recipients, or others can serve to increase the salience of this mode of indebtedness reduction. In order for recipients to believe that they have an opportunity to reciprocate, they must perceive that (1) they have the ability to help the donor, (2) the donor is willing to accept such help, and (3) reciprocation is a more profitable option than doing nothing or reducing the indebtedness by cognitively restructuring the situation. When recipients perceive that one or more of these conditions is absent, they are not likely to believe that an opportunity to reciprocate exists.

Several hypotheses follow from these observations. We would expect that, when recipients perceive that the donor needs assistance, the desire to reduce the indebtedness will motivate them to acquire the necessary ability or skills that will enable them to reciprocate. This is precisely what Greenberg and Bar-Tal (1976) found in two experiments. Recipients were given an opportunity to learn information that their benefactor needed. Compared to those who received no prior help, recipients not only invested more time in obtaining such information, but when study time was controlled, they learned more information. Results of the two experiments are consistent with the proposition that the motivation to reduce indebtedness stimulates exposure to and learning of information that is instrumental for repayment. By doing so, recipients can actively create opportunities for reciprocation.

Of course, recipients can actively create opportunities to reciprocate in other ways. Because the donor's need state is a critical component for such opportunities, we would expect that recipients would maintain a state of heightened vigilance concerning the donor's need for assistance. Recipients may do more than carefully monitor the donor's need for help. They may actively engage in behaviors designed to increase the donor's need state and/ or to enhance the donor's dependency on them. Thus, recipients may withhold from the donor information about other sources of aid, or, in the extreme case, actively prevent others from assisting the donor as such aid would deprive recipients of their opportunity to reciprocate. The premise underlying this reasoning is that recipients are not desirous of seeing the donor benefited by just anyone, as that will not reduce *their* indebtedness. What recipients chiefly desire is that the donor be benefited at their hands. Adam Smith (1892) eloquently described the recipient's state:

> If the person to whom we owe many obligations is made happy without our assistance, though it pleases our love, it does not content our gratitude. Till we have recompensed him, till we ourselves have been instrumental in promoting his happiness, we feel ourselves still loaded with that debt which his past services have laid upon us. (p. 95)

However, under certain conditions the presence of a third party may increase rather than decrease the opportunity to reciprocate. This may come about in two basic ways: (1) the third party can help the recipient supply the donor with needed resources, or (2) the third party can serve as a substitute for the original donor. Let us look at the first of these two functions performed by third parties. Third parties can help recipients repay the donor in a number of ways. For example, in situations in which the recipient possesses resources needed by the donor but is not in a position to aid the donor directly, the recipient may deliver the needed resources to a third party who *is* in a position to assist the donor. Another example of the facilitating role of the third party occurs when the recipient does not possess resources needed by the donor, and the third party does. In this situation, the recipient can provide aid to the third party and direct him or her to reciprocate by helping the donor.

The second way that a third party can increase the opportunity to reciprocate is by acting as a substitute for the donor. The substitute function of a third party occurs when the third party is someone whose welfare is highly valued by the donor, such as members of the donor's family and close friends (Greenberg et al., 1982). By helping such third parties, recipients can benefit the donor, although indirectly.

Third parties can substitute for the donor in yet another way. When recipients anticipate no opportunity to interact further with the donor, they may reduce their indebtedness by helping someone who is similar to the donor but whose welfare is not necessarily valued by the donor. Whether or not a third party can fulfill this role depends on the recipient's perception of the third party's similarity to the donor on relevant dimensions. The recipient is enlarging the number of targets of reciprocation by placing the donor in a category (e.g., professor, classmate). By increasing the number of eligible targets of reciprocation to include all persons in the category, recipients can enhance their opportunities to reciprocate. A series of incidents that involved the first author and his wife illustrate this point. While vacationing in Europe, we were frequently assisted by well-meaning local inhabitants. On one such memorable occasion, when we stopped a Parisian for directions, the person not only gave the directions, but insisted on personally showing us the way. Similar acts of kindness were bestowed upon us by other individuals, but in each instance we had no opportunity for direct repayment. On our flight back to the United States we had occasion to sit next to a gentleman from Greece who was making his first trip to the United States to attend his son's wedding in Philadelphia. Our response was to overwhelm him with assistance. Upon our arrival at Kennedy Airport in New York, we helped him through customs, phoned his son in Philadelphia, and escorted him to the terminal for his connecting flight to Philadelphia. Why did we do this? Because we felt indebted to *Europeans,* and by helping him we were reciprocating for what others in that category had done for us.

Although third parties can substitute for the original donor, they are by no means the preferred choice for reciprocation. Only when recipients are denied access to the original donor will such persons serve this function. Moreover, recent evidence suggests that aiding a third party does not reduce indebtedness as well as does aiding the original donor (Goranson & Berkowitz, 1966; Shumaker & Jackson, 1979).

Our contention that providing aid to a third party can serve to reduce indebtedness raises an interesting conceptual issue. Other theoretical approaches also predict that helping a third party can reduce the discomfort following receipt of a benefit. Austin and Walster's (1975) "equity with the world" interpretation, and Fisher et al.'s (1982) "threat to self-esteem" model are two such approaches. In the Austin and Walster extension of equity theory, recipients may help a third party in order to achieve equity with the "world" rather than equity with the person who originally helped them. The Fisher et al. interpretation assumes that by helping a third party, recipients can reduce the threat to their self-esteem occasioned by their receipt of help. In comparison with these two approaches, indebtedness theory assumes that recipients are motivated to repay their debt and that third parties can help them achieve this goal to the extent that they can be seen as belonging to the same category as the donor. Hence, the perceived *degree of similarity* between the donor and the third party is critical for the indebtedness theory prediction whereas it is inessential to the other two interpretations. We are aware of only one study that has varied the degree of similarity between the donor and the third party and the results tend to support indebtedness theory (Greenglass, 1969). That is, recipients gave more aid to the similar than to the dissimilar third party ($p < .05$, one-tailed test).

In this section we have examined the conditions under which reciprocity is the preferred mode of reducing indebtedness. Central to our reasoning is the belief that recipients must perceive that they have an *opportunity* to reciprocate. When such an opportunity is perceived to be absent, the discomfort is likely to persist, unless it is reduced by other means. Consistent with this reasoning are the results of studies that compare the reactions of individuals who believe that they are unable to reciprocate with those who believe that they are able to do so. These studies show that those who perceive that their chances of reciprocating are low (1) are more reluctant to ask for help when they need it (Greenberg, 1968; Greenberg & Shapiro, 1971; Morris & Rosen, 1973), and when help is received they (2) accept less help (Greenberg & Shapiro, 1971), (3) show less liking for the donor (Castro, 1974; Gergen *et al.,* 1975; Gross & Latané, 1974), and (4) feel less comfortable and more constrained and confined (Gross & Latané, 1974).

Cognitive Restructuring Mode

Recipients can also reduce their indebtedness by first reexamining and then restructuring the cognitions that determine the magnitude of indebtedness. This reexamination may lead recipients to conclude that (1) the magnitude of benefits received was not as large as originally perceived, (2) the donor's costs were smaller than they originally believed, (3) the locus of causality of the donor's actions was more external than they originally thought, (4) the donor's motives were not as altruistic as they formerly believed, or (5) they misperceived the opinions of relevant others concerning the extent to which they are obligated to repay the donor. By restructuring their cognitions in these ways, recipients can reduce their indebtedness and therefore reduce the necessity for reciprocation.

Recipients can also reduce the discomfort of being indebted by enlarging their time perspective. This can be done by selectively searching their memory of previous encounters with the donor in order to find information to help them reduce their indebtedness. The enhanced memorability of such information should, for example, cause recipients to recall more vividly details of past instances in which they had helped the donor. By reassessing the donor's actions in terms of a broader temporal framework, recipients may come to discover that the donor was merely repaying a past debt. Because part of the discomfort associated with indebtedness derives from the uncertainty about if, when, and how the debt can be repaid (Greenberg et al., 1982), recipients may attempt to broaden their future time perspective to include anticipated opportunities to reciprocate. Thus, the couple that has been lavishly wined and dined by some acquaintance, may, as they are driving home, begin to initiate plans to return the dinner invitation. Although contemplating repaying the donor would not by itself reduce the magnitude of indebtedness, it probably would reduce some of the uncertainty about being able to repay and therefore serve to minimize the discomfort and tension associated with this state.

Like the reciprocity mode of indebtedness reduction, the cognitive restructuring mode is more likely to be employed under some conditions than others. Whichever mode is chosen, it is assumed that recipients will prefer the one that they believe is less costly. The major cost in the use of cognitive restructuring derives from the risks inherent in the distortion of reality. The realization that their cognitions are not in tune with reality could cause recipients to have doubts about their objectivity. Moreover, when such distortions come to the attention of others, especially the donor, it is likely to earn them disapproval. Accordingly, we propose that cognitive restructuring will become the preferred mode of reducing indebtedness to the extent that (1) cognitions concerning the magnitude of indebtedness are less subject to objective disconfirmation, (2) there are few witnesses to the helping act, (3) further interaction with the donor and witnesses is not anticipated, and (4) recipients perceive little or no opportunity to reciprocate. That is, when the relevant cognitions are less subject to objective reality testing, recipients can feel freer to engage in cognitive restructuring because it is unlikely that any distortions can be effectively challenged. Similarly, when there are few witnesses to the helping act and further interaction with the donor and witnesses is not anticipated, recipients are less likely to encounter a social reality that contradicts their revised beliefs about the situation. Finally, cognitive restructuring is more likely to be employed when the alternative mode of indebtedness reduction is inaccessible, such as when recipients perceive little or no opportunity to reciprocate.

There is one final issue that needs to be discussed regarding use of the cognitive restructuring mode. Assuming that conditions exist that favor cognitive restructuring over reciprocity, the question remains as to the exact form the restructuring will take. For example, will recipients show a preference for altering their beliefs about the magnitude of help received, will they prefer to alter their perceptions of the donor's motives, or will they show an equal preference for each alternative? As we have stated earlier in this chapter when we discussed the determinants of the magnitude of indebtedness, attempts to reduce indebtedness are far from being random. Rather, such attempts are likely to be directed at what recipients perceive to be the major or salient sources of their indebtedness. Thus, if recipients feel indebted primarily because of the magnitude of aid received, they will direct their restructuring attempts to such questions as, "Did I really need the help that badly?" or "How much did he actually do for me?" Whether or not attempts at cognitive restructuring are successful will depend on the extent to which such cognitive changes are subject to disconfirmation from objective and social reality. In summary, the exact form that successful cognitive restructuring will take depends jointly on the perceived importance of the cognitions for creating indebtedness and the perceived ease of changing these cognitions.

Because researchers have focused their attention almost exclusively on the reciprocity mode of indebtedness reduction, there is little empirical evidence to cite. Only studies by Gergen, Morse, and Bode (1974) and Worchel and Andreoli (1974) provide empirical support for the use of cognitive restructuring as a mode of indebtedness reduction. Gergen et al. found that recipients minimized their net benefits by overestimating the magnitude of their costs, whereas Worchel and Andreoli found that recipients reduced their indebtedness by attributing an external locus of causality for the donor's actions. Clearly, there is a need for additional research on recipients' use of cognitive restructuring to reduce feelings of indebtedness.

INDEBTEDNESS AND INEQUITY COMPARED

With the antecedents and consequences of indebtedness having been described, we now compare and contrast indebtedness with the related state of inequity. Equity theory (Walster, Berscheid, & Walster, 1973; also see Chapter 2 in this volume) and indebtedness theory are tension-reduction theories that assume that people experience distress when they receive more benefits from another than they believe they ought to receive. Although the two theories are similar in this important respect, they differ in a fundamental way. The difference between the two lies in how each theory views the recipient's motivation. Equity theory views recipients as being motivated to *restore equity* to the donor–recipient relationship, whereas indebtedness theory views recipients as motivated to *reduce their indebtedness* to the donor. The implication of this difference in motivation is that actions that help restore equity may not reduce indebtedness motivation but, rather, may add to the recipient's discomfort. Consider, for example, a situation in which the recipient perceives that a third party is responsible for improving the donor's outcomes. Although such third-party-initiated aid will usually suffice to reduce inequity, it will not serve to reduce feelings of indebtedness. In order for indebtedness to be reduced, recipients must perceive themselves and not a third party as responsible for improving the donor's outcomes–inputs ratio. According to indebtedness theory, third-party-initiated aid may actually increase rather than decrease recipients' discomfort, especially when recipients perceive that they have the resources to repay the donor. By helping the donor, the third party is preventing the recipient from reciprocating. However, as we previously noted, a third party can facilitate reciprocation, such as when the third party acts on the recipient's behalf, that is, as the recipient's agent or instrument of reciprocity.

Another instance when an equity-restoring technique is insufficient to reduce indebtedness occurs when recipients actually attempt to (as opposed to psychologically) alter their own outcomes–inputs ratio. That is, indebtedness is not reduced when recipients actually increase their inputs or actually decrease their outcomes. Indebtedness is reduced when recipients actually change the *donor's* ratio of outcomes to inputs by increasing the donor's outcomes and/or reducing the donor's inputs. As a consequence of the differences described in this section, we would, in certain circumstances, expect recipients' responses to vary depending on whether the predominant motive is to reduce indebtedness or to reduce inequity. The question as to when each motive predominates can not be answered here, but must await further empirical research.

VARIABILITY IN RESPONSES
TO INDEBTEDNESS

Differences in responses to indebtedness are likely to exist at the individual as well as at the group level. Although feelings of indebtedness in response to aid have been found in a number of diverse cultures (Greenberg, 1980), we cannot assume that all persons or groups will feel equally indebted in a given situation. The motivation to reduce indebtedness is a product of early socialization (Greenberg, 1980), and because there is a wide diversity of socialization experiences, we would expect to find considerable variability in such motivation. Individual and group differences are likely to be found with regard to the sources of indebtedness, thresholds for perceiving oneself in debt, tolerance for being indebted, and preferred modes of indebtedness reduction. In this section we examine some of these with regard to (1) social class differences, (2) individual differences, and (3) the prior relationship between the donor and recipient.

Social Class Differences

Simmel (1950) suggested that economic conceptions of social interaction derive from the experience with a money economy. Assuming that members of the middle class are likely to have had a greater amount of financial experience than have working-class individuals, we would expect that middle-class individuals would be more inclined to think of their interaction with others in terms of social exchange. In support of this reasoning, Muir and Weinstein (1962) found that middle-class women reported a stronger feeling of obligation to reciprocate favors than did women of lower socioeconomic classes. In addition, more middle-class than lower-class women said that they would eventually quit doing favors for individuals who never repay debts. Berkowitz and Friedman (1967) reasoned that the category "middle class" is too "undifferentiated" and therefore adopted Miller and Swanson's (1958) distinction between the "entrepreneurial" and "bureaucratic" middle classes. Miller and Swanson proposed that individuals growing up in homes in which the principal wage earner is in an entrepreneurial profession (e.g., owner of a small retail store) are more accustomed to thinking about social interaction as an exchange in which favors should be reciprocated and debts repaid, than are those growing up in bureaucratic middle-class homes (e.g., principal wage-earner works for a corporation). An experiment by Berkowitz and Friedman (1967) employing adolescent males confirmed this prediction. Boys from entrepreneurial middle-class homes displayed a stronger reciprocity orientation than did boys from bureaucratic middle-class homes. The entrepreneurial boys gave help to a dependent other only to the extent that they themselves had received help earlier.

Individual Differences

At one time or another we have all known individuals who are highly sensitive to the obligation to repay debts. Similarly, we have all had experience with the opposite number—individuals who seem oblivious to their debts. In this section we speculate about two personality types—the *creditor* personality and the *entitled* personality.

The Creditor Personality

Individuals who are labeled as creditors find being on the recipient side of a social exchange highly aversive, and being on the donor side highly pleasant. Such individuals are strong adherents of the norm of reciprocity (Gouldner, 1960) and, as such, are highly sensitive to owing and being owed. Much of their lives is spent avoiding indebtedness and building up credit with others. When they find themselves indebted, they attempt to repay quickly, and often with interest. When they are on the donor side of an exchange, they discourage others from repaying them, preferring instead to find security in the knowledge that never before has so much been owed by so many to one person. Greenburg's (1964) description of the "Jewish mother" illustrates one strategy sometimes used by creditors to prevent recipients from displaying even the slightest sign of gratitude: "Give your son Marvin two sports shirts as a present. The first time he wears one of them, look at him sadly and say in your Basic Tone of Voice: 'The other one you didn't like?'" (p. 17). These individuals recognize the power advantage that donors have over those in their debt. Although they are reluctant to yield this advantage, they will seek or accept repayment, but only when their need for assistance is very great. On such occasions, they expect recipients to reciprocate immediately and in a manner of the creditor's choosing. Creditors do not rest easily when the debt has been repaid and they quickly look for new opportunities to place the other once again in their debt.

Preliminary efforts to develop a scale to identify the creditor type have recently been undertaken in two studies at the University of Pittsburgh. In the first of these, undergraduates ($n = 71$) were asked to indicate their degree of agreement with 19 statements, using a 6-alternative forced-choice response format (strongly disagree -3, -2, -1, $+1$, $+2$, $+3$ strongly agree). On the basis of results using an interitem consistency measure of reliability, Cronbach's alpha, 8 statements were eliminated. The remaining 11 items comprised the Indebtedness Scale (see Table 1). Cronbach's alpha for the 11-item scale was .59. Because all 11 statements were keyed in the positive direction, the stronger the agreement with each item, the higher the indebtedness score. The validity of the scale was assessed by having subjects read a short story about a hypothetical situation in which the main character is forced to choose between helping someone who had helped him or helping another person who was inequitably treated by the experimenter, and then correlating subjects' scores on the Indebtedness Scale with their responses to two questions concerning the story. Results revealed a significant correlation between subjects' score on the Indebtedness Scale and both their perception of the main character's obligation to help the person who had previously helped him, and their prediction that he would choose to help the benefactor rather than the victim of inequity.

In the second study, which involved 128 University of Pittsburgh undergraduates, the 11 items from the Indebtedness Scale were embedded among items from several other scales: The Belief in a Just World Scale (Rubin & Peplau, 1973), the Social Responsibility Scale (Berkowitz & Lutterman, 1968), and the Social Desirability Scale (Crowne & Marlowe, 1964). Subjects were presented with the same story that was used in the first study with the exception that a series of slides was used to portray the events in

TABLE 1
Indebtedness Scale

	Item–total correlations	
Item	Study 1 ($n = 71$)	Study 2 ($n = 128$)
If someone saves your life, you are forever in their debt.	.30	.36
One should return favors from a friend as quickly as possible in order to preserve the friendship.	.32	.28
Owing someone a favor makes me uncomfortable.	.36	.42
One should not borrow money from a friend unless it is absolutely necessary.	.24	.18
Asking for another's help gives them power over your life.	.05	.31
Never a borrower or a lender be.	.35	.25
I'd be embarrassed if someone had to remind me of a debt I owed them.	.13	.32
As a rule, I don't accept a favor if I can't return the favor.	.39	.32
If someone pays for my dinner or invites me to eat at their place, I feel obligated to buy them dinner the next time or to invite them to eat at my place.	.18	.31
I get very upset when I discover I have forgotten to return something I borrowed.	.24	.33
If someone goes out of their way to help me, I feel as though I should do more for them than merely return the favor.	.29	.25
Cronbach's alpha =	.59	.65

the story. A test of reliability of the Indebtedness Scale yielded an alpha of .65. Although subjects' scores on the 11-item Indebtedness Scale were not significantly correlated with their predictions as to which person the main character in the story would help, scores were, however, significantly correlated with how obligated subjects believed he was to help the person who had previously helped him. In addition, the scale did not correlate significantly with the Belief in a Just World Scale or the Social Responsibility Scale. However, it did correlate positively with the Social Desirability Scale.

The results of these studies offer encouraging support for our attempt at developing an instrument that measures individual differences with regard to indebtedness motivation. The reliability of the scale, as measured by Cronbach's alpha, reached a statistically acceptable level. Significant correlations between subjects' scores on the scale and their perceptions of obligation and predictions about the main character's behavior support the validity of the scale. Although the preliminary results are encouraging, there is clearly a need for additional testing and refinement of the scale.

The Entitled Personality

Robert Coles (1977) has pointed to the emergence of a new character type prevalent among, but not limited to, the economically affluent. He labeled this type of individual the *entitled*. According to Coles, an entitled person is one "who thinks he owns the world, or will one day" (p. 55). The individual "has much, but wants and expects more, all assumed to be his or hers by right—at once a psychological and material inheritance that the world will provide" (p. 55). Coles goes on to describe such a person as "sitting on a throne of sorts—expecting things to happen, wondering with annoyance why they don't, reassuring himself and others that they will, or if they don't, shrugging his shoulders and waiting for the next splendid moment" (p. 56).

Entitled individuals have a high threshold for feeling indebted. Whatever aid they receive from others is their due, and therefore they feel little or no obligation to reciprocate. They exist in a world in which all but one are debtors. One major difference between the entitled personality and the creditor personality lies in the fact that the creditor discourages repayment lest the debt be cancelled, whereas the entitled individual, far from discouraging "repayment," encourages it. For the entitled, the debts that others owe them are limitless and thus can never be cancelled. Therefore, entitled individuals, unlike creditors, are reinforced by what they receive from others and not by the mere knowledge that they are on the creditor side of the relationship.

Relationship between the Donor and Recipient

Recipients' feelings of indebtedness may depend on their relationship with the donor. With one exception (Greenberg et al., 1982), recent studies tend to suggest that when the relationship is between strangers, the receipt of a benefit generates stronger feelings of indebtedness than when the relationship is between friends or relatives (Bar-Tal, Bar-Zohar, Greenberg, & Hermon, 1977; Clark, see Chapter 10 in this volume; Clark & Mills, 1979). In the lone discrepant finding discussed earlier in this chapter, Greenberg et al. (1982) found that when asked to describe an incident in their lives in which they felt indebted to someone, 75% of the respondents identified the donor as a relative or close friend whereas only 10% identified the donor as a stranger. The high frequency with which relatives and friends were cited may simply reflect the fact that people interact more with relatives and friends than they do with strangers and therefore are more likely to receive help from such individuals.

How can we account for the more frequent finding that help from a stranger is more likely to generate feelings of indebtedness than help from a friend or relative? Clark and Mills (1979) argue for the existence of two types of relationships, *exchange* and *communal,* each with a different set of norms. In an exchange relationship, participants give in order to receive, and they reciprocate because debts must be repaid. In contrast, members of a communal relationship assume that each is concerned about the welfare of the other. Participants respond not to the other's benefits but to the other's needs. Unlike recipients in an exchange relationship, recipients in a communal relationship are not obligated to return a comparable benefit, but rather their response is guided by an implicit agreement between members to take care of one another's needs to the best of their ability (Clark, 1981). Clark and Mills (1979) maintain that exchange relationships characterize the relationship between strangers whereas communal relationships characterize the relationship between family members and close friends.

Does the distinction between communal and exchange relationships have to be invoked in order to explain differences in reactions to help rendered by a friend and a stranger, or can such differences be accounted for by indebtedness theory? Let us examine this question. According to the theory, in order to explain the effect of some variable, such as the prior relationship between the donor and the recipient, on the magnitude of indebtedness, one would have to investigate the impact of that variable on the four determinants of the magnitude of indebtedness. When this is done, we can see that the type of prior relationship is likely to have a very strong impact on the locus of causality determinant. Because friends are under greater obligation to help each other than are strangers (Bar-Tal et al., 1977), help given by a friend may be perceived as more externally caused than help given by a stranger, and such help will, therefore, yield less indebtedness.

Differences in reactions to help given by a friend and a stranger may also reflect differences in time perspective in the two situations. Presumably, friends have a longer history of doing favors for each other, as well as a longer future time perspective. Thus, the failure of a recipient to return a favor to a friend may reflect the recipient's belief that the friend is reciprocating a past favor, or the belief that there will be many better opportunities to reciprocate in the future. In contrast, when the donor is a stranger, the recipient has no history of past interactions to invoke, nor can the recipient be sure that there will be future opportunities to reduce the indebtedness. Consequently, we are more likely to observe reciprocation with a stranger than with a friend.

Another interpretation related to the previous one is that, because of the long history of interactions between friends and the sense of trust that such interaction is likely to have built up, friends may not carefully monitor the balance in their exchanges with each other. Moreover, when questioned about such monitoring activities, they may be reluctant to admit that they are keeping track of what each has done for the other because this implies a lack of trust in the other. This is not to say that friends are totally unaware of any imbalance of debts that might exist. Rather, we are merely contending that friends are more relaxed in tracking the exchange of benefits and that social norms prevent them from revealing any monitoring that does occur. As the following example from Whyte's (1955) *Street Corner Society* illustrates, under appropriate circumstances, such as when the friendship is dissolving, participants can sometimes give a detailed accounting of what each has and has not done for the other.

> While Alex and Frank were friends, I never heard either one of them discuss the services he was performing for the other, but when they had a falling-out over the group activities with the Aphrodite Club, each man complained to Doc that the other was not acting as he should in view of the services that had been done for him. In other words, actions which were performed explicitly for the sake of friendship were revealed as being part of a system of mutual obligations. (p. 257)

In summary, the prior relationship between the donor and the recipient may be a source of variability in reaction to indebtedness. Additional empirical work is needed to explicate the precise nature of the mediating mechanism, whether it be in the existence of different norms of helping, differences in the locus of causality, time perspective, monitoring of the exchange, or impression management by the recipient.

APPLICATIONS AND FUTURE DIRECTIONS

There remain a number of theoretical and practical issues in need of additional empirical research. On the theoretical side, more needs to be known about the role played by situational and individual difference variables in determining the salience of the four sources of indebtedness. More generally, we need to collect empirical data on the different qualitative types of indebtedness and their affective, cognitive, and behavioral consequences. There is a need for empirical verification of our hypotheses concerning the conditions under which cognitive restructuring becomes the preferred mode of indebtedness reduction as well as the conditions favoring one mode of restructuring over another. Other theoretical issues in need of empirical investigation relate to our hypotheses regarding the role of third parties in reducing indebtedness, and the effect of individual differences on the arousal, toleration, and reduction of indebtedness. The identification of the creditor personality and the entitled personality types seems to be a promising direction for such research to take. Also needed are empirical investigations concerning the effect of the prior relationship between the donor and recipient on the arousal and reduction of indebtedness.

With regard to practical applications of indebtedness theory, systematic research is needed on the role played by indebtedness motivation in producing negative emotional reactions in welfare recipients and recipients of foreign aid. In a discussion of the sources of negative attitudes manifested by aid recipients, Gross, Wallston, and Piliavin (1979) indicated that feelings of indebtedness were a likely causal factor. Similarly, several writers have commented on the desires of the elderly to avoid feelings of indebtedness (e.g., Kalish, 1967; Lipman & Sterne, 1962), and Bredemeir (1964) noted that hostility was shown by welfare clients toward caseworkers, particularly when the client was expected to show gratitude for the aid.

With regard to international assistance programs, Gergen and Gergen (1971) concluded from their interviews with aid officials in recipient countries that "A majority of aid officials agree that obligating the recipient has important consequences for the success of an aid project. However, considerable controversy surrounds the exact way in which obligation affects the aid process" (p. 95). Whereas one group of officials believe that explicit obligations are onerous because they restrict the recipient's autonomy, others believe that only by successfully meeting one's obligation to reciprocate does one regain the status and dignity of an equal. These studies suggest that indebtedness theory may provide useful insights that can facilitate the delivery of health and social services.

Finally, indebtedness theory can provide some useful insights regarding social influence strategies in the real world. For example, Matthews (1960) describes how United States senators attempt to build up "credit," thereby enhancing their influence over colleagues, lobbyists, and the press. He notes that "every senator, at one time or another, is in a position to help out a colleague. The folkways of the Senate hold that a senator should provide this assistance and that he be repaid in kind" (p. 99). In their relations with friendly lobbyists, senators often devote a great deal of time to providing assistance. "The groups benefit mightily from some of these efforts, of course, but at a cost. They are, as a consequence, indebted to the senator" (p. 190). Likewise, in relations with reporters, a senator might overcooperate by providing leaks and exclusive interviews with the intention of producing not only good will, but a sense of indebtedness as well.

The criminal justice system is another setting in which indebtedness theory can provide some useful insights about strategies of social influence. Police officers, and in particular detectives, have been known to ignore minor offenses committed by drug addicts and prostitutes in order to make them indebted (Rubenstein, 1973; Skolnick, 1975). Later, when important information is needed from these individuals, the debt can be called in. Skolnick (1975) has noted that effective narcotics detectives are those who have built up credit with a number of individuals who can provide them with information when it is needed.

The jury room is another criminal justice setting in which indebtedness can be used as a social influence strategy. During the short lifetime of the jury's existence, members have numerous opportunities to perform favors for fellow jurors. This is particularly true for juries that are sequestered overnight. Zeisel and Diamond (1976) have documented one trial in which feelings of indebtedness may have played a critical role in the final verdict. In the conspiracy trial of John Mitchell and Maurice Stans, one juror was responsible for shifting an initial 8–4 majority for conviction into an acquittal. The juror was a vice-president of a bank who provided fellow jurors with an assortment of benefits during the days that they were sequestered. For example, he used the bank's facilities to entertain fellow jurors with movies and to view the St. Patrick's Day parade, and on several occasions he gave them money for minor jury expenses such as for entertainment. As Zeisel and Diamond (1976) noted, "His fellow jurors could hardly help being obliged to the man who had used his high social position to make their sequestration more bearable" (p. 165). The criminal justice system seems to be an excellent setting for studying the creation of indebtedness as a social influence strategy. Research conducted in real-life settings such as this is likely to yield theoretical understanding as well as practical benefits concerning recipients' reactions to aid.

In this chapter we have attempted to document the ubiquity of in-debtedness and its function as a mediator of reactions to aid. This ubiquity is perhaps best expressed by the German poet and novelist Goethe, who wrote, "Let us live in as small circle as we will, we are either debtors or creditors before we have had time to look around."

REFERENCES

Austin, W., & Walster, E. Equity with the world: An investigation of the trans-relational effects of equity and inequity. *Sociometry,* 1975, **38,** 474–496.

Bar-Tal, D., Bar-Zohar, Y., Greenberg, M. S., & Hermon, M. Reciprocity behavior in the relationship between donor and recipient and between harm-doer and victim. *Sociometry,* 1977, **40,** 293–298.

Bar-Tal, D. & Greenberg, M. S. Effect of passage of time on reactions to help and harm. *Psychological Reports,* 1974, **34,** 617–618.

Berkowitz, L., & Friedman, P. Some social class differences in helping behavior. *Journal of Personality and Social Psychology,* 1967, **5,** 217–225.

Berkowitz, L., & Lutterman, K. Social Responsibility Scale in "The Traditional Socially Responsible Personality." *Public Opinion Quarterly,* 1968, **32,** 169–185.

Bredemeir, H. C. The socially handicapped and the agencies: A market analysis. In F. Reissman, J. Cohen, & A. Pearl (Eds.), *Mental health of the poor.* New York: Free Press, 1964.

Brehm, J. W. *A theory of psychological reactance.* New York: Academic Press, 1966.

Brehm, J. W., & Cole, A. H. Effect of a favor which reduces freedom. *Journal of Personality and Social Psychology,* 1966, **3,** 420–426.

Castro, M. A. C. Reactions to receiving aid as a function of cost to donor and opportunity to aid. *Journal of Applied Social Psychology,* 1974, **4,** 194–209.

Clark, M. S. Non-comparability of benefits given and received: A cue to the existence of friendship. *Social Psychology Quarterly,* 1981, **44,** 375–381.

Clark, M. S. & Mills, J. Interpersonal attraction in exchange and communal relationships. *Journal of Personality and Social Psychology,* 1979, **37,** 12–24.

Coles, R. The children of affluence. *The Atlantic Monthly,* 1977 (September), 52–66.

Crowne, D. P., & Marlowe, D. *The approval motive: Studies in evaluative dependence.* New York: Wiley, 1964.

Festinger, L. A theory of social comparison processes. *Human Relations,* 1954, **7,** 117–140.

Fisher, J. D., DePaulo, B. & Nadler, A. Extending altruism beyond the altruistic act: The effects of aid on the help recipient. In J. P. Rushton & R. M. Sorrentino (Eds.), *Altruism and helping behavior.* Hillsdale, New Jersey: Erlbaum, 1981.

Fisher, J. D., Nadler, A., & Witcher-Alagna, S. Recipient reactions to aid: A review from a theoretical perspective and a new conceptual framework. *Psychological Bulletin,* 1982, **91,** 27–54.

Gergen, K. J., Ellsworth, P., Maslach, C., & Seipel, M. Obligation, donor resources and reactions to aid in three cultures. *Journal of Personality and Social Psychology,* 1975, **31,** 395–400.

Gergen, K. J. & Gergen, M. L. International assistance from a psychological perspective. *The Yearbook of World Affairs, 1971.* New York: Praeger, 1971.

Gergen, K. J., Morse, S. J., & Bode, K. A. Overpaid or overworked? Cognitive and behavioral reactions to inequitable rewards. *Journal of Applied Social Psychology,* 1974, **4,** 259–274.

Gouldner, A. W. The norm of reciprocity: A preliminary statement. *American Sociological Review,* 1960, **25,** 161–178.

Goranson, R. E. & Berkowitz, L. Reciprocity and responsibility reactions to prior help. *Journal of Personality and Social Psychology,* 1966, **3,** 227–232.

Greenberg, M. S. A preliminary statement on a theory of indebtedness. In M. S. Greenberg (Chairman), *Justice in Social Exchange.* Symposium presented at the Western Psychological Association. San Diego, California, March 1968.

Greenberg, M. S. A theory of indebtedness. In K. Gergen, M. S. Greenberg, & R. H. Willis (Eds.), *Social exchange: Advances in theory and research.* New York: Plenum Press, 1980.

Greenberg, M. S., & Bar-Tal, D. Indebtedness as a motive for acquisition of "helpful" information. *Representative Research in Social Psychology,* 1976, **7,** 19–27.

Greenberg, M. S., Bar-Tal, D., Mowrey, J ., & Steinberg, R. Cross-cultural comparisons in the perception of indebtedness. Unpublished manuscript, University of Pittsburgh, 1982.

Greenberg, M. S., Block, M. W., & Silverman, M. A. Determinants of helping behavior: Person's rewards versus Other's cost's. *Journal of Personality,* 1971, **39,** 79–93.

Greenberg, M. S., & Frisch, D. M. Effect of intentionality on willingness to reciprocate a favor. *Journal of Experimental Social Psychology,* 1972, **8,** 89–111.

Greenberg, M. S., & Saxe, L. Importance of locus of help initiation and type of outcome as determinants of reactions to another's help attempt. *Social Behavior and Personality,* 1975, **3,** 101–110.

Greenberg, M. S., & Shapiro, S. P. Indebtedness: An adverse aspect of asking for and receiving help. *Sociometry,* 1971, **34,** 290–301.

Greenburg, D. *How to be a Jewish mother.* London: Wolfe Publishing, 1964.

Greenglass, E. R. Effects of prior help and hinderance on willingness to help another: Reciprocity or social responsibility. *Journal of Personality and Social Psychology,* 1969, **11,** 224–231.

Gross, A. E., & Latané, J. Receiving help, reciprocation, and interpersonal attraction. *Journal of Applied Social Psychology,* 1974, **4,** 210–223.

Gross, A. E., & Somersan, S. Helper effort as an inhibitor of helpseeking. Paper presented at the meeting of the Psychonomic Society, Boston, Massachusetts, November, 1974.

Gross, A. E., Wallston, B. S., & Piliavin, I. Reactance, attribution, equity, and the help recipient. *Journal of Applied Social Psychology,* 1979, **9,** 297–313.

Harvey, J. H., & Weary, G. *Perspectives on attributional processes.* Dubuque, Iowa: Wm. C. Brown, 1981.

Heider, F. *The psychology of interpersonal relations.* New York: Wiley, 1958.

Kalish, R. A. Of children and grandfathers: A speculative essay on dependency. *The Gerontologist,* 1967, **7,** 185.

Kelley, H. H . Attribution in social interaction. In E. E. Jones, D. E. Kanouse, H. H. Kelley, R. E. Nisbett, S. Valins, & B. Weiner (Eds.), *Attribution: Perceiving the causes of behavior.* Morristown, New Jersey: General Learning Press, 1972.

Lerner, M. J., & Lichtman, R. R. Effects of perceived norms on attitudes and altruistic behavior toward a dependent other. *Journal of Personality and Social Psychology,* 1968, **9,** 226–232.

Lipman, A., & Sterne, R. Aging in the United States: Ascription of a terminal sick role. *Sociology and Social Research,* 1962, **53,** 194–203.

Matthews, D. R. *U.S. senators and their world.* New York: Random House, 1960.

Miller, D. R. & Swanson, G. E. *The changing American parent: A study in the Detroit area.* New York: Wiley, 1958.

Morris, S. C. III, & Rosen, S. Effects of felt adequacy and opportunity to reciprocate on help seeking. *Journal of Experimental Social Psychology,* 1973, **9,** 265–276.

Morse, S. J., Gergen, K. J., Peele, S., & van Ryneveld, J. Reactions to receiving expected and unexpected help from a person who violates or does not violate a norm. *Journal of Experimental Social Psychology,* 1977, **13,** 397–402.

Muir, D. E., & Weinstein, E. A. The social debt: An investigation of lower-class and middle-class norms of social obligation. *American Sociological Review,* 1962, **27,** 532–539.

Nemeth, C. Effects of free versus constrained behavior on attraction between people. *Journal of Personality and Social Psychology,* 1970, **15,** 302–311.

Piaget, J. *The moral judgment of the child.* New York: The Free Press, 1965.

Pruitt, D. G. Reciprocity and credit building in a laboratory dyad. *Journal of Personality and Social Psychology,* 1968, **8,** 143–147.

Rubenstein, J. *City police.* New York: Farrar, Staus, & Giroux, 1973.

Rubin, Z., & Peplau, L. A. Belief in a just world and reaction to another's lot: A study of participants in the national draft lottery. *Journal of Social Issues,* 1973, **29**(4), 73–93.

Schachter, S. The interaction of cognitive and physiological determinants of emotional state. In L. Berkowitz (Ed.), *Advances in experimental social psychology* (Vol. 1). New York: Academic Press, 1964.

Schopler, J., & Thompson, V. D. Role of attribution process in mediating amount of reciprocity for a favor. *Journal of Personality and Social Psychology,* 1968, **10,** 243–250.

Shumaker, S. A., & Jackson, J. S. The aversive effects of nonreciprocated benefits. *Social Psychology Quarterly,* 1979, **42,** 148–158.

Simmel, G. *The sociology of George Simmel.* Glencoe, Illinois: Free Press, 1950.

Skolnick, J. H. *Justice without trial: Law enforcement in democratic society* (2nd ed.). New York: Wiley, 1975.

Smith, A. *The theory of moral sentiments.* London: George Bell & Sons, 1892.

Snyder, M. Self-monitoring processes. In L. Berkowitz (Ed.), *Advances in experimental social psychology* (Vol. 12). New York: Academic Press, 1979.

Walster, E., Berscheid, E., & Walster, G. W. New directions in equity research. *Journal of Personality and Social Psychology,* 1973, **25,** 151–176.

Whyte, W. F. *Street corner society.* Chicago, Illinois: University of Chicago Press, 1955.

Wilke, H., & Lanzetta, J. T. The obligation to help: The effects of amount of prior help on subsequent behavior. *Journal of Experimental Social Psychology,* 1970, **6,** 488–493.

Witkin, H. A. Perception of body position and of the position of the visual field. *Psychological Monographs,* 1949, **63,** No. 7 (whole No. 302).

Worchel, S., & Andreoli, V. A. Attribution of causality as a means of restoring behavioral freedom. *Journal of Personality and Social Psychology,* 1974, **29,** 237–245.

Zeisel, H. & Diamond, S. S. The jury selection in the Mitchell–Stans conspiracy trial. *American Bar Foundation Research Journal,* 1976, **1,** 151–174.

CHAPTER 5

Equity Theory and Recipient Reactions to Aid*

Elaine Hatfield
Susan Sprecher

REACTIONS OF RECIPIENTS
IN RECIPROCAL VERSUS
ALTRUISTIC RELATIONSHIPS

Benefits are only acceptable so far as they seem capable of being re-
quited; beyond that point, they excite hatred instead of gratitude (Tacitus,
Annals, Book IV, sec 18).

Equity theory is intended to be a general theory, useful for predicting
human behavior in a wide variety of social interactions. Equity theory has
been applied to predict people's responses in such diverse areas as exploitative relationships, philanthropic relationships, industrial relationships, and

*This research was supported in part by the University of Wisconsin Research Com-
mittee.

intimate relationships (see Berkowitz & Walster [Hatfield], 1976). In this chapter, we will argue that equity theory can provide an orderly framework for understanding the philanthropist–recipient relation and, more specifically, for understanding the recipient's reaction to aid.

In the study of the philanthropist–recipient relationship, much of the research has been concerned with the *philanthropist* and the conditions that facilitate or inhibit helping. [For reviews, see Bar-Tal (1976), Berkowitz (1972a and b), Rushton & Sorrentino (1981), Staub (1978), and Wispé (1978)]. Much less attention has been focused on how the *recipient* feels about seeking and/or receiving aid. However, in order that aid be given under conditions that facilitate harmonious relations between benefactors and recipients and promote the well-being of recipients, it is important to understand the psychology of receiving help.

In this chapter we explore the relevance of equity theory for understanding recipients' reactions to aid. (See also Hatfield, Walster, and Piliavin, 1978.) We show that equity theory provides a useful framework for understanding why recipients may occasionally react negatively to benefit. Recipient reaction to aid is examined in three types of relationships: exploitative relationships, reciprocal relationships, and true "altruistic" relationships.

The first section presents a brief review of equity theory; the second describes the three types of helping relationships and recipients' reactions in each type of relationship; the final section more specifically compares reciprocal relations with altruistic ones.

EQUITY THEORY: AN OVERVIEW[1]

Equity theory is a strikingly simple theory. It is composed of four interlocking propositions. (See Hatfield and Traupmann, 1980.)

1. Individuals will try to maximize their outcomes (where outcomes equal rewards minus punishments).
2. Groups (or rather the individuals comprising these groups) can maximize collective reward by evolving accepted systems for equitably apportioning resources among members. Thus, (a) groups will evolve such systems of equity, and will attempt to induce members

---

[1]For a more detailed explication of equity theory and a review of the voluminous equity research, especially concerning helping relationships, see Walster (Hatfield), Walster, & Berscheid (1978).

to accept and adhere to those systems, and (b) groups will generally reward members who treat others equitably and generally punish members who treat each other inequitably.

3. When individuals find themselves participating in inequitable relationships, they will become distressed. The more inequitable the relationship, the more distress they will feel.

4. Individuals who discover they are in inequitable relationships will attempt to eliminate their distress by restoring equity. The greater the inequity that exists, the more distress they will feel, and the harder they will try to restore equity.

Equity theorists (see Walster, 1975) define an equitable relationship to exist when the person scrutinizing the relationship (who could be Participant A, Participant B, or an outside observer) concludes that all participants are receiving equal relative gains from the relationship, that is, when:

$$\frac{(O_A - I_A)}{(|I_A|)^{K_A}} = \frac{(O_B - I_B)}{(|I_B|)^{K_B}}$$

Where I is inputs of participants[2] O the total outcome of participants, and K a computational device. For a review of the other formulae that have been proposed for calculating equity, see Adams (1965), Alesseio (1980), Harris (1976), Moschetti (1979), or Zuckerman (1975).

Definition of Terms

Inputs (I_A or I_B) are defined as "the scrutineer's perception of the participants' contributions to the exchange, which are seen as entitling them to reward or punishment," (Hatfield & Traupmann, 1980, p. 166–167). The inputs that participants contribute to a relationship can be either assets, which entitle them to rewards, or liabilities, which entitle them to punishment.

Outcomes (O_A or O_B) are defined as "the scrutineer's perception of the rewards and punishments participants have received in the course of their relationship with one another." The participant's total outcomes, then, are

---

[2]The restriction to this formula is that inputs cannot equal zero.

equal to the rewards obtained from the relationship minus the punishments that incurred.

The exponents K_A and K_B take on the value of $+1$ or -1 depending on the sign of A and B's inputs and the signs of their gains (outcomes $-$ inputs). If I and $(I - O)$ are both positive (or both negative) K_A or $K_B = +1$; otherwise K_A and $K_B = -1$.[3]

Who Decides Whether a Relationship is Equitable?

According to the theory, equity is in the eye of the beholder. Observers' perceptions of how equitable a relationship is will depend on their assessment of the value and relevance of the participants' inputs and outcomes. If different observers assess participants' inputs and outcomes differently, and it is likely that they will, it is inevitable that they will disagree about whether or not a given relationship is equitable. For example, an elderly man placed in a public nursing home, focusing on the fact that he devoted many years to his children, may feel mistreated when they refuse to allow him to live with them. His children, on the other hand, focusing on his cantankerous personality, may well feel that they are doing more than enough by visiting him once a week. Moreover, an "objective" observer may perceive the matter in an entirely different way.

The Psychological Consequences of Inequity

According to Proposition 3, when individuals find themselves participating in inequitable relationships they feel distress regardless of whether they are the beneficiaries or the victims of inequity. The overbenefited may label their distress as guilt, dissonance, empathy, fear of retaliation, indebtedness, or conditioned anxiety. The underbenefited may label their distress as anger or resentment. Essentially, however, both the overbenefited and the underbenefited share certain feelings—they both feel *distress*, accompanied by physiological arousal (see Austin & Walster [Hatfield], 1974a, 1974b).

---

[3] The exponents are simply a computational device to make the equity formula work. The exponents' effect is to change the way relative gains are computed; if $k = +1$, then we have $(O - I)/(|I|)$, but if $K = -1$, then we have $(O - I) \times (|I|)$. Without the exponent K, the formula would yield meaningless results when a participant's inputs and profits have opposite signs, that is, when participant inputs are less than zero and profits are greater than zero, or when inputs are greater than zero and profits are less than zero. For a complete description of the assumptions underlying equity theory and its derivation, see Walster (1975).

Techniques by Which Individuals Reduce Their Distress

Proposition 4 states that individuals who are distressed by their inequitable relationships will try to eliminate such distress by restoring equity to their relationships. There are two ways by which participants can restore equity: They can restore either actual equity or psychological equity.

Participants can restore *actual equity* by altering their own or their partner's relative gains in appropriate ways. For example, imagine that an unskilled laborer asks for a much deserved raise from a contractor, but does not receive it. He could reestablish actual equity in various ways: He could neglect his work (thus lowering his own inputs), start to steal equipment from the company (thus raising his own outcomes), make mistakes so that the contractor will have to work far into the night undoing what he has done (thus raising the contractor's inputs), or damage company equipment (thus lowering the contractor's outcomes). The ingenious ways people contrive to bring equity to inequitable relationships are documented by Adams (1963).

Participants can restore *psychological equity* to their relationships by changing their perceptions of the situation. They can try to convince themselves and the other that the inequitable relationship is, in fact, perfectly fair. For example, suppose that a subway rider falls down on the subway and is aided by a nearby passenger. The subway rider could try to convince himself that the relationship with this stranger is equitable in various ways: He could restore psychological equity by minimizing the helper's inputs ("It didn't take him *that* much time to give me a hand"), by exaggerating his own inputs ("I was very appreciative"), by exaggerating the other's outcomes ("He probably enjoyed the chance to look good in front of everyone"), or by minimizing his own outcomes ("Well, I did hurt my knee").

Actual versus Psychological Equity Restoration

At this point, equity theorists confront a crucial question: Can one specify when people will try to restore actual equity to their relationships, versus when they will settle for restoring psychological equity? From equity theory's Propositions 1 and 4, one can make a straightforward derivation: People may be expected to follow a cost–benefit strategy in deciding how they will respond to perceived inequity. Whether individuals respond to injustice by attempting to restore actual equity, by distorting reality, or by doing a little of both, has been found to depend on the costs and benefits participants think they will derive from each strategy (see Berscheid & Walster [Hatfield], 1967; Berscheid, Walster, & Barclay, 1969; and Weick & Nesset, 1968).

THE APPLICATION OF EQUITY THEORY
TO HELPING
RELATIONSHIPS

Relationships between the help giver and the recipient of help may be characterized in one of three ways. In *exploitative* (or excessively profitable) relationships, it is the philanthropist who is really benefiting from the relationship. In *reciprocal* relationships, equity is maintained over the long run, and the participants alternate between being donor and recipient. In *altruistic* relationships, helpers are truly helping by offering the recipients greater benefits than the recipients could ever return. Although all three of these relationships are commonly labeled *helping* relationships, they are, in fact, strikingly different. Let us proceed to describe these three helping relationships in more detail and review what is known about how recipients react in each of these types of relationships.

Exploitative (or Excessively Profitable) Relationships

Exploitative relationships can be diagrammed as follows:

$$\frac{(O_A - I_A)}{(|I_A|)^{K_A}} > \frac{(O_B - I_B)}{(|I_B|)^{K_B}}$$

Philanthropists are sometimes less generous than they appear to be on the surface. Some philanthropists know they are benefiting more than the recipient. They are fully aware that they are "doing well by doing good." For example, the corporate executive may know full well that charitable contributions will increase the company's relative gains (via the tax write-offs) while doing little or nothing for the recipients. These relationships are best labeled *exploitative relationships.*

Other philanthropists are aware that in the past they have received far more than they deserved, and the potential recipient to aid has received far less. The helper gives in an effort to remedy the inequity *partially*; the recipient accepts it as such. This type of relationship may be best labeled as an *excessively profitable* relationship.

According to Proposition 3 of equity theory, when individuals find themselves participating in inequitable relationships, they will become distressed. Recipients of aid in exploitative or excessively profitable relationships may well feel anger or resentment over being given mere token aid while the philanthropist gains from the relationship. They will probably not feel indebted for the aid. They may even try to restore equity by derogating the philanthropist or by taking more of what they feel they deserve from the philanthropist.

Two factors may affect recipients' reactions to the philanthropist who gains more from helping than they do. First, tolerance for inequity probably varies as a function of the balance of costs and rewards involved in receiving help. To the extent that recipients gain more than they lose, they will probably be inclined to tolerate the continuing inequity: They may conclude that "something is better than nothing" and try to ignore the fact that the philanthropist is reaping an even greater benefit. However, once the benefits begin to be exceeded by the costs of receiving help (costs may include such things as lowered self-esteem, restriction of freedom, or an obligation to repay the help with interest), the inequity may become increasingly intolerable.

A second factor that might affect how recipients react to exploitative benefactors is how *comparison others* are being treated. Thus far, we have assumed that recipients are in a relationship only with the philanthropist; whether or not recipients feel inequitably treated is determined solely by comparing their relative gains with the philanthropist's. However, how recipients react to a particular inequity may be tempered—or exaggerated—by their perception of how similar others are being treated. Recipients of aid may be most content with the status quo if they perceive that others are even worse off.

For a more thorough discussion of exploitative (or excessively profitable) relationships, see Walster [Hatfield], Walster, & Traupmann, 1978.

Reciprocal Realtionships

Reciprocal relationship can be diagrammed as follows:

$$\frac{(O_A - I_A)}{(|I_A|)^{K_A}} = \frac{(O_B - I_B)}{(|I_B|)^{K_B}}$$

Any relationship than endures for very long, soon evolves into a reciprocal relationship. Neighbors take turns manning car pools, colleagues exchange advice, lovers comfort one another when things go awry. In such stable relationships, participants alternate between helping others, and being helped themselves.

Mauss (1954) analyzes the impact of such reciprocal giftgiving in primitive societies. Mauss uses the Melansian institution of the *kula* ring as a framework for discussing reciprocal relationships. In the Massim area of the Pacific, tribal chiefs are linked in the *kula*, in which participants travel from island to island doling out and receiving gifts. By custom, a tribal chief is a donor on one occasion and a recipient on the next. Dillon (1968) observes that in the *kula*, as in our society, "People who receive, want to give something in return. Both are involved in the quest for reciprocity" (p. 15). He points out that the reciprocal exchanges are a source of social stability—they breed good feeling, liking, and cooperation. Experimental evidence supports Dillon's contention that *kula*-type reciprocal exchanges solidify social bonds. For example, Nemeth (1970), Berkowitz (1972a, b), and Gross & Latané (1974) provide evidence that reciprocal helping relations stimulate friendly feelings. Other experiments suggest that kindness generates not only liking but also a desire to reciprocate (Greenberg, 1968; Gross & Latané, 1974; Krishnan & Carment, 1979; Pruitt, 1968).

How do recipients of aid in reciprocal, long-term relationships react to being helped? If we can extrapolate from laboratory studies of relatively short-term relationships, evidence exists to suggest that the recipients' reactions to donors are influenced by two factors: (1) Was the donor's help intentional? and (2) Was the help unselfishly motivated?

As suggested by the theories of Heider (1958), Jones and Davis (1965), and Kelley (1967), the recipient of aid may attempt to determine if the benefactor was intentionally motivated to provide help, or if help was either accidentally provided or dictated by role requirements. Heider (1958) has observed, "We do not feel grateful to a person who helps us fortuitously, or because he was forced to do so, or because he was obliged to do so. Gratitude is determined by the will, the intention, of the benefactor" (p. 265). Thibaut and Riecken (1955) experimentally demonstrated that recipients will like a benefactor more if they perceive the benefactor to be internally motivated rather than forced into the helping role.

Other evidence indicates that recipients will also be more inclined to reciprocate if they have been intentionally helped rather than accidently or reluctantly helped. For example, in a study by Greenberg and Frisch (1972), subjects were given aid by another "subject," and were led to believe that they were either intentionally or accidentally helped. Recipients who thought the aid was intentional were more likely to reciprocate than were those who thought it was accidental. Similar results have been found in several other studies (see Garrett & Libby, 1973; Goldner, 1965; Goranson & Berkowitz, 1966; Greenberg, 1968; Gross & Latané, 1974; Leventhal, Weiss, & Long, 1969).

In reciprocal relations, it is important not only that helping behavior is intentional, but also that the help is given for the right reasons. When acquaintances offer to help "out of the goodness of their hearts," our reaction is an immediate one: We feel affection and gratitude; we resolve to return their kindness. If, on the other hand, acquaintances make it brutally clear that they expect a return with interest, we are far less touched by their generosity and may be less concerned about repaying the kindness. This was pointed out by Schopler (1970), who argued that if recipients of help believe that their benefactors were genuinely motivated, they will be appreciative and likely to reciprocate. If, however, recipients believe benefactors were selfishly motivated, they will be less appreciative and less likely to reciprocate. In an experimental illustration of this, Tesser, Gatewood, and Driver (1968) found that the donor's motives had a strong effect on feelings of gratitude expressed. Subjects were given various stories describing the motives a donor had for doing particular acts of helping. Subjects expressed more gratitude for the donor described as giving primarily to benefit the recipient than for the donor described as giving for other, more selfish reasons. Other data in support of this contention come from Brehm and Cole (1966); Broll, Gross, and Piliavin (1974); Krebs (1970); Leeds (1963); Lerner and Lichtman (1978); and Schopler and Thompson (1968).

How do recipients of aid know if donors have selfish or unselfish motives for helping? Schopler (1970) suggests that if the benefit satisfies a real need for the recipient or if the favor is appropriate within the context of that particular relationship, the aid will likely to be perceived as genuinely motivated.

Another indication that the donor is helping for unselfish reasons is if the cost of providing the benefit is high. The greater the cost the recipient appears to incur in rendering aid, the more likely the recipient is to perceive the donor to be altruistically motivated, and the more the recipient will desire to reciprocate. Gergen, Ellsworth, Maslach, and Seipel (1975), for example, found that subjects expressed more attraction to a donor who contributed in spite of having few resources than to a donor who contributed the same amount from a much larger pool of resources. Other studies finding similar results include Fisher and Nadler (1976), Gross and Somersan (1974), and Latané (1973).

Similarly, recipients' attributions as to the donor's generosity may be influenced by the amount of benefit the recipients receive. The more that recipients receive, the more likely they will be to conclude that the donor was altruistically motivated. Several studies have demonstrated a relationship between magnitude of benefit received and desire to reciprocate (Freeman, 1977; Greenberg & Frisch, 1972; Kahn & Tice, 1973; Pruitt, 1968; Stapleton, Nacci, & Tedeschi, 1973; Tesser et al., 1968; Wilke & Lanzetta, 1970).

Why, in equity terms, should recipients have different reactions to givers whose gifts are voluntary and unselfishly given as opposed to givers whose gifts are involuntary or even ulteriorly motivated? First, recipients may feel that goodness and unselfishness, in and of themselves, are positive inputs to a relationship. Thus, they may feel that "good" benefactors deserve a bigger return than "bad" donors, who perform the same acts. Second, the recipients may be more eager to maintain a relationship with a generous person than with a selfish one. Thus, they may be especially willing to treat the others equitably by repaying their kindness.

Intimacy: Special Reciprocal Relationship

A very special type of reciprocal relationship is found between intimates. On almost a daily basis, intimates are involved in a mutual exchange of helping favors. Indeed, more helping (and helping of a more valuable nature) is probably received from intimates than from any other source. Thus, it is surprising that so little research has examined the giving and receiving of help in such relations.

How might helping in intimate relations differ from helping more casual relations? More specifically, how might recipients react if aid is received from an intimate versus a casual acquaintance? We will begin by reviewing the little research that has examined this issue. We will then suggest ways in which intimate relations may differ from casual relations, and the impact of these differences on recipients' reactions to helping behavior.

Clark and Mills (1979) argue that "exchange" (casual) relations are very different from "communal" (intimate) relations. In a communal relationship, members are concerned about one another's welfare; benefits are given in order to meet one another's needs. There is no expectation that the generous giver is entitled to anything in return. In exchange relations, on the other hand, benefits are given with the expectation that they will eventually be reciprocated.

Clark and Mills argue that in a developing social relationship accepting favors and *not* reciprocating is a signal that the individual is interested in forming a truly communal relationship. Accepting favors and immediately reciprocating, on the other hand, is a signal that the individual wants to keep the relationship a casual (exchange) one. This suggests that immediately reciprocating in response to aid received should be welcomed in an exchange relationship, but not in a communal relationship (see Clark, present volume).

Bar-Tal, Bar-Zohar, Greenberg, and Herman (1977) also examined how expectations and obligations for helping differ as a function of how intimate the relationship is. They predicted that the closer the relationship between two people, the more likely one partner would perceive the other as obligated to offer help, and the less the gratitude that would be expressed for the help. They based this prediction on Blau's (1964) contention that expectations and obligations for helping are more intense among family and friends than among acquaintances and strangers. The receiving and the giving of help are perceived as part of the role enactment of an intimate, but not of a casual acquaintance.

How would we, as equity theorists, expect exchange of resources and helping favors to differ in intimate versus nonintimate relationships? Are equity concerns as important in long-term intimate relationships as they are in short-term casual relationships? How might reciprocity differ in casual versus intimate relationships? Let us examine these issues.

1. Is an equitable exchange of resources and helping favors important in intimate relationships? We would argue that it is. In recent years, equity theorists have collected a considerable amount of survey evidence that demonstrates that in intimate relations, people care very deeply about whether or not they are fairly treated (for a review, see Hatfield et al., In press). Researchers have interviewed dating couples (Hatfield, Traupmann, & Walster, 1979; Sprecher-Fisher, 1980; Traupmann et al., In press), newlyweds (Hatfield et al., 1979 and 1982; Utne, Hatfield, Traupmann, & Greenberger (Submitted) couples married an average length of time (Hatfield et al., 1979); couples married for a much longer time (Schafer & Keith, 1980, 1981), and the elderly (Traupmann & Hatfield, 1981; Hatfield and Traupmann (In press); and Traupmann et al., 1981).

The existing data support two contentions: (a) Men and women in equitable relationships are fairly content. Conversely, men and women who feel they've consistently received far more or far less than they deserve are relatively uncomfortable. The more inequitable their relationship, the more distressed they are. (See Figure 1 for a graphic illustration of these results).

At every age and at every stage in a relationship, couples who perceive their dating relationships and marriages to be relatively fair are more content than men and women who feel they are either underbenefited (being "ripped off") or overbenefited (having it "too good"). It is easy to see why men and women who feel they are being "ripped off" by their partners would be furious. They may well feel unloved ("If you really loved me, you would not treat me this way") as well as deprived of real benefits. But on first glance, many are surprised that those who feel they are getting far more than they deserve, are uneasy too. Interviews make it clear why those who have an embarrassment of riches, feel just that—embarrassed. On one hand, they are delighted to be receiving such benefits; on the other hand, they don't deserve them, and this makes them acutely uncomfortable.

(b) Equitable relationships are especially stable relationships. All of the preceding authors found that among dating couples, newlyweds, and the

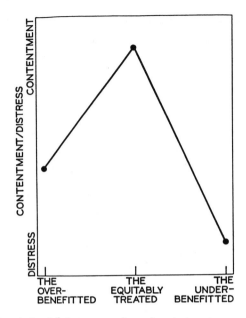

Figure 1. The relationship between equity and contentment.

elderly, equitable relationships were the most stable relationships. People seem to remain in those relationships in which the giving and receiving of helping favors are balanced.

2. How might reciprocity differ in casual versus intimate relationships? If the correlational evidence indicates that equity concerns are important in intimate relationships, why do experimental studies (such Clark & Mills, 1979) suggest just the opposite? We would argue that it is because the type of reciprocity examined in the laboratory is limited to short-term reciprocity that is of an exact form (if one receives aid in the form of chips, it is assumed that one reciprocates with chips rather than with a smile, a thanks, or an offer to meet later). In contrast, in correlational studies, it is assumed that reciprocity operates over a long period of time and comes in many varied forms.

Clark and Mills (1979) have demonstrated that if someone we care about does us a favor, we are hesitant to return exactly the same favor only moments later. We would agree. But the scenerio they describe (aid→non-reciprocation) is not the only possible one. A scenerio that is even more common is the following: Someone we are very interested in gives us a small gift (say flowers). We thank him or her. (This is the first act of reciprocation; not to do so signals ingratitude. We wait a discrete amount of time, searching for exactly the right present to give in return, something to signal we care. Perhaps we escalate a little by giving something of slightly greater value. The next step is then up to the other person. What we think people are signaling in this complex ballet is, "I care for you. We are friends. You can trust me to treat you fair and equitably."

We would argue that had Clark and Mills allowed their study to continue, and had they examined other forms of reciprocity, they would have found this delicate exchange operating in their communal groups. They would have found that intimates *do* reciprocate but over a longer period of time and not necessarily with the same type of aid they received. On the other hand, in groups in which people are not friends and wish to avoid becoming so, the researchers would probably find (as they actually did) that people reciprocate exactly and immediately. (As the old William Hamilton cartoon goes: "Bite for bite, and weekend for weekend, we're even. What do you say we call it quits?")

As suggested by the scenerios above, reciprocity may differ in intimate versus nonintimate relations in several different ways:

1. Type of aid reciprocated: Aid may take several different forms. We can offer others money, information, physical labor, companionship, and a wide variety of other resources. Foa and his associates (Donnenwerth & Foa, 1974; Foa, 1971; Foa & Foa, 1971, 1980) have listed six classes of resources: love, status, information, money, goods, and services. Among casuals, the form aid (and reciprocation of aid) may take is probably limited to money, goods, or services. In contrast, the form aid may take among intimates may span the gamut of resources. Although intimates often provide material benefits for each other, they also deal in the "softer" currencies of love, affection, and tenderness.

2. Immediacy versus nonimmediacy in reciprocating aid: In general, casual relationships are short-term. In contrast, intimate relationships tend to endure over a longer period of time. One of the consequences of being in a long-term relationship is that intimates will be more likely to tolerate inequities in the exchange of helping favors because they know they will have time to set things right. In contrast, casuals will feel that inequities should be set right immediately. Thus, aid received from a casual is likely to be reciprocated within a short period of time. Aid received from an intimate, on the other hand, need not be immediately reciprocated.

3. The impact of *we-ness* on helping: Intimates often come to think of themselves as a *we;* that is, they define themselves as a unit. Casuals, on the other hand, do not. Defining themselves as a *couple* may have a profound impact on the giving, the receiving, and the reciprocation of help among intimates. To the degree that the needs of both members of the

couple blend together, the separation between the helper and the recipient may be blurred; thus, the need to reciprocate is much less salient. Several other theorists have also discussed how defining themselves as a unit may affect exchange between individuals (Hatfield *et al.*, 1979; Hinde, 1979; Walster [Hatfield] *et al.*, 1978).

Unlike other theorists, then, we would argue that *both* casuals and intimates care about the equity of their relationships. However, because of various ways intimates can reciprocate, equity among intimates may be more complicated than among casuals. But in the end, everyone—intimate or nonintimate—cares about equity.

Let us now turn to the last kind of relationship we discussed: altruistic relationships.

Altruistic Relationships

Altruistic relationships can be diagrammed as follows:

$$\frac{(O_A - I_A)}{(|I_A|)^{K_A}} \overset{\text{(Philanthropist)}}{} < \frac{(O_B - I_B)}{(|I_B|)^{K_B}} \overset{\text{(Recipient)}}{}$$

For most people, the true altruistic relationship is evidence of human-kind at its best. In a true altruistic relationship, the individual is giving without expecting anything in return. Yet people's feelings about altruists and beneficiaries are mixed. Let us consider some examples.

1. Society tells people they should/should not behave altruistically. One of society's most perplexing problems is to decide how the needy should be treated. On the one hand, most people acknowldge that if one's fellows are so young, so disabled, so sick, or so old that they are unable to care for themselves, then society should care for them. We feel we *should* give to a plethora of deserving causes: the United Way, Save the Children Fund, Planned Parenthood, Committee for Voter Registration, etc (see Berkowitz, 1972a; Berkowitz & Daniels, 1963; Brickman, Rabinowitz, Coates, Cohn, Kidder, & Karvza, 1979; Gouldner, 1960; Lerner, 1971; Leventhal, Weiss & Buttrick, 1973; Pruitt, 1972).

On the other hand, people do not consider "need" to be an *entirely* legitimate input. They often complain that they cannot be obligated to help all who are in sad straits. At best, many beleaguered givers feel that any help they do cede should be considered not a gift, but a loan. At the very least they feel entitled to the recipient's gratitide. Thus, societal norms provide competing pressures: They say people should behave altruistically toward those in "need"—but that they are entitled to some recognition and thanks for doing so.

Furthermore, there is also a controversy as to whether altruism even helps the recipient—which puts the potential altruist in even a more perplexing position. Some theorists have argued that helping is not good for the recipient *or* for society. Skinner (1978), for example, has argued that by helping we "postpone the acquisition of effective behavior and perpetuate the need for help" (p. 251). Weitman (1978) argues that help is not good for society because it has the potential to alienate those who are not being helped.

Perhaps the pessimism of these theorists is warranted. Reports indicate the high failure rates of such programs as compensatory education (Bentler & Woodward, 1978; Stebbins, St. Pierre, Proper, Anderson, & Cerva, 1978), prisoner rehabilitation (Yochelson & Samenow, 1976), and institutionalized living for such groups as the elderly, the mentally disabled, and foster care children (Glasser, 1978).

Because society's reactions to altruism are mixed, we might expect that altruists would have similarly mixed feelings.

2. Society rewards/punishes people for behaving altruistically. Generally, society encourages and rewards altruistic behavior. In fact, there are even laws to encourage altruists. The state of California, for example, has a Good Samaritan law that compensates citizens for any injuries received while attempting an altruistic deed (reported in Albrecht, Thomas, & Chadwich, 1980). In addition, society may reward altruists with love, praise, their names in the paper, medals, and/or flowery epitaphs. Altruists who have internalized society's norms may also reward themselves for their unselfish behavior (Rosenhan, 1978). Yet, there is often a thin line between being an "altruist" and being a "sap". Sometimes people respond to altruists with ridicule and disdain (Brown, 1968, 1970).

3. Psychologists themselves are ambivalent about whether or not altruism exists. A few scientists believe that people act unselfishly under special circumstances. Some theorists, for example, contend that an empathic arousal predisposes the individual to act altruistically (Aronfreed, 1968; 1970; Aronfreed & Paskal, 1965; Lenrow, 1965; Rosenhan, 1969, 1978). Empathy has been defined as "the self-concious awareness of the consciousness of the other" (Wispé, 1968). Through empathy, people can vicariously experience the other's disappointment over suffering unjust inequities. When individuals experience such an affective arousal to the plight of others, they may sacrifice their own interest for the others'. Much experimental evidence exists to suggest that people do respond empathically

to people in distress and often subsequently offer help (Clark & Word, 1972; Darley & Latané, 1968; Gaertner & Dovidio, 1977; Piliavin, Rodin & Piliavin, 1969; Staub, 1970; Stotland, 1969; Weiss, Boyer, Lombardo, & Stick, 1973).

On the other hand, many other scientists (including equity theorists) are fairly skeptical. They argue that if society wishes to teach children to be generous spirited, it cannot rely on some innate sociobiological impetus to altruism. Instead, society must reward potential altruists with love, praise, or material benefits for acting generously. Society must make it profitable to be good.

Equity theorists interpret apparent altruism in cost–benefit terms; that is, by assuming that individuals learn to perform those acts that are rewarded and to avoid those acts that are not. Reward is whatever people value, and it may include approval from others or from the self. Blau (1968), for example, observes that people may help for social approval: "To be sure, there are men who selfishly work for others without thought of reward, and even without expecting gratitude, but these are virtually saints, and saints are rare. Other men also act unselfishly sometimes, but they require more direct incentive for doing so if it is only . . . social approval" (p. 453). Homans (1961, 1976) argues that if certain people value an image of themselves as altruistic and self-sacrificing, then performing sacrificial behavior will be rewarding to them. Thus, these theorists would argue that the rescuers described above were profiting—in their own idiosyncratic ways—from acting in such seemingly "altruistic" ways.

According to some theorists, even empathy (which was described above as a precursor to altruistic behavior) contains elements of egoism. When experiencing empathic arousal, people may help the one in need primarily to alleviate an aversive state (Gaertner & Dovidio, 1977); Piliavin *et al.*, 1969; Piliavin, Dovidio, Gaertner, & Clark, 1981).

In view of the conflicting pressures on the altruist, it is not surprising that people who voluntarily contribute more than their share to a relationship often feel both pride and distress. And it is no wonder that altruists are often tempted to reduce that distress by restoring actual or psychological equity.

RECIPIENT AMBIVALENCE

If good Samaritans have mixed feelings, their recipients have even more reason to be ambivalent. On the one hand, recipients know that the altruists are showering them with more love and material benefits than they are entitled to and, thus, they cannot help feeling grateful. On the other hand, the recipients cannot help feeling uneasy about their undeserved benefits. There are three reasons for this: The helper–recipient relationship is (1) inequitable; (2) potentially exploitative, and (3) potentially humiliating.[4]

The Recipient Is in an Inequitable Relationship

When benefactors bestow benefits on recipients, they place them in an inequitable relationship. As indicated in Proposition 3, inequitable relationships are unpleasant relationships.

As we saw in the previous section, inequity is disturbing for everyone (see Figure 1 for a graphic illustration of this prediction). Researchers have found that it is more pleasant to be in a reciprocal relationship than in an unbalanced one, regardless of whether one is the benefactor or the beneficiary of largesse.

The distress of being the beneficiary of undeserved reward is also explicated by Greenberg in his theory of indebtedness. According to Greenberg (1968, 1980), indebtedness is an unpleasant motivational state that leads to an obligation to repay the other. Indebtedness is similar to advantageous inequity; the individual feels overbenefited and feels obligated to give something back in return to the other. According to the indebtedness theory, the individual who is "in a state of obligation" will reduce the indebtedness by increasing the donor's outcomes or by reducing the donor's inputs. In contrast to the indebtedness theory, equity theory allows for more options for restoring balance to the relationship—including altering *own* inputs and outcomes (either actually or psychologically). For a more thorough discussion of indebtedness theory, see the chapter by Greenberg in this volume.

The Recipient Is in a Potentially Exploitative Relationship

When philanthropists provide benefits that their recipients cannot repay, the recipients may well feel that they have become obligated to reciprocate in unspecified ways for an indefinite period. As Blau (1968) put it, "giving is, indeed, more blessed than receiving, for having social credits is preferable to being socially indebted" (p. 453). Recipients might reasonably fear that their benefactors may attempt to extract a greater repayment than the recipients would have been willing to give had they been warned of the conditions of the exchange ahead of time. Throughout time and geography,

[4]In any type of helping relationship—exploitative, reciprocal or altruistic—these issues may arise, they are probably most salient in altruistic relationships.

observers have noted that persons often demand repayment at usurious interest.

Dillon (1968) proved a compelling example of how the exploitational gift syndrome works. He describes a French industrialist's (Mr. B's) warm relationship with an Arab worker as follows:

> In June, 1956, an Arab worker at B's factory asked the *patron* for permission to leave work for two days to attend to problems of burying a brother, Ahmed. . . . B. responded by offering to pay for the burial, by arranging to have an Arabic-speaking French officer *des affaires indigenes* (an ex-colonial officer) notify the kinsmen in Algeria, and by hiring an *imam* (Moslem prayer leader) to conduct the services. On July 16, 1956, the end of Bastille Day demonstrations by Algerians at the Place de la Republique, B. summoned Kazan and asked: "If your comrades tell you to go on strike during the vacation, when you are alone guarding the factory, what will you do Kazam?" The *patron* told him that he was aware he would run the risk of being knifed (*coup de couteau*) by other Algerian members of an Islamic fraternal organization who were organizing sympathy strikes to protest French resistance against Algerian rebellion. . . . The *patron,* in describing this understanding with Kazan, his oldest Algerian worker said:
> 'We depend on each other. He has worked for me almost 12 years. Without him I could not count on the work of the other Algerians. He is top man and, being the oldest, I depend on him to control the others. . . . Kzam knows that he can depend on me when he is in trouble.' (pp. 60–61)

When the industrialist offered his favors, he did not state that the price was to risk one's life. Had the Arab known, he may well have concluded that the exchange was not a profitable one. This is the essence of an exploitative relationship.

In addition to the potential cost of having to return the benefit with a high interest, recipients may feel their freedom is limited in such potentially exploitative relationships. This may lead to psychological reactance and negative feelings for the donor (Brehm, 1966; Brehm & Cole, 1966).

Exploitative Relationships Are Potentially Humiliating Relationships

Recipients may be hesitant to accept help for still another reason: They may fear that the gift will establish the benefactor's moral and social superiority. They may be unwilling to accept such menial status. Observational evidence suggests that recipients' fears are probably well founded. Social observers have noted that gift-giving and humiliation are linked. In her analysis of beneficence among East European Jews, Joffe (1953) notes

> For a society within the Western cultural tradition, East European Jewish culture exhibits a minimum of reciprocal behavior. Wealth, learning and other tangible and intangible possessions are fluid and are channeled so that in the main they flow from the 'strong,' or 'rich,' or 'learned,' or 'older,' to those who are 'weaker,'

'poorer,' 'ignorant' or 'younger.' Therefore, all giving is downward during one's lifetime. . . . The concept of the good deed, the Mitzvah, is not voluntary—it has been enjoined upon every Jew by God. . . . It is shameful. . . . to receive succor of any sort from those who are inferior to you in status. To receive any (return gifts) implies that you are in a position to be controlled, for the reciprocal of the downward giving is deference. (pp. 386–387)

Homans (1961) noted that "anyone who accepts from another a service he cannot repay in kind incurs inferiority as a cost of receiving the service. The esteem he gives the other he foregoes himself" (p. 320).

That the individual does forego his self-esteem in accepting help has been documented. For example, it has been observed that welfare has a detrimental effect on the recipient's self-esteem (Haggstrom, 1964). It has also been noted that elderly people who receive help have trouble maintaining their self-esteem (Kalish, 1967; Lipman & Sterne, 1962). Experimentally, it has been shown that there is a detrimental effect on one's self-esteem when help is received and there is little opportunity to reciprocate (Fisher & Nadler, 1974).

These three factors, then, mean that most recipients of help will have serious reservations about having been so blessed. This analysis sheds new light on the perplexing finding that recipients sometimes come to resent their dependence and/or to despise themselves and their benefactors.

REACTIONS OF RECIPIENTS IN RECIPROCAL VERSUS ALTRUISTIC RELATIONSHIPS

In the previous section we described three types of helping relationships and focused more specifically on two types—reciprocal and altruistic. From our comparison of these contrasting types of relationships, it is clear that a single factor seems to have a critical impact on the reactions of recipients; namely, the beneficiary's ability to make restitution.

Researchers who have investigated the interactions of Christmas gift givers, members of the *kula* ring, the kindness of neighbors, and the behavior of intimate lovers, have dealt with donors and recipients who knew that eventually their helpful acts would be reciprocated in kind. Researchers who have investigated the interactions in such dyadic relations as welfare workers and their clients, developed and underdeveloped nations, and the medical staff and the physically handicapped have dealt with recipients who know they will never be able to repay their benefactors. The differing reactions of participants in reciprocal and nonreciprocal relations underscore the importance of the recipient's "ability to repay" in determining how help affects the relationship. Ability to repay seems to determine whether the doing of favors generates pleasant social interactions or resentment and suffering. Research supports the following conclusion: Undeserved gifts produce inequity in a relationship. If the participants know the recipient can and will reciprocate, the inequity is viewed as temporary, and thus it produces little distress. If the participants know the recipient cannot or will not reciprocate, however, a real inequity is produced; the participants will experience distress (Proposition 4).

Ethnographic data demonstrate the importance of the ability to reciprocate in the gift-giving process. Mauss (1954), for example, concluded that three types of obligations are widely distributed in human societies in both time and space: (1) the obligation to give; (2) the obligation to receive; and (3) the obligation to repay. Mauss (1954) and Dillon (1968) agree that, whereas reciprocal exchanges breed cooperation and good feelings, gifts that cannot be reciprocated breed discomfort, distress, and dislike. In support of their contention, the authors surveyed a number of societies that have an exchange system in which everyone is a donor *and* a receiver (the *kula* ring is an example of such an exchange system). Harmonious stable relations are said to be the result of exchange systems of this kind. The authors contrast these societies with those in which no mechanism for discharging obligations is provided. For example, Dillon (1968) notes, "Instead of the Kula principle operating in the Marshall Plan, the aid effort unwittingly took on some of the characteristics of the potlatch ceremony of the 19th Century among North Pacific Coast Indians in which property was destroyed in rivalry, and the poor humiliated" (p. 15). Volatile and unpleasant relations are said to be the result of such continuing inequities (see also Blau, 1955; Smith, 1892).

We present experimental evidence to support the following three contentions concerning the effects of the ability to repay on recipients' reactions to aid: (1) Benefactors are liked more (and derogated less) when their beneficiaries can reciprocate than when they cannot; (2) people prefer gifts that can be repaid over those that cannot; (3) if the recipient cannot directly repay the donor, the ability to benefit a third person may serve to reduce this tension. We examine each contention in turn.

1. Benefactors are liked more (and derogated less) when their beneficiaries can reciprocate than when they cannot. In one study, Gergen (1969) investigated American, Swedish, and Japanese citizens' reactions to reciprocal and nonreciprocal exchanges. The experiment was arranged so that subjects were losing badly in a game. Then, at a critical stage, they received help in the form of needed chips from one of the "luckier" players. For one-third of the subjects, the donor explained that there was no need to return any chips; for another one-third of the subjects, the donor requested

that an equal number of chips be returned later; for the rest of the subjects, the donor asked for the chips to be returned *with* interest. Those partners who provided benefit without obligation or who asked for excessive benefits were liked less than those who proposed that the students make exact restitution later in the game. Similar results were also found by Gergen *et al.* (1975).

In another study by Gergen and his associates (Gergen, Diebold, & Seipel, 1973), subjects received a present of chips at a critical point in the game from another player who requested that an equal number be paid back later. However, in subsequent play, only half of the subjects managed to retain their chips, so that half were unable to return the gift. In evaluations of the donor, recipients who were unable to repay the donor evaluated him less positively than did recipients who were able to repay.

Several other studies have also shown that benefactors are liked more when they can be repaid. In a study by Gross & Latané (1974), it was found that the donor was liked more when the subjects were given an opportunity to return help than when they were not. Castro (1974) also found that the recipient of a benefit will like the donor more if there is an opportunity to repay than if there is no opportunity to make restitution. Schumaker and Jackson (1979) found that if recipients are prevented from directly helping the donor, they end up derogating the donor.

2. People prefer gifts that can be repaid over those that cannot. Gergen and Gergen (1971) questioned citizens in countries that had received U.S. aid as to how they felt about the assistance their country had received. They found that international gifts accompanied by clearly stated obligations are preferred to gifts that are not accompanied by obligations or are accompanied by excessive "strings."

There is also evidence that individuals are more willing to seek and accept gifts that can be reciprocated than gifts that cannot. In one study by Greenberg (1968), subjects were given a temporary handicap (an arm was placed in a sling). This restriction made it almost impossible for the subjects to perform the task they were assigned. The incapacitated student knew, however, that he could solicit help from a fellow worker. Half of the students believed that the fellow worker would need their help on a second task and that they would be able to provide assistance. Half of the students believed that the fellow worker would not need their help in the future and that, in any case, they would not be able to provide much help. The student's expectations about whether or not they could reciprocate any help strongly affected their willingness to request help. Students in the non-reciprocity condition waited significantly longer before requesting help than did those in reciprocity conditions. Greenberg and Shapiro (1971) replicated these findings.

Morris and Rosen (1973), however, questioned whether the procedure used in these studies confounded the lack of opportunity to reciprocate with feelings of inadequacy over a poor performance. They designed an experiment in which the inability to reciprocate was clearly outside of the control of the subject. Subjects were told either they had done well or poorly on the task. In addition, subjects were told either that there would be plenty of time for several tasks to be conducted or that the experiment would have to end immediately after the first task (due to electricity failure). It was found that persons who were led to believe they had performed well were more likely to seek help from another subject than persons who were led to believe they had performed poorly. However, the ability to reciprocate also had an effect: Subjects were reluctant to seek help if they would not be able to reciprocate (for example, if they knew the experiment would end after the first task). Other evidence indicating that people are more willing to seek help if it can be reciprocated comes from Clark, Gotay, & Mills (1974), and DePaulo (1978).

Evidence also exists to indicate that people are less willing to request future aid or gifts if they are unable to reciprocate aid already received (see Castro, 1974).

3. If the recipient cannot directly repay the donor, the ability to benefit a third party may serve to reduce tension. In one study, Goranson and Berkowitz (1966) found that recipients offered to help a third party if prevented from helping the donor. They found, however, that the amount of help given to a third party was significantly less than the amount of help given directly to the donor. Similar results were also found by Kahn and Tice (1973), and Schumaker and Jackson (1979).

Other related evidence suggests that, in the absence of the ability to repay the donor, being able to give to a third party helps prevent possible negative feelings for the original donor. It appears that just the act of donating, even if it is not to the same party who provided the help, serves to reduce the inequity. Castro (1974) found that, in the absence of an ability to reciprocate the donor directly, the recipient will like the donor more and be more willing to request aid in the future if given an opportunity to aid a third party (see also Gross & Latané, 1974; Schumaker & Jackson, 1979).

Some third parties may be more effective substitutes for the original donor than others. For example, evidence exists to suggest that the more similar the third party is to the original donor, the more likely the third party will be to receive help (Greenglass, 1969). In addition, if the third party is perceived to be in a close relationship with the original donor, he or she will be more likely to receive help. In a study by Greenberg Mowrey, Steinberg, & Bar-Tal (1974), subjects were asked the following two questions: (a) "If you were indebted to someone, how indebted would you still feel if you then helped someone with whom the help-giver was not acquainted?" and (b) "If you were indebted to someone, how indebted would you still feel if you helped someone close to the help-giver such as a member of his/her family?" It was found that subjects reported that they would feel less indebted after helping a family member.

In sum, it appears that the critical factor for determining whether or not aid has positive effects for the recipient's well-being and for the recipient's relationship with the benefactor is the ability of the recipient to make restitution.

SUMMARY

In this chapter we explored three types of helping relationships. Although all three relationships are commonly labeled *helper–recipient* relationships, the dynamics of the three are quite different.

In exploitative or excessively profitable relationships, the ostensible donors help others merely because it is the most profitable way to help themselves. In such relationships, the recipients will likely feel resentment over being treated inequitably. In reciprocal relationships, participants alternate between being the donor and being the recipient. Such exchanges seem to build good feelings between the recipient and the helper, probably due to the desire and capacity to repay. Finally, the public's epitome of a good relationship—the altruistic relationship—was considered. In a true altruistic relationship, helpers are offering more help than they expect in return. We reviewed factors that determine whether such relationships breed good feelings or, as they more frequently do, breed hostility, humiliation, and alienation.

Although in this chapter we have concentrated on the recipient's reactions to aid, an interesting and unexplored area of inquiry for future research is to examine the reciprocal and dynamic relation between the recipient and the benefactor, as affected by equity concerns. How do recipients' reactions to aid affect the benefactor and the benefactor's willingness to provide further help? How do benefactors perceive recipients will react to their aid, and how does this perception affect the offer of aid?

REFERENCES

Adams, J. S. Toward an understanding of inequity. *Journal of Abnormal and Social Psychology*, 1963, **67**, 422–436.

Adams, J. S. Inequity in social exchange. In Leonard Berkowitz (Ed.), *Advances in Experimental Social Psychology* (Vol. 2). New York: Academic Press, 1965. Pp. 267–299.

Albrecht, S. L., Thomas, D. L., & Chadwick, B. A. *Social Psychology*. Englewood Cliffs, New Jersey: Prentice-Hall, 1980.

Alessio, J. C. A method of measurement and analysis for equity research. Paper presented at the Midwest Sociological Society Meetings, 1980.

Aronfreed, J. *Conduct and conscience: The socialization of internalized control over behavior.* New York: Academic Press, 1968.

Aronfreed, J. The socialization of altruistic and sympathetic behavior: Some theoretical and experimental analyses. In J. Macauley & L. Berkowitz (Eds.), *Altruism and helping behavior.* New York: Academic Press, 1970. Pp. 103–126.

Aronfreed, J., & Paskal, V. Altruism, empathy, and the conditioning of positive affect. Unpublished manuscript. Philadelphia, Pennsylvania: University of Pennsylvania, 1966.

Austin, W. & Walster, E. Reactions to confirmations and disconfirmations of expectancies of equity and inequity. *Journal of Personality and Social Psychology,* 1974, **30**, 208–216. (a)

Austin, W. & Walster, E. Participants' reactions to "Equity with the World," *Journal of Experimental Social Psychology,* 1974, **10**, 528–548. (b)

Bar-Tal, D. *Prosocial behavior: Theory and research.* New York: Hemisphere, 1976.

Bar-Tal, D., Bar-Zohar, Y. B., Greenberg, M. S., & Hermon, M. Reciprocity behavior in the relationship between donor and recipient and between harm-doer and victim. *Sociometry,* 1977, **40**, 293–298.

Bentler, P. M., & Woodward, J. A. A Head Start re-evaluation: Positive effects are not yet demonstrable. *Evaluation Quarterly,* 1978, **2**, 493–510.

Berkowitz, L. Beyond exchange: Ideals and other factors affecting helping and altruism. Unpublished manuscript, University of Wisconsin, Madison, Wisconsin, 1972. (a)

Berkowitz, L. Social norms, feelings and other factors helping behavior and altruism. In L. Berkowitz (Ed.), *Advances in experimental social psychology* (Vol. 6). New York: Academic Press, 1972. Pp. 63–108. (b).

Berkowitz, L., & Daniels, L. R. Responsibility and dependency. *Journal of Abnormal and Social Psychology,* 1963, **66**, 429–436.

Berkowitz, L., & Walster, E. (Eds.) Equity theory: Toward a general theory of social interaction. *Advances in experimental social psychology,* (Vol. 9). New York: Academic Press, 1976.

Berscheid, E., & Walster, E. When does a harm doer compensate a victim? *Journal of Personality and Social Psychology,* 1967, **6**, 435–441.

Berscheid, E., Walster, E., & Barclay, A. Effect of time on tendency to compensate victim. *Psychological Reports,* 1969, **25**, 431–436.

Blau, P. M. *The dynamics of bureaucracy: A study of interpersonal relations in two government agencies (Rev. ed.).* Chicago, Illinois: University of Chicago Press, 1955.

Blau, P. M. *Exchange and power in social life.* New York: Wiley, 1964.

Blau, P. M. Social exchange. In D. L. Sills (Ed.), *International encyclopedia of the social sciences* (Vol. 7). New York: Macmillan, 1968. Pp. 442–457.

Brehm, J. W. *A theory of psychological reactance.* New York: Academic Press, 1966.

Brehm, J. W., & Cole, A. H. Effect of a favor which reduces freedom. *Journal of Personality and Social Psychology,* 1966, **3**, 420–426.

Brickman, P., Rabinowitz, V. C., Coates, D., Cohn, E., Kidder, L. & Karuza, J. Helping. Unpublished manuscript, University of Michigan, Ann Arbor, Michigan, 1979.

Brock, T. C., & Buss, A. H. Dissonance, aggression, and evaluation of pain. *Journal of Abnormal and Social Psychology,* 1962, **65**, 197–202.

Broll, L., Gross, A. E. & Piliavin, I. Effects of offered and requested help on help seeking and reactions to being helped. *Journal of Applied Social Psychology,* 1974, **4,** 244-258.

Brown, B. R. The effects of need to maintain face on interpersonal bargaining. *Journal of Experimental Social Psychology,* 1968, **4,** 107-122.

Brown, B. R. Face-saving following experimentally induced embarrassment. *Journal of Experimental Social Psychology,* 1970, **6,** 255-271.

Castro, M. A. Reactions to receiving aid as a function of cost to donor and opportunity to aid. *Journal of Applied Social Psychology,* 1974, **4,** 194-209.

Clark, M. S., Gotay, C. C., & Mills, J. Acceptance of help as a function of similarity of the potential helper and opportunity to repay. *Journal of Applied Social Psychology,* 1974, **4,** 224-229.

Clark, M. S., & Mills, J. Interpersonal attraction in exchange and communal relationships. *Journal of Personality and Social Psychology,* 1979, **37,** 12-24.

Clark, R. D., III, & Word, L. E. Why don't bystanders help? Because of ambiguity? *Journal of Personality and Social Psychology,* 1972, **24,** 392-400.

Darley, J. M., & Latané, B. Bystander intervention in emergencies: Diffusion of responsibility. *Journal of Personality and Social Psychology,* 1968, **8,** 377-383.

DePaulo, B. M. Accepting help from teachers—when the teachers are children. *Human Relations,* 1978, **31,** 459-474.

Dillon, W. S. *Gifts and Nations.* The Hague: Mouton, 1968.

Donnenwerth, G. V., & Foa, U. G. Effect of resource class on retaliation to injustice in interpersonal exchange. *Journal of Personality and Social Psychology,* 1974, **29,** 785-793.

Fisher, J. D., & Nadler, A. The effect of similarity between donor and recipient on reactions to aid. *Journal of Applied Social Psychology,* 1974, **4,** 230-243.

Fisher, J. D., & Nadler, A. Effect of donor resources on recipient self-esteem and self-help. *Journal of Experimental Social Psychology,* 1976, **12,** 139-150.

Foa, U. G. Interpersonal and economic resources. *Science,* 1971, **171,** 345-351.

Foa, U. G., & Foa, E. B. *Societal structures of the mind.* Springfield, Illinois: Thomas, 1974.

Foa, E. B., & Foa, U. G. Resource theory: Interpersonal behavior as exchange. In K. J. Gergen, M. S. Greenberg, and R. H. Willis (Eds.), *Social exchange: Advances in theory and research.* New York: Plenum, 1980.

Freeman, H. R. Reward vs. reciprocity as related to attraction. *Journal of Applied Social Psychology,* 1977, **1,** 57-66.

Gaertner, S. L. & Dovidio, J. F. The sublety of white racism, arousal, and helping behavior. *Journal of Personality and Social Psychology,* 1977, **35,** 691-707.

Garrett, J. B., & Libby, W. L., Jr. Role of intentionality in mediating responses to inequity in the dyad. *Journal of Personality and Social Psychology,* 1973, **28,** 21-27.

Gergen, K. J. *The psychology of behavior exchange.* Reading, Massachusetts: Addison-Wesley, 1969.

Gergen, K., Diebold, P., & Seipel, M. Intentionality and ability to reciprocate as determinants of reactions to aid. Unpublished manuscript, Swarthmore College, 1973.

Gergen, K. J., Ellsworth, P., Maslach, C., & Seipel, M. Obligation, donor resources, and reactions to aid in three nations. *Journal of Personality and Social Psychology,* 1975, **3,** 396-400.

Gergen, K. J. & Gergen, M. K. "International assistance from a psychological perspective" in *The Yearbook of International Affairs,* v. 25, London Institute of World Affairs, 1971, 87-103.

Glasser, I. Prisoners of Benevolence. In W. Gaylin, I. Glasser, S. Marcus, and D. Rothman (Eds.), *Doing good: The limits of benevolence.* New York: Pantheon, 1978. Pp. 97-168.

Goldner, F. H. Demotion in industrial management. *American Sociological Review,* 1965, **30,** 714–724.

Goranson, R. E., & Berkowitz, L. Reciprocity and responsibility reactions to prior help. *Journal of Personality and Social Psychology,* 1966, **3,** 227–232.

Gouldner, A. The norm of reciprocity: A preliminary statement. *American Sociological Review,* 1960, **25,** 161–178.

Greenberg, M. S. A preliminary statement on a theory of indebtedness. In M. S. Greenberg (Chem.), *Justice in social exchange.* Symposium held by the Western Psychological Association, San Diego, California, 1968.

Greenberg. M. S. A theory of indebtedness. In K. Gergen, M. S. Greenberg, & R. Willis (Eds.), *Social exchange: Advances in theory and research.* New York: Plenum, 1980.

Greenberg, M. S., & Frisch, D. M. Effect of intentionality on willingness to reciprocate a favor. *Journal of Experimental Social Psychology,* 1972, **8,** 99–111.

Greenberg, M. S., Mowrey, J., Steinberg, R., & Bar-Tal, D. The perception of indebtedness. Unpublished manuscript, University of Pittsburgh, Pittsburgh, Pennsylvania 1974.

Greenberg, M. S., & Shapiro, S. P. Indebtedness: An adverse aspect of asking for and receiving help. *Sociometry,* 1971, **34,** 290–301.

Greenglass, E.R. Effects of prior help and hindrance on willingness to help another: Reciprocity or social responsibility. *Journal of Personality and Social Psychology,* 1969, **11,** 224–231.

Gross, A. E., & Latané, J. G. Receiving help, reciprocation, and interpersonal attraction. *Journal of Applied Social Psychology,* 1974, **4,** 210–223.

Gross, A. E., & Somersan, S. Helper effort as an inhibitor of helpseeking. Paper presented at the meeting of the Psychonomic Society, Boston, Massachusetts, 1974.

Haggstrom, W. C. The power of the poor. In F. Reissman *et al.* (Eds.). *Mental health of the poor.* New York: Free Press, 1964.

Harris, R. J. Handling negative inputs: on the plausible equity formulae. *Journal of Experimental and Social Psychology,* 1976, **12,** 194–209.

Hatfield, E., Greenberger, D, Traupmann, J., & Lambert, P. Equity and sexual satisfaction in recently married couples. *Journal of Sex Research,* 1982, 18–32.

Hatfield, E., & Traupmann, J. Intimate relationships: A perspective from Equity theory. In S. Duck and R. Gilmour (Eds.), *Personal relationships I: Studying personal relationships.* New York, Academic Press, 1980. Pp. 165–178.

Hatfield, E., & Traupmann, J. How important is fairness over the lifespan? *International Journal of Aging and Human Development,* (In press).

Hatfield, E., Traupmann, J., Sprecher, S., Utne, M., & Hay, J. Equity and intimate relations: Recent research. In W. Ickes (Ed.) *Compatible and incompatible relationships.* New York: Springerverlag In press.

Hatfield, E., Traupmann, J., & Walster, G. W. Equity and extramarital sex. In M. Cook and G. Wilson (Eds.), *Love and Attraction: An international conference.* Oxford: Pergamon, 1979. Pp. 323–334.

Hatfield, E., Walster, G. W., & Piliavin, J. Equity theory and helping relationships. In L. Wispé (Ed.), *Altruism, sympathy, and helping.* New York: Academic Press, 1978. Pp. 115–139.

Heider, F. *The psychology of interpersonal relations.* New York: Wiley, 1958.

Hinde, R. A. Towards understanding relationships. New York: Academic Press, 1979.

Homans, G. C. *Social behavior: Its elementary forms.* New York: Harcourt, 1961.

Homans. G. C. Commentary. In L. Berkowitz and E. Walster (Eds.), *Equity theory: Toward a general theory of social interaction* (Vol. 9). New York: Academic Press, 1976. Pp. 231–245.

Joffe, N. F. Non-reciprocity among East European Jews. In M. Mead & R. Matraux (Ed.), *The study of culture at a distance.* Chicago, Illinois: University of Chicago Press, 1953. Pp. 386–387.

Jones, E. E., & Davis, K. E. From acts to dispositions: The attribution process in person perception. In L. Berkowitz (Ed.), *Advances in Experimental Social Psychology* (Vol. 2). New York: Academic Press, 1965. Pp. 219–265.

Kahn, A., & Tice, T. E. Returning a favor and retaliating harm: The effects of stated intentions and actual behavior. *Journal of Experimental Social Psychology,* 1973, **9,** 43–56.

Kalish, R. A. Of children and grandfathers: A speculative essay on dependency. *The Gerontologist,* 1967, **7,** 185ff.

Kelley, H. H. Attribution theory in social psychology. In D. Levine (Ed.), *Nebraska symposium on motivation.* Lincoln, Nebraska: University of Nebraska Press, 1967. Pp. 192–240.

Krebs, D. Altruism: An examination of the concept and a review of the literature. *Psychological Bulletin,* 1970, **73,** 258–302.

Krishnan, L., & Carment, D.W. Reactions to help: reciprocity, responsibility and reactance. *European Journal of Social Psychology,* 1979, **9,** 435–439.

Latané, J. Some determinants of favor acceptance. Paper presented at the meeting of the Eastern Psychological Association, Washington, D.C., 1973.

Leeds, R. Altruism and the norm of giving. *Merrill-Palmer Quarterly,* 1963, **9,** 229–240.

Lenrow, P. B. Studies in sympathy. In S. S. Tomkins & C. E. Izard (Eds.) *Affect, cognition and personality.* New York: Springer, 1965. Pp. 264–294.

Lerner, M. J. Justified self-interest and the responsibility for suffering: A replication and extension. *Journal of Human Relations,* 1971, **19,** 550–559.

Lerner, M. J., & Lichtman, R. R. Effects of perceived norms on attitudes and altruistic behavior toward a dependent other. *Journal of Personality and Social Psychology,* 1968, **9,** 226–232.

Leventhal, G. S., Weiss, T., & Buttrick, R. Attribution of value equity, and the prevention of waste in reward allocation. *Journal of Personality and Social Psychology,* 1973, **27,** 276–286.

Leventhal, G. S., Weiss, T., & Long, G. Equity, reciprocity, and reallocating the rewards in the dyad. *Journal of Personality and Social Psychology,* 1969, **3,** 300–305.

Lipman, A., & Sterne, R. S. Aging in the United States: Ascription of a terminal sick role. *Sociology and Social Research,* 1969, **53,** 194–203.

Mauss, M. *The Gift: Forms and functions of exchange in archaic societies.* Glencoe, Illinois: Free Press, 1954.

Morris, S. C., III & Rosen, S. Effects of felt adequacy and opportunity to reciprocate on help-seeking. *Journal of Experimental Social Psychology,* 1973, **9,** 265–276.

Moschetti, G. J. Calculating equity: Ordinal and ratio criteria. *Social Psychology Quarterly,* 1979, **42,** 172–176.

Nemeth, C. Effects of free versus constrained behavior. *Journal of Personality and Social Psychology,* 1970, **15,** 302–311.

Piliavin, I. M., Rodin, J., & Piliavin, J. A. Good Samaritanism: An Underground phenomenon? *Journal of Personality and Social Psychology,* 1969, **13,** 289–299.

Piliavin, J. A., Dovidio, J. F., Gaertner, S. L., & Clark, R. D. III *Emergency intervention.* New York: Academic Press, 1981.

Pruitt, D. G. Reciprocity and credit building in a laboratory dyad. *Journal of Personality and Social Psychology,* 1968, **8,** 143–147.

Pruitt, D. G. Methods for resolving differences of interest: A theoretical analysis. *Journal of Social Issues,* 1972, **28,** 133–154.

Rosenhan, D. L. Some origins of concern for others. In P. Museen, M. Covington, & J. Langer (Eds.), *Trends and issues in developmental psychology.* New York: Holt, 1969. Pp. 132–153.

Rosenhan, D. L. Toward resolving the altruism, paradox: Affect, selfreinforcement and cognition. In L. Wispé (Ed.), *Altruism, sympathy and helping.* New York: Academic Press, 1978. Pp. 101–114.

Rushton, J. P., & Sorrentino (Eds.) *Altruism and helping behavior.* Hillsdale, New Jersey: Erlbaum, 1981.

Schafer, R. B., & Keith, P. M. Equity and depression among married couples. *Social Psychology Quarterly,* 1980, **43,** 430–435.

Schafer, R. B., & Keith, P. M. Equity in marital roles across the family life cycle. *Journal of Marriage and the Family,* 1981, **43,** 359–367.

Schopler, J. An attribution analysis of some determinants of reciprocating a benefit. In J. Macauley & Berkowitz (Eds.), *Altruism and helping behavior.* New York: Academic Press, 1970.

Schopler, J. & Thompson, V. D. Role of attribution processes in mediating amount of reciprocity for a favor. *Journal of Personality and Social Psychology,* 1968, **10,** 243–250.

Schumaker, S. A., & Jackson, J. S. The aversive effects on nonreciprocated benefits. *Social Psychology Quarterly,* 1979, **42,** 148–158.

Skinner, B. F. The ethics of helping people. In L. Wispé (Ed.), *Altruism, sympathy, and helping.* New York: Academic Press, 1978. Pp. 249–262.

Smith, A. *The Theory of Moral Sentiments.* London and New York: Bell and Sons, 1892.

Sprecher-Fisher, S. Men, women, and intimate relationships: A study of dating couples. Unpublished Master's thesis, University of Wisconsin–Madison, 1980.

Stapleton, R. E., Nacci, P., & Tedeschi, J. T. Interpersonal attraction and the reciprocation of benefits. *Journal of Personality and Social Psychology,* 1973, **28,** 199–205.

Staub, E. A child in distress: The influence of age and number of witnesses on children's attempts to help. *Journal of Personality and Social Psychology,* 1970, **14,** 130–140.

Staub, E. *Positive forms of social behavior.* New York: Academic Press, 1978.

Stebbins, L. B., St. Pierre, R. G., Proper, E. C., Anderson, R. B., & Cerva, T. R. An evaluation of follow through. In T. D. Cook, M. L. Del Rosario, K. M. Hennigan, M. M. Mark, & W. M. K. Trochim (Eds.), *Evaluation studies review annual* (Vol. 3). Beverly Hills, California: Sage Publications, 1978.

Stotland, E. Exploratory investigations of empathy. In L. Berkowitz (Ed.), *Advances in Experimental Social Psychology* (Vol. 4). New York: Academic Press, 1969.

Tacitus. *Annals,* Book IV, sec. 18.

Tesser, A., Gatewood, R., & Driver, M. Some determinants of gratitude. *Journal of Personality and Social Psychology,* 1968, **9,** 233–236.

Thibaut, J. W., & Riecken, H. W. Some determinants and consequences of the perception of social causality. *Journal of Personality,* 1955, **24,** 113–133.

Traupmann, J., & Hatfield, E. Love and its effect on mental and physical health. In E. Fogel, E. Hatfield, S. Kiesler and E. Shanas (Eds.), *Aging: Stability and change in the family.* New York: Academic Press, 1981.

Traupmann, J., Hatfield, E., & Sprecher, S. The importance of "fairness" for the marital satisfaction of older women. Unpublished manuscript, University of Wisconsin–Madison, 1981.

Traupmann, J., Hatfield, E., & Wexler, P. Equity and sexual satisfaction in dating couples. *British Journal of Social Psychology,* In press.

Utne, M. K., Hatfield, E., Traupmann, J., & Greenberger, D. Equity, marital satisfaction and stability. *Basic and Applied Social Psychology.* (submitted)

Walster (Hatfield), E., Walster, G. W., & Berscheid, E. Equity: *Theory and research*. Boston, Massachusetts: Allyn and Bacon, 1978.

Walster (Hatfield), E., Walster, G. W., & Traupmann, J. Equity and premarital sex. *Journal of Personality and Social Psychology*, 1978, **37**, 82–92.

Walster, G. W. The Walster *et al.* (1973) Equity formula: A Correction. *Representative Research in Social Psychology*, 1975, **6**, 65–67.

Weick, K. E., & Nesset, B. Preferences among forms of equity. *Organizational Behavior and Human Performance*, 1968, **3**, 400–416.

Weiss, R. F., Boyer, J. L., Lombardo, J. P., & Stick, M. H. Altruistic drive and altruistic reinforcement. *Journal of Personality and Social Psychology*, 1973, **25**, 390–400.

Weitman, S. R. Prosocial behavior and its discontents. In L. Wispé (Ed.), *Altruism, sympathy, and helping*. New York: Academic Press, 1978. Pp. 229–246.

Wilke, H., & Lanzetta, J. T. The obligation to help: the effects of amount of prior help on subsequent helping behavior. *Journal of Experimental Social Psychology*, 1970, **6**, 488–493.

Wispé, L. G. Sympathy and empathy. In D. L. Sills (Ed.), *International encyclopedia of the social sciences* (Vol. 15). New York: Macmillan, 1968, Pp. 415–420.

Wispé, L. G. (Ed.) *Altruism, sympathy, and helping*. New York: Academic Press, 1978. Pp. 303–328.

Yochelson, S., & Samenov, S. F. *The criminal personality* (Vol. 1). New York: Jason Aronson, 1976.

Zuckerman, M. A comment on the equity formula by Walster, Berscheid and Walster. (1973) *Representative Research in Social Psychology*, 1975, **6**, 63–64.

CHAPTER 6

The Social Construction
of Helping Relationships*

Kenneth J. Gergen
Mary M. Gergen

Inquiry into the antecedents and consequences of helping behavior typically treat the existence of *help* itself as unproblematic. That is, such actions are assumed to be among the normal constituents of social life; helping behavior falls within the inventory of everyday events such as aggressing, working, loving, and so on that the typical behavioral scientist hopes to understand, predict and perhaps control. Given the existence of helping behavior, systematic inquiry can begin to examine the conditions that enhance or reduce its occurrence (cf. Bar-Tal, 1976; Gergen, Gergen, & Meter, 1972; Krebs, 1970; Latané & Darley, 1970; Staub, 1978, 1979; and Wispé, 1978) and the conditions under which it may be accepted, rejected, sought,

*The present chapter was facilitated by a grant from the National Science Foundation (7809393) and by the supportive environment furnished by Professor Carl F. Graumann, Psychologisches Institüt, Universität Heidelberg.

143

or avoided (cf. Fisher & Nadler, 1976; Gergen & Gergen, 1972; Greenberg, 1980; Nadler, Altman, & Fisher, 1979). It is to this presumption of objective helping behavior that the present paper first addresses itself. That which has been treated as an unproblematic cornerstone of traditional inquiry proves, on closer inspection, to be an insubstantial pretender. What has been accepted as an event in nature is shown to have no existence independent of a meaning system. Helping is thus not an objective occurrence, but an integer in an interpretive system. Further, when the grounds for this reassessment are elucidated, we find that they furnish the rationale for an alternative theoretical approach to the issue of help and its consequences. This sociorationalist alternative (Gergen & Morawski, 1980) centers on the negotiation of meaning and the specific place of help-giving and help-receiving within this process. After exploring this orientation, we consider its relationship to current research and application.

HELP: FROM OBJECT
TO OBJECTIFICATION

We may begin with a focus on observable behavior. If we consider what is given in observation, perhaps the most accurate description of such activity would be rendered in a physical language made possible through sophisticated instrumentation. That is, for example, photographic devices might be used to determine the velocity and direction of bodily movement at specified times. With sensitive recording devices one could plot the precise movements of each limb; with a sound spectograph one could capture each nuance of sound emitted by the individual from one second to the next; further instruments might inform us of the individual's angle of visual gaze, the curvature of the mouth, and so on. Yet, it must be asked, how, in this panoply of observational data, could one go about locating a specimen of helping behavior? Which particular displacements of the arms, the fingers, or the mouth, which arrangement of phonemes, and which particular velocities of bodily movement are to be properly identified as instances of helping behavior?

It might be responded that instances of helping are lost in this microscopic account of activity. Helping behaviors are more molar in character; they take place over a more extended period and require sequences of coordinated activities. This reply seems reasonable until one attempts to enumerate those particular sets of coordinated activities that would unequivocally count as help. Are there certain patterns of extended movement (NE at 10 mph for 22 minutes with limbs moving rhythmically, and then SE at 2 mph with limbs moving arhythmically) that might be recognized by most people as help? And wouldn't the very same action (placing a coin in a plate) be counted as help on some occasions (e.g., when donations are being collected at a religious service) and not in others (e.g., when a magician is about to cause the coin's disappearance?) Again there is nothing in extended sequences of observable action that seems to enhance one's capacities to identify instances of help.

Given the opacity generated by an inductive approach, let us approach the problem deductively. Let us consider an action that most people would identify as help and then attempt to locate the observable markings, signs, or indicators used to justify the classification. Consider a motorist who brings his car to a halt on a busy motorway, exits from the vehicle, smiles and talks to the driver of a stranded vehicle, tinkers with the engine of the disabled vehicle until it is functioning, talks for two additional minutes, and then departs. One is inclined to call this particular sequence an act of help. Yet, we may ask again, do the observable actions furnish the cues enabling us to reach this conclusion? If the details of the actions were altered, would we still be permitted to call it help? That is, if the actor did not smile, or tinkered with the engine with one instead of two hands, would such variants also constitute acts of help? If so, on what grounds? Let us consider aspects of the situation other than the activity itself. What if the actor were a virile male and the stranded motorist an inviting female; if he had recently been released from a hospital for the criminally insane; if he had a long history of attempted rapes; or he had been travelling for four days without human contact? Would the very same performance constitute an act of help?

As should be clear from this exploration, it is not the motions of the individual moving through space and time that enable us to identify his actions. And, in principle, how could they be? The particular motions described above never occurred before, and will never be replicated in precisely this manner. In effect, we would have no previous training in matching word with observable pattern. Previous learning of this kind could not thus furnish a basis for identifying the act in the present case. Further, our identification of the action appears vitally dependent on what we know about both the events preceding and following the activity in question. As we may thus conclude, when we speak of acts of helping we are not referring to the precise character of the action. Help is not part of the inventory of real world events available for study.

How, then, would one go about determining the circumstances under which the concept of help may be properly employed? On what basis can one justifiably call a given pattern of action *helping* and another pattern a *reaction to help?* Let us return to the ostensible helper in the above instance and play the role of jurors. It is the judicial process that perhaps best illustrates the means of behavioral identification implicit within a culture more generally. Juries must typically determine whether an action constitutes a murder, an accident, a rape, an arson, a suicide, and so on, and the results of their decisions are often substantial. In most such instances, the chief concern of the jury is whether the individual in question knew what he or she was doing and could or could not have selected an alternative action. In effect, the jury is typically concerned with the meaning of the action for the actor—its intentional basis. Murder, rape, and suicide, after all, are matters of intention. By definition, one cannot engage in such actions unintentionally. In the same way we may properly examine the meaning or the intent of the motorist's actions. Was he intending to help? Or was he flirting, scanning the scene in hopes of a later theft, practicing his mechanical skills in hopes of gaining future employment, seeking relief from his loneliness, or something else? The way in which we interpret the action depends importantly on what we ascertain to be the meaning of the act for the individual. If he intended robbery, and the stranded motorist believed he was giving help, we should have to conclude that she was mistaken. The help was only a charade and the action was "actually" something other.[1]

In this light we see that the relationship between the identity of an action and its observable properties is fundamentally indeterminate (see also Rommetveit, 1980). The very same behavioral act may be seen as part of a sequence that may properly be called flirtation, rape, theft, help, and so on. We cannot determine from the act itself what particular meaning it has for the actor, and thus to which of these classifications it should be assigned. In the same way, patterns that differ in exterior features may all be identified as one kind of act. Repairing an engine, picking up the coins someone has dropped, or plunging a dagger into another's heart may all be classified as acts of help within a particular meaning system. Of course, some might disagree with a particular classification; for example, can the plunging of the dagger properly be identified as help? It is also possible for others to see the actor as "getting it wrong."[2] It is precisely this potential for disagreement that will furnish the basis for our later treatment of the relationship between the giver and the receiver in the helping relationship.

In general, however, it may be said that social ontology is a product of meaning systems and not of observable activities. It is the meaning of actions, and not actions themselves, that furnish the individual with a sense

---

[1]For a related discussion of the problem of identifying aggressive behavior [see Mummenday (1979, 1982) and Tedeschi, Smith, & Brown (1974).]

[2]Whether the actor can even "get it right" with respect to an empirical anchoring remains moot. The weight of contemporary argument is contrary to the assumption that actors can "know" in any objective sense the intentional grounds or meaning of their acts (cf. Anscombe, 1976; Gergen, 1980; 1982; Nisbett & Wilson, 1977).

of "what is happening." What has traditionally been viewed as an act of helping is thus an objectification of a meaning system—the treatment of the meaning system as if its constituents were palpable.[3]

Before proceeding, we must ensure clarity regarding our premises. The attempt is not to deny either the existence or the importance of human activity. It is the traditional treatment of the relationship between activity and the language of person description that is being challenged. Although we are proposing that terms of person description do not generally refer to actual observations, it is clear that observations of ongoing activities do furnish the context for using descriptive terminology. In effect, such observations serve as excuses for using descriptive terms without providing the referents for the terminology itself. This point may seem especially difficult to accept in many instances. Don't many descriptive terms refer to the actual patterns? Wouldn't the observable pattern of "combing one's hair" be discriminably different from the act of "milking the cow"? In such cases it may be said that there are certain recurring patterns of activity that have been so repeatedly identified by the same term that their subsequent occurrence virtually ensures the use of a particular terminology. One simply knows what "combing one's hair" looks like (within a broad range), and can reliably discriminate between such patterns and those one might typically call "milking the cow." Under such circumstances, one simply employs the term with little concern for what is intended or meant by the actions. Much social interaction can proceed with relative ease on this account; surely if query into underlying intention were continuous, social life would soon stagnate. Yet, it is also important to avoid the tempting and pervasive conclusion that the descriptive terms are therefore anchored in, or ultimately justified by, the observations.[4]

[3]Although there are significant similarities between the present arguments and those which may be made from a radical extension of symbolic interactionism, there is one difference of fundamental significance. Whereas symbolic interactionists generally consider symbols as psychological entities, constituents of an "inner world," the present orientation locates interpretive integers within language systems. What kinds of underlying or inner processes are involved in producing language remains unspecified. In this sense, the present analysis is more compatible with ethnomethodological research (Antaki, 1980; Garfinkel, 1967) and certain aspects of social constructionist theory (Berger & Luckmann, 1967; Zimmerman & Pollner, 1970).

[4]To illustrate, on what objective basis, for example, can one say that a person has fired a pistol? Is the motion of the finger squeezing around the trigger the essential and unmistakable cue? Consider the instance in which another's hand is pressing one's finger around the trigger. Could one continue to say that the individual has still fired the pistol? Chances are, the individual would reject this description. His fingers may have been instrumental, he might argue, but it was not he who fired the pistol. It was the individual who squeezed his finger who did so. Or, if one were hunting and tripped over a fallen tree, whereupon the pistol was discharged, could one say of the individual that he fired the pistol? The overt action of squeezing the trigger was the same, but the individual might well argue that this was not, in fact,

HELP AND ITS CONJOINT RELATIONS

Now that we have removed the act of help from the world of observation and placed it within a system of meanings, we are in a position to
explore its relationship with other symbolic entities. What, then, is the relationship between help, for example, and the recipients' gratitude, reciprocity, resentment, retaliation, and the wide range of other activities of
typical concern to investigators of helping relationships? As is rapidly dis-
cerned, all such reactions are also to be removed from the realm of objectification and reconstituted as symbolic integers. The question we thus
confront is, what is the relationship between the concept of help and other
concepts in the system of shared meanings? To put it another way, if help
is said to occur, what limits are placed over one's descriptive vocabulary
for subsequent occurrences? It would appear that an answer to this question
requires inquiry into the common sense constructions available within a
culture. If someone is described as giving help, how must one be able to
describe the recipient's actions if they are to make sense within the common
framework of understanding?

Based on common cultural experience (cf. Cicourel, 1974), it might be
suggested that actions described as helping may properly be followed by
actions understood, for example, as "gratitude," "reciprocity," and "cooperation" (see Figure 1). These descriptions may be contrasted with a variety of others that presumably would not be understood within large
segments of the culture. For example, if it were said of Stan that he helped
his friend, Lisa, our sense of propriety would be upset if it were said of
Lisa that she responded by "moping," "committing suicide," "aggressing," "running in circles," or "treating Stan like a dog." At a minimum,
Lisa would be said to have failed to display the level of skill required for
acceptable participation in the culture; at a maximum, she might be said to
be mentally deranged. This is not to say that such descriptions cannot be
made of Lisa's actions. However, given common conventions of understanding, they cannot generally be offered without some form of extenuating communication. One would be required to furnish some form of

---

his doing. He did not mean to fire the weapon; it was discharged by "circumstances." Or, if
the individual were asked to squeeze the trigger as a test of his strength, and he found to his
surprise that he had been tricked into squeezing the trigger of a pistol that subsequently fired,
could it be said of the individual that he fired the pistol? Surely, he would argue that he was
testing his strength; it would be unfair to say of him that he fired the pistol. As can be seen,
then, even when actions are recognizable and widely repeated, the adequacy of description
cannot be judged by the overt movements themselves, but depends importantly on judgments
about the individual's state of mind—his or her intentions, meanings, or aims. The superficial
movements count only so long as they furnish an occasion for an interpretive practice. However, the referent of such practices is essentially an unseen construction.

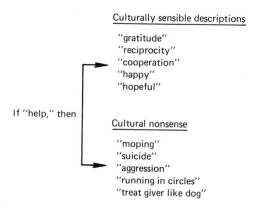

Figure 1. Appropriate and inappropriate descriptions of responses to help.

justification enabling the description to fit once again into the acceptable range of interpretations. Thus, it might be said of Lisa's suicidal reaction, "Stan's help was such a magnanimous act that it served as a crowning indication of her longstanding sense of inferiority. Under the circumstances, she couldn't bear to live with herself any longer." Or it might be said of Lisa's aggressive reaction, "The help was seen by Lisa as Stan's attempt to show her she was an inferior person. For Lisa, it was not an act of help but an act of vengeance on Stan's part." With these added remarks, one can now make sense of the description of Lisa's actions. Such accounting is not required if Lisa's reactions were characterized as "gratitude" or "friendliness."

Thus far we have confined our analysis to two simple descriptive integers, a helping term and a descriptive term for the reaction. We must now extend the analysis in an important way. In particular, we must consider the manner in which these descriptive tendencies are embedded within a broad network of understandings. This network may be said to possess both a *synchronic* and a *diachronic* aspect (cf. Collett, 1980; Gergen & Gergen, 1983; Harré, 1979). In the former case, the terms of description applied to the present exchange are embedded within the broader structure of understanding pertaining to the present or contemporaneous segment of time. The way in which one understands the identity of the individuals, their psychological makeup, the context of the interaction, and so on, all bear on the allowances that can be made in describing the acts in question. There are, for example, an array of other descriptive terms that, when applied to Stan in this situation, would favor the use of "help" as an account of his action, along with a battery of terms that would favor certain accounts regarding Lisa's reaction. If Stan were said to be a "pleasant," "nurturant," "optimistic," or "fatherly" person, it would be sensible to use the term "help" to describe his action. In contrast, if he were said to be "self-centered," "miserly," or "aggressive," his "help" would be less evident. Additional accounting would be necessitated in order to demonstrate that a "self-centered" person does "help." Likewise, if Lisa were described as "pleasant" and "affable," we would generally be more willing to accept "gratitude" as a description of her reaction than we would "resentment." The use of the latter term would require again a form of explanation that would mend the fissure in common sense.

With respect to the diachronic dimension of understanding, it may be said that the manner in which the contemporary activities can be described depends importantly on one's understanding of the history of the participants. That is, one's description of the moment is embedded within a historical narrative. Actions do not generally appear to us as isolated in time, but rather, are understood as constituent elements in broader historical sequences. The elements are essentially understood as they are related to other elements within a structure; that is, they possess a narrative form (Gergen & Gergen, 1983). Thus, in the present instance, the exchange between Lisa and Stan may be viewed within a narrative account of their relationship. If the two are described as having a long friendship in which Lisa has often rescued Stan from the throes of despair, then Stan's present action may sensibly be described as help. Within this narrative account of their relationship, an action of helping would be plausible by conventional standards. If, in contrast, narrative accounts of the relationship demonstrated it had been one of continuous conflict, intrigue, and perfidy, an act of "help" on Stan's part would fail to be sensible. Additional accounting would be necessitated before this characterization would seem reasonable.

To formalize the implications of this discussion, it may be said that the actions of any moment serve as candidates for identification. One wishes to know "what X is doing" at the moment. Such identification requires that one consult a vocabulary of potentially relevant descriptors. The potential relevance of any descriptor is first dependent upon the network of descriptive and explanatory terms employed within the present situation. Depending on the way in which this network of synchronic understandings is elaborated, the range of possible descriptors for the action in question may be progressively narrowed or broadened. In effect, one may say that, with the elaboration of the meaning of the present situation, variations occur in the "logical force" (Cronen & Pearce, 1981) undergirding the use of particular descriptors. Thus, for example, if our understanding of the situation is such that Stan is known to be a "warm," "generous," and "loving" person, and Lisa is his "friend," it becomes increasingly "logical" to view the act in question as "help." If it is also said that Lisa is "in need" and is "displaying this need" to Stan, the logical force demanding the use of "help" as a descriptor is further increased. By the same token, one might reduce the logical force underlying the "help" descriptor if it were pointed out that Stan has a migraine headache, is preoccupied with concerns of his health, or is angry with Lisa and suspicious of her intentions.

We can further extend the analysis by viewing the synchronic description as importantly dependent upon the network of diachronic understandings. Whether we can properly call Stan a "warm and friendly" person or "angry" with Lisa depends upon how we understand the history of their relationship. If Stan had never been known as a warm and friendly person, it would be difficult to justify the use of such descriptors in the present instance. If the narrative account demonstrated Lisa's continuous good will toward Stan, the logical force behind the use of "aggressive" to describe Stan would be diminished. More generally, then, synchronic understanding stands in a similar relationship to diachronic understanding as the action in question stands to the synchronic network (see Figure 2). As the diachronic account is elaborated, the logical force behind a particular synchronic account is affected, and as the synchronic account is elaborated, the logical force behind a particular description of the action itself is affected. With full elaboration of both the synchronic and diachronic domains, a particular descriptor for the action in question could become virtually inevitable (cf. Fish, 1979; Wieder, 1970).

It is but a short step from this analysis to understanding what is involved in identifying reactions to help. Once the action serving as a candidate for "help" is identified, that which we have termed a *reaction* takes a focal position. It now serves as the candidate in question, and all we have said about engendering understanding of the helping action now becomes relevant to identifying its sequelae. The only additional feature is that the candidate for identification as help now has entered the ledger of synchronic understanding. It now serves as one of the integers to be taken into account in judging whether the subsequent reaction is to be taken as "gratitude," "cooperation," "hostility," "moping," and so on. In the same way that the logical force underlying the employment of the helping label may wax and wane with the elaboration of the synchronic and diachronic contexts, so now does the description of the reaction become more or less

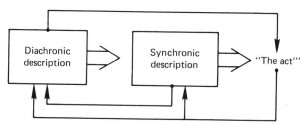

Figure 2. Act description as synchronically and diachronically embedded.

constrained. If Stan and Lisa have long been friends, Lisa has often helped Stan, Stan is now prosperous, Lisa is in need, Stan has been friendly, and has now offered "help," it must be said of Lisa that she was "grateful," "cordial," "friendly," or the like in her reaction. To say that she "attacked" Stan under these descriptive constraints would require a great deal of explanatory work. This is to say that Lisa could go through a variety of reactions that are typically viewed as unfriendly (e.g., failure to smile, diminished verbal expression) if she were to explain that she was suffering from anxiety or pain. This would inform Stan that these patterns did not count as reactions to him and that the true, underlying reaction was one of friendliness and gratitude.

Finally, it should be pointed out that although our analysis has emphasized the linear effects of description—beginning with the diachronic effects on the synchronic interpretation and the synchronic account on the identification of the action in question—a multidirectional system of effects must ultimately be entailed. That is, an interpretive stand at any point in the array may have reverberating effects on the remainder of the network. For Lisa to announce that she is "exceedingly grateful" for Stan's help, for example, is to invite Stan to reassess his actions ("Did I help that much?"), to consider himself and Lisa in a particular way ("I guess we are a friendly pair") and to review their history with certain constraints ("I think she has always been a good friend"). In effect, the entry of any descriptive integer into the ledger of understanding may have repercussions throughout the interpretive network.

NEGOTIATING REALITY
IN HELPING RELATIONSHIPS

Based on this preliminary sketch, we may begin inquiry into the determination of help and related entities in ongoing relationships. If we confine ourselves to the dyadic encounter, it is quickly seen that we have not one contextual array for determining the meaning of the action sequence, but two. That is, each party brings to the occasion a particular understanding of both the diachronic and the synchronic contexts within which the action sequence is occurring. Although such perspectives could be identical in principle, given the immensely varied forms of understanding available in any culture (or across cultures), conflict in understanding may be considered the general rule (Ricoeur, 1979). With full and obdurate conflict in understanding, a precipitous termination of interaction might be anticipated. It may be assumed that two parties, each of whom believes the other to be mad, would not wish to sustain a relationship. However, we may commonly anticipate a sufficient overlap and flexibility in practices of understanding that the two parties can, with sustained communication, approach an agreement as to how common actions are to be understood. This process of forming a common reality is essentially one of negotiation (cf. Strauss, 1979; Turner, 1970).

By using the term *negotiation* in this case, we intend to point up vital aspects of the process. Each party in the relationship may be viewed as interest-invested, that is, as favoring a certain range of interpretive outcomes and attempting to avoid others. Interest investment may be dependent on the ontological commitments with which the individual enters the relationship. To the extent that one places continued reliance on a particular world view, and to the extent that this employment yields satisfaction, one may sustain it across social encounters and avoid reaching agreements posing logical threats to it. For example, those who enter a relationship with a strong belief in their magnanimity might favor an interpretation of their actions as "helping," and demonstrate antipathy to others' definitions of the same action as "manipulation." Individuals who believe themselves to be gracious persons might readily accept a description of their reaction to help as "gratitude," and actively avoid the ascription of "craven dependency."

It is because of this interest relevance of each negotiator that the interaction should properly be viewed as a bargaining process. Participants may rapidly be able to reach an agreeable decision as to "what is taking place" providing the interpretation does not pose a strong challenge to previous commitments. However, to the extent that such challenges are apparent, the participants may adopt tactics for minimizing their losses. It is useful to consider four of these tactics.

1. Statement: the logic of preemption. A bargainer may attempt to build a case for a given interpretation that, once accepted, will block or discourage later attempts of the other to identify this or a related action in a disagreeable way. That is, if one can gain initial agreement over the identification of one major aspect of the interpretive network, the possibilities are thereby restricted for interpreting related actions. In effect, certain options are preempted. For example, if Stan can succeed in convincing Lisa that they have had a deep and enduring friendship, it will be exceedingly difficult for Lisa to address Stan as if she has been exploited. Exploitation is not, by common definition, a constituent of a deep and enduring friendship. Exploitation as an identification is thus preempted.

2. Partial statement: the logic of concession making. In addition to preemption, the participants in a relationship may also make interpretive concessions. They may sacrifice particular aspects of their interest-relevant

formulations in order to enhance or protect others. Thus, for example, in the case of international aid, recipient governments may desire to strengthen their domestic positions by securing outside funds or resources. However, they may also have a vested interest in not being seen as pawns to the developed nations. The strength of the first interest may be sufficient to accept the donor nation's identification of its transfer of resources as "aid" even when its preferred interpretation would be that the resources are a form of "manipulation." And, at times, donor nations wish to demonstrate on the domestic scene that their international policies have been both generous and moral. On this basis they extract token gestures of "gratitude" from recipients. For the public, such acts are interpreted as "gratitude" when privately they are acknowledged as acts of "forced compliance." They only seem to be gratitude.

3. Nonstatement: the logic of ambiguity. At times participants in a relationship may blunt each other's interpretive strategies or veil their own by generating ambiguity. Perhaps the simplest form of ambiguity production is that of letting candidates for interpretation pass without articulation. Essentially, through silence, the social world becomes uneventful.[5] Or, one may also create ambiguity by multiplying the number of available and legitimate interpretations so that no one candidate seems overwhelmingly compelling. One simply doesn't know what to make of the event any longer.

4. Restatement: the logic of reformulation. Through reformulation of interpretations, participants attempt to demonstrate how existing interpretations are faulty. For example, welfare workers often confront recipients who do not wish to see themselves as needy and sometimes may avoid offers of what is viewed as help (Broll, Gross, & Piliavin, 1974). If the welfare program is to succeed, the worker must combat this interpretation. Specifically, the worker may reformulate the case for the recipient. It could be demonstrated, for example, how the program is designed to help, not the individual, but the society as a whole, or to show how the program is not attempting to fulfill needs, but to fulfill an obligation.[6]

Against this backdrop, let us now examine a hypothetical scenario from the domestic sphere. Such consideration will enable us to vivify more directly the processes described previously. Let us consider the interaction

[5]White House aides tell the story of the way in which "Ford's fiasco" in his television debate with Carter was produced by news analysts. During the debate, Ford indicated that Poland was not an Iron Curtain country, clearly an error in judgment. Immediate telephone surveys of the public revealed, however, that the statement in no way damaged Ford's presentation. After the debate, news analysts discussed the event and called attention to Ford's unforgivable error. Subsequent surveys revealed a dramatic decline in Ford's popularity.

[6]See also Nelson Goodman's (1978) discussion of the means by which "worldmaking" can proceed.

between a 35-year-old married male and his neighbor, a divorced 37-year-old mother of three who has recently lost her job:

Don: "It's been 12 years or so since you moved in next door, hasn't it, Donna? We've been friends since practically the first day. Gee, we've been through a lot. You must be one of the best friends Janie and I have!"

In this initial fragment we find the rudiments of a diachronic interpretation. The history of the relationship is being described in such a way as to enhance the logical force of an interpretation that Don is to make of a contemplated action. If Donna accepts Don's interpretation of the relationship, certain forms of subsequent interpretation are preempted.

Donna: "Yes, it's true that we have really been through a lot in these 12 years together. You both have been great neighbors."

Here Donna reformulates the definition Don has made of their relationship. She shifts its meaning from one of "best friends" to "great neighbors." This reformulation enables her to increase her options for subsequent interpretation. Presumably the interpersonal obligations placed on a "best friend" are more onerous and less casual than those posed by a "great neighbor." However, she does not negate fully Don's identification of the relationship. The ambiguity leaves her options flexible.

Don: "I realize things have been really difficult for you since Rick left, especially since you lost your job. Well, things have been going pretty well for me at the shop, so it just seemed, well, . . . like it was a good idea to share a little. What I mean is that I would like to give you a little money each month until you get your job back. Consider it a gift."

Here Don has moved from a definition of the diachronic context (i.e., "We have been in a relationship which makes you a best friend") to the synchronic context. She is defined as in need, and he is defined as having resources. The logical force for identifying the act as a "gift" is now established. Given a relationship of friendship, the need of one friend and the resources of the other, the rationality of giving is highly favored.

Donna: "Oh, look, Don, that's really going too far! Certainly beyond the duty of a good neighbor. I'm not sure how Janie would feel about it, either."

Donna does not deny her need or his resources. Further she lets Don's interpretation stand ambiguously by referring to his offer of "sharing" a "gift" as "it." Her comment on "duty" also enables her to blunt the initial interpretive thrust and thus gain space for alternative interpretations. Raising the issue of Don's wife, Janie, may play at least two important functions. First, it has the precautionary effect of insuring that a third party, with differing interest-relevant interpretations will not enter at a later point to reformulate or possibly destroy the reality being constructed in the present moment. However, the query also has the effect of preempting later formulations that Don may wish to inject into the relationship, namely that the action in question is in reality an expression of love, a solicitation of affection or the first move in a seduction. In effect, Donna is not now ready to accept the offer if it is identified as a gift, and she wishes to ensure that it will not subsequently be reformulated as an integer in a differing form of relationship.

Don: "Oh, Jane is quite happy with the idea. She suggested it, in fact. Look, you don't have to see this as a gift from us to you. If you accept it, it will really be your gift to us. We would feel good about it, like you trusted us to be the kind of people we really want to be. *You* would be doing *us* a great favor."

Don fully accedes to the effect of the preemption in denying that the initiation of the act is his responsibility. In addition, realizing that the definition of his gift to her will not be accepted, he begins to reformulate the action. This reformulation gains a certain credibility from the previously established definition of their relationship as a deep friendship. However, it lacks other logical supports, such as a rationale for their being in particular need for this kind of gift (e.g., an enhanced self-concept).

Donna: "Look, Don, I really could use the money, and you and Janie are really sweet to offer it to me. But let's make it a loan. I'll pay you when I get my job back."

At this point Donna is making an interpretive concession. She is essentially agreeing to the action that Don has proposed, but on the condition that it be termed a loan and not a gift. This concession may enable her to maintain a certain kind of definition of herself ("provider for the children") but requires that she abandon another possible definition of herself ("one who is not dependent upon others"). It also allows her to escape the implications of Don's initial proposal that the relationship is one of "best friends" (presumably good neighbors are persons who make loans to one another), and to reassert her initial definition of a "good neighbor" relationship.

Don: "Well, let's call it a loan, but I may never ask you for the money."

Don is willing to make the interpretive concession as a means of furthering the transaction. He concedes to her definition while reserving the option to reassert his initial interpretation.

Donna: "Don, I am really grateful to you. You are very thoughtful. but you will get your money back."

At the conclusion of this episode Donna is carrying through with an action that might, given the interpretive context, be viewed by both of them as a form of appropriate gratitude. In addition she reaffirms that the money should be viewed as a loan, and not as a gift.

POST HOC RECONSTRUCTION OF HELP

Thus far we have described a variety of central tactics that may be used to influence the definition of an action, along with the constraints placed upon the interpretation of associated actions. The formulation must now be expanded in one important way. Our chief emphasis thus far has been on the negotiation of reality within a single episode, in which participants strive for mutually acceptable accounts during a single period of time. We must now take into account the recursive character of negotiation, that is, the manner in which interpretations may be transformed through reconsideration over time.

The significance of such transformations of interpretation were made apparent to us in a series of interviews with foreign aid officials (Gergen & Gergen, 1972). As discovered in this context, upon a variety of occasions, foreign aid programs had succeeded at the outset in generating enthusiastic responses among recipients. In effect, the donor nations succeeded in defining their actions as aid or help, and recipients responded with actions that were viewed as appropriate gratitude. However, years later, when such programs reached their termination point, recipient reactions frequently took a different course. The donor nation was now held in disrepute, as it had now "taken something from the people that was rightfully theirs." What had been viewed as aid, or help, was now considered an "obligation" by the recipients. In effect, the meaning of the program was now renegotiated.

Such post hoc reformulations, like the rewriting of history, may be considered a normal condition of social life. Their frequent occurrence may be anticipated for two major reasons. First, as one confronts new information sources over time, the character of one's interpretive commitments may shift. What was interest-relevant interpretation in one period of time may cease to be at a later point, and new interpretations may simultaneously gain in favor. Thus, at the time of receiving resources from abroad, it may be important for a recipient nation to agree to its definition as "aid" and to react with appropriate "gratitude." Yet, as the recipient is informed over time, for example, that the "donor" is reliant upon the "recipient" for a political voice in the Third World, a reassessment of the action's meaning may occur. Such reassessment may be particularly attractive in this case as it allows one to escape the negative implications of receiving "help" or of being "dependent," "inferior," or "obligated" (Gergen & Gergen, 1972; Greenberg, 1980), and to gain positive self-ascriptions, such as "needed," "significant," and "autonomous."

Post hoc reformulations may be favored for a second important reason. The negotiation process is essentially an interdependent one. Like a game of chess, it requires more than one participant to proceed (cf. Shotter's 1980 discussion of "joint action"). As persons negotiate, they may succeed in constructing an interpretive reality that is as significant to the actions of the participants as a concrete wall or a stone bridge. The essential problem is, however, that each relationship requires its own construction of reality, and the joint constructions in which an individual is enmeshed may differ considerably from one relationship to another (cf. Schutz, 1962). Thus, a participant in a relationship may agree that "help" and "gratitude" have occurred within the relationship, but within the context of a second relationship may "come to see" that he or she did not "really" receive "help" but a "bribe," and that the "gratitude" was not really as it seemed but only a "platitude." In effect, because of the engagement in multiple relationships, each requiring its own form of negotiation, early forms of reality may be continuously subject to replacement. Any form of constructed reality may be of brief duration.

INQUIRY INTO REACTIONS TO HELP

This chapter has outlined the rationale for viewing help and the consequences of help as social constructions, and to touch on processes essential to such construction. This sociorationalist orientation stands in sharp contrast to traditional inquiry into helping relationships inasmuch as the latter is premised on the assumption of help and its conjoint relations as objective entities. Although empirical studies also abound in the latter arena, little has been said about the kinds of research that are favored in the sociorationalist frame. In remedying this situation, two questions may be addressed: What contribution, if any, does previous research make toward understanding the helping relationship in the sociorationalist frame? What other forms of inquiry might be favored from this perspective? Let us examine each of these issues in turn.

With respect to traditional inquiry into help an its consequences, it may be argued that such research does not deliver as promised. That is, the assumption that investigators are testing hypotheses about the real-world conditions giving rise to helping behavior and the conditions under which various reactions to help occur seems unwarranted. If help and its reactions are essentially integers in meaning systems, and not constituents of the real world, and if the relationship between these integers and observation is fundamentally indeterminate, then one is ill disposed to argue that investigators are studying the "real thing." Yet, it may be responded, investigators are concerned with actual phenomena. Consider the scores of studies on by-stander help in an emergency, the effects of moods on helping activities, altruism among children, modeling and help, and the dozens of studies on tensions of obligation, equity, justice, and self-esteem maintenance as they influence reactions to help. Surely there are real activities at stake in such research. In response to this defense, let us consider more closely that which the investigation discloses. To be sure, the investigator is observing human behavior—persons moving about at certain velocities in certain directions, with limbs displaced in various positions. However, it is not such behaviors that are reported in the literature. Rather, the investigator transforms such observations into a language of understanding and, more precisely, into languages that make sense within the culture of the readers. What the in-vestigators serve up, then, is sophisticated interpretation. And, it may be argued, such interpretation must be guided by existing conventions of un-derstanding. The investigator does possess choice in interpretation. There are many languages available with which the investigator could make sense of the given observations. However, if the investigator furnishes a full dis-closure of this multiplicity—one that might be approached, for example, by having subjects describe their own activities or by having a board of observers each render an independent account—the investigator would be engaging in the kind of ambiguity production described earlier. Usually, however, it is supposed that the function of science is not to enhance but to reduce ambiguity. In effect, a strong case is typically made by the in-vestigator for one and only one intelligible interpretation.

This account of the research process furnishes us with a key to appre-ciating one important outcome of existing empirical studies.[7] From the so-ciorationalist perspective, such studies furnish examples of intelligible accounts. That is, the investigator, as a member of a language community, is providing instantiations of acceptable conventions of understanding. The investigator is telling us what is permissible to say about helping and its consequences within this culture. Thus, for example, one outcome of the early research on bystander helping in an emergency (Latané & Darley, 1968) is the general conclusion that, as feelings of personal responsibility are de-creased, people are less inclined to help. This statement can be rendered neither true nor false with respect to observables, but it does stand as an exemplar of the language of understanding. Thus, from the present per-spective, it informs us that to say of someone that "he feels personal re-sponsibility for helping" will increase the logical force behind the conclusion that "he has helped." To say of someone that he "feels no responsibility

[7]In this analysis we are much indebted to Smedslund's (1978, 1980) innovative work.

to help and therefore gave help'' would be nonsensical by present standards unless accompanied by further explanatory material. Or, to consider
research on reciprocity and reactions to help (Gouldner, 1960; Pruitt, 1968;
Schwartz, 1977; Staub & Sherk, 1970; Wilke & Lanzetta, 1970), investigators conclude that to receive help generates a tension of obligation, which
eventuates in a reciprocity of the helping act. Seen in the present context,
such a conclusion informs us that it is appropriate to label oneself as obligated when one has ''received help'' and that when one experiences a ''tension of obligation'' one helps those from whom help has been received.
Thus, to say of someone, ''the help he has received from X made him
feel less obligated to X'' would be unusual, if not obtuse. Or to say of a
person, ''he felt no obligation and therefore he reciprocated'' would be
unacceptable as an explanation; additional theoretical work would be required in order to make the statement intelligible. In effect, then, the theoretical conclusions reached through the research process begin to lay
foundations for further elaboration of the interpretive practices in which
they are embedded.

Yet, as this analysis also reveals, if the explication of such practices
entails the burdensome activity of controlled experimentation, its progress
will be slow indeed. These practices could have been generated without the
experiments themselves; the process of experimentation essentially furnished the excuse for offering an existing interpretation but served neither
as its source nor its boundary. Much needed at this point are means of
explicating these interpretive practices more directly and systematically. Interview procedures, text analyses, questionnaires and other means for elic-
iting accounts of the helping relationship might all be usefully employed.
The work of Davis and his colleagues (Davis & Todd, 1981; Roberts, 1981)
on the concept of friendship and intimacy, the research of Mummenday
(1979, 1982) and colleagues on the interpretation of aggression, the Silver
and Sabini (1978) analysis of envy, and Shweder's analysis of personality
structures (1975, 1982) may all furnish useful leads in this regard.

Yet, mere documentation also has its limitations. Practices of social
definition are clearly dynamic in character, changing continuously and differentially in various cultures and subcultures. Required are more general
theoretical formulations concerning the possible fundamentals of the interpretive process and its functions and alteration. In effect, the documentation of interpretive practices may thus serve applied as well as theoretical
interests. It may inform the professional helping agent about means for
enhanced intelligibility, and thus increase efficacy of action. At the same
time, it may encourage and vivify broad theoretical accounts of the interpretive process in general and understanding of the accountability of help
in particular.

REFERENCES

Anscombe, G. E. M. *Intention.* Oxford: Basil Blackwell, 1976.

Antaki, C. (Ed.) *The psychology of ordinary explanations.* New York: Academic Press, 1980.

Bar-Tal, D. *Prosocial behavior: Theory and research.* Washington, D.C.: Hemisphere, 1976.

Berger, P., & Luckmann, T. *The social construction of reality.* New York: Doubleday/Anchor, 1966.

Broll, L., Gross, A. E., & Piliavin, I. Effects of offered and requested help on help-seeking and reactions to being helped. *Journal of Applied Social Psychology,* 1974, **4**, 244–258.

Cicourel, A. V. *Cognitive sociology: Language and meaning in social interaction.* New York: Free Press, 1974.

Collett, P. Segmenting the behaviour stream. In M. Brenner (Ed.), *The structure of action.* Oxford: Basil Blackwell, 1980. Pp. 150–167.

Cronen, B. E., & Pearce, W. B. Logical force in interpersonal communication A new concept of necessity in social behavior. *Communication,* 1981, **31**, 13–33.

Davis, K. E., & Todd, M. Friendship and love relationships. In K. E. Davis & T. O. Mitchell (Eds.), *Advances in descriptive psychology* (Vol. 2). Greenwich, Connecticut: JAI Press, 1981.

Fish, S. Normal circumstances, literal language, direct speech acts, the ordinary, the everyday, the obvious, what goes without saying, and other special cases. In P. Rabinow & W. Sullivan (Eds.), *Interpretive social science: A reader.* Berkeley, California: Univ. of California Press, 1979. Pp. 243–266.

Fisher, J. D., & Nadler, A. Effect of donor resources on recipient self-esteem and self-help. *Journal of Experimental Social Psychology,* 1976, **13**, 139–150.

Garfinkel, H. *Studies in ethnomethodology.* Englewood Cliffs, New Jersey: Prentice-Hall, 1967.

Gergen, K. J. Toward intellectual audacity in social psychology. In R. Gilmour & S. Duck (Eds.) *The development of social psychology.* New York: Wiley, 1980.

Gergen, K. J. *Toward transformation in social knowledge.* New York: Springer-Verlag, 1982.

Gergen, K. J., & Gergen, M. M. International assistance from a psychological perspective. In *Yearbook of world affairs, 1971,* (Vol. 25). London: Institute of World Affairs, 1972.

Gergen, K. J., & Gergen, M. M. Understanding foreign assistance through public opinion. In *Yearbook of world affairs, 1974.* (Vol. 28). London: Stevens and Sons, 1974.

Gergen, K. J., & Gergen, M. M. Narratives of the self. In K. Scheibe & T. Sarbin (Eds.), *Studies in social identity.* New York: Praeger, 1983.

Gergen, K. J., Gergen, M. M., & Meter, K. Individual orientations to prosocial behavior. *Journal of Social Issues,* 1972, **28**, 105–130.

Gergen, K. J., & Morawski, J. An alternative metatheory for social psychology. In L. Wheeler (Ed.), *Review of personality and social psychology.* San Francisco, California: Sage, 1980.

Goodman, N. *Ways of worldmaking.* Indianapolis, Indiana: Hackett, 1978.

Gouldner, A. V. A norm of reciprocity: A preliminary statement. *American Sociological Review,* 1960, **25**, 161–178.

Greenberg, M. S. A theory of indebtedness. In K. J. Gergen, M. S. Greenberg, & R. H. Willis (Eds.) *Social exchange: Advances in theory and research.* New York: Plenum Press, 1980.

Harré, R. *Social being.* Oxford: Basil Blackwell, 1979.

Krebs, D. Altruism: An examination of the concept and a review of the literature. *Psychological Bulletin,* 1970, **73**, 258–302.

Latané, B. & Darley, J. M. *The unresponsive bystander: Why doesn't he help?* New York: Appleton-Century-Crofts, 1970.

Mummendey, A. Anmerkungen zur "Prädikationsanalyse des Aggressionsbegriffs" von Jüttemann. *Zeitschrift für Sozial-Psychologie,* 1979, **10,** Heft 4.

Mummendey, A. Zum nutzen des Aggressionsbegriffes für die psychologische Aggressionsforschung. In R. Hilke & W. Kempf (Eds.) *Menschliche Aggression. Naturwissenschaftliche und kulturwissenschaftliche Perspektiven der Aggressionsforschung.* Bern-Stuttgart-Wien: Hans Huber. 1982.

Nadler, A., Altman, A., & Fisher, J. D. Helping is not enough: Recipient's reactions to aid as a function of positive and negative information about the self. *Journal of Personality,* 1979, **47,** 615–628.

Nisbett, R. E., & Wilson, T. D. Telling more than we can know: Verbal reports on mental processes. *Psychological Review,* 1977, **84,** 231–259.

Piliavin, I. M., Piliavin, J. A. & Rodin, J. Costs diffusion and the stigmatized victim. *Journal of Personality and Social Psychology,* 1975, **32,** 429–438.

Pruitt, D. G. Reciprocity and credit building in a laboratory dyad. *Journal of Personality and Social Psychology,* 1968, **8,** 143–147.

Ricoeur, P. The model of the text: Meaningful action considered as a text. In P. Rabinow & W. Sullivan (Eds.), *Interpretive social science: A reader.* Berkeley, California: Univ. of California Press, 1979. pp. 73–102.

Roberts, M. K. Men and women: Partners, lovers, friends. In K. E. Davis & T. O. Mitchell (Eds.), *Advances in descriptive psychology* (Vol. 2). Greenwich, Connecticut: JAI Press. 1981.

Rommetveit, R. On "meanings" of acts and what is meant and made known by what is said in a pluralistic social world. In M. Brenner (Ed.), *The structure of action.* Oxford: Basil Blackwell, 1980. Pp. 108–149.

Schutz, A. *Collected papers: I. The problem of social reality.* The Hague: Martinus Nijhoff, 1962.

Schwartz, S. H. Normative influences on altruism. In L. Berkowitz (Ed.), *Advances in experimental social psychology* (Vol. 10). New York: Academic Press, 1977.

Shotter, J. Action, joint action and intentionality. In M. Brenner (Ed.) *The structure of action.* Oxford: Basil Blackwell, 1980, pp. 28–65.

Shweder, R. A. How relevant is an individual difference theory of personality? *Journal of Personality,* 1975, **43,** 455–484.

Shweder, R. A. Fact and artifact in trait perception: The systematic distortion hypothesis. In B. A. Maher & W. B. Maher (Eds.), *Progress in experimental personality research* (Vol. 11). New York: Academic Press. 1982.

Silver, M., & Sabini, J. P. The social construction of envy, *Journal for the Theory of Social Behavior,* 1978, **8,** 313–332.

Smedslund, J. Bandura's theory of self-efficacy: A set of common sense theorems. *Scandinavian Journal of Psychology,* 1978, **19,** 1–14.

Smedslund, J. Analyzing the primary code: From empiricism to apriorism. In D. R. Olson (Ed.), *The social foundations of language and thought. Essays in honor of Jerome S. Bruner.* New York: Norton, 1980. Pp. 47–73.

Staub, E. *Positive social behavior and morality* (Vol. 1), Social and personal influences. New York: Academic Press, 1978.

Staub, E. *Positive social behavior and morality* (Vol. 2), Socialization and development. New York: Academic Press, 1979.

Staub, E., & Sherk, L. Need for approval: Child's sharing behavior. *Child Development,* 1970, **14,** 243–253.

Strauss, A. *Negotiations,* San Francisco, California: Jossey-Bass, 1979.

Tedeschi, J. T., Smith, R. B., & Brown, R. C. A reinterpretation of research on aggression. *Psychological Bulletin,* 1974, **81,** 540–562.

Turner, R. Words, utterances and activities. In J. Douglas (Ed.) *Understanding everyday life.* Chicago, Illinois: Aldine, 1970. Pp. 169–187.

Wieder, D. L. On meaning by rule. In J. Douglas (Ed.) *Understanding everyday life.* Chicago, Illinois: Aldine, 1970. Pp. 107–135.

Wilke, H., & Lanzetta, J. T. The obligation to help: The effects of amount of prior help on subsequent helping behavior. *Journal of Experimental Social Psychology,* 1970, **6,** 488–493.

Wispé, L. (Ed.) *Altruism, sympathy and helping.* New York: Academic Press, 1978.

Zimmerman, D. H., & Pollner, M. The everyday world as a phenomenon. In J. Douglas (Ed.), *Understanding everyday life.* Chicago, Illinois: Aldine, 1970. Pp. 80–104.

PART III

Individual Differences

CHAPTER 7

Recipient Self-esteem
and Reactions to Help

Arie Nadler
Ofra Mayseless

INTRODUCTION

As the chapters in the present volume show, the phenomenon of receiving help is a complex psychological event. Although it is often a favorable experience for the recipient, leading to positive affect and favorable self-evaluations, it can at other times highlight the recipient's relative inferiority and lead to negative affect and unfavorable recipient self-evaluations. Beyond its effects on the recipient's affect and self-evaluations, receiving help may or may not generate positive perceptions of the helper. Both observations in the field (e.g., Briar, 1966; Gergen & Gergen, 1974; Kalish, 1967) and data from the social psychological laboratory (Broll, Gross, & Piliavin, 1974; Gross, Wallston, & Piliavin, 1979; Morse & Gergen, 1971; Nadler, Fisher, & Streufert, 1974), point to instances in which the recipient 'bites the hand that feeds,' and helping serves to poison rather than to enhance the quality of interpersonal relations between the recipient and the helper (Nadler, Fisher, & Ben-Itzhak, in press). Finally, receiving help under different conditions has differential effects on recipients' post-aid behaviors, such as reciprocity or self-help efforts (e.g., Bar-Tal, Zohar, Greenberg, & Hermon, 1977; Fisher & Nadler, 1976).

From an overall perspective, receiving help affects recipients' (1) self-perceptions (e.g., affect and self-evaluations), (2) external perceptions (e.g., evaluations of help and helper), and (3) postaid behaviors (e.g., reciprocity, self-help, help-seeking). Further, differential reactions on all these dimensions are dependent on aid-related conditions. For example, whether the helper is socially distant or close (Clark, present volume), poor or rich (Gergen, Ellsworth, Maslach, & Seipel, 1975), whether the task on which help is given is or is not ego-relevant (Nadler & Fisher, in press), and whether reciprocity is or is not foreseeable (Hatfield & Sprecher, present volume), are all important determinants of recipients' reactions. In fact, it seems that knowing the *situational* variables that surround the helping interaction (i.e., characteristics of the *help, helper,* and *helping* context) enables the prediction of how the recipient will respond to a particular form of help.

Yet, do all individuals react similarly to receiving help in a given context? Common sense and daily life experiences suggest a negative answer. We are all familiar with individuals for whom receiving help is a painful experience, individuals who find it hard to murmur the obligatory "thank you," and who make every effort to avoid meeting with their benefactors. On the other extreme, we may find people who find dependency quite comfortable. As students, these people may 'adopt' helpers, rely on their advice in exams and class assignments, and finally graduate feeling as unconfident about their own abilities as ever. The present chapter deals with these differential reactions to help. More specifically, our chapter centers on how individuals who have high and low self-esteem respond to receiving help.

This emphasis on the recipient's level of self-esteem is neither arbitrary nor accidental. In fact, recipient reactions to being helped have been recently conceptualized as determined by the relative weight of the self-supporting (e.g., signs of donor's concern for the recipient) and self-threatening elements (e.g., information about helper's relative superiority) that are inherent in receiving help (Fisher, Nadler, & Whitcher-Alagna, 1982; Fisher, Nadler, & Whitcher-Alagna, present volume). Deriving from this conceptual framework, research has examined how the level of recipient self-esteem plays a role in determining the weight of the self-support or the threat inherent in receiving help, thereby determining recipient reactions. The present chapter outlines these findings and examines their overall implications.

Having laid out the general framework within which the present chapter is placed, we shall now describe in more detail the general plan of the chapter. First, a brief exposition of two theoretical concepts that are at the core of the research of self-esteem and recipient reaction to being helped will be made: (1) the threat to self-esteem conceptualization (Fisher *et al.*, 1982) provides the conceptual base for the links between self-esteem and reactions to receiving help; and (2) vulnerability versus consistency predictions have served as the base for specific hypotheses regarding the direction of such links. After these theoretical concepts are discussed, empirical findings that support consistency predictions will be described. This section will include a review of data regarding the effects of self-esteem on recipient affect, evaluations, and behaviors. Following this, we shall describe data that support the opposite, "vulnerability" prediction. We conclude by proposing integrative explanations.

LEVEL OF RECIPIENT SELF-ESTEEM: CONCEPTUAL BACKGROUND

The Threat to Self-esteem Model of Recipient Reactions to Aid

The early discussions of phenomena associated with receiving help note that it affects one's feelings of self-worth and esteem. Ladieu, Hanfman, and Dembo (1947) discuss how disabled veterans resent the elements of inferiority and inability that are inherent in receiving help, and Lipman and Sterne (1962) note that the elderly view being helped by others as inconsistent with their wish to maintain a self-image of competence and self-reliance.

Based on these and other observations (e.g., Kalish, 1967) Fisher *et al.* (1982) proposed a model of the threat to self-esteem posed by receiving aid. Although this model is more fully presented elsewhere in this volume (Chapter 3), a brief exposition of its major postulates seems necessary here because it serves as a conceptual base for the research on levels of recipient self-esteem. The model suggests that receiving help is a mixture of self-supporting and self-threatening elements for the recipient. Elements of material gain and the donor's concern are the primary sources of potential support, whereas elements of relative inferiority and dependency are the major potential sources of threat. Further, this model suggests that if aid-related conditions render the receipt of help a supporting experience for the recipient, a cluster of positive recipient reactions (e.g., positive affect and self-evaluations, increased liking and favorable evaluations of the helper) and positive nondefensive behaviors (e.g., willingness to seek help, low degree of self-help efforts) occurs. If, however, help is self-threatening, a cluster of negative reactions (i.e., negative affect and self- and other evaluations) and ego-defensive behaviors (e.g., unwillingness to seek help, increased self-help efforts to terminate the dependency) occurs.

Consistency versus Vulnerability

This view of receiving aid as a mixture of self-threatening and self-supporting elements has been corroborated by studies that have shown that, under situations that highlighted the self-threat (relative inferiority and dependency) inherent in help, individuals experienced the receipt of help as a stressful event (Fisher & Nadler, in press; Nadler & Fisher, in press). These findings, which emphasized the threat to feelings of self-esteem as a major determinant of recipient's reactions, led to the suggestion that individuals who have different levels of self-esteem would be differentially sensitive to the self-threat–support in the receipt of help (cf. Underwood, 1975). However, when the issue of how high and low self-esteem individuals respond to the receipt of help is considered, two opposite predictions present themselves.

Based on Bramel's (1968) conception of the ways in which individuals with different levels of self-esteem respond to self-threatening situations, a consistency and a vulnerability prediction are suggested (cf. also Tessler & Schwartz, 1972). The *consistency prediction* relies on the assumption that negative information about the self is disturbing only when it is inconsistent with one's existing self-cognitions. This approach indicates that receiving help under conditions that highlight the self-threatening aspects in aid (i.e., elements of relative inferiority and dependency), will be inconsistent with the positive self-cognitions of high self-esteem individuals and, therefore, a self-threatening event for them. For low self-esteem persons, the information about relative inadequacy that is inherent in receiving help should be consistent with existing negative self-cognitions, and help should be an overall positive self-supporting experience.

Opposite predictions stem from the *vulnerability prediction*. This approach suggests that low self-esteem individuals are more vulnerable to self-threatening situations than are high self-esteem individuals. This is because, for low self-esteem persons, who have few positive cognitions about themselves, each additional unit of negative information about the self is far more disturbing than it is for high self-esteem persons who are less vulnerable because they possess relatively many positive self-cognitions. This approach suggests that receiving help under conditions that highlight the negative self-threatening aspects in aid will be more aversive for low than high self-esteem recipients.

In all, predicting how high and low self-esteem individuals respond to help seems a difficult task. The consistency approach suggests that high self-esteem individuals are more sensitive to the self-threat in aid, whereas the vulnerability approach suggests that low self-esteem individuals are more sensitive to this self-threat.

SELF-ESTEEM AND RECEIVING HELP: EVIDENCE FOR CONSISTENCY

Recipient Affect and Self-evaluation

Two studies have taken up the issue of self-esteem and reaction to aid directly. In the first, Nadler, Fisher, and Streufert (1976) examined how individuals who differ on levels of self-esteem respond to the different levels of self-threat that are inherent in help from an overall similar and dissimilar other. This was based on an earlier finding that only a receipt of help from an attitudinally similar other is a relatively self-threatening experience because, in line with social comparison theory (Brickman & Bullman, 1977; Festinger, 1954), the recipient's relative inferiority to, and dependency on, the donor is more salient and psychologically meaningful when a high degree of donor–recipient similarity exists. Thus, it was reasoned that individuals with different levels of self-esteem would be differentially sensitive to this self-threat.

To test this, Nadler et al. (1976) used a median split to divide their subjects into high and low self-esteem individuals. The division was made on subjects' scores on the Coopersmith Self-Esteem Inventory (Coopersmith, 1967). Following that, subjects were introduced to a Stock Market Game (SMG) and were told that they could win large sums of money if they made correct investment decisions. Further, subjects were told that in later stages of this stock market simulation they would be playing with another participant who was supposedly sitting in an adjoining room. This individual was presented to half the subjects as attitudinally similar, and to the other half as attitudinally dissimilar.

After a few investment trials, all subjects were in a losing position, and in danger of being barred from further participation in the game. At this point, half the subjects received from the other individual an envelope that contained enough help to enable them to continue their participation in the SMG. Thus, the resulting experimental design was a 2 (aid–no aid) × 2 (similar–dissimilar helper) × 2 (high–low self-esteem recipient) between subjects experimental design. Following the receipt of help from their "partner," subjects were asked to respond to the paper and pencil dependent measures. Subjects were asked to rate their current mood on six 7-point bipolar-adjective scales (e.g., pleasant–unpleasant; good–bad). These ratings were summed to obtain a single affect score. Also, subjects were asked to rate themselves on self-evaluation scales (i.e., "confident–not confident in myself" and "intelligent–unintelligent") and indicate to what degree they thought that their performance on the experimental task (i.e., failure for all the subjects) was due to lack of ability, bad luck, lack of effort or task difficulty. In all, data on (1) affective state, (2) self-evaluations, and (3) attributions for the state of need which precipitated the help, were collected.

First, in line with earlier findings (Fisher & Nadler, 1974), subjects had lower ratings of affect and self-evaluations when the donor was an overall similar other. This is so because the relative degree of threat to self-esteem is higher when the helper is an overall similar other who serves for comparison purposes (cf. Nadler & Fisher, in press). But, are individuals with high and low self-esteem differentially sensitive to this self-threat? The data provide an affirmative answer. In fact, a three-way 2 (similar–dissimilar helper) × 2 (high–low self-esteem recipient) × 2 (aid–no aid) interaction indicates that only high self-esteem recipients were sensitive to the differential levels of self-threat and self-support inherent in aid from a similar or dissimilar other. Relative to the no-aid control condition, individuals characterized as high in self-esteem had relatively unfavorable affect and low self-evaluations when the helper was an overall similar other. On the other hand, for individuals characterized as low in self-esteem, receiving help had mildly favorable effects, regardless of the donor–recipient similarity.

These data support the consistency prediction in this context. It seems that the inferiority and dependency cues inherent in aid from a similar other are inconsistent with the positive self-cognitions of the high self-esteem individual, and therefore these individuals experienced lower affect and less favorable self-evaluations after the receipt of help. For the low self-esteem individuals, the cues about inferiority relative to an overall similar other seem to have been consistent with the low self-image and therefore were not self-threatening. Consequently, such a receipt of help was not associated with similar affective and or self-evaluative changes. This view of the meaning of help for the low self-esteem recipient is supported by the finding that low self-esteem individuals who were helped, attributed their failure less dispositionally than did low self-esteem individuals who did not receive help (means for attributions of lack of ability for the failure are 66.7 and 92.4, respectively, $F(1,42) = 5.08$, $p < .05$). Conversely, high self-esteem recipients who received help from a similar other tended to make more lack of ability attributions for their performance than did high self-esteem individuals in the control condition who did not receive help (the aid × self-esteem interaction was, $F(1,41) = 3.08$, $P < .09$). Thus, for the high self-esteem person, the receipt of help from a similar other seems to highlight their relative inadequacy and inferiority and they, therefore, tend to see their lack of ability as more of a cause for their poor performance than did their counterparts in a control group that failed, but did not receive help.

Although these findings support the importance of considering the recipient's level of self-esteem in this research context, they cannot be seen as providing conclusive evidence. In fact as is often the case in research dealing with effects of self-esteem, one cannot be certain whether the observed effects are to be attributed to self-esteem or to some other variable that is correlated with self-esteem (e.g., need for achievement). In fact, Wells and Marwell (1976) note that because high and low self-esteem individuals differ from each other on many qualities associated with self-esteem, one cannot be sure whether observed differences in responses of high and low self-esteem individuals are due to different levels of self-esteem or to other variables. In order to surmount this problem, Wells and Marwell suggest that investigators try to replicate the effects observed with a chronic definition of self-esteem (i.e., defined as a score on a personality scale) in studies where self-esteem is experimentally manipulated. They note that if chronic and manipulated levels of self-esteem show parallel patterns, one could be more confident about the exact meaning of observed differences.

In an effort to deal with this issue in the present context of recipient self-esteem, Nadler, Altman, and Fisher (1979) experimentally manipulated high and low levels of self-esteem and compared the reactions of these two groups to receiving help. In this experiment, male subjects filled out a bogus personality inventory 1 week prior to the experimental session. At the beginning of the experimental session, half the participants received negative feedback about themselves, and the other half received positive feedback. The feedback included references to qualities such as emotional maturity, intelligence, and overall mental health. Following this manipulation of self-esteem, subjects continued to play the SMG. As in the previous experiment, here, too, subjects were in a losing position and received help from their partner. After the receipt of help, relevant dependent measures were collected. Subjects in no-aid control conditions did not receive help, and were not aware that anyone else had received help.

The results closely parallel the findings of Nadler et al. (1976). Thus as can be seen in Table 1, subjects who had received positive information about themselves (i.e., high manipulated self-esteem) and later received help had more negative moods and lower self-evaluations than did individuals in the high manipulated self-esteem–no-aid control group. This was not the case with individuals who had received negative information about themselves (i.e., low manipulated self-esteem). These individuals had better mood ratings and more favorable self-evaluations than did subjects who had received negative information about themselves (i.e., low manipulated self-esteem) but who did not receive help.

These findings lend further support to the consistency prediction, and extend the earlier data in two important respects. First, they show that the greater sensitivity of the high self-esteem individual to the self-threatening elements in aid is not unique to the comparison between groups that received help from highly similar and dissimilar helpers. Rather, it seems that individuals high in self-esteem find the receipt of help from an anonymous peer as self-threatening even without the magnifying effects of manipulated interpersonal similarity. Second, the fact that the effects of self-esteem on recipient reactions portray a similar pattern when self-esteem is "chronically" defined (i.e., on the basis of a median split on a self-esteem scale [Nadler *et al.,* 1976], or experimentally manipulated) (i.e., Nadler *et al.,* 1979) lends further support to the contention that different levels of self-esteem, and not other associated dimensions, are the explanatory constructs in this regard.

Taken together, these two experiments suggest that in line with a consistency formulation in this regard, high self-esteem individuals are more sensitive than low self-esteem individuals to the self-threatening information about relative inferiority and dependency which are inherent in a receipt of help. They, therefore, report such an event as affectively unpleasant and suffer a decrement in their self-evaluation. Theoretically, in line with Underwood's (1975) approach, the fact that individuals who differ from each other in their self-esteem respond differentially to the receipt of help in a conceptually consistent manner corroborates the presumed role of self-threat and self-support as the psychological mechanisms linking aid-related conditions and recipient reactions (Fisher *et al.,* 1982).

TABLE 1

Mood Ratings and Self-Evaluation Scores

Information about self	Mood ratings		Self-evaluation	
	Aid	No aid	Aid	No aid
Positive (high manipulated self-esteem)	20.0	27.7	20.8	22.3
Negative (low manipulated self-esteem)	24.0	21.2	21.4	18.3

Note. (Adapted from Nadler, A., Altman, A., & Fisher, J. D. *Journal of Personality,* 1979, **47,** 615–628.

The data reviewed above pertain to the effects of recipient self-esteem on recipient affect and self-evaluation. The effects of recipient level of self-esteem on recipient evaluation of benefactors (i.e., external perceptions) and behavior after help has been received (e.g., reciprocity) will be attended to in the following sections.

Considering the joint implication of (1) the assertion that self-threatening help is associated with unfavorable evaluations of the helper, and defensive postaid behaviors (Fisher *et al.,* 1982) and (2) the finding that high self-esteem individuals are more sensitive to the self-threat in aid, suggests that they are also more likely than the low self-esteem recipient to resent the helper and display defensive postaid behaviors. Specifically, high self-esteem recipients should show relative dislike and unfavorable evaluations towards their benefactors, be less willing to seek further help, reciprocate more, and should invest more in self-help efforts in order to avert the self-threatening dependency.

Recipient Self-esteem and External Perceptions

The data regarding the effects of recipient level of self-esteem on external perceptions (i.e., evaluations of helper and help) do not support the prediction that high self-esteem recipients are more resentful toward their benefactor than are low self-esteem individuals. In fact, in both of the experiments described above (Nadler *et al.,* 1976, 1979), subjects high and low in self-esteem who received help from their partner evaluated him more favorably than did subjects in control conditions who did not receive help from their partner. Yet, as pointed out in the discussion of these findings (Nadler *et al.,* 1976, 1979), these data cannot be seen as conclusive because of the strong normative pressure to rate one's benefactor favorably. Such pressures could have obscured the possible effects of recipient self-esteem on evaluations of helper. In line with similar discussions in this context (e.g., Morse, 1972), other less obtrusive measures may be needed to detect differential degrees of liking of high and low self-esteem individuals toward their benefactors. For example, one may detect different levels of liking and evaluations of one's benefactor via the conformity that the recipient displays with opinions voiced by the helper (Morse, 1972).

Recipient Self-esteem and Behavioral Responses

Regarding the effects of recipient self-esteem on recipient behaviors, several behavioral indices seem relevant here: (1) willingness to seek help; (2) degree of reciprocity engaged in by the recipient; and (3) recipient postaid self-help behaviors (i.e., amount of effort invested in order to regain independence). As noted before, relative to low self-esteem recipients, high self-esteem recipients should engage more in defensive behaviors that are designed to avoid the self-threatening dependency and/or to restore equality between oneself and one's helper. Thus, they should (1) seek less help; (2) engage in more reciprocity; and (3) invest more self-help efforts in order to regain independence. We shall now examine the evidence that pertains to each of these three behaviors.

In regard to *help-seeking* behavior, Tessler and Schwartz (1972) observed that high, but not low, self-esteem individuals sought less help when the task on which help was needed was said to reflect inadequacy on a psychologically central dimension than when it was not. In a similar vein, Nadler and Kolker (as described in Nadler & Fisher, in press) have observed that high self-esteem individuals showed the least amount of help-seeking when being helped was said to reflect inadequacy on a psychologically central dimension, and the helper was said to be an overall similar other. Further, Wallston (1976) reports that high self-esteem traditional males sought less help when the task on which help was needed was described as a female task. Taken together, these studies indicate that when aid-related conditions render the receipt of help a self-threatening event (i.e., high degree of donor–recipient similarity; psychologically central task), the recipient's self-esteem is a major determinant of help-seeking behavior. Relative to low self-esteem individuals, high self-esteem individuals refrain from seeking help because of the inconsistency between their positive view of themselves, and the admission of failure and dependency which may be inherent in such an act.

Regarding *reciprocity,* no direct evidence exists to support the presumed greater need of the high self-esteem individual to reciprocate, but Nadler, Mayseless and Perri (1982) have recently obtained data which are relevant to this issue. In this experiment, seventh-grade children were given an opportunity to ask for help that they could or could not reciprocate. Further, based on an upper- and lower-thirds division of their scores on the Coopersmith Self-Esteem Inventory (Coopersmith, 1967), half these children were designated high, and half designated low, in self-esteem. The data show that high but not low self-esteem individuals were affected by the expected ability to reciprocate manipulation (Table 2). Specifically, a significant self-esteem × expected opportunity to reciprocate interaction, $F(1,36) = 4.73$, $p < .05$, indicates that least help was sought by high self-esteem children who did not foresee an opportunity to reciprocate. It seems that for the high-esteem children the prospects of receiving help which they did not expect to be able to reciprocate conflicted with their self-cognitions of independence and self-reliance and they therefore refrained from the seeking of help. Put otherwise, the feelings of indebtedness associated with help that can not be reciprocated (Greenberg & Westcott, present volume) appears to be more intense for the high than for the low self-esteem person. This suggests that, if given help, high self-esteem individuals would engage in more immediate reciprocity than would low self-esteem persons. However, a direct assessment of this prediction awaits further research.

Finally, in line with the preceding discussion, recipient self-esteem should affect recipient *self-help behavior*. Based on (1) the findings that high self-esteem recipients are more sensitive to the self-threat in aid and (2) the theoretical prediction that self-threatening help leads the recipient to invest in more self-help efforts (Fisher *et al.*, 1982), it can be expected that, relative to low self-esteem individuals, high self-esteem persons who are more self-threatened by receiving help would invest more self-help efforts in order to regain independence and to restore a positive self-image. Based on similar reasoning, De Paulo, Brown, Ishii, and Fisher (1981) have suggested that, compared to the postaid task performance of low self-esteem individuals, post-aid task performance of high self-esteem individuals would be enhanced. In general, the results of De Paulo *et al.* (1981) support this prediction. In fact, high self-esteem individuals performed relatively better when helped, whereas low self-esteem individuals performed relatively worse when helped. In further support of the link between self-threat in aid, self-esteem, and self-help behavior, De Paulo *et al.* (1981) found that an improvement in postaid performance of high self-esteem subjects did not occur when situational conditions rendered the receipt of help a self- supporting favorable experience, (i.e., the helper conveyed sympathy with the help). Overall, assuming that better performance is a consequence of more self-help efforts, these results support the presumed link between recipient self-esteem and self-help efforts. However, it should be noted here that this study does not provide a direct assessment of the presumed link between recipient self-esteem and self-help efforts. Although it would seem safe to assume that increased self-help efforts would lead to better performance, a direct test of the links between (1) recipient level of self-esteem,

TABLE 2

Help-seeking Scores of High and Low Self-esteem Individuals in the Two Reciprocity Conditions ($N = 40$)

Self-esteem	Opportunity to reciprocate	No opportunity to reciprocate
High	6.6	3.9
Low	6.7	7.0

(2) self-help efforts, and (3) postaid task performance awaits the scrutiny of future research.

The "Receiving Paradox"—
Can Help Be Made to Work?

The suggestion that only high self-esteem individuals invest in self-help efforts after the receipt of self-threatening help, leads to some intriguing implications for interpersonal helping relations. In fact, it suggests that for the high self-esteem individual, receiving help motivates self-help efforts that are likely to result in improved performance and renewed independence. On the other hand, for the low self-esteem individual, the receipt of help fosters relative passivity and dependency. This is especially noteworthy because most recipients are helped at a low point in their lives (e.g., financial, emotional, familial) and are therefore expected to possess a relatively unfavorable image of themselves. Based on the above, it seems that these low self-esteem individuals are not likely to utilize the help as a spring-board to regain competence and independence. Rather, at this low point in one's life, help is likely to foster one's passivity and self-cognitions of incompetence and dependency. In fact, the receipt of help may be interpreted by recipients as indicating that they are indeed helpless and that things are to be accomplished by relying on others rather than on oneself.

This state of affairs presents a problem for the helper(s). In fact, if helping others is to be effective in the sense of encouraging recipients to take responsibility for their own fate and "pull themselves by their bootstraps" (Brickman *et al.,* present volume), help given to low self-esteem individuals, who are likely to be overrepresented in a population of needy persons, seems counterproductive. How can this circle be broken? How can helping help people to help themselves?

The data and theory discussed in this section suggest that if helpers want help given to a low self-esteem person to work, they need to devise ways to raise the recipients' self-esteem, even temporarily, before providing the help. Only then, after the helpers have modified the negative self-esteem of the individuals in need, should help be given. If help is given after efforts toward self-esteem enhancement have been successful, it is more likely to precipitate adaptive behaviors (e.g., self-help efforts and subsequent improved performance) than if given before such efforts are attempted. Admittedly, general and sweeping changes in self-esteem are probably a matter of lengthy psychotherapy and/or other major life events, but more modest changes can be obtained. Thus, if one could give the individual in need a significant success experience in another area, a temporary yet sufficient change in the needy individual's self-esteem may occur (Koocher, 1971). If the goal of the helping encounter is to enable recipients to regain their independence, helpers should differentiate between high and low self-esteem recipients and adopt different helping strategies for members of the two groups. For high self-esteem recipients, the threat to self-esteem should be enhanced in order to challenge their current favorable self-cognitions, and thereby motivating these recipients to invest in self-help efforts. For low self-esteem individuals, the helper should enhance self-esteem before helping. After feelings of competence have been implemented, help can be perceived as a challenge to the newly installed cognitions of competence and can motivate the recipient to invest in self-help efforts.

Before concluding this discussion, two issues should be noted. First, self-threat and subsequent self-help efforts are not viewed as being in a perfect linear relationship. In fact, under conditions of extreme self-threat, help may be debilitating even for the high self-esteem person. Our discussion does not pertain to such extreme events. Second, there seems to be a delicate balance between the costs and rewards inherent in self-threatening help. In fact, by providing help that threatens self-esteem, one is likely to cause a temporary state of bad feelings and unfavorable self-evaluations in the recipient. However, if a way out of the dependency is provided (e.g., the helper indicates to the recipient an effective way for self-help), the overall rewards for the individuals who have confidence in their abilities (either as a consequence of a chronically high level of self-esteem, or manipulated high self-esteem) and who therefore perceive the help as a challenge rather than as an affirmation of relative inadequacy, are likely to transcend these temporary costs.

From an overall perspective, the research described in previous sections shows that recipient level of self-esteem is an important moderator of recipient reactions to help. This corroborates the view that recipient reactions to aid can be parsimoniously accounted for via differential degrees of self-threat or support as explanatory mechanisms (Fisher *et al.*, 1982). Further, recipient self-esteem affects recipient self-perception (i.e., affect and self-evaluations) and behavioral response (i.e., help-seeking, need to reciprocate, and postaid task performance). Finally, these effects are all conceptually congruent and lend support to the consistency prediction. Specifically, because elements of dependency and relative inferiority that are inherent in a receipt of help are more inconsistent with the high than the low self-esteem individual's view of self, the high self-esteem individual seems more sensitive than the low self-esteem recipient to the self-threat inherent in receiving help.

SELF-ESTEEM AND RECEIVING HELP: EVIDENCE FOR THE VULNERABILITY PREDICTION

Although the research reviewed thus far supports the consistency pre-diction in this research context, several studies exist that provide support for the vulnerability prediction. To reiterate, the vulnerability prediction states that the low self-esteem individual, who has fewer positive self-cog-nitions than the high self-esteem individual, is more vulnerable to incoming self-threat and should therefore be more sensitive to the self-threat inherent in receiving help. In the following sections we shall examine this evidence.

In a study within the help-seeking literature, Morris and Rosen (1973) investigated how felt adequacy and perceived opportunity to reciprocate affect willingness to engage in help-seeking behavior. Subjects were in-structed to construct paper boxes under simulated disability conditions (e.g., one arm was tied behind the back). Feelings of adequacy were manipulated by telling half the subjects that their performance was superior, whereas the other half were told that their performance was inadequate. Subjects were then asked to perform the box-building task and were told that they could ask for help to complete the required quota. In addition, half the subjects expected an opportunity to reciprocate to the helper and the other half did not. A main effect for the expected reciprocity variable indicates that more help was sought when the individuals in need expected that they could reciprocate than when they could not. However, of greater relevance in this context is that individuals who were made to feel inadequate on the experimental task sought less help, and the latency of their help-seeking response was greater, than individuals who had been made to feel adequate on the task in question. These results are in line with the vulnerability pre-diction. In fact, these data suggest that individuals who felt less adequate were more vulnerable to a self-threat associated with a public admission of failure associated with the seeking of help than were individuals who felt adequate on the task in question. The "inadequates" were therefore more reluctant to seek help, even if this abstention was to lead to a continued state of failure.

Another study that is relevant here is a field study that examined pat-terns of help-seeking and receiving in disabled individuals (male paraple-gics) as a function of their acceptance of physical disability (Nadler, Sheinberg, & Jaffe, 1981). This study will be described in some detail be-cause it is one of the very few studies that have systematically considered reactions to help in a severely handicapped population, a population for which seeking and receiving help is a grim daily necessity.

In the psychological literature dealing with the physically disabled, a successful rehabilitation process is said to be associated with a high degree of acceptance of one's physical disability. Such a psychological state is characterized by the fact that the individuals no longer perceive the disability as central to their feelings of esteem (i.e., they have moved the disability from the center into the periphery of their egos), and accept themselves as worthwhile individuals in spite of the severe handicap. The disabled persons who do not accept the disability continue to view their lost abilities as central to their egos, continue mourning their losses, and therefore do not accept themselves as worthwhile individuals. Operationally, feelings of acceptance of disability are assessed by a score on the "acceptance of physical disability" scale developed by Linkowski (1971) and used by several researchers working in the area (e.g., Grand, 1972).

An examination of the links between degree of acceptance of physical disability and self-esteem suggests that the former is a major facet of the disabled individual's self-esteem. In fact, an individual who is severely handicapped (e.g., a paraplegic) and accepts the disability, is likely to have higher feelings of esteem than the disabled person who does not accept the disability. Considered with the previous data, this suggests that the degree of acceptance of physical disability should affect the disabled individual's reaction to help in an important way. Specifically, if the consistency prediction is adopted, disabled individuals who accept the disability (i.e., have higher self-esteem) should be more hesitant to seek help and be more bothered by its receipt than disabled individuals who have not yet accepted their disabilities. This is because the seeking and receiving of help may serve as reminders of disability and, as such, are likely to be inconsistent with overall feelings of competence and self-worth. If, however, the vulnerability prediction is adopted, disabled persons who accept their disability should be *less* vulnerable to incoming self-threat and therefore more willing to seek and to receive help than the ones who do not accept the disability.

To test this prediction, Nadler *et al.,* (1981) conducted structured interviews with 38 male paraplegics. In these interviews, several questionnaires were administered: (1) a questionnaire tapping the individual's degree of acceptance of physical disability (Linkowski, 1971); especially constructed instruments that assess (2) the individual's willingness to seek help in daily situations (e.g., asking a passerby to help with entering an office that has several steps at the entrance); and (3) the feelings that are expected to be aroused after receipt of help in such situations.

The results support the derivations from the vulnerability prediction. In fact, higher levels of acceptance of physical disability were associated with greater willingness to seek help actively ($r = .78$) and positive feelings after its receipt ($r = .46$). In line with the vulnerability approach, these data indicate that the vulnerable paraplegic who does not accept the physical disability seems more sensitive to the self-threat inherent in the receipt of help and is therefore less likely to seek help and to respond favorably to its receipt.

CONSISTENCY VERSUS VULNERABILITY REVISITED: RECONCILIATION AND INTEGRATION

Taken together, both Morris and Rosen (1973) and Nadler *et al.* (1981) indicate that the high self-esteem individual is more willing to seek and to receive help than is the low self-esteem person. This suggests that, contrary to the research reviewed in the earlier parts of this chapter, low self-esteem individuals are more sensitive than are high self-esteem recipients to the self-threatening elements of relative inferiority and dependency that are inherent in help. In line with the vulnerability approach this greater sensitivity is to be attributed to the fact that the low self-esteem person has relatively few positive self-cognitions, and therefore the relative weight of the incoming self-threatening elements in aid is high. How can this be reconciled with the earlier data showing that in line with the consistency approach, the high self-esteem recipient is more sensitive to the self-threat in aid? In the following section we shall propose that this empirical inconsistency may be resolved through a consideration of the ego-relevance of the task on which help is given, or through a better definition of the meaning of self-esteem in the helping context.

Ego-relevance of Task As Determinant

A variable that may affect recipient reactions in an important way is the ego-relevance of the task on which help is given. One may receive help that reflects one's inferiority and inadequacy on an ego-relevant central dimension (e.g., intelligence) or a non-ego relevant dimension. In the first case, the receipt of help has a self-threat potential (i.e., serving as evidence of one's inferiority on a central dimension), whereas in the second case, aid does not carry such a self-threat potential.

Viewing the issue of recipient self-esteem with this variable in mind suggests that the consistency prediction may be applied only when the help is given on an ego-relevant dimension and therefore carries self-threat potential. In fact, the inconsistency between the high self-esteem individual's positive self-cognitions and the receipt of help may arise only when such help reflects on central self-cognitions. Thus, only in this case of ego-relevance should high self-esteem individuals be more sensitive to the self-threat in receiving aid (i.e., a consistency prediction) (Nadler & Kolker, as described in Nadler & Fisher, in press; Tessler & Schwartz, 1972).

If, however, the receipt of help does not reflect on an ego-relevant dimension (e.g., manual dexterity), there is no logical ground to assume that the inconsistency between one's positive self-cognition and the inferiority inherent in aid should hurt. This is because such inferiority is not psychologically relevant. In this case, the high self-esteem individual should respond more favorably to the receipt of help than does the low self-esteem person. This is because, relative to the recipient with low self-esteem, the one with high self-esteem has higher expectations for success (Korman, 1967) and therefore the instrumental value of the aid (i.e., completion of task), which is not overwhelmed by the self-threatening aspects in aid, is more salient. This logic suggests that in non-ego-relevant conditions, the high self-esteem person will be more receptive to the receipt of help than the low self-esteem person (i.e., the vulnerability prediction).

An examination of the studies discussed in earlier sections supports this analysis. In fact, the studies that reported that high self-esteem individuals are more sensitive to receiving help than are low self-esteem individuals have all used ego-relevant tasks. In Nadler *et al.* (1976, 1979), subjects were under the impression that their "investment abilities" were being tested; in Nadler, Mayseless, and Perri, (1982), subjects were working on an "intellectual word-game." In a more direct test of the above, Tessler and Schwartz (1972) and Wallston (1976) compared help-seeking responses of high and low self-esteem individuals in ego-relevant task conditions. In these studies, it was observed that the greater sensitivity of the high self-esteem individual to the self-threat in aid occurred only under central conditions. Only under such conditions were high self-esteem individuals more reluctant to seek help.

Studies that support the vulnerability prediction have employed a non-ego-relevant aid condition. In Morris and Rosen (1973), adults worked on a paper box-building task, under simulated handicap conditions. In Nadler *et al.* (1981), a closer examination of the concept *acceptance of disability* suggests that the paraplegic individual who accepts the disability regards help related to the physical handicap as noncentral. In fact, this individual is likely to have transferred the activities associated with the disability from the center to the periphery of the ego (Linkowski, 1971).

In sum, this explanation of the data calls for a study in which recipient self-esteem, and the ego-relevance of the task will be considered simultaneously. Although the help-seeking literature contains data congruent with this analysis (Nadler & Kolker, as described, in Nadler & Fisher, in press; Tessler & Schwartz, 1972), an investigation of the interactive effects of these two dimensions on recipient reactions to help awaits future research.

Self-esteem and Defensiveness:
What is a High Self-esteem Score?

Another way of looking at the conflicting evidence about self-esteem and the individual's sensitivity to the self-threat in aid involves a closer examination of the meaning of high self-esteem. Recent research has indicated that the individual who appears to have high self-esteem may be either one with genuinely high self-esteem or one with defensive high self-esteem. The meaning of a high self-esteem score should be considered in light of the person's ego-defensiveness (Dion & Dion, 1975; Turkat & Schneider, 1974). In the first case, one is dealing with "true" high self-esteem individuals whose high scores on the self-esteem scale reflects the fact that they have many positive self-cognitions. In the second case, one deals with individuals who in actuality have fairly low self-esteems, but because they have strong needs to defend themselves those persons project an image of high self-esteem. Operationally, the *genuine-high* and *defensive-high* person have been identified by their respective scores on self-esteem and defensiveness scales (e.g., The Marlow-Crowne Social Desirability Scale). The person having a high score on both the self-esteem and the defensiveness scales was labeled the defensive high, whereas the individual having a high self-esteem score, but a low defensiveness score was labeled the genuine high. More important, data indicate that the genuine high and defensive high self-esteem individuals display different responses to interpersonal events (Dion & Dion, 1975).

Applied to the present context, the above leads to the question of the differential effects of defensiveness and self-esteem in determining recipient reactions to help. More specifically, because a positive correlation exists between self-esteem and defensiveness scores (Fux & Nadler, 1983), the possibility that defensiveness rather than self-esteem is the major determinant of recipient's reactions cannot be ruled out. This would suggest that the aforedescribed greater sensitivity of the high self-esteem individual to the self-threat in ego-relevant aid reflects the responses of the defensive-high but not the genuine-high recipients. If this were the case, it could have been due to the stronger need of defensive-high but not genuine-high self-esteem individuals to defend themselves against incoming self-threatening information. Furthermore, it may be that individuals who possess genuinely high self-esteem, and are not guided by strong needs to defend their self-esteem, may indeed be less vulnerable to the self-threat in aid.

The above suggests a more complex view of the consistency versus vulnerability issue. It indicates that consistency may be an ample way to conceptualize the effects of defensiveness on recipient reactions to being helped. Specifically, individuals who have strong needs to defend themselves will be more threatened by the negative implications that receiving help may hold, and this defensiveness is aroused only when the self-threat potential is high (i.e., when help reflects inadequacy on an ego-relevant dimension). Accordingly, the aforedescribed data that high self-esteem individuals find help given on an ego-relevant dimension self-threatening may be due to the association between defensiveness and self-esteem, and reflects ego-defensive processes. Furthermore, based on this logic, one would expect that the vulnerability prediction would hold when the net effects of self-esteem are considered: specifically, that genuine-high self-esteem individuals would indeed be less sensitive to the self-threat in aid than either low self-esteem or defensive-high self-esteem persons. Further research can validate this analysis by investigating the joint effects of defensiveness and self-esteem on reactions to receiving help.

CONCLUDING REMARKS

The present chapter has assessed the role of recipient self-esteem as a determinant of recipient reactions to being helped. The data reviewed in the previous sections point to the importance of considering recipient self-esteem as a major determinant of recipient reactions. Importantly, in line with Underwood's approach (1975), these findings corroborate the assertion made by Fisher et al. (1982) that the receipt of help has important self-threatening–supporting implications for the recipient.

Data have been presented to support vulnerability and consistency predictions in this context. In fact, whereas some of the studies have shown that high self-esteem recipients are more self-threatened by help than are low self-esteem recipients (i.e., consistency), others indicate that low self-esteem recipients are more self-threatened by help than are high self-esteem recipients. Further, it has been suggested that this empirical incongruence may be resolved by considering (1) the meaning of the task on which help is given (i.e., ego-relevance of task), and (2) the meaning of a high self-esteem score (i.e., genuine versus defensive high). Yet, it should be noted that the empirical examination of these two explanations awaits future research.

Another main avenue for future research in this context is the presumed link between recipient self-esteem and subsequent self-help behavior. In this regard, we have noted the *receiving paradox* that may be responsible for encouraging passivity and dependency among recipients. It seems to us that conceptual and applied considerations should direct future research to elucidate more fully the situational and personality variables that interact with the level of recipient self-esteem to determine the way in which the recipient perceives the meaning of the helping relations. More specifically, research that will center on conditions that will explain when the receipt of help is perceived by the recipient as (1) a challenge and stimulus for future self-help or (2) an affirmation of relative inadequacy that fosters future passivity and dependency (see De Paulo, Brown, & Greenberg, this volume) should have many conceptual and applied implications.

REFERENCES

Bar-Tal D., Zohar, Y. B., Greenberg, M. S., & Hermon, M. Reciprocity in the relationship between donor and recipient and between harm-doer and victim. *Sociometry,* 1977, **40,** 293–298.

Bramel, D. Dissonance, expectation and the self. In R. Abelson, E. Aronson, T. M. Newcomb, W. J. McQuire, M. H. Rosenberg, & Tannenbaum (Eds.), *Scorebook of cognitive consistency.* New York: Rand-McNally, 1968.

Briar, S. Welfare from below: Recipients' view of the public welfare system. In J. Brock (Ed.), *The law of the poor.* San Francisco, California: Chandler Publ., 1966.

Brickman, P., & Bullman, R. J. Pleasure and pain in social comparison. In J. M. Suls & R. L. Miller (Eds.), *Social comparison process: Theoretical and empirical perspectives.* Hemisphere Publ., Washington, D.C., 1977.

Broll, L., Gross, A. E., & Piliavin, I. Effects of offered and requested help on help-seeking and reactions to being helped. *Journal of Applied Social Psychology,* 1974, **4,** 244–258.

Coopersmith, S. *The antecedents of self-esteem.* San Francisco, California: Freeman, 1967.

De Paulo, B. M., Brown, P., Ishiis, S., & Fisher, J. D. Help that works: The effects of aid on subsequent task performance. *Journal of Personality and Social Psychology,* 1981, **41,** 478–487.

Dion, K. K., & Dion, K. L. Self-esteem and romantic love. Journal of Personality, 1975, **43,** 39–54.

Festinger, L. A theory of social comparison processes. *Human Relations,* 1954, **1,** 117–140.

Fisher, J. D., & Nadler, A. Effect of donor resources on recipient self-esteem and self-help. *Journal of Experimental Social Psychology,* 1976, **12,** 139–150.

Fisher, J. D., & Nadler, A. Donor-recipient similarity and one's beliefs about the nature of their problem as determinants of recipient reactions to aid. In T. A. Wills (Ed.), *Basic processes in helping relationships.* New York: Academic Press. In press.

Fisher, J. D., Nadler, A., & Whitcher-Alagna, S. Recipient reactions to aid: A conceptual review. *Psychological Bulletin,* 1982, **91,** 27–54

Fux, D., & Nadler, A. Self-esteem and social desirability as determinants of help seeking behavior, Unpublished Manuscript, Tel-Aviv University, 1983.

Gergen, K. J., Ellsworth, P., Maslach, C. L., & Seipel, M. Obligation, donor resources and reactions to aid in three nations. *Journal of Personality and Social Psychology,* 1975, **31**, 390–400.

Gergen, K. J., & Gergen, M. Understanding foreign assistance through public opinion. *Yearbook of world affairs,* (Vol. 27). London: Institute of World Affairs, 1974.

Grand, S. A. Reactions to unfavorable evaluation of the self as a function of acceptance of disability: A test of Dembo, Leviton & Wright's misfortune hypothesis. *Journal of Counseling Psychology,* 1972, **19**, 87–93.

Gross, A. E., Wallston, B. S., & Paliavin, I. Reactance, attribution, equity, and the help recipient. *Journal of Applied Social Psychology,* 1979, **9**, 297–313.

Kalish, R. A. Of children and grandfathers: A speculative essay on dependency. *The Gerontologist,* 1967, **7**, 185ff.

Koocher, G. P. Swimming, competence and personality change. *Journal of Personality and Social Psychology,* 1971, **18**, 275–288.

Korman, A. K. Self-esteem as a moderator of the relationship between self-perceived abilities and vocational choice. *Journal of Applied Psychology,* 1967, **51**, 65–67.

Ladieu, G., Hanfman, E., & Dembo, T. Studies in adjustment to visible injuries: Evaluation of help by the injured. *Journal of Abnormal and Social Psychology,* 1947, **42**, 169–192.

Linkowski, D. C. A scale to measure acceptance of disability. *Rehabilitating Counseling Bulletin,* 1971, **19**, 226–244.

Lipman, A., & Sterne, R. Aging in the United States: Ascription of a terminal sick role. *Sociology and Social Research,* 1962, **53**, 194–203.

Morris, S. C., III, & Rosen, S. Effects of felt adequacy and opportunity to reciprocate on help-seeking. *Journal of Experimental Social Psychology,* 1973, **9**, 265–276.

Morse, S. Help, likeability and social influence. *Journal of Applied Social Psychology,* 1972, **2**, 34–46.

Morse, S., & Gergen, K. Material aid and social attraction. *Journal of Applied Social Psychology,* 1971, **1**, 150–212.

Nadler, A., Altman, A., & Fisher, J. D. Helping is not enough: Recipient's reactions to aid as a function of positive and negative self-regard. *Journal of Personality,* 1979, **47**, 615–628.

Nadler, A., & Fisher, J. D. Effects of donor-recipient relationships on recipient's reactions to being helped. In E. Staub, D. Bar-Tal, J. Reykowski, & J. Karylowski (Eds.), *Development and maintenance of pro-social behavior: International perspectives.* New York: Plenum Press. In press.

Nadler, A., Fisher, J. D., & Ben-Itzhak, S. With a little help from my friend: Effect of single or multiple act aid as a function of donor and task characteristics. *Journal of Personality and Social Psychology,* in press.

Nadler, A., Fisher, J. D., & Streufest, S. The donor's dilemma: Recipient's reactions to aid from friend or foe. *Journal of Applied Social Psychology,* 1974, **4**, 275–285.

Nadler, A., Fisher, J. D., & Streufert, S. When helping hurts: The effects of donor-recipient similarity and recipient self-esteem on reactions to aid. *Journal of Personality,* 1976, **44**, 392–409.

Nadler, A., Mayseless, O., & Perri, N. Self-esteem and perceived opportunity to reciprocate as determinants of help seeking behavior, Unpublished Manuscript, Tel-Aviv University, 1982.

Nadler, A. Sheinberg, L., Jaffe, Y. Coping with stress by help seeking: Help seeking and receiving behaviors in male paraplegics. In C. Spiel-berger, I. Sarason and N. Milgram (Eds.): *Stress and Anxiety (Vol. 8),* Washington, D.C., Hemisphere Publishing Corp., 1981, pp. 375–386.

Schneider, D. J., and Turkat, D. Self-presentation following success or failure: Defensive self-esteem models. *Journal of Personality,* 1975, **43**, 127–135.

Tessler, R. C., & Schwartz, S. H. Help-seeing, self-esteem, and achievement motivation: An attributional analysis. *Journal of Personality and Social Psychology,* 1972, **21,** 318–326.

Underwood, B. J. Individual differences as a crucible in theory construction. *American Psychologist,* 1975, **30,** 128–134.

Wallston, B. S. The effects of sex-role ideology, self-esteem and expected future interactions with an audience on male help-seeking. *Sex Roles,* 1976, **2,** 353–356.

Wells, E., & Marwell, G. *Self-esteem: Its conceptualization and measurement.* Beverly Hills, California: Sage Publ. 1976.

CHAPTER 8

Developmental Aspects
of Recipients' Reactions to Aid

Nancy Eisenberg

In the past 15 years, the study of prosocial behavior has become a major area of empirical and theoretical investigation. However, despite the considerable interest in this topic, few investigators have attended to recipients' reactions to being assisted. This lack of attention to recipients' responses is especially striking in the developmental research.

It is interesting to speculate why this neglect has occurred. One likely reason is that the investigation of prosocial behavior is quite recent; thus, most researchers have been dealing with the salient issues—the development and elicitation of prosocial behavior—rather than with more subtle issues, such as others' reactions to being helped. A second possible reason has its roots in Western society's attitudes toward prosocial behavior. In general, we seem to assume that prosocial behavior is a meritorious, desirable mode of behavior. A corollary of such reasoning is the assumption that the effects of prosocial behavior generally are positive, and probably are viewed as such by recipients. Assumptions of this type may have precluded the ex-

Copyright © 1983 by Academic Press, Inc.

penditure of much energy to verify recipients' perceptions of and responses to aid.

Although there currently is little research regarding children as recipients of aid, research on this issue is important for several reasons. First, it is impossible to develop a thorough understanding of the helping process without information regarding the origins and developmental course of individuals' reactions to aid. Equally important, however, is that research on children's reactions to aid has important implications for understanding both the role of peers in the socialization of positive behaviors and the development of children's social cognition regarding themselves and others. For example, children's responses to peers' prosocial behaviors can serve as reinforcers or as punishment for prosocial action, and, consequently, can play a major role in the socialization of positive behaviors (Staub, 1979).

The purpose of the present chapter is to present relevant research on the development of children's reactions to aid and to stimulate thinking and research regarding this issue. In the first section of the chapter, the few studies directly pertaining to the topic are reviewed. Next, factors that may influence developmental changes in reactions to aid (subdivided into characteristics of the donor, the recipient, the positive behavior itself, and the situation) are discussed. Given the paucity of relevant data and theory, this discussion is, by necessity, rather speculative. Finally, the major theories concerning adult recipients' reactions to aid are analyzed briefly from a developmental perspective.

REVIEW OF THE LITERATURE

In a recent comprehensive review of the research, Fisher, Nadler, and Whitcher-Alagna (1982) cited less than a dozen studies concerning either help-seeking or recipients' responding to aid that involved at least some subjects younger than college age. Few of these studies included children younger than junior high school age, and few were developmental in nature, that is, involved the examination of changes in behavior with age. The Fisher *et al.* review provides a fairly accurate picture of the current state of the literature—as was mentioned previously, research on children's reactions to aid is extremely sparse. This meager literature is now examined.

Infants

There are few data on infants' help-receiving behavior. Pastor (1981) found that 18–24-month-olds were more likely to ignore peers' offers of objects and social interaction if their relationships to their mothers were insecure, anxious, and resistant than if they either were securely attached to or avoided their mothers. However, the various groups of infants did not differ in acceptance or rejection of offers. Lamb (1978a, b) found that infants (12 and 18 months) were more likely to accept toys from their pre-school siblings (approximately 1½–4 years older) than vice versa. However, because the older siblings were much more likely to *offer* objects (or show or point out) than were the younger siblings, the infants had more opportunities to accept toys than did their older siblings. Thus, it is not clear whether or not infants accepted a higher proportion of toys offered to them than did their preschool siblings. Both the infants and preschoolers were stable in their tendencies to accept objects over a 6-month period, but the frequencies of older and younger siblings' acceptances were not related (Lamb, 1978b).

The data on infants' reactions to aid are too sparse to clarify the early development of these behaviors. The need for further research is clear.

Preschool and Elementary School-aged Children

Reciprocity Responses

Most of the data regarding children's reactions to aid concern reciprocity in the helping process. Researchers who have done this work generally have been testing hypotheses derived from social psychological theories related to social exchange in human interactions (Gouldner, 1960; Walster, Walster, & Berscheid, 1978), such as the notion that people who receive aid will be likely to return the favor due to either social norms supporting such action or discomfort produced by inequity in the interaction. In such research, other alternative reactions to aid aside from reciprocation seldom have been examined.

In general, the literature on this issue is consistent with the conclusion that children who receive assistance are more likely to reciprocate the favor if given the opportunity than are children who have not received prior aid. This conclusion is based on several types of data. First, in studies of peer interaction, researchers have found that preschoolers and school-aged children who perform positive behaviors receive more positive behaviors from peers (and, frequently, vice versa for negative acts) (e.g., Charlesworth & Hartup, 1967; Eisenberg, Cameron, Tryon, & Dodez, 1981; Marcus & Jenny, 1977; Staub & Feinberg, 1980). However, although these data seem to indicate that children who receive help often respond with positive behavior directed toward the benefactor, in reality the data are ambiguous with regard to this issue. It is not clear in these studies that children who were recipients of aid actually reacted by emitting a positive behavior, or that a given recipient ever responded positively to the benefactor. It is possible that children who behave positively toward others receive more positive behavior in general (at various times), and that they do not necessarily elicit positive reactions for their prosocial behaviors. Most likely, much of the reciprocity noted in children's behaviors reflects broad patterns of interpersonal interactions and not the fact that children frequently react to one prosocial behavior with another positive act.

Although the data on reciprocity in children's social interactions is ambiguous with regard to children's reactions to aid, some researchers have provided support for the conclusion that children frequently will react directly to positive acts with reciprocation (Dreman, 1976; Peterson, Hartmann, & Gelfand, 1977; Staub & Sherk, 1970). Unlike the primarily naturalistic research on reciprocation in children's ongoing social interactions, this research tends to be of an experimental or interview nature. For example, Peterson *et al.* (1977), in an experimental study, found that kindergarteners and third graders who had not been aided by a peer donated less to that peer than did children who had received prior assistance from the peer, and less than a control group who had not been given an opportunity to receive help from the peer. Kindergarteners donated less than third graders to a peer who had previously refused to help them.

In nonexperimental studies, children also report such sequences of behavior as common among friends. Youniss (1980) told 6- to 14-year-olds a story about a child or an adult who did something kind for a child story protagonist and then asked the children what the protagonist was likely to do in the subsequent interaction with the benefactor. Most of the children's responses regarding the peer's kindness could be coded as expressions of gratitude, direct reciprocity (the recipient would perform the same act as the helper for the helper), or approximate reciprocity (the recipient performed some act approximating but not exactly duplicating the actor's original prosocial behavior). The children gave direct reciprocity responses most frequently (62 times), followed by gratitude (32 times) and approximate reciprocity responses (22 times). In contrast, when the children predicted what a child recipient would do in response to an adult's kindness, the children generally mentioned either gratitude or approximate reciprocity, not direct reciprocity. Youniss suggested that the difference in responses to stories about adults' and children's kindness was due to the fact that peer interactions are more reciprocal than are adult–child interactions.

Other Types of Responses

In general, researchers who have examined reciprocity as a response to prosocial behavior seldom have assessed other possible modes of recipient responses to a benefactor. Thus, there have been few attempts to delineate the diversity of children's reactions to aid, or the conditions under which they occur.

Although they were not explicitly studying prosocial behavior, Charlesworth and Hartup (1967) did assess preschoolers' responses to peers' positive reinforcements (including the giving of positive attention, approval and tokens, affection and personal acceptance, and submission). They found that 58% of the time, reinforcement was followed by the recipients' continuing the activity in which they were engaged at the time of reinforcement. Sixteen percent of reinforcements were followed by a change in behavior; 6% were rejected by the recipient; 8% were ignored; and 12% could not be rated. Although it is difficult to draw many conclusions from these data, they do suggest that children infrequently respond negatively to positive reinforcement from peers.

Furman and Masters (1980) also examined preschoolers' reactions to peers' positive, neutral, and negative behaviors. Positive behaviors included help-giving, gift giving, protection, and giving a reward, as well as behaviors such as smiling, compliance, and giving permission or praise. They found that 27% of the time that a child performed a positive behavior, the recipient of the act responded with overt signs of pleasure. Negative reactions such as crying, frowning, screaming, or disapproval occurred only 2% of the time, whereas peers reacted neutrally (with a blank look or no overt reaction) to 71% of their peers' positive behaviors. Although the category of "positive behaviors" in this study included more than prosocial behaviors, the results are consistent with the conclusion that children seldom react negatively to others' positive acts.

Iannotti (1981) examined 4- and 5-year-olds' reactions to the receipt of prosocial behaviors (sharing, helping, comforting, cooperation). Seventy-five percent of prosocial acts were followed by no apparent consequences; 12% by an expression of gratitude; 6% by a prosocial act; and 2% by affectionate behavior. Iannotti reported no instances of negative reactions; however, it is unclear if he coded negative reactions if they occured.

In a study of preschoolers of age 4–5 years, Eisenberg et al. (1981), like Iannotti, specifically examined children's reactions to a peer's prosocial behaviors in the classroom. They videotaped 33 children's naturally occurring prosocial behavior in the preschool classroom during free play time (over a 9-week period). A variety of social behaviors, including prosocial behaviors, were coded, as well as peers' reactions to these behaviors. Positive, neutral, and negative reactions were defined as follows:

Positive reactions—the recipient smiles, approves of the act, thanks the benefactor, reciprocates, initiates social interaction with the benefactor, or sustains interaction with the benefactor.

Neutral reaction—the recipient does not notice the action, acts puzzled, or accepts the object or help with no other reaction.

Negative reaction—the recipient ignores the benefactor, grabs something from the benefactor, or reacts negatively; for example, by pushing or yelling.

Note that positive reinforcement was defined broadly as including not only obvious positive reactions such as "thank-you" or smiles, but also events such as positive social interaction that may be viewed as reinforcing.

According to the data, preschool children responded positively to helping or sharing approximately 34% of the time if the benefactor's prosocial behavior was spontaneous (unsolicited), and 48% of the time if the behavior was asked for (solicited by the recipient of the aid). Neutral, nonresponsive reactions occurred approximately 50% of the time for both categories of behavior, whereas negative reactions occurred for approximately 16 and 1% of spontaneous and asked-for behaviors, respectively. Most of the children's positive reactions consisted of initiating or sustaining social interaction, rather than explicit thanks, praise, or other reactions clearly linked to the prosocial behavior. The low frequency of positive reactions such as verbal thanks and smiles is consistent with Rogers-Warren and Baer's (1976) findng that preschoolers seldom verbally compliment one another, and with Barton, Olszawski, and Madsen's (1979) research indicating that preschoolers infrequently reinforce sharing by peers with smiles or praise.

The fact that most of the children's negative reactions were elicited by spontaneous rather than asked-for behaviors is probably due to the fact that a spontaneous behavior can be easily misinterpreted. For example, it may be seen as an attempt to interfere with the recipient's ongoing behavior. In contrast, the occurrence of an asked-for behavior is anticipated (indeed initiated) by the potential recipient of aid. This conclusion is supported by Eisenberg et al.'s finding (unpublished data) that children who most frequently received negative responses for their spontaneous prosocial behaviors were those who were most likely to grab or otherwise try to take a peer's possession.

Eisenberg et al. also examined the relation between a child's characteristics and how other children responded to that child's prosocial behavior. Frequency of emitting spontaneous prosocial behaviors was unrelated to type of response received for such behaviors. However, children who frequently performed asked-for behaviors (especially males) received fewer positive reactions and somewhat more ($p < .10$) negative reactions (girls only) from peers than did less compliant children who were not as likely to respond to requests for help or sharing.

Again, children who frequently performed asked-for behaviors tended to receive fewer positive and more negative reactions than did children who exhibited fewer asked-for behaviors. A possible explanation for this finding can be derived from other data collected by Eisenberg and her students. Children who perform many asked-for behaviors appear to be relatively submissive (Eisenberg-Berg & Giallanzo, 1980), dependent and compliant (Eisenberg *et al.*, 1981), and perhaps are seen as easy targets by peers. Indeed, those children who exhibit many asked-for behaviors are those who are asked to share or help more frequently. This pattern of findings in the Eisenberg *et al.* study was stronger for males than for females (as was the association between frequency of asked-for behavior and type of feedback received), suggesting that dependent, compliant boys are especially unlikely to elicit positive reactions from peers for prosocial behaviors that can be interpreted as acts of compliance. This may be because the behavior of these boys does not conform to the independent, dominant, masculine stereotype, and preschool children tend to ignore and respond negatively to boys who engage in feminine behavioral patterns (Fagot, 1977; Roopnarine, 1981).

According to Eisenberg *et al.*'s (1981) data, the type of reaction emitted by a child also was correlated with the type of response received from peers. Children who responded positively to others' spontaneous prosocial behaviors received positive reactions when they themselves behaved prosocially. Similarly, neutral reactions to peers were associated with neutral reactions received from peers (neutral and positive reactions were highly, negatively correlated). Moreover, type of feedback received for prosocial behavior was associated with children's sociability (frequency of positive social contacts). Children who received positive reactions when they responded to another's request for aid were relatively social with both peers and teachers. Children who were less social, when they were asked to assist, tended to receive nonresponsive reactions from the recipient of their aid. The type of reaction received by children for spontaneous prosocial behaviors was not significantly related to their general sociability. Furthermore, according to unpublished data, children who were relatively social with peers tended to respond positively rather than neutrally to peers' prosocial behaviors, especially their asked-for behaviors. Overall, these data indicate that a recipient's response to a benefactor's attempt to help may be strongly related to aspects of both the benefactor's and the recipient's personalities.

In one of the very few studies containing data on elementary school children's reactions to aid, Bryant and Crockenberg (1980) found that fourth- and fifth-grade girls accepted help less frequently from their younger sisters (2–3 years younger) than vice versa. However, because older siblings made more offers of help than did younger siblings, the younger girls had more opportunities to accept assistance. Nevertheless, the ratio of acceptance of help to refusals of help or sharing was much higher for younger children (no statistical test was used to compare these ratios), suggesting that the older sisters were more likely to refuse aid than were younger sisters. Whether this differences was due to merely age or to the nature of the relationship between younger and older sisters cannot be determined from the data in this study.

Adolescents' Reactions to Aid

Although quite limited in quantity, there are more data relating to adolescents' reactions than to children's reactions to aid. Some of these data, however, are not useful to the individual who is interested in delineating developmental progress because the responses of adult and adolescent samples are combined. Moreover, nearly all of the adolescent research has been conducted with social psychological experimental paradigms in which specific, contrived manipulations were instituted. Although such controlled manipulations frequently served to provide information regarding the researchers' hypotheses, the resultant data include little information regarding the diversity of possible reactions in different situations. Thus, the few data available provide a very spotty picture of adolescents' reactions to aid.

In this section, the limited research on adolescents' responses to aid is briefly reviewed. Several studies relating to help-seeking also are discussed because of their implications for understanding adolescents' reactions to aid. Only studies in which the responses of adolescents were not combined with those of adults are reviewed.

As for the research with children, investigators frequently have examined adolescent recipients' reactions to aid in the context of studying reciprocation of prosocial behavior. In general, the results of this research indicate that adolescents often reciprocate a benefactor's aid (Cox, 1974). However, socioeconomic status of the adolescent recipient seems to be related to degree of reciprocation. In two studies with high school students, Berkowitz (Berkowitz, 1968; Berkowitz & Friedman, 1967) has found that the helping of boys whose fathers worked at bureaucratic middle-class occupations was relatively unaffected by how much prior help they themselves had received, whereas American boys from middle-class entrepreneural families and English working-class boys (but not American working-class boys) were influenced in their reciprocation by the amount of aid previously received.

As might be expected, adolescents apparently are more likely to respond to another's prosocial behavior with reciprocation if the other individual's behavior is perceived as intentional and voluntary (Garrett & Libby, 1973; Nemeth, 1970). These findings are consistent with the predictions of attribution theorists (e.g., Jones & Davis, 1965) who contend that reactions to others are a function of both the consequences of the other's behavior and the perceived intentionality of the actor. Further, according to other research (Morse, Gergen, Peele, & VanRyneveld, 1977), adolescents perceive assistance that is unexpected as more valuable and, thus, more worthy of reciprocation, than help that is expected and therefore produces no more than the expected outcome (as long as the help-giving does not violate any rules).

Other studies with adolescents have produced additional information relevant to their reactions to aid. Nadler and Porat (1978) found that 15–16-year-olds were unlikely to ask for assistance on a general knowledge task unless their identity was kept anonymous *and* they could attribute their need for help to external rather than internal factors (that is, they had been told that 90% of people rather than 10% could not answer all of the test questions correctly). These data are consistent with the conclusions that (1) adolescents sometimes perceive help-seeking as an admission of inadequacy and avoid such behavior as long as anyone will know, and (2) in some circumstances, it is easier for adolescents to seek help if they feel they are not responsible for their state of need. In another study DePaulo (1978a) found no direct association between adolescents' acceptance of art lessons from a child and measures of self-esteem and need for approval. However, self-esteem and need for approval seemed to be important moderator variables influencing acceptance of help. In sum, the findings from these studies indicate that an adolescent's self-esteem sometimes moderates behavior in a help-seeking or help-receiving situation and that in some circumstances the adolescent will respond negatively to receiving assistance.

The fact that adolescents view help as less desirable in some situations than in others is also evident in another study. DePaulo (1978c) asked junior-high- and high-school students and adults how likely they would be to seek help in a variety of situations. In some circumstances, the subjects reported that they would be reluctant to ask for help. For example, males were especially unwilling to ask for help in unimportant situations. Further, subjects were less likely to seek help if they were unable to reciprocate. These data are consistent with the postulates of social exchange theorists (Walster *et al.,* 1978) in indicating that adolescents are sometimes uncomfortable when they are involved in an inequitable relationship. The adolescents in this study also preferred help from nonthreatening others such as from same-sex, same-age peers who liked them. Adults and junior-high-school students were more likely to turn to family than friends for help; the reverse pattern was true for high-school and college students. Adults were more likely than adolescents to prefer help from an opposite-sex peer. Furthermore, junior-high- and high-school students reported liking a benefactor who helped in a serious situation more than did older subjects. Junior-high students, in comparison to older subjects, found it important to get help in frivolous situations, whereas older subjects reported that it was more important to get help in task-oriented situations. Finally, adolescents and adults did not differ overall in willingness to seek help, in the perceived importance of obtaining help, or in that they both preferred to ask for help when they felt the potential benefactor would not mind assisting.

To summarize, adolescents' reactions to aid frequently seem to be governed by reciprocity considerations and concern for the effects of receiving aid on one's own and others' evaluations of the self. These concerns also seem to be important determinants of adults' reactions to aid (Fisher et al., 1982). Although adolescents prefer to seek help from different people than do adults in some situations (DePaulo, 1978c), based on the sparse available data, there is no reason to believe that adolescents' (particularly high-school students') responses to assistance differ substantially from those of adults. Of course, significant differences between adolescents' and adults' responses may be delineated in future research.

Comparison of the Data for Children and Adolescents

It is difficult to compare the results of research concerning children's and adolescents' reactions to aid because the data are so limited, and the studies vary greatly in terms of design, methodology, and the issues addressed. For example, in research with children, real-life peer benefactors have been employed and the studies usually have been either experimental or naturalistic in design. In contrast, researchers who have studied adolescents generally have conducted experimental studies structured to test social psychological principles and frequently have used a benefactor who is a stranger. However, despite the differences in the research, a review of the existing data for children and adolescents does raise some questions.

One question that is easily derived from a review of the literature concerns developmental changes in frequency of negative reactions to aid. It appears that young children respond negatively to aid relatively infrequently and, when they do, it often seems to be in situations in which the helping act can be misinterpreted as interference or an attempt to take something from the child (Eisenberg et al., 1981). In contrast, in the limited adolescent literature, there are numerous indications that adolescents, like adults (cf. Fisher et al., 1982), frequently respond negatively to aid and are reluctant to seek help. It is possible that the difference in findings for children and adolescents is due primarily to noncomparability of the research. However, it is more likely that children, with age, are more sensitive to a number of possible negative interpretations of help-seeking behavior (for example, that the receipt of help implies incompetent or dependent behavior), and that they become increasingly aware of the fact that help-giving can be used to ingratiate or to create an unwanted indebtedness on the recipient. Moreover, adolescents may internalize more strongly than do children norms and interpersonal expectations related to reciprocity and equity between individuals. Consequently, adolescents may be more sensitive than children to the negative consequences (internally or externally caused) for acting in violation of these norms and expectations.

There is one study that is directly relevant to the issue of developmental changes in reactions to aid from childhood to adolescence. However, the results of the study are difficult to interpret. Northman (1978) asked children in Grades 3, 6, 9, and 12 to indicate how "uncomfortable" they would feel accepting help from a variety of helpers in seven different situations. He found that the older children (Grades 9 and 12) were more open to receiving help than were young children in four of the seven situations, whereas younger children (Grades 3 and 6) were more comfortable receiving aid in one situation.

These data are not consistent with the hypothesis that older children are more sensitive to the implications of receiving help and, thus, are more likely to react negatively to aid. However, it is quite possible that older children's apparent willingness to accept help in this study reflected a social desirability effect. Older children, more than younger children, may have felt that there was something undesirable about saying that they would not be comfortable accepting help—that experiencing discomfort would indicate defensiveness and lack of self-confidence.

Although questions related to children's reactions to aid and developmental changes in these responses seldom have been addressed directly, there are data on a variety of topics that indirectly relate to these issues. By attending to these data, as well as to the research that is more directly linked to the issue at hand, it is possible to make some reasonable predictions concerning children's reactions to assistance. Some of the potential factors influencing childrens reactions to aid are now reviewed.

FACTORS OF POTENTIAL SIGNIFICANCE IN CHILDREN'S REACTIONS TO AID

Characteristics of the Benefactor

Relationship to the Recipient

It is clear that the manner in which children respond to aid must be a function, in part, of whomever provides the aid. Certainly, it is common knowledge that once children can distinguish between individuals, distressed infants and young children more readily respond to the comforting efforts of familiar, loved others than to the efforts of strangers. In fact, an attachment figure's presence and comforting behavior are an important benefit for the child, serving to reduce the child's anxiety in stressful, novel, or fear-inducing situations (Ainsworth, 1973; Ainsworth, Blehar, Waters, & Wall, 1978).

According to the limited data, children and adolescents seem to prefer assistance from either those similar to the self (for example, peers), or persons with whom the child has a relationship (Bachman, 1975). Preference for peer rather than adult benefactors seems to increase somewhat with age. For example, in a study with elementary school children, Boehm (1957) found that with increasing age children tended to prefer advice regarding a problem from a talented peer rather than from an adult who was described as having no expertise relevant to the problem. Similarly, in a study with adolescents, DePaulo (1978c) noted a preference for same-age, same-sex donors who were liked and who liked them. Preference for help from a friend rather than from family members increased from junior-high to high-school age. Finally, in a study with students in Grades 3, 6, 9, and 12, Northman (1978) found that children in Grade 6 and high school said they would be most comfortable accepting aid from a female peer or a girl 3 years older than themselves. The order of preference for other helpers from most to least was teacher, other adults, boy, parent, and older boy. Thus, Northman obtained only partial support for the assertion that peers are preferred helpers.

If children do prefer help from peers and/or liked others, it is likely that they will usually attend to and respond more positively to help from those individuals than from others. However, to my knowledge there are few data directly pertaining to this prediction.

The one relevant study that is available suggests that help from similar others can, at times, be threatening to children's self-esteem and, consequently, aversive. Fisher and Nadler (1982) reported a study in which fifth graders who were tutored in math by another fifth grader expressed less liking toward the tutor and evaluated the tutoring more negatively than did children who were tutored by a nonpeer (a seventh grader). Apparently, help from similar others is less favorably received when the fact that a similar other can provide the needed assistance could be interpreted as evidence of the recipient's incompetence.

According to some research, children apply norms of reciprocity less to interactions with friends than to interactions with other peers—they seem to feel less obligated to reciprocate immediately a friend's prosocial behavior than a nonfriend's (Floyd, 1964; Staub & Noerenberg, 1981; Staub & Sherk, 1970; also see Clark, present volume). In seeming contrast, in a naturalistic study of preschool children, Marcus and Jenny (1977) found more correspondence between amount of help received and amount of help given if the recipient of aid was liked than if the recipient was disliked. However, because reciprocation between friends need not occur immediately—with an ongoing relationship reciprocation can occur over time—children may feel little need to respond immediately to a friend's kindness with kindness. Because Marcus and Jenny did not obtain information relating to immediacy of the child's reciprocation, their data do not conflict with those of Floyd or Staub and Sherk. Thus, the limited data are consistent with the conclusion that children do reciprocate aid from a friend, but that reciprocation may occur at a later time.

Age Status

Age status of the donor appears to influence the likelihood that a child will respond to another's prosocial behavior with reciprocity. As was previously mentioned, Youniss (1980) found that 6- to 14-year-olds, when asked to complete scenarios about a child's reaction to aid, reported that children usually would respond to a peer benefactor's prosocial action with a similar or comparable prosocial behavior. In contrast, most of Youniss' 6- to 8-year-old group reported that a child would react to an adult benefactor with expressions of gratitude; only a few mentioned reciprocity. Some 9- to 14-year-olds also said that a child would react to an adult's behavior with gratitude; however, most gave answers indicating a reciprocal response. Apparently, due to an inequity in resources and competencies, children, especially young children, often cannot or do not respond with reciprocity to adults' aid. In contrast, because peers are more equal in their capacities, resources, and interests, there seems to be more reciprocity in their social interactions. However, with age, children's responses to adults' prosocial behaviors seem to become more similar to their reactions to peer benefactors.

Sex of the Benefactor

It is likely that sex of the benefactor is a variable associated with effectiveness of helpers' strategies and, consequently, with mode of a child's reactions to aid from a given benefactor. For examples, DePaulo (1978b) found that, as reported by other subjects of the same age, female adolescents and adults were more accurate than males in predicting the feelings of persons asking for aid in a variety of situations. Recall, also, that both school-aged children and adolescents reported that they would prefer the help of a female peer to assistance from a variety of other persons (Northman, 1978). DePaulo (1978c) also found that adolescents (and adults) preferred female helpers in some situations (in serious circumstances and in feminine sex-typed situations). These findings are consistent with the data indicating that women are more sensitive to nonverbal cues than are men (Hall, 1978). Apparently, females are socialized to be more interpersonal in their orientation than are males (Block, 1973; Hoffman, 1977) and, therefore, are more sensitive and/or effective benefactors. Fagot (1978) found, for example, that female toddlers are encouraged both to accept and to give more help than are males.

Level of Cognitive Functioning

Due to differences in individuals' levels of sensitivity, role-taking, and more general knowledge, some benefactors are more capable of providing appropriate assistance than are others. For example, Barnett, Darcie, Holland, and Kobasigwa (1982) interviewed kindergartners and third and sixth graders to assess their awareness of a variety of variables that affect the quality of helping behaviors. According to their data, even kindergarten children appeared to understand the relevance of a helper's willingness and competence for effective helping, the role of helpees' cooperativeness in the helping process, and the necessity of using different helping techniques in different situations. However, kindergarteners were less likely than older children to realize that effective helping is a consequence of more than one attribute of the helper—that either willingness, competence, or empathic ability, by itself, is not sufficient. Furthermore, young children were less aware than older children that initial knowledge about the requirements of a helping situation can be used to determine task difficulty and appropriate helping strategies. Finally, young children also were less sensitive to the fact that constraints in a situation can be used to evaluate the suitability of various strategies of intervention (direct intervention, indirect intervention, or no intervention). For example, young children were relatively impervious to the fact that direct intervention may not be an appropriate strategy for assisting a child who wants to do a task unaided.

Not only do children's abilities to analyze strategies for effective helping change with age, but their capacity to assess difficulty of a task (Nicholls, 1978) and to analyze others' cognitive processes and affective reactions become increasingly sophisticated with age (Shantz, 1975). These developmental changes should enable older children to be more sensitive and effective helpers than are younger persons.

Although there are few data concerning this issue, it is logical to assume that differences in helpers' capacities will influence the quality (appropriateness and effectiveness) of helpers' strategies and, consequently, recipients' reactions to an individual's interventions. In general, recipients of aid would be expected to react more positively if aid is sensitively rendered. Further, as will be discussed later, it is reasonable to assume that children will become more reactive to the subtle differences in helper's capacities and strategies as they themselves develop the ability to comprehend these differences.

Personality of the Benefactor

Another factor that would seem to influence how children react to aid is the donor's personality. For example, Raviv, Bar-Tal, Ayalon, and Raviv (1980) found that sixth graders reported that they preferred to receive help from popular rather than unpopular peers. Furthermore, Eisenberg *et al.* (1981) found that socially active and responsive preschool benefactors were more likely to elicit positive reactions from recipients of their helping and sharing behaviors. Moreover, according to unpublished data, Eisenberg *et al.* found that when children did respond negatively to peers' spontaneous prosocial behaviors, it tended to be in interactions with peer benefactors who, in other circumstances, were relatively likely to take objects in another's possession and to emit negative verbal reactions when others attempted to obtain objects from them. These findings are consistent with the conclusion that preschoolers may mistrust or misinterpret the unsolicited assistance of peers who typically try to take possessions but are reluctant to give them up.

Other personality characteristics of the benefactor undoubtedly also influence the valence and mode of recipients' responses. In the future, researchers may profit by not assuming that all benefactors are comparable. Furthermore, children's conceptions of individuals' personalities and characteristics become more sophisticated with age—indeed, the concept of a stable personality develops with age (Feldman & Ruble, 1981; Rotenberg, 1982; Ruble & Rholes, in press; Shantz, 1975). Therefore, it is likely that the personality of a benefactor assumes increasing significance as the age of the recipient increases.

Socioeconomic Status and Race of the Benefactor

The limited relevant research is consistent with the assertion that social class of a benefactor influences children's reactions to aid, but in a complex manner. Berkowitz (1968; Berkowitz & Friedman, 1967) found that social class of a prior benefactor influenced the amount of help reciprocated both by American boys from entrepreneural families (but not bureaucratic families) and by English adolescent males from working-class and bureaucratic families. For these boys, middle-class subjects were more likely to expend low effort on behalf of a peer who had previously provided little assistance to the subject only if the peer had a working-class background. The working-class English boys followed a reciprocity principle primarily when dealing with middle-class peers—they worked hardest for a middle-class person who previously had provided them with aid and expended the least energy for a middle-class peer who had given them little help previously.

There also is evidence that children's social judgments about themselves and others are influenced by race, with Caucasians generally being viewed by Blacks and Caucasians as superior (Clark & Clark, 1974; Clark, Hocevar, & Dembo, 1980; Stephen, 1977). However, due to lack of data, it is unclear whether the influence of race of the benefactor on children's reactions to aid is substantial or not, and whether it increases or decreases with age. Because white children's reports of negative attitudes toward Blacks seem to peak at age 5½–7 and decrease subsequently (Clark *et al.,* 1980), it is possible that young Caucasian school-aged children react more negatively to aid from minorities than do preschoolers or older children. Because of the superior status of Caucasians in our culture, the reverse relationship may not hold (minorities may not react especially negatively to aid from Caucasians).

Characteristics of the Recipient

Characteristics of a recipient may be even more important in determining a recipient's reactions to aid than are characteristics of the benefactor. This is because the effects of developmental advances in children's thinking processes on reactions to aid are likely to be very pronounced. The potential influence of a recipient's level of cognitive functioning will be examined after discussion of other characteristics of recipients that may color their reactions to aid.

Sex of the Recipient

Many benefactor characteristics that are associated with children's reactions to aid are also important potential correlates of a given recipient's reaction to aid. For example, sex of the recipient seems to be associated with preschoolers' responses to assistance, albeit in a complex manner. Although preschool boys did not ask for aid more frequently than did girls, Eisenberg *et al.* (1981 study, Note 1) found that males were more likely than females to respond positively rather than neutrally (passively) to a peer's solicited prosocial behavior. In contrast, the data in two other studies are consistent with the conclusion that females should respond more favorably to the receipt of aid than do males. In Northman's (1978) study of students in Grades 3, 6, 9, and 12, females were much more likely to say that they would be comfortable receiving help. Furthermore, DePaulo (1978c) found that adolescent females were more likely than males to say they would seek help, and to feel it is important to get help. It is possible that the inconsistencies in the research findings are due to developmental changes in males' and females' reactions to aid; however, it is also possible that the discrepancies in findings are the result of differences in the type of aid being considered. The Eisenberg *et al.* study involved naturalistic observations of children's actual reactions to peers' aid; the Northman and DePaulo studies employed a self-report format in which children and/or adolescents stated their preferences for various types of helpers and/or help in hypothetical situations. Social desirability factors may have influenced the subjects' responses in the self-report studies; furthermore, in the Northman and DePaulo research, the subjects reported hypothetical *preferences* for aid, not reactions to aid. Moreover, only in the Eisenberg *et al.* study were reactions to (or preferences for) solicited versus unsolicited helping distinguished.

It is clear that more research regarding the relation between sex of the recipient and children's reactions to aid is merited. However, even if consistent sex differences in reactions to aid are noted, interpretation of this fact must be made judiciously. Because there is evidence that females' reactions to various types of aid are easier to predict than are reactions of males (DePaulo, 1978b), benefactors may find it easier to deduce how and when to assist females. Thus, females' more positive responses to aid may reflect qualitative differences in the aid that is received by males and females.

Personality of the Recipient

It is likely that the personality of a recipient, including interactive style, values, level of self-esteem, and need for approval plays a role in determining children's responses to aid. However, as a reader might now suspect, data relevant to this issue are not available. Eisenberg *et al.* (1981 study, Note 1) did find that the children who were sociable (engaged in many peer interactions), in comparison to less social children, tended to react positively rather than passively to peers' assistance (when the assistance had been solicited). Furthermore, although Pastor (1981) found no differences in securely and insecurely attached 18–24-month-olds' acceptance or rejection of peers' offers of objects and social interaction (combined), insecurely attached, anxious, resistant toddlers were more likely to ignore peers' offers than were securely attached or avoidant toddlers. Unfortunately, Pastor did not analyze the toddlers' reactions to sharing behavior separately from reactions to offers to be social.

Although it is likely that characteristics such as need for approval and self-esteem moderate or directly influence children's reactions to aid, at the present time one can only hypothesize regarding the relation between these variables and modes of response. It is probable that relatively young children, as well as adolescents and adults (DePaulo, 1978a), will respond in a positive manner if they are high in need for approval and if it is apparent that seeking and/or acceptance of aid is the approved behavior in a particular situation. Furthermore, the adult literature (Fisher *et al.*, 1982) suggests that older children with high self-esteem may be more sensitive to self-threat than are low self-esteem individuals because they benefit more from maintaining a consistent image of themselves as competent. It is difficult to predict the relation between self-esteem and reactions to aid for young children with a less consistent image of the self. However, it is unlikely that the relations of need for approval, self-esteem, and other personality variables to behavior are simple.

Socioeconomic Status and Race of the Recipient

Socioeconomic status of the recipient is another factor that seems to covary with children's reactions to aid, but seldom has been examined, especially developmentally. As was previously discussed, in research concerning adolescent boys' reciprocation of help, Berkowitz found that American boys from entrepreneural families were more influenced by amount of help received previously than were boys from working-class and middle-class bureaucratic families (Berkowitz & Friedman, 1967). In a comparable study, English working-class boys were more responsive to the principles of reciprocity (that is, were more likely to base their own helping on the amount of helping previously obtained from a peer) than were middle-class bureaucratic English boys (Berkowitz, 1968). Although Cox (1974) found no effect of race on adolescents' tendencies to reciprocate help, it is also likely that race of a recipient, especially in interaction with race of the benefactor, has some effect on children's reactions to aid.

Need State of the Recipient

It is logical to assume that the level of a recipient's need affects how that recipient responds to aid. However, the association between need state and recipients' reactions probably varies as a function of age. Young children tend to focus on hedonistic costs to the self and/or others' concrete needs when making judgments regarding prosocial behavior (Eisenberg-Berg & Hand, 1979; Eisenberg-Berg & Neal, 1981), and not on the possible negative effects of assistance on a recipient (Barnett *et al.*, 1982). Thus, it is reasonable to hypothesize a positive relation between neediness of recipients and positiveness of their reaction to aid. In contrast, among older school-aged children who are more likely to compare their own competence with that of others (Ruble, Feldman, & Boggiano, 1976), high need may be associated both with desire for assistance and resentment toward the benefactor. It is also possible that the relation between the need state of the recipient and the recipient's reaction is not linear. This is a matter for future investigation.

Level of Recipient's Social Cognitive Capacities

Variations in children's reactions to aid are probably more a function of the recipient's current level of social cognition than any other recipient characteristic. In a given situation, a recipient's reaction to aid can be expected to be strongly influenced by the recipient's evaluation of the benefactor and the benefactor's motives, by the recipient's perceptions regarding others' evaluations of the self, and by the recipient's self-evaluation as a consequence of seeking and/or receiving assistance. Furthermore, because evaluations of one's own and others' intentions and motives change dramatically with age, it is likely that level of social cognition has a profound influence on the development of reactions to aid.

Attributions Regarding Others It is logical to assume that a recipient's evaluations of a helpers' kindness is a major determinant of that recipient's reaction to the helper. Thus, examination of the aged-related changes in the criteria used by children to evaluate kindness should throw some light on the ways in which children's judgments of, and reactions to, recipients change with age.

A number of researchers have examined causal schemes used by children and adults to make inferences regarding the kindness of an act. Among the schemes that have been studied are the discounting, augmentation, and additive principles (Kelley, 1967). According to the discounting principle, a given cause (e.g., the assumption that an act was motivated by kindness) is minimized when another plausible facilitory cause (e.g., a formal obligation or duress) is present. In contrast, according to the augmentation principle, the presence of an inhibiting cause (e.g., previous refusal to help by the potential recipient of aid, or threats of bodily harm to potential benefactors if they help) leads to the inference that the facilitating cause (e.g., kindness of an act) is greater. Finally, according to the additive principle, intentions are believed to be positively related to outcomes; thus, the person who is rewarded for helping another is perceived as wanting or liking to help more than a person who is not rewarded (e.g., Karniol & Ross, 1979).

Researchers interested in attributions concerning kindness of an act or a benefactor also have sought to apply tenets of Kelley's (1967) covariation theory pertaining to the inference of stable dispositions. According to these tenets, people are likely to attribute behavior to the person rather than to the situation if the person acts consistently toward a particular stimulus (high consistency), responds the same way toward many difference stimuli (low distinctiveness), and if everyone else does not behave in the same manner as the actor (consensus information).

In general, investigators have consistently noted that young children use the additive principle (and, thus, judge rewarded behaviors as more meritorious than unrewarded behaviors) when evaluating prosocial behaviors (Cohen, Gelfand, & Hartmann, 1981; DeVitto & McArthur, 1978; Jensen & Hughston, 1973; Leahy, 1979). Conversely, use of the discounting and augmentation principles apparently increases in use with age (Baldwin & Baldwin, 1970; Benson, Hartmann, & Gelfand, 1981; Cohen et al., 1981; Leahy, 1979; Peterson, 1980; Shure, 1968; Suls, Witenberg, & Gutkin, 1981). Generally, children's use of the additive principle has been found to decrease significantly by second or third grade. In contrast, use of the discounting principle seems to increase significantly during the early school years until approximately third grade, and gradually thereafter. In some studies, researchers have found that application of the discounting principle improves past the age of 12 or 13 (Baldwin & Baldwin, 1970; DiVitto & McArthur, 1978); in other research, there was no significant change in the use of this principle after age 12 or 13 (Cohen et al., 1981). Although use of the discounting principle usually is not reliable before age 7-9, younger children (for example, kindergarteners) will discount an actor's internal motivation when they are helped to attend to and/or understand the inducement value of interpersonal causes (Benson et al., 1981; Karniol & Ross, 1979). Ways of increasing children's understanding of the inducement value of various factors seem to include making the ulterior motive of an actor more salient, either by explicitly pointing out possible manipulative intents or external pressures (Benson et al., 1981; Karniol & Ross, 1979) or by visually depicting the course of events (Shultz & Butkowsky, 1977).

There also appear to be developmental changes in children's understanding of covariation information. By first grade, children seem to be relatively adept at using some covariation information (consistency and distinctiveness information) to make judgments about an actor other than themselves (DiVitto & McArthur, 1978; Leahy, 1979; Ruble & Rholes, in press). However, it is not until middle childhood or later that children develop the requisite skills to make similar inferences using consistency and consensus information regarding the role of the target individual in producing a behavior (DiVitto & McArthur, 1978). In summary, although very young children have some understanding of motives (even 3-year-olds appear to be able to differentiate between good and bad motives, Keasey, 1978), mastery of the various attributional competencies occurs over time, with various skills developing on different time schedules.

How is this attribution research relevant to the predictions regarding children's reactions to aid? According to the adult literature, people seem to react more positively to aid when they believe it is voluntary and intentional and not due to nonaltruistic ulterior motives (see Fisher et al., 1982). Because the role of choice in children's judgments of kindness has been found to increase in importance from kindergarten to the fourth grade (Baldwin & Baldwin, 1970), it is likely that children in early elementary school increasingly attend to the voluntary–involuntary nature of the helping act when reacting to a behavior. Similarly, although even preschool children seem to have some concept of intentionality (Karniol, 1978), children's understanding of the intentionality of prosocial (Baldwin & Baldwin, 1970) and other moral behaviors (Keasey, 1978) seems to improve until at least age 6 or 7. Thus, one would predict that children's reactions to a benefactor are not influenced by perceived or actual intentionality of the actor's behavior until the early school years.

Because young children do not use the discounting principle, they should evaluate more instances of helping as kind and altruistically motivated than should older children and adults. Thus, one would expect young children to react more positively than adults to benefactors who, based on information embedded in the situation, could logically be assisting to avoid punishment, to earn a reward, or for some other nonaltruistic reason. Around mid-elementary school, and progressively thereafter, as children become more capable of making inferences regarding motives, children should begin to respond negatively in many of the same situations as do adults. Research testing this hypothesis is badly needed.

Attributions Relating to the Self It frequently has been demonstrated that adults react negatively to aid when receipt of help might damage their self-esteem and/or others' perceptions of the self (Fisher et al., 1982). Feelings of self-threat should be unlikely to result from help-receiving unless one or more of several conditions occur. These conditions include the following: (1) recipients must be aware of the possibility that receipt of assistance in a particular situation could imply recipient incompetence; (2) recipients must be able to use information embedded in a situation (such as the fact that the recipients need help) to evaluate their own competence;

and (3) recipients should be capable of using information regarding others' performances to evaluate themselves.

Based on the limited empirical data, young children seem to be less adept than older children in the kinds of information processing just listed. In the Barnett *et al.* (1982) study described earlier, kindergarteners were significantly less likely than third or sixth graders to recognize that providing direct assistance is inappropriate when a child wants to do a task without help. It was not clear if older children thought direct helping was less appropriate in this situation because they were aware of the possible negative effects of assistance on a child's self-evaluation of competence or merely because they felt that one should comply with another's desires. Nonetheless, these data suggest relative insensitivity among young children with regard to both analyzing helping situations and recognizing the consequences of helping behaviors on a recipient. Furthermore, DiVitto and McArthur (1978) found that children, unlike adults, were less able to make attributions regarding the target (e.g., recipient) in a social interaction than attributions regarding the actor. This finding is consistent with the conclusion that early elementary school-aged children generally do not understand some aspects of the role of a recipient in a helping interaction. Of course, children's abilities to make attributions about hypothetical recipients of aid may not be an accurate indication of their ability to make inferences regarding themselves when they are recipients of aid.

Young children also seem to be relatively unable or unmotivated to use information embedded in a situation to evaluate their own performances (Nicholls, 1979; Rholes, Blackwell, Jordan, & Walters, 1980). For example, in a study with 4–5- and 7–9-year-olds, Ruble, Parsons, and Ross (1976) experimentally manipulated children's success and failure at a task and then questioned them regarding both task difficulty and their own ability and effort. For the younger children, consistent failure or success had no effect on self-attributions (but did influence self-affect ratings). Children who consistently failed on a task rated themselves as no less capable than did peers who experienced success. Moreover, only the older children's ratings were influenced by information regarding task difficulty.

Young children seem as unlikely to use others' performances as a basis for making self-evaluations as they are to use situational and outcome information. Ruble *et al.* (1967a) found that kindergarten children were less interested than elementary school children in seeking out information concerning their peers' performance that would aid in evaluation of their own work. Furthermore, young children do not seem to use social comparison data (even if it is readily available) to make competence-related judgments about themselves (Boggiano & Ruble, 1979; Ruble, Boggiano, Feldman, & Loebl, 1980). For example, Ruble *et al.* (1980) found that children's achievement-related self-evaluations were not significantly influenced by relative comparisons until at least 7–8 years of age.

The data reviewed above are consistent with the conclusion that children younger than 7 or 8 years are unlikely to make negative, self-esteem threatening self-attributions as a result of receiving aid. This conclusion is based on the observation that young children seem to evaluate their own behaviors positively and frequently do not use information on others' performances or even their own histories of success or failure to evaluate their own competence. In addition, it is likely that young children are oblivious to contextual cues that would influence older children's and adults' inferential processes. However, once children are capable of the inferential processes discussed previously, it is likely that they will begin to discern the implications of help-receiving for their own self-esteem and self-image, and that sensitivity to potential negative consequences for receiving aid will increase accordingly.

Characteristics of the Helping Act

As is true for adults (Fisher et al., 1982), it appears that children's and adolescents' reactions to aid are influenced by characteristics of the helping act. For example, in studies with adolescent boys, Berkowitz found that quantity of prior aid from a peer influenced adolescents' reciprocity responses (Berkowitz, 1968; Berkowitz & Freedman, 1967). It is also likely that benefits and costs of a helping behavior, as well as quantity, influence children's reactions; children's moral judgments regarding prosocial behaviors vary somewhat as a function of cost of the behavior (Eisenberg-Berg & Neal, 1981), and young children probably highly value prosocial behaviors that produce large benefits for the self. However, it is not clear at what age children begin to realize that cost and/or yield of aid influences others' attributions concerning the recipient's competence and also has implications regarding the recipient's future obligation to the benefactor.

Another characteristic of the helping act that seems to affect even young children's reactions to aid is whether or not a particular helping behavior was solicited. As was mentioned previously, Eisenberg et al. (1981) found that nearly all of their preschoolers' negative reactions to aid occurred when the aid was spontaneously emitted rather than solicited by the recipient. However, because adults sometimes value spontaneous aid more than solicited aid (Broll, Gross, & Piliavin, 1974), it is likely that children's evaluations of spontaneous aid change somewhat with age. Spontaneously rendered assistance may be judged more positively as age increases because helping that is involuntary or emitted in response to external factors is not as highly valued by either adults or older children as voluntary aid (Baldwin & Baldwin, 1970; Leahy, 1979).

The type of prosocial behavior rendered (for example, helping, sharing, or comforting) also may influence children's reactions to aid. However, due to lack of data, one can only hypothesize regarding the nature of this influence. It is evident that children's conceptions of relationships such as friendship change with age, with young children frequently defining friendship in terms of playing together, sharing of possessions, and helping one another, and older children conceptualizing friendship more in terms of provision of psychological support and interest in one another's emotional welfare (e.g., Youniss, 1980). Based on these data, it is reasonable to hypothesize that comforting and other prosocial behaviors that provide psychological support should become more valued with age, at least in the context of close relationships. It is unclear if task-oriented aid should be more or less valued with age. Additionally, factors such as sex-role stereotypes may influence which types of aid are most unambivalently valued by recipients. For example, boys may become increasingly reluctant with age and sex-role socialization to accept emotional help. Acceptance of such aid is likely to be interpreted as a sign of weakness and emotional dependence and, consequently, is inconsistent with the stereotypic masculine role (Block, 1973).

The Helping Context

It is safe to assume that recipients' reactions to aid, like other social behaviors, are shaped, in part, by the context in which they are embedded. Certainly this seems to be the case for adults' responses to assistance; in the social psychological literature, it is clear that adults' reactions to receiving and seeking aid are influenced by a number of contextual factors. Among these are anonymity of the recipient, whether or not aid was expected, if there is an opportunity to reciprocate, and whether the need for assistance can be attributed to external (situational) or internal (personal) causes (see Fisher *et al.*, 1982). In addition, according to the limited database on adolescents reviewed earlier, these contextual variables also influence adolescents' reactions to aid. In general, adolescents appear to react more positively to receiving help if it is unexpected (but does not also violate a norm; Morse *et al.*, 1977) and can be reciprocated (DePaulo, 1978c). They are more likely to seek help (at least from a stranger) if their identity will be anonymous and if the situation is such that the need for help can be attributed externally (Nadler & Porat, 1978).

Researchers have not systematically examined the effects of any of these situational variables on children's reactions to aid. By age 5, children do seem to be responsive to reciprocity consdierations (e.g., Dreman, 1976; Dreman & Greenbaum, 1973; Peterson *et al.*, 1977), but this responsiveness frequently may be based merely on desire for self-gain, not upon more subtle motives such as the desire to maintain equity in relationships and / or the protection of self-esteem or one's image. At this time, it simply is unclear why young children frequently reciprocate a benefactor's kindness and under what conditions they are most likely to reciprocate. Moreover, it also is unclear when, developmentally, many of the situational variables such as anonymity of the recipient begin to influence the quality of children's reactions to aid.

Psychologists often have accounted for the effect of various contextual variables on adult recipients' reactions with explanations grounded in equity theory, attribution theories, reactance theory, or a threat to self-esteem theory (see Fisher *et al.*, 1982). If any of these theoretical frameworks, in combination or separately, does account for the pattern of findings concerning adults' reactions to aid, then one would expect children to begin to react to contextual variables in the same way adults do when the psychological processes hypothesized as a basis of each of these various theories become operational. As will be discussed further in a later section of this chapter, many of the relevant processes and abilities are not evident until the elementary school years, and may continue development into adolescence. Thus, it is likely that children do not interpret many situational variables as do adults, and, consequently, do not vary their behaviors as a function of many of the situational cues that influence adults' behaviors until at least middle childhood. Further, because young children seem to attend to the outcomes or consequences of a process more than to the process itself (Brown, 1976; Piaget, 1965), it is likely that young children do not react as much to the situation in which aid is embedded as to the characteristics and consequences of the helping act itself. The subtle implications of receiving aid in various situations should be increasingly processed with age as children become more skilled at identifying and interpreting others' motives, intentions, and attributional processes.

Thus far in this chapter, situational influences on children's reactions to aid have been discussed separately from other potential influences (benefactor characteristics, recipient characteristics, characteristics of the helping act). Of course, in real-life situations, children's reactions to aid probably are simultaneously a function of a number of factors. Thus, it is reasonable to assume that situational factors interact with other factors in shaping children's reactions to aid. Researchers must attend to these interactions if they are to understand the complexity of children's reactions to aid.

A DEVELOPMENTAL PERSPECTIVE
ON MODELS CONCERNING
REACTIONS TO AID

In general, researchers who have examined adults' reactions to aid have been influenced in both design of studies and interpretation of the data by one of several social psychological theoretical perspectives (equity, reactance, attribution, and threat to self-esteem theories). In a recent paper, Fisher *et al.* (1982) have extensively reviewed the adult research literature and evaluated the usefulness of each theoretical perspective for explaining the patterns in the literature. They concluded that a threat to self-esteem model most parsimoniously and comprehensively accounts for the data, and that such a theoretical model actually incorporates the other theoretical perspectives. In this chapter, the relative strengths of the various models with regard to the adult literature are not evaluated. Rather, the potential of each theory for predicting children's reactions to aid and developmental changes in these reactions is briefly discussed.

Equity Theories

According to theoretical formulations concerning equity and social exchange (Walster *et al.*, 1978; see Greenfield and Hatfield chapters in this volume), people attempt to maintain equity in their interpersonal interactions. Inequitable relations are viewed as producing discomfort that motivates individuals to try to dispel their negative feelings by either actually restoring equity (e.g., by reciprocating) or distorting one's own cognitive perceptions of a situation so as to achieve psychological equity. As applied to helping situations, recipients of aid are believed to experience negative effect when they have a more favorable ratio of outputs to inputs than does the benefactor (especially if the aid is costly and valuable).

The fact that children tend to reciprocate prosocial behaviors is consistent with equity theory's predictions but also can be explained by means of other mechanisms (e.g., norms relating to reciprocity or the desire for future rewards). Thus, at this time, I know of no research in which the relevance of equity theory's predictions for interpreting children's reactions to aid has been directly tested. However, based on the data concerning children's allocations of a reward, one can make some tentative comments concerning the relevance of equity theory for understanding children's help-receiving behaviors.

Hook and Cook (1979) demonstrated via a review of the literature that children younger than 6 years generally make allocations that reflect either self-interest or the desire for equality (rather than equity in the relation of rewards to inputs). In contrast, 6- to 12-year-olds most often distribute rewards based on *ordinal equity* (their allocations are in the direction that would be predicted by equity theory—i.e., according to deservedness of the various individuals—but rewards are not directly proportional to deservedness). Individuals 13 years of older may be capable of allocating rewards according to *proportional equity* (i.e., their rewards accurately reflect the various individuals' inputs). If these data are interpreted as indicative of how much children's behaviors are influenced by equity considerations, one would conclude that children younger than 6 years of age infrequently will react to aid in ways consistent with equity theory's predictions. In addition, one would expect that application of the theory's postulates would be increasingly evident in behavior with age. Thus, as was previously suggested, it is unlikely that young children's reciprocity of prosocial behavior is due solely to equity considerations, and equity theory probably does not, by itself, account for the variations in even elementary-school children's reactions to aid. Of course, it is possible that equity considerations influence children's reactions to aid at a different point in development than when they affect the distribution of rewards. Little is currently known about the role of equity considerations across various circumstances.

Reactance Theory

According to reactance theory formulations (Brehm, 1966), individuals are motivated to maintain their freedom of choice, and perceived threats to that freedom result in a negative psychological state (reactance). As applied to individuals' reactions to aid, the theory suggests that recipients will react negatively to aid that is perceived as limiting present or future actions (for example, by inducing feelings of indebtness on the part of the recipient that would force the recipient to behave positively toward the benefactor in the future).

The literature on reactance in children is limited in quantity. However, the existing data are consistent with the conclusion that elementary school children and adolescents sometimes exhibit reactance in response to threats to their freedom (Brehm, 1981; Staub, 1979). Furthermore, there is evidence consistent with the conclusion that even preschool children (particularly boys) sometimes exhibit reactance; for example, they oppose physical barriers or the agent who has implemented the barrier (see Brehm, 1981). Thus, it is possible that young children might react negatively to assistance because they feel that receipt of aid will restrict their freedom. However, the ability of young children to make inferences regarding implicit threats to their own freedom and others' manipulativeness is questionable because children's inferential skills are relatively limited until the middle elementary school years (Karniol & Ross, 1979; Ruble & Rholes, in press; Shantz, 1975). Moreover, once children are able to process potential threats to their freedom, it is questionable how much they will weigh such threats against the concrete benefits received from help. It is questionable also whether threats to one's freedom as a result of help are, indeed, an important motivator of children's behavior.

Attribution Theories

The attributional theories of Jones and Davis (1965), Kelley (1967), and others frequently have been used to predict the conditions under which adults attribute different motives to a donor for his or her behavior, and if the recipient's state of need is attributed to the environment or to personal characteristics of the recipient. These attributional processes have been used to explain why adult recipients behave in different ways in different situations. Much of the relevant literature related to children's inferences regarding helpers and recipients of help has been reviewed earlier in this chapter. Although there is little empirical evidence directly linking children's inferential capacities to their own behavioral reactions to aid, it is likely that their reactions reflect their understanding of others and others' motives. Furthermore, because children can make some simple inferences regarding motives even in the preschool years, attributional models may have predictive potential for even very young children.

It is likely that the tenets of attribution theories will prove to be extremely useful in delineating and explaining children's reactions to aid and developmental changes in these reactions. This prediction is based on the facts that attributional theories are relevant to a wide range of social behaviors produced in a variety of environments and that attributional processes go through marked changes during childhood. As was attempted earlier in this chapter, one can use information regarding these developmental changes in children's inferential abilities to make a range of predictions regarding children's reactions to aid in different circumstances. However, at this time, the fruitfulness of attributionally based predictions awaits empirical verification.

Threats to Self-esteem Theory

The threat to self-esteem perspective has been most clearly articulated by Fisher and Nadler (see Fisher, Nadler, & Whitcher-Alagna in this volume). According to this model, the consequences of aid for the self are critical in determining a recipient's reaction. More specifically, aid potentially contains a mixture of self-threatening and supportive elements. Assistance sometimes is perceived as threatening because it seems to imply inferiority on the part of the recipient in relation to the benefactor, and because help-receiving is not consistent with the values of self-reliance and independence that are stressed during socialization in Western culture. Conversely, aid may be viewed as supportive because it frequently involves instrumental benefits (for example, possessions, suggestions) and the act of assisting may communicate concern on the part of the benefactor for the recipient. Whether aid is perceived as threatening or supportive is presumed to be due to a number of factors, such as situational conditions and recipient or donor characteristics. Furthermore, according to the model, help that is interpreted as self-supportive elicits positive, nondefensive responses, whereas aid that is viewed as threatening tends to produce defensive reactions. Attributional processes frequently are involved in determining whether a situation is perceived as threatening or supportive but, unlike in attributional theories, these attributions are more focused on the self than on others' behaviors and motives.

The threat to self-esteem theory, like attributional theories, has the advantage of being applicable to a diverse range of situations and can be linked to several processes involving clear, dramatic developmental changes. Thus, as for attributional theories, it is likely that the threat to self-esteem model will prove to be productive to the researcher examining the developmental course of children's reactions to aid. However, as was previously discussed, young children infrequently use situational and social comparison information to draw conclusions about the self and one's own performance (at least in achievement situations; Boggiano & Ruble, 1979; Nicholls, 1979; Ruble et al., 1980), although occasionally they do make such comparisons (Mostache & Bragonier, 1981). Moreover, they appear to be somewhat oblivious to both the implications and the appropriateness of helping in various situations (Barnett et al., 1982). These data suggest that children younger than 7–8 years of age should be relatively impervious to the self-threatening components of aid, at least to those aspects processed by adults. It is possible, however, that young children are threatened by the actual receipt of (or offer of) aid in a domain in which they feel they should be competent. Actual offers of aid may be less subtle cues of incompetence than are other situational and social comparison cues. At this time, the usefulness of self-esteem theory for explaining young children's reactions to aid is unclear.

CONCLUSIONS

Undoubtedly, more questions regarding the development of children's reactions to aid are raised by the literature reviewed in this chapter than are answered. Although there is sufficient research on which to formulate some hypotheses regarding children's reactions, there are few data to either verify or disprove predictions. Indeed, if the study of recipients' reactions to aid is characterized as being in its infancy, the examination of the development of reactions to aid during childhood must be viewed as being in the early stages of embryonic development.

At this time, much of the research involves self-report and, therefore, is vulnerable to social desirability effects and unintentional inaccuracies. Furthermore, many of the studies concern children's help-seeking rather than their reactions to receiving help. Moreover, the few studies in which children's reactions to aid have been assessed tend to be experimental in nature and concern reciprocity; consequently, these studies provide little information regarding the range of responses to aid emitted in the natural environment.

What kinds of data are needed to further our understanding of the development of recipients reactions to aid? Clearly, both descriptive and explanatory data are lacking. At the present time, we do not even know at what age children react to receiving aid, in which circumstances they react positively versus negatively, and what age-related changes in their responses can be observed. In brief, we do not even have the data to describe the form or shape of the phenomenon of interest.

The dearth of relevant data is especially evident for infants and very young children; although there is a limited amount of data on help-seeking behaviors, systematic observation of very young children's reactions to aid has been extremely rare. Thus, at this time, the greatest need would seem to be for descriptive data regarding children's (especially infants' and very young children's) reactions to aid in the natural environment; for example, their reactions to parents' and teachers' attempts to assist them at home and school. When such data are available, researchers will be better able to formulate hypotheses regarding the determinants of children's reactions to aid and to test their predictions. Only if researchers are aware of the origins of reactions to aid—that is, the frequency, mode, and quality of children's reactions to aid—can they accurately trace the progression from childhood to adult modes of responding.

REFERENCE NOTE

1. Eisenberg, N., Cameron, E., Tryon, K., & Dodez, R., Socialization of prosocial behavior in the preschool class. Unpublished data, Arizona State University, 1981.

REFERENCES

Ainsworth, M. D. S. The development of infant–mother attachment. In B. M. Caldwell & H. N. Ricciuti (Eds.), *Review of child development research* (Vol. 3). Chicago, Illinois: University of Chicago Press, 1973.

Ainsworth, M. D., Blehar, M. C., Waters, E., & Wall, S. *Patterns of attachment: A psychological study of the strange situation.* Hillsdale, New Jersey: Lawrence Erlbaum Associates, 1978.

Bachman, R. Elementary school children's perception of helpers and their characteristics. *Elementary School Guidance and Counseling,* 1975, December, 103–109.

Baldwin, C. P., & Baldwin, A. L. Children's judgments of kindness. *Child Development,* 1970, **41**, 29–47.

Barnett, K., Darcie, G., Holland, C. J., & Kobasigawa. Children's cognitions about effective helping. *Developmental Psychology.* 1982, **18**, 151–173.

Barton, E. J., Olszewski, M. J., & Madsen, J. J. The effects of adult presence on the prosocial behavior of preschool children. *Child Behavior Therapy,* 1979, **1**, 271–286.

Benson, N. C., Hartmann, D. P., & Gelfand, D. M. *Intentions and children's moral judgments.* Paper presented at the Biennial meeting of the Society for Research in Child Development, Boston, Massachusetts, April, 1981.

Berkowitz, L. Responsibility, reciprocity, and social distance in help-giving: An experimental investigation of English social class differences. *Journal of Experimental Social Psychology,* 1968, **4**, 46–63.

Berkowitz, L., & Friedman, P. Some social class differences in helping behavior. *Journal of Personality and Social Psychology,* 1967, **5**, 217–225.

Block, J. H. Conceptions of sex-role: Some cross-cultural and longitudinal perspectives. *American Psychologist,* 1973, **28**, 512–526.

Boehm, L. The development of independence: A comparative study. *Child Development,* 1957, **28**, 85–92.

Boggiano, A. K., & Ruble, D. N. Perceptions of competence and the overjustification effect: A developmental study. *Journal of Personality and Social Psychology,* 1979, **37**, 1462–1468.

Brehm, J. W. *A theory of psychological reactance.* New York: Academic Press, 1966.

Brehm, S. Oppositional behavior in children: A reactance theory approach. In S. S. Brehm, S. M. Kassin, & F. X. Gibbons (Eds.), *Developmental social psychology: Theory and research.* London and New York: Oxford University Press, 1981.

Broll, L., Gross, A. E., & Piliavin, I. Effects of offered and requested help on help-seeking and reactions to being helped. *Journal of Applied Social Psychology,* 1974, **4**, 244–258.

Brown, A. L. Semantic integration in children's reconstruction of narrative sequences. *Cognitive Psychology,* 1976, **8**, 247–262.

Bryant, B. K., & Crockenberg, S. B. Correlates and dimensions of prosocial behavior: A study of female siblings with their mothers. *Child Development,* 1980, **51**, 529–544.

Charlesworth, R., & Hartup. W. W. Positive social reinforcement in the nursery school peer group. *Child Development,* 1967, **38**, 993–1002.

Clark, A., Hocevar, D., & Dembo, M. H. The role of cognitive development in children's explanations and preferences of skin color. *Developmental Psychology,* 1980, **16**, 332–339.

Clark, K. B., & Clark, M. P. Racial identification and preference in Negro children. In T. M. Newcomb & E. L. Hartley (Eds.), *Readings in social psychology.* New York: Holt, 1947.

Cohen, E. A., Gelfand, D. M., & Hartmann, D. P. Causal reasoning as a function of behavioral consequences. *Child Development.* 1981, **52**, 514–522.

Cox, N. Prior help, ego development, and helping behavior. *Child Development,* 1974, **45**, 594–603.

DePaulo, B. M. Accepting help from teachers—When the teachers are children. *Human Relations,* 1978, **31**, 459–474. (a)

DePaulo, B. M. Accuracy in predicting situational variations in help-seekers' responses. *Personality and Social Psychology Bulletin,* 1978, **4**, 330–333. (b)

DePaulo, B. M. Help-seeking from the recipient's point of view. *JSAS Catalog of Selected Documents in Psychology,* 1978, **8**, 62 (MS. No. 1721). (c)

DiVitto, B., & McArthur, L. Z. Developmental differences in the use of distinctiveness, consensus, and consistency information in making causal judgments. *Developmental Psychology,* 1978, **14**, 474–482.

Dreman, S. B. Sharing behavior in Israeli school children: Cognitive and social learning factors. *Child Development,* 1976, **47**, 186–194.

Dreman, S. B., & Greenbaum, C. W. Altuism or reciprocity: Sharing behavior in Israeli kindergarten children. *Child Development,* 1973, **44**, 61–68.

Eisenberg, N., Cameron, E., Tryon, K., & Dodez, R. Socialization of prosocial behavior in the preschool classroom. *Developmental Psychology.* 1981, **17**, 773–782.

Eisenberg-Berg, N., & Giallanzo, S. J. Components of successful proprietary behavior among preschool children. Unpublished manuscript, 1981.

Eisenberg-Berg, N., & Hand, M. The relationship of preschoolers' reasoning about prosocial moral conflicts to prosocial behavior. *Child Development,* 1979, **50**, 356–363.

Eisenberg-Berg, N., & Neal, C. The effects of person of the protagonist and costs of helping on children's moral judgment. *Personality and Social Psychology Bulletin,* 1981, **7**, 17–23.

Fagot, B. I. Consequences of moderate cross-gender behavior in preschool children. *Child Development,* 1977, **48**, 902–907.

Fagot, B. I. The influence of sex of child on parental reactions to toddler children. *Child Development,* 1978, **49**, 459–465.

Feldman, N. S., & Ruble, D. N. The development of person perception: Cognitive and social factors. In S. S. Brehm, S. M. Kassin, & P. X. Gibbons (Eds.), *Developmental social psychology: Theory and research.* London and New York: Oxford University Press, 1981.

Fisher, J. D., & Nadler, A. Donor similarity and one's beliefs about the nature of their problem as determinants of recipient reactions to aid. In T. A. Wills (Ed.), *Basic processes in helping relationships.* New York: Academic Press, 1982.

Fisher, J. D., Nadler, A., & Whitcher-Alagna, S. J. Recipients' reactions to aid. *Psychological Bulletin,* 1982, **91**, 27–54.

Floyd, J. M. K. Effects of amount of reward and friendship status of the other on the frequency of sharing in children. Unpublished doctoral dissertation, University of Minnesota, 1964.

Furman, W., & Masters, J. C. Affective consequences of social reinforcement, punishment, and neutral behavior. *Developmental Psychology,* 1980, **16**, 100–104.

Garrett, J., & Libby, W. L. Role of intentionality in mediating responses to inequity in the dyad. *Journal of Personality and Social Psychology,* 1973, **28**, 1–27.

Gouldner, A. W. The norm of reciprocity: A preliminary statement. *American Sociological Review,* 1960, **25**, 161–178.

Hall, J. D. Gender effects in decoding nonverbal cues. *Psychological Bulletin,* 1978, **45**, 845–959.

Heider, F. *The psychology of interpersonal relation.* New York: Wiley, 1958.

Hoffman, M. L. Sex differences in empathy and related behaviors. *Psychological Bulletin,* 1977, **54**, 712–722.

Hook, J. G., & Cook, T. D. Equity theory and the cognitive ability of children. *Psychological Bulletin,* 1979, **86**, 429–445.

Iannotti, R. J. *Prosocial behavior, perspective taking, and empathy in preschool children: An evaluation of naturalistic and structured settings.* Paper presented at the Bieenial Meeting of the Society for Research in Child Development, Boston, Massachusetts, April, 1981.

Jensen, L. C., & Hughston, K. The relationship between type of sanction, story content, and children's judgments which are independent of action. *The Journal of Genetic Psychology*, 1973, **122**, 49–54.

Jones, E. E., & Davis, K. E. From acts to dispositions: The attributional process in person perception. In L. Berkowitz (Ed.), *Advances in experimental social psychology* (Vol. 2). New York: Academic Press, 1965.

Karniol, R. Children's use of intention cues in evaluation behavior. *Psychological Bulletin*, 1978, **85**, 76–85.

Karniol, R., & Ross, M. Children's use of a causal attribution schema and the inference of manipulative intentions. *Child Development*, 1979, **50**, 463–468.

Keasey, C. B. Children's developing awareness and usage of intentionality and motives. In H. E. Howe, Jr. (Ed.), *Nebraska symposium on motiviation*. Lincoln, Nebraska: University of Nebraska Press, 1967.

Kelley, H. H. Attribution theory in social psychology. In D. Levine (Ed.), *Nebraska symposium on motivation*. (Vol. 15). Lincoln, Nebraska: University of Nebraska Press, 1967.

Lamb, M. E. Interactions between eighteen-month-olds and their preschool-aged siblings. *Child Development*, 1978, **49**, 51–59. (a)

Lamb, M. E. The development of sibling relationships in infancy: A short-term longitudinal study. *Child Development*, 1978, **49**, 1189–1196. (b)

Leahy, R. L. Development of conceptions of prosocial behavior: Information affecting rewards given for altruism and kindness. *Developmental Psychology*, 1979, **15**, 34–37.

Marcus, R. F., & Jenny, B. A naturalistic study of reciprocity in the helping behavior of young children. *The Alberta Journal of Educational Research*, 1977, **23**, 195–206.

Morse, S. J., Gergen, K. J., Peele, S., & Van Ryneveld, J. Reactions to receiving expected and unexpected help from a person who violated or does not violate a norm. *Journal of Experimental Social Psychology*, 1977, **13**, 397–402.

Mostache, H. S., & Bragonier, P. An observational study of social comparison in preschoolers. *Child Development*, 1981, **52**, 376–378.

Nadler, A., & Porat, I. When names do not help: Effects of anonymity and locus of need attribution on help-seeking behavior. *Personality and Social Psychology Bulletin*, 1978, **4**, 624–626.

Nemeth, C. Effects of free versus constrained behavior on attraction between people. *Journal of Personality and Social Psychology*, 1970, **15**, 302–311.

Nicholls, J. G. The development of the concepts of effort and ability, perception, and the understanding that difficult tasks require more ability. *Child Development*, 1978, **49**, 800–814.

Nicholls, J. G. The development of perception of own attainment and causal attributions for success and failure in reading. *Journal of Educational Psychology*, 1979, **71**, 94–99.

Northman, J. Developmental changes in preferences for help. *Journal of Clinical Child Psychology*, 1978, 129–132.

Pastor, D. L. the quality of mother–infant attachment and its relationship to toddlers' initial sociability with peers. *Developmental Psychology*, 1981, **17**, 326–335.

Peterson, L. Developmental changes in verbal and behavioral sensitivity to cues of social norms of altruism. *Child Development*, 1980, **51**, 830–838.

Peterson, L., Hartmann, D. P., & Gelfand, D. M. Developmental changes in the effects of dependency and reciprocity cues on children's moral judgments and donation rates. *Child Development*, 1977, **48**, 1331–1339.

Piaget, J. *The moral judgment of the child.* New York: Free Press, 1965. (First published in London: Keagen Paul, 1932).

Raviv, A., Bar-Tal, D., Ayalon, H., & Raviv, A. Perception of giving and receiving help by group members. Unpublished manuscript, Tel-Aviv University, 1980.

Rholes, W. S., Blackwell, J., Jordan, C., & Walters, C. A developmental study of learned helplessness. *Developmental Psychology,* 1980, **16**, 616–624.

Rogers-Warren, A., & Baer, D. M. Correspondence between saying and doing: Teaching children to share and praise. *Journal of Applied Behavior Analysis,* 1976, **9**, 335–354.

Roopnarine, J. L. *Consequences of peer and teacher responses to the sex-typed activities of preschoolers.* Paper presented at the Biennial Meeting of The Society for Research in Child Development, Boston, Massachusetts, April, 1981.

Rotenberg, K. J. Development of character constancy of self and other. *Child Development,* 1982, *53,* 505–515.

Ruble, D. N., Boggiano, A. K., Feldman, N. S., & Loebl, J. H. Developmental analysis of the role of social comparison in self-evaluation. *Developmental Psychology,* 1980, **16**, 105–115.

Ruble, D. N., Feldman, N. S., & Boggiano, A. G. Social comparison between young children in achievement situations. *Developmental Psychology,* 1976, **12**, 192–197.

Ruble, D. N., Parsons, J. E., & Ross, J. Self-evaluation responses of children in an achievement setting. *Child Development,* 1976, **47**, 990–997.

Ruble, D. N., & Rholes, W. S. The development of children's perceptions and attributions about their social world. In J. H. Harvey, W. J. Ickes, & R. F. Kidd (Eds.), *New directions in attributional research* (Vol. 3). Hillsdale, New Jersey: Lawrence Erlbaum and Associates, in press.

Shantz, C. U. The development of social cognition. In E. M. Heatherington (Ed.), *Review of child development research* (Vol. 5). Chicago, Illinois: University of Chicago Press, 1975.

Shultz, T. R., & Butkowsky, I. Young children's use of the scheme for multiple sufficient causes in the attribution of real and hypothetical behavior. *Child Development,* 1977, **48**, 464–469.

Shure, M. B. Fairness, generosity, and selfishness: The naive psychology of children and young adults. *Child Development* 1968, **30**, 857–886.

Staub, E. *Positive social behavior and morality: Socialization and development* (Vol. 2). New York: Academic Press, 1979.

Staub, E., & Feinberg, H. K. *Regularities in peer interaction, empathy, and sensitivity to others.* Paper presented at the Annual Meeting of the American Psychological Association, Montreal, September, 1980.

Staub, E., & Noerenberg, H. Property rights, deservedness, reciprocity, friendship: The transactional nature of children's sharing behavior. *Journal of Personality and Social psychology,* 1981, **40**, 271–289.

Staub, E., & Sherk, L. Need for approval, children's sharing behavior, and reciprocity in sharing. *Child Development,* 1971, **41**, 243–252.

Stephen, W. G. Cognitive differentiation in intergroup perception. *Sociometry,* 1977, **40**, 50–58.

Suls, J., Witenberg, S., & Gutkin, D. Evaluating reciprocal and nonreciprocal prosocial behavior: Developmental changes. *Personality and Social Psychology Bulletin,* 1981, **7**, 25–31.

Walster, E., Walster, G. W., & Berscheid, E. *Equity: Theory and research.* Boston, Massachusetts: Allyn and Bacon, 1978.

Youniss, J. *Parents and peers in social development: A Sullivan–Piaget perspective.* Chicago, Illinois: University of Chicago Press, 1980.

PART IV

Determinants of Reactions to Aid

CHAPTER 9

The Effects of Help
on Task Performance
in Achievement Contexts*

Bella M. DePaulo
Pamela L. Brown
James M. Greenberg

Ordinarily, help is meant to work. Tutors want their tutees to learn, teachers want their classes to excel, and study counselors want their clients to face their academic challenges confidently and effectively. Benevolent interests are also assumed to govern helping transactions that are not role required —for example, classmates helping each other with homework. Al-

*Preparation of this chapter was supported in part by grants from the Foundation for Child Development and the National Academy of Education. We thank Judith Harackiewicz, James Pennebaker, Timothy D. Wilson, and Steve Worchel for their comments on earlier drafts.

Correspondence should be addressed to Bella M. DePaulo, Department of Psychology, Gilmer Hall, University of Virginia, Charlottesville, Virginia, 22901.

223

though perversions of the helping process are plentiful (as, for example, when a co-worker's assistance serves more to flaunt his or her own competence than to aid the recipient), it is generally assumed that these are the unfortunate exceptions rather than the rule, and that help not only is meant to work, but often really does work.

Indeed, help sometimes does work well. Recipients solve their current problem (or attain their current goal), and they sometimes go on to attempt other problems that are even more difficult than the one for which help was received. Other times, however, help seems to be markedly ineffective. It is the purpose of this chapter to explore some of the conditions under which help is most likely to be effective in facilitating rather than impairing task performance, in stimulating interest in the problem at hand (and related problems) rather than undermining it, and in furthering long-term self-sufficiency rather than dependency. Although the issue of effectiveness is relevant to all helping domains, the primary focus in this chapter will be on informal helping transactions in achievement-related contexts (see also Allen's review [in press] of research and theory on peer tutoring and Rosen's analysis [in press] of the role of competence concerns in helping interactions).

Occasionally, the most "helpful" type of help that individuals can receive is that which enables them to accept unavoidable failure at a task, or to redirect their energies toward a different and more suitable task than the one in which they are currently engaged. In this chapter, however, we deal primarily with the effects of help on task performance when successful task performance is an appropriate and attainable goal.

The major thrust of the chapter is theoretical. We begin by discussing some basic definitional issues, then proceed to outline a preliminary formulation for predicting the effects of help on task performance. An experimental investigation of several of the predictions generated from the formulation will also be reported.

DEFINITIONAL ISSUES

Effectiveness

Implicit in the foregoing discussion were certain criteria for ascertaining effectiveness (see also Brickman, Kidder, Coates, Rabinowitz, Cohn, & Karuza, this volume, and Coates, Renzaglia, & Embree, this volume). One such criterion is concrete and immediate: the recipients improve in their attempts to solve the problems for which they received help. This criterion—enhanced problem-solving success—will often be the most important indicator of the effectiveness of help. However, other performance-relevant reactions might also be regarded as telling indexes of the effectiveness of aid. For example, subsequent to receiving help, students might solve problems more quickly, more easily, and with greater enthusiasm. Help that is effective, then, might make problem solving a more pleasant experience.

If the problems for which students receive help are the only ones they will ever need to solve, then the effectiveness of aid can be assessed exhaustively by measures of performance taken on that particular problem set at that particular point in time. More often, however, recipients receive help with only a limited subset of the total set of problems that they might need to solve, and the problems are of a sort that the recipients will need to solve on other occasions as well as in the present context. This suggests that in assessing the effectiveness of aid, two types of generalizability should be considered: (1) generalizability across problem types, and (2) generalizability over time and context. Thus, if a student in a tutoring session received help on one particular type of problem, then showed improvement in solving that type of problem and another type of problem, generalizability across problem types would be demonstrated. Further, if the student performed especially well on both types of problems not only on the quiz given in that particular tutoring session, but also on the exam given in class, then generalized effectiveness over time and context would also be evidenced.

In sum, help can facilitate or impair task performance in the present and in the future, on the particular problems for which help was given, and on other types of problems.

Help

Instrumental Help

We discuss two major forms of help that occur in achievement contexts: instrumental help and noninstrumental help (see also Gergen and Gergen, this volume, and Morse, this volume, for other discussions of definitional issues). Task-relevant instrumental elements are the defining feature of *instrumental help*. Instrumental elements are cues that are directly relevant to the solution of the problem at hand. They are cues that give the recipient an answer, an explanation, or a hint as to how to do the task. Occasionally, a cue that appears to have instrumental qualities is actually misleading—as, for example, when an incorrect answer is given. We would still regard this as an instance of instrumental help if the instrumental element (i.e., the answer) was intended by the helper to facilitate the recipient's task performance, or if it was perceived by the recipient as potentially facilitative of task performance.

Help is indirectly instrumental if it allows the recipient increased opportunities to work at the problematic task, without at the same time providing any indication as to how to achieve greater success at the task. For example, a number of studies conducted by Nadler, Fisher, and their associates (e.g., Fisher & Nadler, 1974; Nadler, Altman, & Fisher, 1979) involved a stock market game in which poker chips were used as investment currency. The subjects, who were led to believe that they were losing badly (i.e., they had very few chips left at the end of the first investment period), received help in the form of additional chips sent to them by their pairmate. These chips enabled the recipients to remain in the game, but they provided no information as to how to invest more wisely.

When help is instrumental, the extent to which it works should be determined, to a considerable degree, by the value of its instrumental elements. (*Value* is defined by criteria such as accuracy, informativeness, and suitability to the recipient's current level of task competence; see following discussion.) However, the contribution of this relatively objective factor (value) to the eventual effectiveness of help might be less than one might at first expect. This is because help rarely, if ever, includes only instrumental cues. Instead, help tends to be infused with a variety of affective and evaluative meanings other than those that pertain directly to the mechanics of task performance. From the way in which the help is given, from the characteristics of the person who is giving it, and from the context in which it is given, as well as from the help itself, recipients often try to infer answers to such questions as, What does the helper think of me? What do other observers of the helping interaction think? Why did I need the help? Why did the helper give me help? What should I think of myself now that I've received help on this task? If I am successful in solving these kinds of problems in the future, will people attribute my success to the help? Could I have solved these problems without the help? Will I able to solve them even with the help?[1] The impact of these affective and evaluative overtones on the help-recipient's task performance can be quite substantial, enhancing or dampening the effect that might have resulted from the instrumental cues alone.

---

[1] We acknowledge that the effects of help on recipients' expectations for success might be considered to be a cognitive consequence of aid rather than an affective, evaluative, or motivational implication of aid. We use terms such as *affective and evaluative implications* as convenient shorthands that are already a bit too inconvenient and long.

Noninstrumental Help

Instrumental help usually includes both instrumental cues and evaluative cues.[2] However, messages that do not provide the recipient with task-relevant cues or resources can still be regarded as help if they are intended by the helper to facilitate the recipient's task performance, or if they are perceived by the recipient as potentially facilitative of successful task performance. This class of help is called *noninstrumental help.*

The category of noninstrumental help subsumes a wide variety of urgings, prods, exhortations, and words of encouragement. For example, a teacher or friend could suggest to floundering students that they simply are not trying hard enough (e.g., see Dweck & Licht, 1980), or that they need to take a more active role in figuring out for themselves how to solve challenging problems (see also Brickman, Rabinowitz, Karuza, Coates, Cohn, & Kidder, in press; Brickman *et al.,* this volume; Coates *et al.,* this volume); or that many other students have also had similar difficulties at first, but eventually did quite well (Wilson & Linville, 1982). Finally, the teacher or friend could decide that the distraught problem-solver simply needs to be distracted for a while, or to be coaxed into a better mood; efforts might then be initiated toward those ends. Not one of these diverse forms of help includes any instrumental cues or task-relevant resources. Thus, the power of noninstrumental help to affect task performance inheres entirely in its affective, evaluative, and motivational aspects.

PREDICTORS OF EFFECTIVENESS

In the following sections, we argue that the extent to which help works depends on three factors: (1) the *value* of the instrumental components of the help; (2) the recipient's relative *attentiveness* to the instrumental elements of the help, as compared to the affective and evaluative components; and (3) the *motivational properties* of the help—that is, the degree to which help is perceived by the recipient as having the potential to increase the probability or desirability of goal attainment. The value and attentiveness factors are relevant primarily to instrumental help, whereas the motivational factors are important predictors of the effectiveness of both instrumental and noninstrumental help.

---

[2]This is because the instrumental components of help almost always carry evaluative implications. For example, a very detailed explanation is an instrumental cue that can carry the implication that the recipient is not capable of benefiting from an explanation that is less detailed.

Value of the Instrumental Cues

The degree to which help works is of course determined in part by the value of the instrumental components of the help. Several straightforward criteria can be used to establish the instrumental value of help. These include informativeness, accuracy, appropriateness, clarity, and generality.

Informativeness refers to the extensiveness of the instrumental benefits conveyed by the help. For example, a tutor who explained three of the four steps in a problem solution would be giving more informative help than someone who explained only one or two of the steps. The *accuracy* criterion is satisfied if the instrumental cues are valid rather than misleading. *Appropriateness* encompasses several criteria: For help to be effective, its instrumental components should be (1) constructed at a level of complexity that is appropriate to the recipient's sophistication at the task, and (2) well adapted to the recipient's specific needs. Thus, even a valid and informative explanation is likely to be of little instrumental value if it is too difficult for the recipient to understand, or if it refers to an aspect of the problem that the recipient had already solved.

Clarity is a characteristic of the way that the instrumental benefits are conveyed. Messages that are carefully structured and well timed will tend to meet the clarity criterion. Finally, an instrumental benefit characterized by a high level of *generality* is one that can be applied to the solution of other problems in addition to the troublesome ones in question.

Attention to Instrumental versus Evaluative Cues

In order for instrumental cues to be effective, the help recipient must attend to these cues and to their relationship to the task at hand. Often, however, attention to instrumental cues competes with attention to affective and evaluative cues. Affective and evaluative cues can either facilitate or impair task performance. When evaluative cues are potential enhancers of task performance, they detract from recipients' attention to the instrumental aspects of the help and of the task only momentarily; this is because the eventual effect of motivating (enhancing) evaluative cues is to return the recipient's attention to the problem-solving task (see following discussion). To the extent that evaluative cues are potentially detrimental to task performance, however, the recipient would do well to ignore those cues and focus instead on the instrumental cues and on the task. It will be important, then, to begin to determine the predictors of attentiveness to instrumental versus evaluative cues.

In developing a framework for predicting relative attentiveness to af-fective–evaluative versus instrumental aspects of help, it is important to acknowledge that recipients' attention may also be turned toward cues that are not inherent in the help itself. For example, recipients might focus on the task (e.g., they might try to figure out alternative problem-solving strat-egies), or on their performance at that task (e.g., how well they are doing compared to others, and how much they are improving), or on the im-plications of their performance (e.g., what it implies about their general level of intelligence; what others will think of it) or on their bodies (e.g., signs of anxiety, arousal, physical symptoms, or specific emotions), or on the possibilities for escape (e.g., how much longer they have to work on the problems, and what they plan to do when they finish the problems). We expect that attention to instrumental aspects of help will be correlated with attention to the task itself, and to changes in one's own level of success at that task over time. Attention to evaluative aspects of help, on the other hand, should correlate positively with attention to the performance of oth-ers, to the evaluations that others might be making of oneself, to one's own bodily sensations, and to the possibilities of escape.

Individual Differences

Certain individual differences may be important predictors of recipi-ents' focus of attention. The strongest theoretical and empirical foundation from which to make predictions about the impact of recipient character-istics on attentiveness is the literature on test anxiety. That literature is es-pecially relevant to the present formulation because it makes predictions about task performance in achievement contexts, and because it, too, ac-cords an important status to variables such as evaluative concerns and focus of attention.

Early research documented marked performance deficits among highly test-anxious people in stressful and evaluative testing situations (Wine, 1971). Differential performance of high versus low test-anxious individuals was attributed to differences in their focus of attention. Whereas lows con-centrate primarily on the task, highs tend to be preoccupied with themselves (particularly their inadequacies) and with other concerns that are irrelevant to the task itself. Subsequent studies showed that the characteristic behav-iors of highly test-anxious people are not specific to formal testing situa-tions; rather, "Persons who score high on measures of test anxiety . . . typically interpret a wide range of situations as evaluative and react with cognitive concern and performance deficits" (Wine, 1980, p. 351). From the test-anxiety literature, then, it can be predicted that high test-anxious help recipients, compared to lows, will (1) focus more on the evaluative aspects of aid than on the instrumental elements; (2) be biased toward interpreting the evaluative aspects of the aid in a self-deprecatory manner; and (3) tend to perform more poorly after receiving help.

Other kinds of individuals who might be expected to be particularly attentive to evaluative aspects of aid are people who are seeking approval, who look to others for cues to appropriate behavior, who are sensitive to subtle interpersonal messages (perhaps particularly negatively tinged messages), and who respond to failure by giving up rather than by trying harder. Thus, need for approval (Crowne & Marlowe, 1964), self- monitoring (Snyder, 1974), differential nonverbal sensitivity (DePaulo & Fisher, 1981; see also DePaulo, Brittingham, & Kaiser, in press) and a problem-solving orientation of helplessness rather than mastery (Dweck & Licht, 1980) should predict evaluative concern in helping interactions and relative deficits in performance subsequent to the receipt of help. Attentiveness to instrumental cues, on the other hand, should be predicted by achievement motivation (Atkinson & Raynor, 1974; McClelland, Atkinson, Clark, & Lowell, 1953), feelings of self-efficacy (Bandura, 1977), intellectual self-esteem, and preferences for challenge and independent mastery (Harter, 1981).

Although no research has directly tested any of the above predictions regarding individual differences in focus of attention during helping interactions, several studies are suggestive. Two studies have demonstrated that individuals who are reluctant to ask for help (compared to more willing help-seekers), as measured either by their own reports (DePaulo & Rosenthal, 1979), or by their behaviors (DePaulo & Fisher, 1981), are especially sensitive to covert nonverbal cues. In helping interactions, covert cues include cues that a helper is trying to hide—e.g., signs of resentment at being asked to help. It was suggested that helping interactions might be especially aversive to recipients who are particularly sensitive to certain kinds of affective and evaluative cues.

The other suggestive study was one in which subjects were given an opportunity to ask for help after their self-esteem had been experimentally manipulated (Morris & Rosen, 1973). In their open-ended responses to a questionnaire asking why they had or had not asked for help, subjects who were made to feel competent tended to give instrumental, task-oriented responses (e.g., they asked for help in order to facilitate task-completion, or refrained from seeking help in order to meet the challenge of the task completely independently), whereas those who were made to feel inadequate tended to describe feelings of embarrassment and incompetence, and concerns about how the helper might respond to their help request.

Situational Variables

Complementing individual-difference variables is an array of situational variables that can ward off certain evaluative concerns before they develop, or make affective aspects of help less salient. Among the most important situational variables in achievement contexts may be those that foster in the problem-solving individuals an orientation of either ego-involvement or task-involvement. Task- involvement is defined somewhat differently in the literatures on achievement and intrinsic motivation. Achievement researchers such as Ames (in press) and Nicholls (1979) describe task-involvement as the orientation of problem solvers who are attempting to learn new tasks and to improve upon their own past performance. These problem solvers tend to focus on the task itself and on information relevant to the task. They should be particularly attuned to the instrumental aspects of help when the help that they receive is well timed and well adapted to their specific needs.

From a motivational perspective, task-involved problem solvers are captivated by the *process* of learning and mastery. Tasks that are interesting, challenging, and novel often foster this orientation by engaging people's intrinsic urge for mastery (e.g., de Charms, 1968; Harter, 1982; Ryan, 1982; White, 1959). Help offered to such intrinsically motivated problem solvers is likely to be perceived by recipients as subtly pressuring them to abandon their highly pleasurable process-oriented activity in favor of a perhaps less attractive outcome-oriented mode. In these instances, recipients' attention will be drawn to the affective and evaluative implications of aid rather than its task-relevant benefits. The instrumental aspects are likely to be noticed and utilized effectively only if help is carefully designed to bring a task that is already somewhat engaging to a level of interest, challenge, or novelty that is optimal for the recipient.

Ego-involvement is an orientation toward problem solving that can be fostered by situational cues that elicit a concern about being evaluated by others.[3] Compared to achievement-oriented task-involved individuals, ego-involved persons are more interested in comparing their performance to the performances of others than to their own prior performance (Ames, in press). Compared to intrinsically motivated task-involved people, they are more interested in the outcomes of their efforts than in the process of learn-

---

[3]Problem solvers who are concerned with self-evaluation, or who perceive the problem-solving task as relevant to important personal values, are also ego-involved (Greenwald, 1982). However, in this chapter, we deal primarily with the type of ego-involvement that is fostered by a concern with evaluation by others.

ing and mastery. According to Ames (in press), the affective reactions of ego-involved individuals are more extreme than those of task-involved individuals. In reacting to an offer of help, then, ego-involved recipients are likely to be more attentive to the affective and evaluative components of the aid than to its instrumental aspects.

Motivational Properties of the Help

We have argued that the affective and evaluative components of help can be either motivating or debilitating. We have also noted that when these cues are motivating they have the effect of returning the recipient's attention to the task. In this section we describe some of the mechanisms by which help produces this effect.

Briefly, we argue that the motivational properties of help "work" by increasing recipients' expectations that: (1) successful task performance is possible; (2) one of their current goals can be achieved via successful task performance; and/or (3) a different goal, which also can be attained via successful task performance, is worth striving for. The motivational properties of help can also work by (4) increasing the desirability to recipients of successful task performance, or of a goal that can attained via successful task performance, or (5) enhancing recipients' affect or self-image.

One of the most important ways in which the affective and evaluative components of help redirect attention to the task is by establishing or underlining the link between successful task performance and goal-attainment (as perceived by the recipient). When successful task performance *is* the recipient's goal (as is often the case in achievement contexts), help that works is help that increases the recipient's expectations for successful task performance. This kind of help may be particularly important to recipients who lack self-confidence. In other instances, however, successful task performance is a necessary, but not sufficient, condition for goal attainment. Perhaps the most common example of this in achievement contexts occurs when the recipient's goal is that of mastering the task completely independently. When independent task mastery is the recipient's goal, the conferring of instrumental help by another person or agent severs the link between successful task performance and goal attainment. As a result, the recipient is unlikely to derive maximal benefit from the instrumental components of the help, and may suffer a decrement in intrinsic interest in the task.

When the recipient's goal is to evaluate accurately self-competence, the receipt of help may again be detrimental to task performance. For example, when the instrumental components of help are clear, accurate, and informative (as when the helper tells the recipient in precise and explicit detail exactly how to solve the problems), performance on those problems is no longer highly diagnostic of the recipient's ability. Thus, the recipient's motivation to work on those problems, and other problems like them, may wane. In order for help to facilitate the goal of self-assessment, it would have to provide enough information to nudge the bewildered recipient back onto the right track, but not so much information that eventual success at the task would be completely undiagnostic.

In addition to increasing recipients' expectations of attaining their current goals, help can also work by creating a new goal that can be attained via successful task performance. For example, a tutor who helps a student in a particularly endearing way may create for that student a new goal—that of pleasing the tutor, and earning his or her respect. Showing improvement in one's task performance may be perceived by the recipient as a potentially effective way of attaining that goal.

Finally, the motivational aspects of help can also work by making successful task performance (or some goal that can be attained via successful task performance) seem more interesting, desirable or worthwhile, or by enhancing recipients' affect or self-image.[4] For recipients who have the necessary ability to master the task, but who are uninterested in the task, unwilling to make much of an effort to master it, or too depressed to concentrate on it, attention to these types of affective and evaluative cues may be essential.

Identifying Recipients' Motives and Goals

Research on achievement-related strivings has identified a number of goals and motives that are often operative in achievement contexts. These include self-assessment (e.g., Trope, in press), self-enhancement (e.g., Greenwald, 1980; Snyder, Stephan, & Rosenfield, 1978), and the motives to achieve success and avoid failure (Atkinson & Raynor, 1974; McClelland et al., 1953). From the point of view of the researcher, a difficult and important task is that of identifying the particular goal that is predominant in the situation under investigation. Two familiar methods can be used toward this end: (1) assessing individual difference characteristics that are defined by their relationship to particular goals or motives; and (2) constructing the experimental scenario in such a way as to make salient a particular goal or motivational scheme.

For example, various related lines of research on constructs such as

---

[4]Although an improvement in affect or self-image may sometimes be necessary in order for successful task performance to occur, it will not always be sufficient.

self-esteem, achievement motivation, and test anxiety (e.g., Brockner, 1979; Sigall & Gould, 1977; Weiner, 1980; Wine, 1980) suggest that individuals who are fairly confident about their task-relevant abilities, and those who are very achievement oriented, may be most effectively motivated by cues that describe a challenge. Sources of this challenge (which can be built into an experimental scenario) might range from innuendo (e.g., an intimation of doubt about the recipient's ability to perform successfully) to other more "objective" aspects of the situation (e.g., the difficulty level of the problems that the recipient is trying to solve). For these self-confident and achievement-oriented individuals, the effect of a challenging offer of help should be to focus their attention on the instrumental aspects of the help, and to increase their interest in mastering the task.

The same cues that are challenging and motivating to a self-confident recipient may be threatening and debilitating to one who is anxious or insecure. Instead of redirecting attention to the task, such cues might serve instead to exacerbate recipients' nervous ruminations over the affective and evaluative implications of aid. For recipients low in task-relevant self-esteem, or high in anxiety, reassuring cues might be most effective in quelling their evaluative concerns and in facilitating performance. As was true of challenging cues, reassuring cues might be inherent in the task (e.g., problems that are simple and straightforward), the context (e.g., unlimited time is allowed for problem completion), the helper (e.g., the helper is known to be supportive and encouraging), or the way that the help is given. With regard to the latter variable, attributional models suggest that recipients will make less-damaging self-attributions if the help is given in such a way as to suggest that the recipient probably needs help only on this one task and at this one point in time, and that many other people have needed help at this task, too (Kelley's distinctiveness, consistency, and consensus criteria; 1967).

Brickman and his colleagues have suggested that the most effective form of help is that which reassures recipients that they are not responsible for needing help, but that they are responsible for solving their problems so as to be free of the need for help in the future (Brickman *et al.,* in press; this volume; Coates *et al.,* this volume). We think that for highly anxious or insecure recipients, the injunction to take responsibility for problem solution is best coupled with some reassurance that problem-solving efforts are likely to meet with success.

Motivational Intensifiers

Help that is motivating, we have argued, has the effect of redirecting the recipient's attention back to the task, and to the instrumental aspects of the help. In these instances, recipients' postaid task attentiveness is marked by a heightened level of interest, concentration, and determination. On the other hand, when help is debilitating, it has the effect of dampening recipients' interest and enthusiasm for the task. Recipients in these situations focus on the evaluative implications of the help (usually the negative implications), and they continue to mull over these and other task-irrelevant considerations, rather than returning their full attention to the task.

Two factors serve to intensify the effects of help. One is the *importance* to the recipient of goal attainment. As importance increases, motivating help becomes even more effective, and debilitating aid becomes even more disastrous.

The second factor is the degree to which help is *personalized*. Personalized help is help that points to the person helped as a special and individuated recipient. This can occur in a variety of ways. For example, help given to a single student is more personalized than is help given to an entire class of students. Help that is administered contingently upon the recipient's need for it is more personalized than is help that is given before the recipient has even begun to work on the task, and it is more personalized than is help given by a helper who is unaware or unsure of the nature or extent of the recipient's need state. Many manipulations that induce or increase ego-involvement also foster personalization. For example, when help is given in the presence of others, the beneficiary's status as a help-recipient is again underlined, and the help is therefore more personalized (and more ego-involving) than it would be if it were given privately. Even if the helper merely interacts with the recipient in a more intimate or immediate way (e.g., using the recipient's name, talking in more affectively laden tones), help is more personalized than if the helper had adopted a more businesslike manner. The effect of personalized help, in all of its manifestations, is always the same; as help becomes more personalized, motivating help becomes even more motivating, and debilitating help becomes even more debilitating.

Boundary Conditions

Several qualifications need to be added to the formulation we have described. The first and most obvious qualification is that help cannot always be made to work. The task may be generally impossible, or it may be impossible for the particular recipient in question in his or her particular situation.

Second, there will be situations in which the instrumental value of help is so high that help almost has to work (for example, when helpers tell recipients the correct answers to all of their unsolved problems). In these situations, there may be virtually no variance in performance on the problems for which help was received. However, the fact of having received help may still have very powerful effects on recipients' levels of motivation, interest, and performance when they encounter the same or similar problems in other contexts and on other occasions.

Third, although attentiveness to the instrumental aspects of help may generally be beneficial to task performance, negative consequences may occur when attention becomes too narrowly focused. For example, instrumentally oriented problem solvers may demonstrate very low levels of incidental learning (Easterbrook, 1959; see also Harackiewicz, 1979).

Fourth, although the formulation we have described does make general predictions regarding the effects of help on task performance, it does not make a systematic set of *differential* predictions regarding the effects of help on (1) immediate task performance versus subsequent task performance, or (2) performance on the particular problems for which help was received versus other types of problems. This may well be one of the most interesting directions for future work.

In its broad outlines, the formulation that has been proposed is similar to empirically validated theories from related areas of inquiry. For example, our distinction between the instrumental and evaluative aspects of help is like certain distinctions that have proved useful in research and theory on intrinsic motivation; most notably, Deci's distinction between the informational and controlling aspects of rewards (Deci, 1975; Deci & Ryan, 1980; see also Harter, 1982). Further, to the extent that the receipt of help can be construed as an externally imposed interruption of self-regulatory processes, predictions for the effects of help on task performance could be generated from Carver and Scheier's theory of attention and self-regulation (1981). We think that many of those predictions (and their theoretical justifications) would be similar to those that we have described. Although such similarities are encouraging, the fact remains that—with the exception of the study to be reported in the next section—the formulation we have described has yet to be tested empirically. It should therefore be regarded as a working model in need of further testing and refinement.

THE EFFECTS OF NONINSTRUMENTAL HELP ON PERFORMANCE: AN EXPERIMENTAL INVESTIGATION

In this section, we describe an experimental investigation of the effects of noninstrumental help. Although originally derived from Fisher, Nadler, and Whitcher-Alagna's (1982) threat to self-esteem model, the study addresses several of the hypotheses generated from the present formulation.

In the experiment (DePaulo, Brown, Ishii, & Fisher, 1981), subjects received a problem-solving hint relevant to an achievement task that they had tried to master with little success. The hint, however, turned out to be irrelevant to the next set of problems that they would face. Thus, any effect of the help on subsequent task performance would be due to the affective and evaluative components of the aid, rather than any instrumental value.

The effects of noninstrumental help on task performance depend importantly on the match between the affective, evaluative, and motivational aspects of the help and the recipients' motives or goals. As noted earlier, recipients' motives or goals can be defined by arranging aspects of the situation so as to make salient a particular motive or goal, or by selecting individuals characterized by a particular orientation toward achievement goals. In the present investigation, we did both. We constructed an experimental setting in which successful task performance would presumably be an important goal for all subjects, and we recruited subjects who varied systematically in their orientations toward achievement goals—that is, subjects low and high in self-esteem.

The experimental scenario was designed to resemble a highly evaluative achievement context. Subjects were recruited from a college population and worked on timed tasks (similar to those that appear in Scholastic Aptitude Tests) that were described as predictive of intellectual ability and professional success. They then received feedback indicating that they had performed quite poorly, whereas their respective "partners" had performed extremely well. Moreover, all subjects were led to believe that their partners, who performed far more competently than they had, were highly similar to themselves in task-relevant ability and experience. In this context, the receipt of help from the partner should underline the recipient's relative inferiority and increase the potential for evaluative concerns.

According to the conceptualization described previously, help that works is help that increases recipients' expectations that successful task performance is possible, or that their goals (e.g., meeting a challenge) can be attained via successful task performance. Further, help that works is help that puts to rest recipients' anxious ruminations about task-irrelevant concerns, and returns their attention to the task.

Individuals with low self-esteem already have a self-concept of incompetence. Receiving help can reinforce that self-concept (as, for example, when it implies that they cannot succeed without help or when it leads them to fear that they may not succeed even with help), thereby lowering their expectations for successful task performance, increasing their evaluative concerns, and further distracting them from the task. Low self-esteem subjects, then, should suffer performance decrements subsequent to the receipt of help. Only if the context is made more reassuring (e.g., if the partner offers words of encouragement without at the same time providing help, or if the problems that the subject is given to solve are obviously easy ones) should low self-esteem subjects perform well.

High self-esteem individuals, by definition, enter the experimental context feeling more self-confident than low self-esteem individuals. Although highs might perceive their partner's offer of help as a statement of relative superiority, to them it is a statement that can be disproved by subsequent task performance. In this context, the receipt of help constitutes a challenge to high self-esteem individuals. Further, it is a challenge that they are motivated to meet and that they believe they can meet. Aspects of the situation that highlight that challenge (e.g., facing a difficult set of problems, or a subtle insinuation of incompetence issued by one's partner) should serve to facilitate further the subsequent task performance of these high self-esteem subjects.

These predictions are consistent in a general way with research and theory in areas such as achievement motivation (e.g., Atkinson & Raynor, 1974), text anxiety (e.g., Sarason, 1980), self-esteem (e.g., Nadler & Mayseless, this volume), reactance and helplessness (e.g., Wortman & Brehm, 1975), and even with certain clinical case histories (e.g., Watzlawick & Coyne, 1980). They are also bolstered by a study that focused specifically on the relationship between self-esteem and effort expenditure. In that study, Sigall and Gould (1977) showed that people in whom a high level of self-regard had been induced exerted a great deal of effort to improve their performance when situational cues were challenging (e.g., when they knew that the person who would evaluate their performance was particularly demanding). Low self-regard subjects, on the other hand, exerted more effort when the evaluator was known to be easy to please. Sigall and Gould (1977) concluded from their research that people whose competence is challenged may not make an active attempt to meet that challenge unless they are reasonably certain that their attempt will be successful.

In the present study, recipients who were high or low in dispositional self-esteem (i.e., above or below the median on the Coopersmith Self-Esteem Inventory; Coopersmith, 1967) were given failure feedback, then were given help by their partner in a neutral, supportive, or challenging way. In the neutral help condition, the helper simply conveyed to the recipient a hint for solving the problems, with no further comment. In the supportive-help condition, the helper gave the same hint, and also expressed positive affect ("Good luck on the next task!"). In the challenging-help condition, the helper conveyed, along with the hint, a remark indicating the helper's perception of the recipient as incompetent ("I guess this is hard for you"). In a parallel set of "no help" conditions, the helper conveyed the supportive message, the challenging message, or no message at all, without giving the hint. After receiving help, the recipients worked on a set of easy problems and a set of difficult problems. Both sets were unrelated to the problems with which they received help. Thus, there were two sources of challenge in this experimental context: (1) the helpers who communicated in a challenging way provided a greater challenge to the recipients' sense of competence than those who communicated in a neutral or supportive way, and (2) the difficult problems were more challenging than the easy problems.

As we expected, high self-esteem subjects performed relatively more successfully after they had been helped; low self-esteem subjects, on the other hand, performed relatively better when they did *not* receive help. In the conditions in which no help had been received, the performance of the high and low self-esteem subjects did not differ significantly; in the help conditions, in contrast, the high self-esteem subjects peformed substantially more successfully than did the low self-esteem subjects (see Table 1).

Our results (see Table 2) also showed that high self-esteem subjects rose to the challenge and performed especially well in the most challenging conditions; that is, when working on the most demanding problems after having received help from a partner who said nothing at all or who suggested that the task was probably too difficult for the recipient to handle successfully. Low self-esteem subjects, on the other hand, tended to perform most adequately under conditions of maximum supportiveness and reassurance; that is, when working on easy problems, after their partner had passed along an encouraging word without at the same time giving any help. The low self-esteem subjects, relative to the highs, also performed especially well when working on the difficult problems after receiving no feedback at all (i.e., no help and no other comment). Thus, on the difficult problems, it was not the supportive feedback, but instead the neutral feedback, that most enhanced the performance of the low self-esteem subjects.

Performance on cognitively complex tasks might be disrupted by any kind of added arousal, even that which presumably results from a response that clarifies the helper's motivation. For low self-esteem subjects, the extra

TABLE 1
Effects of Help on Task Performance

	Self-esteem	
Help	Low	High
No help	$.102^{ab}$	$-.027^{ab}$
Help	$-.363^a$	$.504^b$

Note. Cell entries are performance scores (number of problems right) that have been z-scored separately for the easy and difficult problems. The scores in this table are collapsed across problem difficulty. Scores with different superscripts differ from each other at $p < .05$ or less.

TABLE 2
Effects of Help, Evaluative Cue, and Problem Difficulty on
Task Performance of Low and High Self-esteem Subjects

	Evaluative cue					
	Easy problems			Difficult problems		
Help	Supportive	Neutral	Challenging	Supportive	Neutral	Challenging
No help	−.767	−.401	.295	.555	−.799	.388
Help	.465	.404	.866	.080	1.711*	1.676*

Note. Performane scores (number of problems right) were z-scored separately for the easy and difficult problems. Cell entries are high self-esteem advantage scores (i.e., score of high self-esteem subjects minus score of low self-esteem subjects), which indicate the degree to which the high self-esteem subjects outperformed the lows in each condition.

*$p < .01$, two-tailed, for the difference in performance between high and low self-esteem subjects.

comment that they received, with all of its affective and evaluative implications, may have had a more general distracting (or arousing) effect, independent of the particular content or affective valence of the comment. Subjects who each received a supportive or threatening comment from their partner (compared to those who received no comment) may have expended considerable mental effort thinking about the comment or about the person who sent it. This may have interfered with performance on the difficult problems, which demanded more intense concentration and for which high arousal inhibits performance.

Further Refinements: Performance in the Service of What?

Response to Challenge and Reassurance

We have explained the adept performance of the high self-esteem subjects subsequent to receiving help as a response to the challenging aspects of the help. That is, their competent task performance may have served to disprove any negative evaluations of their competence that might be implied by the help. We have also argued that for high self-esteem subjects—but not for lows—the challenge posed by the receipt of help is a welcome one because it is a challenge that they believe they can meet. If this interpretation is correct, then high self-esteem subjects should suffer no decrements in perceived intelligence or self-confidence after receiving aid, and they should exhibit increments in task performance. Further, those who feel especially self-confident and intelligent under challenging circumstances should perform especially well.

We suggested earlier that for low self-esteem subjects, the receipt of challenging help provides further evidence for their feelings of incompetence, which are then exacerbated by the aid. Thus, they are more motivated to be reassured than to be challenged. They will try hard to do well only in those contexts in which they think they *can* do well. In these nonthreatening situations, the more reassured (e.g., comfortable, happy) they feel, the better they should perform. Thus, for low self-esteem subjects in reassuring contexts, positive affect should be positively correlated with performance.

Right after subjects received help, and before they performed the easy and difficult tasks, we collected affect ratings (summed ratings on "happy," "positive," "comfortable," "good," "pleasant," and "high" scales) and self-evaluations (ratings of self-confidence and intelligence). Although, over all conditions, high self-esteem subjects reported more positive affects and self-evaluations than did low self-esteem subjects, self-esteem did not interact significantly with help on either of these measures. However, a marginally significant self-esteem $\times$ help interaction ($p = .10$, $d = .41$) on the ratings of intelligence tended to support the challenge formulation. Low self-esteem subjects perceived themselves as less intelligent after they received help ($M = 2.24$), compared to when they did not receive help ($M = 3.00$), whereas the high self-esteem subjects saw themselves as relatively, but not significantly, more intelligent when they did receive help ($M = 3.45$) than when they did not ($M = 3.25$).

Although we had too few subjects to compute correlations separately for each of the 12 cells of the design (low–high self-esteem $\times$ help–no help $\times$ supportive–neutral–challenging evaluative cue), we did compute correlations separately for subjects high and low in self-esteem for the easy and difficult problems (see Table 3). Although these correlations should be regarded only as suggestive, we think they are interesting.

For high self-esteem subjects, positive self-evaluations were directly correlated with performance; thus, the more confident and intelligent these subjects felt, the more successfully they performed. This relationship was especially strong for the difficult problems. In fact, for the difficult problems, the correlation between self-evaluation and performance was significantly more positive for the high self-esteem subjects than for the lows. (This is shown in the bottom row of Table 3.)

For low self-esteem subjects, on the other hand, performance on a nondemanding task was predicted by affect. Thus, among the low self-esteem subjects working on easy problems, those who felt most comfortable and content performed most successfully. For these easy problems, the correlation between affect and performance was significantly more positive for the low self-esteem subjects than for the highs.

TABLE 3
Correlations with Task Performance

| Self-esteem | Problem Difficulty | | | |
| | Easy | | Difficult | |
	Affect	Self-evaluation	Affect	Self-evaluation
Low	.29*	.10	.04	−.13
High	−.14	.23	−.07	.40***
High minus low	−.43**	.13	−.11	.53**

*p < .10
**p < .05
***p < .01

In sum, high self-esteem subjects showed no evidence of suffering a decrement in self-evaluation subsequent to the receipt of help. Compared to low self-esteem individuals, they felt slightly more intelligent after they were helped, and the more intelligent and self-confident they felt, the better they performed, particularly on the difficult problems. These subjects, then, did seem to be motivated by the challenging cues built into the experimental context.

Interestingly, in several previous studies, high self-esteem subjects have reported lowered self-evaluations subsequent to the receipt of help from a similar other (Nadler et al., 1979; Nadler, Fisher, & Streufert, 1976). One way that those studies differed from the present investigation is in the type of help that was given. In the present study, help was a hint for solving problems. At the time when they received this hint (which is the same time that self-evaluations were assessed), high self-esteem subjects may have felt particularly confident that they would be able to use the hint effectively in a later phase of the experiment. In the Nadler et al. studies, on the other hand, "help" was a number of poker chips that subjects could use to continue to invest in a simulated stock market game in which they had been performing quite poorly. The chips, however, provided recipients with no indication whatsoever as to how to invest more wisely than before. High self-esteem subjects who received this kind of help felt even worse about themselves than those who received no help at all.

Furthermore, the specific hint that was used in the present study may have been particularly advantageous to high self-esteem recipients. The hint ("There is a pattern within each page. I think the problems that are diagonally across from each other use the same kinds of relationships, such as counting, matching, etc. If you solve one, you know what to do with the rest") was vague and unpromising. In order to be able to make any use of it at all, recipients would have to figure out at least one problem per page on their own. Perhaps only high self-esteem recipients were confident that they could do so. If instead the hint were very precise, explicit, informative, and clear, such that recipients knew as soon as they received it that it would be very useful, the results may have been very different. Because of its reassuring qualities, such a hint may have been motivating for low self-esteem individuals. For high self-esteem recipients, however, such a hint may have robbed the task of the challenging aspects which to them were most motivating.

Across all types of help, then, the relationship between instrumental value and level of motivation may be curvilinear. When help has no instrumental value at all (e.g., a poker chip), high self-esteem subjects have very little reason to believe that they can now succeed on the exact same task at which they have been failing badly; when help is very high in instrumental value, they have very little reason to think that they might not succeed. It is when help teasingly offers a possible, but not certain, chance for success that high self-esteem subjects (relative to lows) may be most motivated.[5]

Public Identity, Private Identity, and Self-sufficiency

One function of improved task performance might be to bolster the self-concepts of subjects whose esteem was damaged by the receipt of help. This esteem-restoration hypothesis is unlikely to account for the results of the present study because the only subjects who showed any evidence at all of self-esteem decrements subsequent to the receipt of help (i.e., low self-esteem subjects) did not show postaid performance increments. Nonetheless, the esteem-restoration mechanism could be more definitively ruled out by interjecting an esteem-bolstering experience between the receipt of help and the performance of the postaid tasks. If problem-solving success serves primarily to bolster a sagging self-percept, then there should be a less marked increment in success in conditions in which esteem has already been bolstered by some other event.

The esteem-restoration hypothesis just described assumed that subjects are concerned primarily with their own private identities. Alternatively, they might be more concerned with how the helper (and others) are evaluating them, rather than with how they feel about themselves. According to this

---

[5]A second potentially important difference between the Nadler et al. studies and the present study is that the former involved only male subjects, whereas the latter involved only females. Perhaps the positive self-image of high self-esteem males (unlike that of high self-esteem females) is based on their ability to master problems completely independently. Whenever success is facilitated by some external source (e.g., help given by someone else), esteem is lost rather than gained.

public identity hypothesis, successful task performance serves to disprove *to others* any implication of incompetence implicit in the prior offer of help. If this is true, then a privately experienced esteem-bolstering event would not reduce the motivation to perform well on the tasks. Such motivation would be reduced if subjects were convinced that no one would ever find out about their scores on the postaid tasks.

If either private or public esteem-enhancement were an important motivator of task performance in the present study, then the fact that the postaid tasks were very different from the tasks with which subjects were helped may have been very important. If all tasks were alike, then subjects and observers might be tempted to attribute any increment in performance to the help rather than to the recipient's competence. This suggests that for high self-esteem subjects—or perhaps for any individuals who value independently achieved success—help can lead to increments in interest and performance on very different tasks, and at the same time undermine interest and performance on tasks that are too similar to the one for which help was received.

Another potentially important motivator of successful postaid task performance is the desire to avoid receiving any more help in the future. Subjects who perform especially well are particularly unlikely to be offered any more aid. If this dynamic is important, then the performance increments found in the present study should not occur if subjects are told that there will be no further opportunities to receive help from their partner or anyone else.

Indebtedness-reduction and Equity-restoration

One common consequence of receiving help is a feeling of indebtedness (Greenberg & Westcott, this volume). Indebtedness has been shown to be an aversive state that recipients are motivated to reduce. In certain contexts, effective task performance can facilitate indebtedness-reduction. Experimental support for this proposition comes from a study in which subjects received varying amounts of help from fellow subjects on a problem-solving task, then were given an opportunity to learn information that would be instrumental to repayment. The more help subjects received, the more they learned—presumably in an effort to be in a better position to repay the helper and to reduce their indebtedness (Greenberg & Bar-Tal, 1976).

In the present study, too, subjects may have performed especially well in order to increase their ability to repay their helper in subsequent phases of the experiment. The option of reducing indebtedness behaviorally, that is, via reciprocity, may have seemed like a reasonable option only to subjects high in self-esteem—subjects who believe that they could perform better if they tried. The less self-confident subjects may have felt forced to rely on cognitive forms of indebtedness reduction (e.g., belittling the helpfulness of the help, the costs incurred in rendering it, or the helper's motivations).

If indebtedness were the key mediator of the obtained performance results, such results should be obviated in conditions in which subjects anticipate no opportunity to reciprocate to their helper. In such conditions, subjects should show evidence of alternative forms of indebtedness-reduction.

Related to indebtedness motivation is equity motivation. According to equity formulations (e.g., Hatfield & Sprecher, this volume), people in a relationship are motivated to achieve equal relative gains (roughly, equal ratios of outcomes to inputs). Persons who receive help may perceive their relationship with their helper as no longer equitable; increments in task performance may serve to increase recipients' inputs, and thereby reduce inequity. (To reduce *indebtedness* it is not sufficient merely to alter the recipient's relative gains; instead, the *helper's* outcome–input ratio must be altered; see Greenberg & Westcott, this volume). Again, improving one's performance may be an equity-restoration device that is available only to subjects with high self-esteem, who believe that they can do better than they have in the past. Other subjects may rely more on cognitive restorations. If inequity-reduction were the primary motivating force in the research under discussion, then it should be possible to find evidence of equity-restoration attempts even in the absence of any opportunity to increase one's performance inputs. For example, if, after receiving help, subjects were led to expect that there would be no further tasks to work on, they might then attempt to restore equity by altering their perceptions of their own inputs and outputs or those of their helper.

The indebtedness and inequity formulations do not seem to be the best models for explaining the results of the DePaulo *et al.* (1981) study. Neither model appears to explain straightforwardly the effects of the evaluative-cue variable (i.e., whether the partner says "I guess this is hard for you," "Good luck on the next task," or makes no evaluative comment). Also, there is no evidence for nonbehavioral modes of indebtedness-reduction or equity-restoration among the low self-esteem subjects. For example, the effects of help on perceptions of the helper were not different for high versus low self-esteem subjects.

The effects of the evaluative-cue variable and of problem difficulty are in closer accord with other formulations that have been discussed. For instance, when a helper says, "I guess this is hard for you," recipients are likely to feel especially challenged, and especially motivated to disprove the intimation of incompetence, to bolster their own feelings of self-esteem, and to increase their level of self-sufficiency. All of these goals (e.g., meeting the challenge, disproving the negative evaluation) are more effectively realized by successful performance on problems that are particularly difficult.

Nonetheless, it does not necessarily follow that recipients' reactions to aid are always more accurately predicted by competence-type formulations (e.g., those stressing challenges or self-sufficiency) than by other formulations, such as those relevant to inequity and indebtedness. The DePaulo *et al.* (1981) study was derived from a competence formulation, and thus the experimental scenario was infused with elicitors of competence-concerns. For example, subjects worked on timed tasks consisting of problems similar to those found in tests of intelligence and achievement. Further, they were told that success at the task was in fact relevant to intelligence and professional success, and they were given performance feedback expressed in raw scores and percentile ranks. Asking whether the results of such research are better predicted by competence concerns or inequity is somewhat akin to giving people a game board featuring Boardwalk and Marvin Gardens, then recording whether they play Monopoly or Backgammon.

SUMMARY

Instrumental help is a complex event consisting of instrumental cues that are directly relevant to goal attainment and a diversity of social, affective, and evaluative meanings that are inferred from the help itself, the way the help is given, the context in which it is given, and the characteristics of the persons who give and receive it. Insofar as the instrumental aspects of help are well suited to the task on which help is needed and to the recipient's level of sophistication, and assuming that the recipient is attentive to the instrumental cues in the help, is motivated to master the task, and is confident that the task can be mastered, then help should work. Effective help—help that works—facilitates performance on the immediate task, and sometimes even enables the recipient to perform other tasks at other times completely independently.

Help, however, does not always work. Help can fail to work even when its instrumental elements are potentially quite useful and when the recipient really does want to benefit from the help. We have suggested that when help is ineffective, the potency of the surplus meanings that pervade helping events is often to blame. The affective and evaluative aspects of help—which can carry implications relevant to recipients' public and private identities, and to their relationships with their helpers—can wrestle attention away from the instrumental elements of help and subvert recipients' problem-solving efforts. Thus, it will sometimes be advisable to arrange aspects of the helping situation so as to minimize the salience of these surplus cues.

However, affective and evaluative cues are not all bad. For certain recipients, in certain situations, the effect of particular kinds of evaluative cues is to enhance task-relevant motivation, interest, and determination. In these situations, then, the evaluative cues which at first grabbed attention away from the task, immediately direct that attention back to the task in an energizing and facilitating way. Thus, in attempting to make help more effective, one alternative to dampening the affective and evaluative implications of help is to tailor those implications in such a way as to facilitate task performance.

We also suggested that help can affect performance even when it contains no instrumental cues at all or when its instrumental elements cannot be directly utilized. In these situations, the affective and evaluative implications of help become even more important. These implications are often relevant to important recipient goals, such as demonstrating competence, attaining self-sufficiency, avoiding indebtedness, and maintaining positive interpersonal ties. To the extent that (1) successful task performance serves (or is seen as serving) to facilitate these goals, and (2) recipients believe that they *can* perform more successfully, then task performance should improve subsequent to the receipt of help. Further, this increment in performance should be even more pronounced as the goal becomes more important and the help becomes more personalized. *Importance* and *personalization* are general intensifiers of the motivational consequences of aid. Thus, if help is debilitating rather than motivating, then its effects are even more damaging when the goal is more important and the help is more personalized.

In an experimental investigation of the effects of the affective and evaluative components of help, only subjects high in self-esteem (who presumably believed that they were capable of competent performance) responded to help by performing particularly well on a subsequent task (DePaulo *et al.,* 1981). It was suggested that high self-esteem subjects were motivated by the challenge to their competence implied by the offer of help. Consistent with this explanation, aspects of the helping context that highlighted the challenge posed by aid further increased the difference in performance between the high and the low self-esteem recipients.

REFERENCES

Allen, V. L. Reactions to help in peer tutoring: Roles and social identities. In A. Nadler, J. D. Fisher, & B. M. DePaulo (Eds.), *Applied research in help-seeking and reactions to aid.* New York: Academic Press. In press.

Ames, R. Help-seeking and achievement orientation: Perspectives from attribution theory. In B. M. DePaulo, A. Nadler, & J. D. Fisher (Eds.), *New directions in helping* (Vol. 2), Help-seeking. New York: Academic Press. In press.

Atkinson, J. W., & Raynor, J. O. (Eds.). *Motivation and achievement*. Washington, D.C.: Winston, 1974.

Bandura, A. Self-efficacy: Toward a unifying theory of behavioral change. *Psychological Review*, 1977, **84**, 191–215.

Brickman, P., Rabinowitz, V. C., Karuza, J., Coates, D., Cohn, E., & Kidder, L. An attributional analysis of helping behavior. In L. Berkowitz (Ed.), *Advances in experimental social psychology* (Vol. 15). New York: Academic Press. In press.

Brockner, J. The effects of self-esteem, success-failure, and self-consciousness on task performance. *Journal of Personality and Social Psychology*, 1979, **37**, 1732–1741.

Carver, C. S., & Scheier, M. F. *Attention and self-regulation*. Berlin and New York: Springer-Verlag, 1981.

Coopersmith, S. *The antecedents of self-esteem*. San Francisco, California: Freeman, 1967.

Crowne, D., & Marlowe, D. *The approval motive*. New York: Wiley, 1964.

de Charms, R. *Personal causation: The internal affective determinants of behavior*. New York: Academic Press, 1968.

Deci, E. L. *Intrinsic motivation*. New York: Plenum Press, 1975.

Deci, E. L., & Ryan, R. M. The empirical exploration of intrinsic motivational processes. In L. Berkowitz (Ed.), *Advances in experimental social psychology* (Vol. 13). New York: Academic Press, 1980.

DePaulo, B. M., Brittingham, G. L., & Kaiser, M. K. Receiving competence-relevant help: Effects on reciprocity, affect, and sensitivity to the helper's nonverbally-expressed needs. *Journal of Personality and Social Psychology*, in press.

DePaulo, B. M., Brown, P. L., Ishii, S., & Fisher, J. D. Help that works: The effects of aid on subsequent task performance. *Journal of Personality and Social Psychology*, 1981, **41**, 478–487.

DePaulo, B. M., & Fisher, J. D. Too tuned-out to take: The role of nonverbal sensitivity in help-seeking. *Personality and Social Psychology Bulletin*, 1981, **7**, 201–205.

DePaulo, B. M., & Rosenthal, R. Ambivalence, discrepancy, and deception in nonverbal communication. In R. Rosenthal (Ed.), *Skill in nonverbal communication*. Cambridge, Massachusetts: Oelgeschlager, Gunn, Hain, 1979.

Dweck, C. S., & Licht, B. G. Learned helplessness and intellectual achievement. In J. Garber & M. E. P. Seligman (Eds.), *Human helplessness*. New York: Academic Press, 1980.

Easterbrook, J. A. The effect of emotion on cue utilization and the organization of behavior. *Psychological Review*, 1959, **66**, 193–201.

Fisher, J. D., & Nadler, A. The effect of similarity between donor and recipient on reactions to aid. *Journal of Applied Social Psychology*, 1974, **4**, 230–243.

Fisher, J. D., Nadler, A., & Whitcher-Alagna, S. Recipient reactions to aid. *Psychological Bulletin*, 1982, **91**, 27–54.

Greenberg, M. S., & Bar-Tal, D. Indebtedness as a motive for acquisition of "helpful" information. *Representative Research in Social Psychology*, 1976, **7**, 19–27.

Greenwald, A. G. The totalitarian ego. *American Psychologist*, 1980, **35**, 603–618.

Greenwald, A. G. Ego task analysis. In A. H. Hastorf & A. M. Isen (Eds.), *Cognitive social psychology*. New York: Elsevier, 1982.

Harackiewicz, J. M. The effects of reward contingency and performance feedback on intrinsic motivation. *Journal of Personality and Social Psychology*, 1979, **37**, 1352–1363.

Harter, S. A model of intrinsic mastery motivation in children: Individual differences and developmental change. In W. A. Collins (Ed.), *Minnesota symposium on child psychology* (Vol. 14). Hillsdale, New Jersey: Lawrence Erlbaum Associates, 1981.

Harter, S. A developmental perspective on some parameters of self-regulation in children. In P. Karoly & F. H. Kanfer (Eds.), *Self management and behavior change.* Oxford: Pergamon, 1982.

Kelley, H. H. Attribution theory in social psychology. In D. Levine (Ed.), *Nebraska symposium on motivation* (Vol. 15). Lincoln, Nebraska: University of Nebraska Press, 1967.

McClelland, D. C., Atkinson, J. W., Clark, R. W., & Lowell, E. L. *The achievement motive.* New York: Appleton, 1953.

Morris, S. C. III, & Rosen, S. Effects of felt adequacy and opportunity to reciprocate on help-seeking. *Journal of Experimental Social Psychology,* 1973, **9**, 265–276.

Nadler, A., Altman, A., & Fisher, J. D. Helping is not enough: Recipient's reactions to aid as a function of experimentally induced self-regard. *Journal of Personality,* 1979, **47**, 615–628.

Nadler, A., Fisher, J. D., & Streufert, S. When helping hurts: Effects of donor–recipient similarity and recipient self-esteem on reactions to aid. *Journal of Personality,* 1976, **44**, 392–409.

Nicholls, J. G. Quality and equality in intellectual development. *American Psychologist,* 1979, **34**, 1071–1084.

Rosen, S. Perceived inadequacy and help-seeking. In B. M. DePaulo, A. Nadler, & J. D. Fisher (Eds.), *New directions in helping* (Vol. 2): Help-seeking. New York: Academic Press. In press.

Ryan, R. M. Control and information in the intrapersonal sphere: An extension of cognitive evaluation theory. *Journal of Personality and Social Psychology,* 1982, **43**, 450–461.

Sarason, I. G. (Ed.). *Test anxiety.* Hillsdale, New Jersey: Lawrence Erlbaum Associates, 1980.

Sigall, H., & Gould, R. The effects of self-esteem and evaluator demandingness on effort expenditure. *Journal of Personality and Social Psychology,* 1977, **35**, 12–20.

Snyder, M. Self-monitoring of expressive behavior. *Journal of Personality and Social Psychology,* 1974, **30**, 526–537.

Snyder, M. L., Stephan, W. G., & Rosenfield, D. A. Attributional egotism. In J. H. Harvey, W. Ickes, & R. F. Kidd (Eds.), *New directions in attribution research* (Vol. 2). Hillsdale, New Jersey: Lawrence Erlbaum Associates, 1978.

Trope, Y. Self-assessment in achievement behavior. In J. M. Suls and A. G. Greenwald (Eds.), *Psychological perspectives on the self* (Vol. 2). Hillsdale, New Jersey: Lawrence Erlbaum Associates. In press.

Watzlawick, P., & Coyne, J. C. Depression following stroke: Brief, problem-focused family treatment. *Family Process,* 1980, **19**, 13–18.

Weiner, B. *Human motivation.* New York: Holt, 1980.

White, R. W. Motivation reconsidered: The concept of competence. *Psychological Review,* 1959, **66**, 297–333.

Wilson, T. D., & Linville, P. W. Improving the academic performance of college freshmen: Attribution therapy revisited. *Journal of Personality and Social Psychology,* 1982, **42**, 367–376.

Wine, J. D. Cognitive-attentional theory of test anxiety. In I. G. Sarason (Ed.), *Test anxiety.* Hillsdale, New Jersey: Lawrence Erlbaum Associates, 1980.

Wine, J. D. Test anxiety and direction of attention. *Psychological Bulletin,* 1971, **76**, 92–104.

Wortman, C. B., & Brehm, J. W. Responses to uncontrollable outcomes: An integration of reactance theory and the learned helplessness model. In L. Berkowitz (Ed.), *Advances in experimental social psychology* (Vol. 8). New York: Academic Press, 1975.

CHAPTER 10

When Helping Backfires:
Help and Helplessness*

Dan Coates
Gary J. Renzaglia
Marlowe C. Embree

Help is usually given in the hope that it will do some good, that is, move recipients closer to a goal of theirs. Indeed, research has shown that people are less willing to help when they can provide only a partially successful solution rather than a completely successful one (Weiss, Boyer, Lombardo, & Stich, 1973). It would follow that potential donors would be even more disturbed by the prospect that their help will not only fail, but will actually leave the recipient even worse off. Yet, there is strong evidence that well-meaning helpers may often do more harm than good (Coates & Wortman, 1980; Fisher, DePaulo, & Nadler, 1981; McCord, 1978; Nadler,

*Work on this chapter and the research reported here were supported by grants to the first author from the Biomedical Committee of the University of Wisconsin.

251

Fisher, & Streufert, 1976; Rodin & Langer, 1977; Taylor, 1979; Wortman & Dunkel-Schetter, 1979).

In this chapter we focus on one potential negative consequence of helping: helplessness among recipients. The phenomenon of learned helplessness was originally observed in animals. When dogs were first exposed to inescapable shock, then later placed in a different situation in which they could actually avoid shock, they just gave up and made no attempt to escape the aversive stimulus (Overmier & Seligman, 1967; Seligman, 1975; Seligman & Maier, 1967). This behavior was interpreted by the researchers as the result of a learning process. During the inescapable shock, the dogs learned that no response they made would end the shock, that they had no control over the shock. Later, although it was possible to escape, the dogs, in effect, saw no point in trying to do so. If outcomes are uncontrollable, it is obviously futile to try to control them.

Humans also give up and show performance decrements when they are exposed to noncontingent aversive outcomes (Hiroto & Seligman, 1975), at least some of the time (Baum & Gatchel, 1981; Wortman & Brehm, 1975). But humans can become helpless even if they do not directly experience failure or a lack of control. In a reformulated version of learned helplessness theory, Abramson, Seligman, and Teasdale (1978) argue that people may feel helpless even though they believe important outcomes are within human control. According to these theorists, people can experience personal helplessness, believing that others can influence events through their behavior, but that they personally are incapable of doing so. It follows from this reasoning that not only threats to perceived control in general, but also threats to perceived self-competence in particular, can lead to the development of helplessness in humans. Indeed, research by Garber and Hollon (1980) suggests that those individuals who show the most serious helplessness decrements believe that others can control certain consequences, but that they lack the ability to do so themselves. Other experiments have shown that indirect threats to perceived self-competence, such as witnessing others of similar ability fail at a task (Brown & Inouye, 1978) or being placed in a dependent position (Langer & Benevento, 1978; Langer & Imber, 1979), can lead people to act helpless even though they have had no direct experience with noncontingent outcomes. Clearly, a variety of factors may cause us to feel incapable, with the consequence that we also see our situation as hopeless and consider further effort futile.

In an unfortunate irony of human social interaction, help can reduce both the actual and the perceived capabilities of recipients, and thereby render them helpless. In this chapter, we begin by reviewing past research on recipients' reactions to aid that points out some of the ways that help can undermine perceived competence and control. This research indicates that help frequently carries with it at least an implicit threat to the self-esteem and perceived efficacy of recipients. Because this threat so commonly accompanies help, whether recipients will become helpless may depend as much on their interpretation of the help as the nature of the help that is given. For example, in a study by Farina, Fisher, Getter, and Fischer (1978), two groups of female college students received the same kind of help, a psychotherapy session. However, the group that had been led to view psychotherapy as a treatment for illness later tended to exert less effort toward solving their own personal problems than did the group that believed psychotherapy was a treatment for learning problems. Brickman, Rabinowitz, Karuza, Coates, Cohn, and Kidder (1982) have proposed a system of help orientations, which are in some ways comparable to those employed by Farina *et al.* (see Farina & Fisher, 1982), but intended to apply much more generally to problems besides mental disorders or social learning failures. We briefly describe these helping models and discuss how these orientations may be related to the development of helping-produced helplessness. We then present a study that explores the extent to which the acceptance of certain models is associated with helplessness among help recipients. Finally, we consider the implications of our results for professional helpers and for future research on recipients' reactions to aid.

HOW HELP UNDERMINES COMPETENCE
AND CONTROL

Research on recipients' reactions to aid suggests that, indeed, good intentions may be the paving stones on the road to hell. Despite the benevolence of donors, their attempts to improve the lot of unfortunate others may leave those others feeling out of control, incompetent, and incapable of overcoming their present or future problems. How is it that such good intentions can lead to such bad results?

First of all, the help may be so overwhelming that it directly reduces the control that recipients have over their own lives. This type of help is most clearly exemplified in total care institutions, such as hospitals (Taylor, 1979) and homes for the aged (Mullins, 1982; Wack & Rodin, 1978). Although the goal of such institutions may be to make clients' lives as easy as possible by doing as much as possible for them, such complete care may actually serve the same macabre function as inescapable shock (Seligman, 1975). Taylor (1979) argues that hospital patients frequently respond to the lack of control they experience by becoming helpless. She further notes that such helplessness impairs the patients' ability to make crucial contributions to their own health maintenance. A recent study by Raps, Peterson, Jonas, and Seligman (1982) provides empirical support for this argument, demonstrating that patients' cognitive deficits and related feelings of helplessness increased with length of hospitalization. When aged residents are provided with somewhat less care, for example when they are expected to arrange their own rooms or to attend to their own plants rather than to have someone else do it, they show dramatic improvement in both physical and emotional well-being (Langer & Rodin, 1976; Rodin, 1980; Rodin & Langer, 1977). Help sometimes promotes helplessness, then, by directly reducing the actual control that recipients have over important events and outcomes in their lives.

Of course, we may not ordinarily think of helping on such an overwhelming, institutionalized scale. But even the little acts of kindness we perform for one another can be killing by directly undermining the acquisition of new skills or the maintenance of old ones. Skinner (1978) provides the example of well-intentioned parents who rush to tie a fumbling child's shoe, but thereby deprive the child of an opportunity to learn how to tie his or her own shoes. The physically disabled, who often must learn new ways of mastering the environment, raise similar complaints about unrequested help on simple tasks they would rather do themselves (Davis, 1961; Goffman, 1963; Ladieu, Hanfman, & Dembo, 1947). Even when skills are already well learned, help may impair the extent to which people are able to apply those skills. Research by Langer and Benevento (1978) and Langer and Imber (1979) shows that when labels that imply inferiority are applied to them, people are less able to succeed at tasks that they had previously performed quite well. These researchers suggest that allowing others to do things for us will lead to similar performance decrements. So, help may foster helpless recipients by directly hindering the acquisition and maintenance of important and useful skills.

Even when help does not directly reduce control or impair the development of certain abilities, it can indirectly undermine the perceived self-efficacy of recipients. Help frequently carries with it the implication that recipients are relatively inferior and incapable of solving problems on their own (Brickman et al., 1982; Broll, Gross, & Piliavin, 1974; Nadler & Porat, 1978; Tessler & Schwartz, 1972). Fisher, Nadler, and Whitcher-Alagna (1982) review a series of studies suggesting that in many situations, such as when the donor is similar to the recipient, or has been much more successful than the recipient at earning useful resources, receiving help seems to prompt people to make more negative self-evaluations (e.g., Fisher, Harrison, & Nadler, 1978; Fisher & Nadler, 1974, 1976; Nadler, Altman, & Fisher, 1979). Abramson et al. (1978) contend that low self-esteem is frequently accompanied by feelings of personal helplessness. Because needing, seeking, or accepting help often implies inferiority, people may come to think less of themselves and their general capability for having done so.

Finally, help can undermine competence and control by creating confusion as to who should get credit or blame for the way things turn out. If the help is successful in resolving or lessening the problem, the recipients may attribute this outcome to the helper, with the result that they feel no more capable of dealing with problems on their own. Coates and Wortman (1980) review evidence that suggests that depressed people, for example, often attribute the more constructive behaviors they engage in to others' demands that they stop acting depressed. As a result, they continue to feel depressed and apathetic, even though they may be acting more cheerful and interested. Brickman et al. (1982) discuss a long list of studies showing that, in general, people are less likely to maintain improvements that are attributed to external agents rather than to themselves (e.g., Chambliss & Murray, 1979; Davison & Valins, 1969; Liberman, 1978). So, recipients may have their problem solved by the help, but still become helpless, convinced they could not succeed on their own.

If the help fails, and the recipients' problems remain, it might seem beneficial for them to have another party to blame. Some research has shown that people are relieved when they can attribute problems or failures to external rather than internal causes (e.g., Ross, Rodin, & Zimbardo, 1969; Storms & Nisbett, 1970), but other research has failed to replicate this general finding [Chambliss & Murray (1979); see also Storms, Denney, McCaul, & Lowery (1979) for a review]. Although it may be somewhat comforting for us to see problems as the fault of someone else, this view also has the discomforting implication that those problems are not under our own control. Although they did not explictly measure attributions, Ellis, Atkeson, and Calhoun (1981) found that rape victims who had been attacked under conditions in which they would be most obviously blameless, that is, by a complete stranger, were more depressed and showed more long-term deficits than did rape victims who might have felt more at fault, that is those attacked by an acquaintance or dating partner. Other researchers have found that accident victims cope better with their problems when they accept responsibility for them (Bulman & Wortman, 1977), and have argued that at least certain types of internal attributions for difficulties enhance perceived control (Dweck, 1975; Janoff-Bulman, 1979). We are less likely to feel we can learn from our mistakes when we are not sure they are really ours. By providing a potential external explanation for failure, then, help can undermine perceived control and encourage helplessness.

Clearly, help can undermine recipients' competence and control in a variety of ways. In fact, help is so frequently threatening to the efficacy of recipients, whether they will be positively or negatively affected by it may be determined as much by their interpretation of it as by the type of help offered. The work of Farina *et al.* (1978), described earlier, supports this argument (see Farina and Fisher (1982) for a review of related studies). But with the exception of the illness and social learning models these researchers have explored, very little work has been directed at understanding how recipients' models or theories of helping might influence their reactions to aid. Recently, Brickman *et al.* (1982) have proposed a system of help orientations that recipients, among others, are likely to adopt, and that have important implications for responses to help. Brickman *et al.* focus most directly on the attributional confusion help creates, that is, the problem of who should get credit or blame, but suggest that this is an overriding issue in determining how recipients will deal with the variety of threats that help can carry. Because these models are discussed in detail elsewhere in this volume (see Brickman *et al.*), we describe them only briefly and then discuss their ramifications for helping-produced helplessness.

HELP ORIENTATIONS AND HELPLESSNESS

The helping models proposed by Brickman *et al.* (1982) are anchored by different types of responsibility attributions, but these authors emphasize that they are talking about moral responsibility and not the causal responsibility most social psychologists have been concerned with (Kelley, 1967; Weiner, 1974). Heider (1958) pointed out that people may be held responsible either because they could produce some outcome, or because they should produce some outcome. The issue of *could* is a principal question in determining causal responsibility, whereas the issue of *should* is a principal question in determining moral responsibility. People may frequently assign causal and moral responsibility to the same source, but they do not always do so. For example, individuals may be seen as morally innocent for events they clearly caused, as when a defendant is excused for admitted criminal acts on the grounds of insanity. They may also feel morally responsible for events they did not cause, as when a father pays a neighbor for a window his son shattered. Brickman et al. argue that it is moral responsibility rather than causal responsibility that people are most directly concerned with in evaluating social events, especially helping. People want to know who, if anyone, should be blamed for a problem and who, if anyone, should be expected to solve it. Causal information is often insufficient or unnecessary to answer these moral concerns.

In helping situations, the answers that donors, recipients, and observers find for these moral questions define the help orientation or helping model that they apply. Under one such model, which Brickman *et al.* call the *moral model,* recipients are seen as responsible both for creating their problems and for solving them. Under this model, recipients are considered capable, but lazy or misdirected in their efforts. They do not expect or want very much help, and they do not actually need any at all. What help they do get is minimal, and consists primarily of a kick in the pants or some other reminder that they have to take care of themselves and better begin doing so. Advice columnists such as Ann Landers provide an example of helping in the moral model. They point out to readers how they got themselves into trouble, and suggest steps for getting themselves out of trouble.

In a second model that people sometimes use, the *compensatory model,* recipients are not blamed for problems, but are seen as responsible for solutions. Recipients are seen as capable but unfairly deprived of important earlier training or resources. Help is given as compensation for this past deprivation and, once it is supplied, recipients are expected to do as well as those who were never deprived. This model has the important advantage of releasing recipients from any guilt or shame about having problems, although not releasing them from a sense of responsibility for dealing with those problems. Project Headstart is an example of helping under the compensatory model. Children who, through no fault of their own, had grown up in intellectually unstimulating environments were given extra training and tools to make up for their disadvantaged backgrounds. They were then expected to hold their own, and do as well in school as more advantaged children.

The third, and perhaps most familiar, model is the *medical model.* Under this model, recipients are not responsible for either problems or solutions. Recipients are considered sick or incapacitated, the victims of disease or other overwhelming negative forces that are and will be beyond their control. Recipients are incapable of helping themselves and need considerable help from others. This help must come from experts, who have talents or skills that recipients do not have. The best example of medical model helping is obviously hospital care, but as Brickman *et al.* point out, some distinctly nonmedical problems may be treated with this model.

In the final model, called the *enlightenment model,* recipients are blamed for problems but are not expected to solve them, at least not on their own. Under this model, recipients have a very negative image of themselves and are expected to submit to a higher authority in order to be helped. Recipients are guilty and sinful, capable of getting themselves into trouble but incapable of getting themselves out of it. Recipients must commit themselves to a new way, a new system of living, and will be able to maintain this commitment only with the constant emotional support and encouragement of helpers. An example of enlightenment model helping is Alcoholics

Anonymous. Members are forced to admit that they are compulsive drinkers, responsible for their drinking problems but unable to stop drinking on their own. They can overcome their alcoholism, but only if they rely heavily on other ex-alcoholics and God.

Brickman *et al.* point out that effective helping, help that lessens or eliminates recipients' presenting problems, can and does take place under all of these models. What determines whether help will be effective in this sense is the extent to which the model fits with the problem and the extent to which donors and recipients share the same or compatible models. But even when help is effective in eliminating certain problems, it can still lead to helpless recipients, as the literature on hospital patients suggests (Taylor, 1979 Raps *et al.,* 1982). So, although any of the models can be applied to resolve problems successfully certain models may be more likely to produce helpless recipients.

We predict that recipients who hold more strongly to models that reduce their responsibility for solutions will be most likely to respond to help by becoming helpless. Researchers have found that certain types of internal causal attributions for problems are associated with better coping, but they usually account for this relationship in terms of the implications those attributions have for solutions (Bulman & Wortman, 1977; Dweck, 1975; Janoff-Bulman, 1979; Peterson, Schwartz, & Seligman, 1981). People who attribute their problems to lack of effort rather than to lack of ability, or to their behavior rather than to their character, are more persistent and less helpless because they believe they can, and perhaps should, solve the problems themselves. This reasoning suggests that recipients' willingness to keep trying or to give up will be more directly determined by how responsible they feel for solutions than how responsible they feel for problems. Although other features of the helping situation are affected when recipients are blamed for problems, such as donors' willingness to assist them, Brickman et al. specifically state that models under which recipients are held responsible for solutions are more likely to foster competent recipients. These authors also review empirical evidence that indicates that people are sometimes helped and sometimes hurt by making external attributions for problems, but consistently and clearly benefit when they see themselves as responsible for solutions. Some of this research suggests that when people feel more responsible for solving their problems, they work harder and more creatively at doing so (Alkire, Collum, Kaswan, & Love, 1968) and are more likely to maintain and extend improvements (Chambliss & Murray, 1979). When help recipients forfeit this responsibility, as in the medical and enlightenment model, it would follow that they will be less inclined to work for themselves and more inclined to just give up when the help ends.

If it could be demonstrated that recipients who endorse the medical and enlightenment models are more likely to respond to help by becoming helpless, this would not only support the theoretical arguments of Brickman *et al.*, it would also have important practical implications. Perhaps, by directly addressing them, the less functional models that recipients adopt could be changed to more functional ones. Or, if this is impossible, at least knowing recipients' models could aid in determining who might respond poorly to help and who might need some special intervention such as mastery training (Seligman, 1975). We conducted a study to test the relationship between help recipients' models, their feelings of helplessness, and some related issues. This study is described in the following section.

LEARNING SKILLS TRAINING:
WILL IT HELP OR HURT?

In order to investigate the relationship between recipients' help orientations and the development of helplessness, we (Renzaglia & Coates, 1981) decided to study people who signed up for the Learning Skills Program at the Counseling Center of the University of Wisconsin. This seemed an interesting and appropriate helping situation to study for a variety of reasons. First of all, it is real life help, offering greater external validity than the contrived types of aid that laboratory studies are often necessarily limited to (Krebs, 1970). The Learning Skills Program is comparable to study skills training at other universities, and consists of four to six weekly small group meetings, at which counselors discuss effective strategies for studying and tips on how to organize and use time more effectively. Students join the program on a strictly voluntary basis after an initial interview with an intake counselor who recommends the program to students for whom it seems appropriate. Occasionally, students come to the Counseling Center specifically requesting the Learning Skills Program after finding out about it from other students, their professors, or from an explanatory brochure that is distributed regularly to all undergraduate dormitories. As with much of the help that people offer, the program provides aid only for a limited, temporary period. The recipients' problem, dissatisfaction with their academic progress, is a fairly serious and important one. It is also a problem that is likely to become worse unless recipients feel that they can and should actively contribute to its solution (Dweck, 1975).

In addition, this is a helping situation that recipients could conceivably approach from any of the helping models. Some helping situations, such as hospitals, fit so well with a particular model that we would expect most of the recipients in those situations to adopt that model. But, more often, help is offered and received under more ambiguous conditions. In the present case, students dissatisfied with their grades or academic progress could reasonably interpret their situation in a number of ways. Adopting the moral model, they may decide that they are just lazy. They will seek help primarily to confirm that laziness is indeed the source of their troubles and to be reminded that they need to buckle down and get to work. Alternatively, students could feel that they have not had the opportunity to develop the organizational or time management skills that others seem to have, and with a little training in these areas, they will do as well in school as anyone else. Such students would be endorsing the compensatory model. Dissatisfied students might also apply the medical model, believing that their failures and academic inadequacies stem from some underlying neuroses or psychological disturbances that only experts can cure. Finally, students could take an enlightenment model approach. For example, they might consider themselves compulsive procrastinators, television addicts, or just plain stupid and slow. They will only make it in school if they have someone constantly available to keep their noses to the grindstone and to help them along. To the extent that recipients endorse models that remove their responsibility for improving, we would expect them to feel hopeless and incapable of doing better in school when the Learning Skills Program ends.

On the other hand, we did not expect much variability in the models adopted by the counselors who led the study groups. We did not measure help orientations among the group leaders, in part because there were only eight of them. But in discussions with these counselors, most agreed that the Learning Skills Program fit best with the compensatory model, although a few thought the moral model was most appropriate. Both these models are consistent with the limited, fixed nature of the help the program provides.

Recipients who adopt the enlightenment or medical models have already conceded that they alone are unable or unwilling to control an important outcome. Consistent with this reasoning, research by Fisher and his associates (Farina *et al.,* 1978; Fisher & Farina, 1979) has shown that when subjects are led to believe that mental illness is a disease rather than a learning difficulty, they see attempts to think about and to work on solving personal emotional problems as less valuable. Recipients who strongly endorse these models might already feel helpless (Abramson *et al.,* 1978) were it not for their strong faith in helpers. Under these models, recipients see helpers as people with greater knowledge or skills than the recipients themselves possess (Brickman *et al.,* 1982). Helpers know "the way" or are highly trained "experts." They have the power to cure the recipients and to carry them down the right path. Some support for the notion that at least medical model recipients will have strong faith in helpers is provided in a study reported by Morrison, Bushell, Hanson, Fentiman, and Holdridge-Crane

(1977). They found that the more strongly psychiatric outpatients agreed that mental disorders were a form of illness, the more dependent the outpatients felt on mental health professionals to solve their problems. Ironically, then, those recipients who adopt a medical or enlightenment model, and who would be expected to feel most hopeless when the helping ends, would also be expected to feel most hopeful when the helping begins.

Of course, people who enter the Study Skills Program expecting the counselors to solve their problems for them may not need to stay in the program very long before they realize that this is not going to occur. Recipients who approach helping from a moral or compensatory model only expect limited and temporary help, whereas medical and enlightenment recipients are looking for more total or long-term care. Because the Learning Skills Program offers only short-term help, we would expect that those recipients who approach the program with a medical or enlightenment model would be most likely to drop out before the program is finished.

So, to reiterate our predictions, we expect that to the extent that recipients endorse the medical or enlightenment models, they will begin the Learning Skills Program with high expectations for receiving effective help and for making substantial improvements in their academic progress. However, the program cannot provide the complete or long-term aid that these models imply, so recipients who are inclined to these models will also be likely to drop out of the program. Finally, students who stay in the program but still maintain an enlightenment or medical model are most likely to feel hopeless and helpless at its conclusion. The procedures we used to see whether the Brickman *et al.* helping models can tell us who will be helped and who will be hurt by study skills training are detailed in the next section.

Method

In all, 57 subjects participated in this project. They were all students who signed up for the Learning Skills Program at the Counseling Center, and who attended at least the first meeting of this program. Only 23 of these original 57 students stayed in the program until its completion.

At the first Learning Skills meeting, all participants filled out measures aimed at assessing their endorsement of each of the help orentations, as well as their expectations for receiving effective help and improving in school. Again at the final meeting of the program, which was either 4 or 6 weeks later, participants filled out the help-orientation measures, and some questions intended to tap their feelings of helplessness. The specific measures we used are described in detail in the next section.

Measuring Recipients' Models

In developing a measure of recipients' helping models, we began with the Help Orientation Test originally constructed by Rabinowitz (see Brickman *et al.*, 1982). This is a generally applicable instrument, consisting of 40 items with four subscales of 10 items each, measuring each separate model. Because of their generality, we felt it would be appropriate to reword the items to fit more specifically with the counseling program. So, for example, rather than having subjects rate "people receiving help," we ask them to rate "people who come to the Learning Skills Program". Like the Help Orientation Test, our test, which we titled "Counseling Perspectives," also had 40 items with four subscales of 10 items each. Subjects answered each item by circling a number on a scale running from 0 to 6, and anchored by "Disagree Strongly–Agree Strongly" at the extremes.

Because we were using a modified version of the Help Orientation Test, we were concerned about the internal consistency of the subscales. So, first we conducted a factor analysis of the initial responses to our Counseling Perspectives Test. We did this solely for the purpose of identifying those items from each subscale that seemed to be interrelated, and to eliminate items that were unrelated or nondiscriminating among the models. An abbreviated form of the items that emerged as the most useful measures of each of the models are presented in Table 1. We also calculated Chronbach's Alpha for each separate model, and these are included in Table 1 too. Although the size of the Alphas is not large, they are apparently within acceptable limits. Nunnally (1967 p. 266) writes that, in early work on "hypothesized measures of a construct," reliabilities of .50 or greater are sufficient standards. Because there are different numbers of items associated with different models, the model scores we report represent the sum of subjects' ratings on each set of items divided by the number of items.

Measuring Expectations and Helplessness

At their first Learning Skills meeting, along with the Counseling Perspectives Test, subjects answered two other questions concerning their expectations. They were asked to indicate how much they expected to be helped with their school problems, and how much they expected their academic performance to improve, by circling a number on a 9–point scale anchored "Not At All–Very Much."

Again at their last session, participants filled out the Counseling Perspectives Test. They also filled out a general, standard evaluation of the program, which included four items intended to measure their feelings of

TABLE 1

Items Measuring Each Helping Model with the Corresponding Alpha for People in the Learning Skills Program

Model	Standardized item Alpha[a]
Moral	.61
Need only to discover their own strength	
Would benefit most from good advice	
Just need a chance to think and re-evaluate	
Need only to find out how to solve their own problems	
See counselors as people who enjoy helping others who are similar to the counselors	
Compensatory	.72
Need opportunities or resources they have not had in the past	
Have a disadvantaged background that is the biggest barrier to solving their problems	
Must have the training and resources they have been denied in order to improve	
See counselors as people who enjoy helping those who have not had a fair chance	
Without help, would consider illegitimate means of getting what they need	
Will need help again only if they are further deprived	
Enlightenment	.75
Lack willpower, which is the biggest barrier to solving their problems	
Need help till cured	
Need a long term helping relationship	
Need prolonged care and attention	
Will fail if they try to solve problem without help	
Medical	.58
Have poor psychological health, which is the biggest barrier to solving their problem	
Lack insight into their problems	
Need help from someone like a therapist	
Do not know how to rely on themselves	
Will need help again if they suffer from further psychological problems	

[a] The Alphas reported here are based on the responses of 57 subjects.

helplessness. Subjects were asked to rate how hopeful they felt about doing better in school in the future, the extent to which they felt they would continue to make the same mistakes and errors they used to make in courses, the extent to which they felt they might as well give up on school, and the extent to which they expected to be successful in school in the future. Subjects answered all these questions on 9-point scales marked "Not At All–Very Much."

Results

We had predicted that to the extent recipients endorsed the medical or enlightenment models, they would begin the Learning Skills Program with high hopes of being helped and doing better in school. As Table 2 shows, this prediction was supported. There was no statistically significant relationship between moral or compensatory model scores and expectations of helping or improvement. However, both of these expectation measures were significantly related to both the medical and enlightenment model scores.

Despite the high hopes associated with the enlightenment and medical models, we had anticipated that recipients who more strongly endorsed these models would be more likely to drop out of the Learning Skills Program. We conducted an analysis of variance comparing the initial model scores of those who completed the program ($N = 23$) with those who left the program ($N = 34$). These two groups differed significantly only on their medical model scores. The mean medical model score for the drop-outs was 2.70, whereas the mean for those who completed the program was 1.97 ($F(1,55) = 5.57$, $p < .01$). Because the medical and enlightenment models imply more complete or sustained help than the Learning Skills Program provides, we had expected that both of these models would be associated with dropping out. Perhaps, though, recipients who endorse the medical model are especially prone to leave the program because they are looking

TABLE 2

Correlations among Initial Model Scores and Expectations of Help and Improvement[a]

Model	Expect help	Expect to improve
Moral	−.14	−.04
	(n.s.[b])	(n.s.)
Compensatory	.15	.12
	(n.s.)	(n.s.)
Enlightenment	.34	.43
	($p < .006$)	($p < .001$)
Medical	.30	.26
	($p < .014$)	($p < .031$)

[a]For all correlations, $N = 54$. Three subjects who failed to answer one or more items were eliminated from the analysis.

[b]N.S. = not significant.

for the quick fix or the easy cure, something like a pill to ease their problem. Consistent with this view, Fisher and Farina (1979) found that students who believed mental illness was a disease were more likely to use drugs or alcohol when they felt upset. The enlightenment model, on the other hand, implies prolonged, long-term help. Recipients who endorsed the enlightenment model may have realized that the Learning Skills Program was not going to provide quite the kind of help they were looking for, but still stayed in to get as much help as they could.

We had also predicted that endorsement of the medical and enlightenment models would be related to feelings of helplessness and hopelessness at the end of the counseling program. Among the 23 students who completed the program, there was only one statistically significant correlation between any of the initial model scores and any of the four helplessness measures. Endorsement of the enlightenment model was negatively related with expectations for greater success in school ($r = -.49$, $p < .009$). However, these students also filled out the Counseling Perspectives test again at the end of the program, and we calculated the model scores from this second testing the same way we had done initially. The post-test model scores were more generally related to the helplessness measures, as might be expected, because they were administered at the same time and place. The correlations among the final model scores and the helplessness measures are presented in Table 3.

As Table 3 shows, there is no relationship that reaches conventional levels of statistical signficance between the moral or enlightenment model scores and any of the measures of helplessness. However, moral model scores do tend to be negatively related to expectations for success, which is not a finding we had predicted. Because recipients who more strongly

TABLE 3
Correlations among Final Model Scores and Measures of Helplessness[a]

Model	Hopeful	Give up	Mistakes	Expect success
Moral	−.13 (n.s.)	−.14 (n.s.)	.24 (n.s.)	−.32 ($p < .08$)
Compensatory	−.16 (n.s.)	.18 (n.s.)	.21 (n.s.)	−.16 (n.s.)
Enlightenment	−.22 (n.s.)	.25 (n.s.)	.33 ($p < .06$)	−.39 ($p < .03$)
Medical	−.35 ($p < .05$)	.34 ($p < .05$)	.24 (n.s.)	−.23 (n.s.)

[a] For all correlations, $N = 23$. N.S. = not significant.

endorse the moral model are, theoretically at least (Brickman *et al.,* 1982), inclined to view themselves as lazy, perhaps this finding is not so surprising. Obviously, it is quite possible to believe that one can and should do better in school, while still doubting that one actually will. In any case, the fact that the moral model scores are not significantly related to any of the other helplessness measures indicates that the association between agreement with this model and lower expectations of success reflects concerns other than general feelings of hopelessness or incompetence.

Only the enlightenment and medical model scores are related to more than one of the helplessness measures. The more strongly participants endorsed the medical model, the more inclined they were to give up on school, and the less hopeful they felt about doing better at school. Greater agreement with the enlightenment model was associated with lower expectations for future success and tended to be related to higher expectations of repeating the same old academic mistakes. So, the overall pattern of findings presented in Table 3 is quite consistent with our initial predictions. Apparently, those students who more strongly held to a medical or enlightenment model at the close of the Learning Skills Program were more inclined to feel hopeless about improving their grades and incapable of doing better in school.

Obviously, with such high attrition rates in this study, the findings from the 23 people who actually completed the Learning Skills Program must be viewed with caution. These people are most likely different on many dimensions from most people who sign up for study skills training. But the attrition here is not completely uninterpretable. The one way we know these people differed from those who dropped out is that they agreed less strongly with the medical model at the beginning of the program. This suggests that the range of medical model scores, at least, may have been rather low and restricted in the sample of program completers. This restricted range would, of course, limit the size of correlations between these scores and less restricted measures. Had the sample of completers been more like the sample of starters, the relationship between endorsement of the medical model and feelings of helplessness may have emerged as even stronger.

Finally, we also considered the possibility that people who stayed in the program did so because they changed their initial models more toward the compensatory or moral orientations that the group counselors seemed to hold. However, there is little evidence that the people who stayed in the program were moving as a group toward any particular model. We conducted a repeated measures analysis of variance on the pretest and post-test models, and did not find any significant changes in any of the model scores. In addition, the pretest measures of each model correlate fairly well with their post-test counterparts (pre–post compensatory $r = .74$; pre–post moral r = .60; pre–post enlightenment r = .64; pre–post medical r = .41; N = 23). With the possible exception of the medical model, participants tended to end the Learning Skills Program endorsing the same help orientations they began with.

Discussion

Our results suggest a disturbing picture of what happens to help recipients when they are more inclined to models that minimize their own moral responsibility for solving problems. Although they already tend to feel unable or unwilling to control an important outcome, they seek help feeling anything but helpless. Endorsement of the medical or enlightenment models was associated with high expectations for effective help and high hopes for improvement. But such high expectations are very vulnerable to disconfirmation. Recipients who more strongly endorse the medical orientation are apparently particularly prone to becoming dissatisfied with the help they receive and are more likely to withdraw from the helping relationship. By the time the help ends, the more strongly recipients hold to a medical or enlightenment model, the less hopeful they seem to feel. Rather, they are inclined to say that they might as well give up, or that they are doomed to repeating their past mistakes. In short, such recipients appear to be worse off after being helped than they were before.

Our findings indicate that the helping models proposed by Brickman *et al.* (1982) can be useful theoretical tools for understanding recipients reactions to aid. On a more practical level, they also suggest that some measure of applicants' help orientations would be useful to counselors, at least in determining who is likely to stay with and benefit from a learning skills program. But before we draw too many conclusions from our findings, it is important to recognize that there are many limitations on this study and some basic questions about the helping models that remain unanswered. Among the limitations are the correlational nature of the study, the fact that the relationship between certain models and feelings of helplessness has been observed in only one helping situation, and that we have so far only self-reports of helplessness and no actual performance data. The questions that these findings raise include: Can we, and should we, tailor helping programs to suit the models of all recipients, or should we try to change the models of some recipients to ones that seem more functional? Can recipient's models even be changed? Can we determine more specifically how endorsement of the medical or enlightenment models may interfere with personal problem-solving efforts? In the remainder of this chapter we discuss the limitations on our study and some possible answers to these questions.

CLARIFYING THE CAUSAL IMPACT
OF RECIPIENT ORIENTATIONS

Because we have only looked at the correlation between the help orientations and feelings of helplessness among recipients, we obviously have no basis for assuming that adopting certain models causes people to give up and feel hopeless at the termination of helping. In our particular study, it is quite possible that a third variable might explain both why certain recipients adopt the medical or enlightenment model and why they feel helpless. Brickman *et al.* (1982) argue that people high in self-esteem are most inclined to apply the compensatory model to themselves, whereas those who have a lower opinion of themselves are more likely to favor the medical model and particularly the enlightenment model. Therefore, those people who ended the program feeling incapable of improving may have also felt that way before they started the program. The high expectations associated with these models at the first learning skills session probably reflected recipients' faith in helpers more than it reflected any confidence in themselves. So, perhaps those recipients who endorsed the medical or enlightenment models were not actually any worse off for having participated in the Learning Skills Program. In a sense, they may just be back to where they started before the program began, but with one important exception.

When people try to get help for school problems, but do not find the help very useful, the consequences could be quite devastating or quite positive. On the one hand, they may be all the more convinced that their success in school is beyond anyone's control, and subsequently experience universal helplessness (Abramson *et al.,* 1978). On the other hand, they may eventually realize that no one can solve their problems for them, and reevaluate their approach to dealing with their academic difficulties in a way that leads them to take more personal responsibility (Wortman & Dintzer, 1978). It is interesting that in our sample, endorsement of the medical model was most strongly associated with general feelings of hopelessness and an inclination to give up on school. The enlightenment model, on the other hand, was more strongly related to recipients' feelings that they would continue to repeat the same old mistakes they used to make. Perhaps, then, endorsement of the medical model is more likely to lead to universal helplessness among recipients, whereas the enlightenment model is more strongly associated with feelings of personal helplessness (Abramson *et al.,* 1978). Because personal helplessness implies individual failure rather than general uncontrollability, those recipients who initially endorsed the enlightenment model may be more inclined eventually to escape their feelings of helplessness by deciding that the problem is in them and should be solved by them. We plan to follow up the subjects in this study, to see if those who left the program with an enlightenment model move to a more moral model, and to investigate whether any of those models are associated with better or worse performance in classes.

It may be possible to assess more clearly both the causal impact of adopting certain models and the generality of any consequences associated with them by more directly manipulating the orientations that recipients hold for a variety of problems and solutions. The techniques used by Fisher and his associates (Farina *et al.*, 1978; Fisher & Farina, 1979) in leading subjects to view mental illness as a medical or learning problem suggest some ways in which such manipulations might be accomplished. If subjects could be led to view helping situations in different ways, it might be interesting to see how the different orientations affect their approach to the problem-solving steps proposed by Dewey (1933). These steps consist of recognizing that one has a problem, specifying the nature of the problem, considering alternative solutions, selecting the optimal solution, and then implementing and testing that solution. These five steps are theoretically involved in overcoming any problem (Dewey, 1933; Urban & Ford, 1971). Quite possibly, different helping models imply different degrees of recipient and donor responsibility for taking each of these steps. If so, studying the impact of the various orientations on recipients' feelings about the steps might allow us to pinpoint more precisely how certain models may interfere with recipients' attitudes and behaviors toward helping themselves. We are currently conducting some pilot studies along these lines.

STRATEGIC FUNCTIONS OF CLAIMING TO BE HELPLESS

Collecting actual academic performance data is important for another general reason. Because, so far, we only have people's public self-reports of their feelings of helplessness, we cannot be certain how accurately those reports reflect private experience. The helplessness measures we administered were included in a questionnaire entitled "Learning Skills Evaluation". Participants may have correctly realized that both their counselors and their counselors' superiors would be hearing about the results from these questionnaires. Under such conditions, a number of strategic functions could be served by claiming to feel helpless, whether or not participants actually felt that way.

First of all, some recipients may have used such claims as a way of getting back at counselors they did not like. Given that counselors were more inclined to compensatory or moral orientations, the more strongly recipients endorsed the medical or enlightenment models, the more conflicted their relationships with the group leaders may have been. As a result, they could have felt fairly optimistic about their academic future, but claimed to feel hopeless so that it would appear the counselor was doing a poor job. This seems rather unlikely, though, because over 95% of the participants who finished the program wrote very positive comments about their counselors on open-ended sections of the evaluation questionnaire (Renzaglia & Coates, 1).

Another strategic function that claims of hopelessness and helplessness may serve is to lower the expectations of important observers. People may say they expect to fail, when actually they have high hopes of succeeding, because they want observers to view any minimal success they do have as quite an accomplishment. This might be particularly true of recipients who more strongly endorsed the moral model, and who also tended to report lower expectations for their future academic performance. Because people who adopt the moral model want to be seen as generally capable of taking care of themselves (Brickman *et al.,* 1982), they may also try to maintain such a public view of themselves by keeping observers' expectations of their performance rather low. It will be interesting to see whether, contrary to their stated expectations, people who more strongly endorse the moral model actually show greater academic improvement. Recent research by Schachter (1982) suggests they well might because people seem quite good at solving some very difficult problems when they decide to do so on their own.

Finally, claiming to be helpless might be seen by recipients as a good way of getting more help. Believing that their counselors would be seeing their answers, participants who agreed more strongly with the medical or enlightenment models may have felt that if they appeared pitiful enough, their group leaders would have mercy on them and continue to work with them. It is quite interesting, and rather paradoxical, that many religious belief systems seem to maintain as a basic tenet that a greater or ultimate control can be obtained through apparent helplessness. The comforting notion from the New Testament that "the meek will inherit the earth" and the more cynical notion from Karl Marx that "religion is the opium of the masses" both express the point that religious belief systems promise rewards for the weak and unassertive while often threatening punishment for the strong and aggressive. This notion is not unique to Christianity and, in fact, seems to reach a rather dramatic pinnacle in the traditional religion of Ojibwa Native Americans (Hay, 1971, 1973). This religion teaches that the most effective way of obtaining the aid of the gods is to starve oneself into a state of literal physical helplessness. Recipients who are inclined to the medical or enlightenment model, and who are therefore also inclined to see helpers as almost godlike in their power, may well employ a somewhat similar, if more moderate, tack. Of course, even if recipients' claims of hopelessness actually reflect high hopes of getting more help, they still are not likely to be feeling very capable of helping themselves.

RECIPIENT RESPONSIBILITY, RECIPIENTS' PROBLEMS, AND HELP-ORIENTATION CONFLICT

Another limitation on our findings is the specific helping situation we studied. We had initially suggested that even if help is effective in solving certain problems, recipients who adopt models that minimize their responsibility for solutions will be more inclined to feel helpless. But maybe those recipients in our study who were more inclined to a medical or enlightenment model really did suffer from some psyhological disturbance or destructive compulsive behaviors and so were not very effectively helped by the limited, temporary training offered by the Learning Skills Program. Recipients' feelings of helplessness, then, may be more strongly related to the failure of the help offered to address their problems than it is to the models that recipients endorse. However, the Counseling Center does screen applicants to the Learning Skills Program for possible mental illness, and makes referrals to other types of professional services where appropriate. This minimizes the likelihood that recipients who endorsed the medical or enlightenment models were suffering from problems that were much different from recipients who endorsed other models. In addition, the medical model, at least, has been associated with feelings of lack of control among recipients in other situations (Fisher & Farina, 1979), and even under conditions where the help is very effective in solving problems (Raps *et al.*, 1982). So, it would appear that recipients' help orientations may be better predictors of eventual helplessness than the actual effectiveness of the help provided across a variety of situations.

A related possibility, alluded to earlier, is that there was a clash between the models that counselors held and the enlightenment or medical models of participants. It could be that endorsement of models that minimize recipient responsibility for solutions does not necessarily promote helplessness, but rather that recipients are not likely to feel very "helped" when donors are taking much different approaches to the situation than they do. Consistent with the latter point, some clinicians (e.g., Haley, 1963) have argued for the importance of using the client's language in psychotherapy. A study reported by Claiborn, Ward and Strong (1981) indicates that when counselors interpret their clients' problems in terms that are consistent with the clients' initial beliefs, healthy adjustment becomes more likely. In a series of experiments that seem particularly pertinent to the present study, Forsyth and Forsyth (1982) found that when individuals who had a high internal locus of control were provided with internal–controllable explanations for social problems they had encountered, they reported feeling more competent and capable of dealing with similar problems in the future. However, individuals who had a high external locus of control were generally unaffected by such explanations, and even tended to report lower perceived self-competence on some measures after being told their problems were due to internal–controllable causes. As these authors suggest, when people are presented with information that is inconsistent with many of the beliefs and attitudes they hold, they usually reject or ignore it. But, in some instances, they may start to doubt those previously held opinions and begin to question generally the correctness of their thoughts and behaviors. The learning skills counselors, consistent with the moral and compensatory models they favored, may well have stressed the participants' own responsibility for doing better in school. And some recipients, who were more inclined to medical or enlightenment models, which are generally consistent with a perceived external locus of control, may have begun to doubt all they thought they knew about how grades are given in school. As a result, they may have felt more stupid than ever, and less capable of dealing with academia.

However, at least in a study skills context, participants' refusal to take much responsibility for solving their own problems and the conflict between their views and those of counselors are basically two sides of the same coin. After all, what the clients and counselors are likely to differ on is the issue of responsibility. If counselors had reinforced participants' medical and enlightenment leanings, recipients may well have felt more comforted and assured (Claiborn et al., 1981). But, there seems a fair probability they still would have ended up dependent and unable or unwilling to help themselves. For instance, the more strongly participants endorsed the medical model, the more pleased they probably would have been if the counselors could just hand them a "smart pill" that would have improved their intellectual performance. This is not such an outlandish idea as it may seem because research by Davis, Mohs, Tinklenberg, Pfefferbaum, Hollister and Kopell (1978) indicates that the drug, physostigmine, has considerable potential for improving memory and increasing general mental capacity. But research suggests that the more people believe a pill will solve their problems, the less effort they apply toward solving their own problems (see Farina & Fisher, 1982, for a review). Similarly, Nentwig (1978) found that subjects who believed a placebo would help them stop smoking showed considerable immediate reduction in cigarettes consumed. But 6 months later, a group who had been led to believe they could control their smoking only through their own efforts were doing much better than the drug group was. Even when problems, such as serious disease, are in fact largely beyond the control of help recipients, they are still more likely to get well if they believe they can and should work at maintaining good health practices (Taylor, 1979).

Taken together, this research strongly suggests that a medical model treatment for study skills problems is likely to turn out physostigmine addicts, with a lot of faith in the power of the treatment but little faith in their own skills and abilities without the treatment. A pill may make it easier to study, but people still have to do the work of studying in order to get good grades. This reasoning indicates, then, that even if counselors had agreed with participants' points of view, we would still find that endorsement of models that minimize recipient responsibility for solving problems is associated with greater feelings of personal incompetence and lack of control.

CHANGING RECIPIENTS' MODELS

The preceding discussion indicates that tailoring helping programs to suit the medical or enlightenment orientation of recipients is not likely to be a very effective way of avoiding helplessness among recipients. An alternative solution might be to change recipients' models in a direction favoring greater responsibility for solving problems. This may not be an easy task, however. In our pilot work relating these models to the problem-solving steps, we have found it very difficult to get subjects to adopt different models by simply describing helping situations in different terms. In the learning skills study, there was also little evidence that recipients changed models over the course of the program. It may be that certain types of problems, or certain recipient characteristics such as self-esteem or perceived locus of control, will lead people to hold quite strongly to a particular type of model (Brickman et al., 1982). If so, helpers may well find that rather special interventions are needed to move recipients from less functional to more functional models.

Aside from the difficulties involved in getting people to change their orientations, there is also the issue of knowing what model fits best with a particular helping situation. In our own study we found that stronger endorsement of the medical or enlightenment models was related to greater feelings of hopelessness, but no evidence that endorsement of the moral or compensatory models was associated with higher expectations for improvement or success. This is to some extent understandable because recipients who endorse these latter models have only themselves to rely on in the future, and may have high or low expectations depending on the level of their own self-discipline, self-esteem, etc. Although generally favoring the compensatory model, Brickman *et al.* (1982) point out that it is not at all evident just what model might be best for students to adopt in educational settings. To the extent that students feel more responsible for solving their own problems, they may feel less responsible for following their teachers' instructions. Likewise, the reactive hospital patient may be more willing to contribute to his or her own health care, but less willing to submit to demands or requests of hospital staff (Taylor, 1979). By encouraging recipients to adopt moral or compensatory models, we may be able to minimize their feelings of helplessness, but only by undercutting the effectiveness of the help that donors provide.

One solution to this dilemma may be to encourage certain models while recipients are being helped, but then to attempt to change those models at the termination of the help. Helping programs might be followed up with something like mastery training (Seligman, 1975) or therapy aimed at changing recipients' causal attributions to ones that imply more personal control (Dweck, 1975; Forsyth & Forsyth, 1982). Such interventions may help recipients to feel that they can solve their own problems, or at least maintain the solution provided by the helpers. However, even if recipients believe that they can solve their own problems, they may continue to feel that they should not need to, that it is the helper's job to take care of that. It may be necessary to change recipients' moral attributions along with their causal attributions. Unfortunately, at this point, we can only speculate on how this might be accomplished. But, moral attributions do seem to be a particularly social phenomenon (Brickman *et al.,* 1982; Hamilton, 1978) and so perhaps can be most effectively manipulated through special types of social interaction.

To change people's moral attributions, something like paradoxical therapy may be effective (Haley, 1963; Raskin Klein, 1976). A common paradoxical technique is prescribing the symptom, or in other words, encouraging clients to engage in symptomatic or troublesome behaviors rather than trying to avoid them. For example, depressed clients may be concerned because they lie in bed for 12 hours a day doing nothing. The therapist might say that the clients could be genuinely fatigued and should try staying in bed for 14 instead of 12 hours each day. If clients follow the prescription and stay in bed longer, they can share responsiblity for the symptom with the therapist. On the other hand, if they feel like getting up before 14 hours have passed, they have no one but themselves to credit for the apparent improvement. Some practitioners of paradoxical therapy have been quite explicit in suggesting that it encourages clients to rely on themselves rather than on the therapist (Haley, 1963) and to feel shame for failing to maintain improvements (Rosen, 1953). Perhaps paradoxical techniques could be applied in helping situations other than psychotherapy to move recipients from enlightenment or medical models to compensatory or moral models.

Another type of social interaction that may be particularly effective in altering recipients' moral attributions involves turning recipients into donors. There is fairly consistent evidence that teaching is probably a more effective way of improving abilities and general competence than is being taught (Allen, 1976; Zajonc & Bargh, 1980; Zajonc, Markus, & Markus, 1979). Although teachers may be motivated by a moral responsibility to help their students rather than themselves, the improved sense of competence they develop may well lead to more favorable self-evaluations (Goodman, 1967) and perhaps therefore to better self-care too. As Brickman *et al.* (1982) suggest, part of the reason Alcoholics Anonymous may be fairly successful is because it emphasizes mutual help among members. The moral responsibility of setting a good example may aid many members in maintaining their alcohol abstinence. At the same time, when members help with others' problems, they are able to operate under the compensatory model. They are taking responsibility for solving problems they did not create. This may help to counteract some of the more negative consequences of the enlightenment model approach that Alcoholics Anonymous otherwise stresses. Indeed, a similar technique might be very useful with study skills participants who are inclined to an enlightenment model. At the close of the formal program, participants could be set up in pairs or small groups of "study buddies" who will continue to meet and work together on school problems. This might provide enlightenment-oriented people with the continued help they want, while making it all the more likely that they will develop their own competence, abilities, and improved self-concept.

We have presented the results from a study that indicates that the more strongly help recipients endorse a medical or enlightenment model, the more inclined they are to feel helpless and hopeless at the termination of the help. We have argued that, in general, the best way to deal with this problem might be to change recipients' models when the help ends, and we have made some specific suggestions as to how this might be accomplished. But sometimes helpers will do better by those they help by leaving their models alone. As both Wortman and Brehm (1975) and Janoff-Bulman and Brickman (1981) point out, sometimes giving up is the best thing we can do. Not every one can succeed at some important tasks, and no one can succeed at all important tasks. We are all, in some domains at least, genuinely helpless. Painful though this may be to accept, accepting it is much more functional than wasting a lot of energy and resources on a pursuit we will never fulfill.

Both Wortman and Brehm, and Janoff-Bulman and Brickman, further indicate that helpers may help most, not by convincing recipients that they will always be in control, but rather by assisting them in sorting out what areas they can control and what areas they cannot. This may be difficult for helpers to do because confronting people with their own helplessness will quite possibly be rather depressing for them (Abramson et al., 1978). Perhaps, at such times, religion or other shared value systems that remind us of our unavoidable limitations as humans, and the worthiness of accepting those limitations, will be rather comforting. At least, sayings such as, "There are no atheists in a foxhole", imply that such belief systems can be reassuring when we are faced with the inevitable fact of our own lack of control. Of course, helpers want to avoid making recipients so comfortable with their failures that their helplessness begins to generalize, becoming like the opium Karl Marx complained about. Still, too often it seems, both researchers and helpers may forget that we can all use a little fix now and then.

REFERENCES

Abramson, L. Y., Seligman, M. E. P., & Teasdale, J. D. Learned helplessness in humans: Critique and reformulation. *Journal of Abnormal Psychology,* 1978, **87**(1), 49–74.

Alkire, A. A., Collum, M. E., Kaswan, J., & Love, L. R. Information exchange and accuracy of verbal communication under social power conditions. *Journal of Personality and Social Psychology,* 1968, **9**, 301–308.

Allen, V. L. *Children as teachers: Theory and research in tutoring.* New York: Academic Press, 1976.

Baum, A., & Gatchel, R. J. Cognitive determinants of reaction to uncontrollable events: Development of reactance and learned helplessness. *Journal of Personality and Social Psychology,* 1981, **40**(6), 1078–1089.

Brickman, P., Rabinowitz, V. C., Karuza, J., Coates, D., Cohn, M., & Kidder, L. Models of helping and coping. *American Psychologist,* 1982, **37**(4), 368–384.

Broll, L., Gross, A. E., & Piliavin, I. Effects of offered and requested help on help-seeking and reactions to being helped. *Journal of Applied Social Psychology,* 1974, **4**, 244–258.

Brown, I., & Inouye, D. K. Learned helplessness through modeling: The role of perceived similarity in competence. *Journal of Personality and Social Psychology,* 1978, **36**(8), 900–908.

Bulman, R. J., & Wortman, C. B. Attributions of blame and coping in the "real world": Severe accident victims react to their lot. *Journal of Personality and Social Psychology,* 1977, **35**, 351–363.

Chambliss, C. A., & Murray, E. J. Efficacy attribution, locus of control, and weight loss. *Cognitive Therapy and Research,* 1979, **3**, 349–353.

Claiborn, C. D., Ward, S. R., & Strong, S. R. Effects of congruence between counselor interpretations and client beliefs. *Journal of Counseling Psychology,* 1981, **28,** 101–109.

Coates, D., & Wortman, C. B. Depression maintenance and interpersonal control. In A. Baum and J. E. Singer (Eds.), *Advances in environmental psychology: Applications of personal control* (Vol. 2). Hillsdale, New Jersey: Lawrence Erlbaum, 1980.

Davis, F. Deviance disavowal: The management of strained interaction by the visibly handicapped. *Social Problems,* 1961, **9,** 120–132.

Davis, K. L., Mohs, R. C., Tinklenberg, J. R., Pfeiferbaum, A., Hollister, L. E., & Kopell, B. S. Physostigmine: Improvement of long term memory processes in normal humans. *Science,* 1978, **201,** 272–274.

Davison, G. C., & Valins, S. Maintenance of self-attributed and drug-attributed behavior change. *Journal of Personality and Social Psychology,* 1969, **11,** 25–33.

Dewey, J. *How we think.* New York: Heath, 1933.

Dweck, C. S. The role of expectations and attributions in the alleviation of learned helplessness. *Journal of Personality and Social Psychology,* 1975, **31,** 674–685.

Ellis, E. M., Atkeson, B. M, & Calhoun, K. S. An assessment of long-term reaction to rape. *Journal of Abnormal Psychology,* 1981, **90**(3), 263–266.

Farina, A., & Fisher, J. D. Beliefs about mental disorders: Findings and implications. In G. Weary & H. L. Mirels (Eds.), *Integrations of clinical and social psychology.* London and New York: Oxford University Press, 1982.

Farina, A., Fisher, J. D., Getter, H., & Fischer, E. H. Some consequences of changing people's views regarding the nature of mental illness. *Journal of Abnormal Psychology,* 1978, **87**(2), 272–279.

Fisher, J. D., DePaulo, B. M., & Nadler, A. Extending altruism beyond the altruistic act: The mixed effects of aid on the help recipient. In J. P. Rushton & R. M. Sorrentino (Eds.), *Altruism and helping behavior: Social, personality, and developmental perspectives.* Hillsdale, New Jersey: Erlbaum, 1981.

Fisher, J. D., & Farina, A. Consequences of beliefs about the nature of mental disorders. *Journal of Abnormal Psychology,* 1979, **88,** 320–327.

Fisher, J. D., Harrison, C., & Nadler, A. Exploring the generalizability of donor–recipient similarity effects. *Personality and Social Psychology Bulletin,* 1978, **4,** 627–630.

Fisher, J. D., & Nadler, A. The effect of similarity between donor and recipient on reactions to aid. *Journal of Applied Social Psychology,* 1974, **4,** 230–243.

Fisher, J. D., & Nadler, A. Effect of donor resources on recipient self-esteem and self-help. *Journal of Experimental Social Psychology,* 1976, **12,** 139–150.

Fisher, J. D., Nadler, A., & Whitcher-Alagna, S. Recipient reactions to aid. *Psychological Bulletin,* 1982, **91**(1), 27–54.

Forsyth, N. L., & Forsyth, D. R. Internality, controllability and the effectiveness of attributional interpretation in counseling. *Journal of Counseling Psychology,* 1982, **29**(2), 140–150.

Garber, J., & Hollon, S. D. Universal versus personal helplessness in depression: Belief in uncontrollability or incompetence? *Journal of Abnormal Psychology,* 1980, **89**(1), 56–66.

Goffman, E. *Stigma: Notes on the management of spoiled identity.* Englewood Cliffs, New Jersey: Prentice-Hall, 1963.

Goodman, G. An experiment with companionship therapy: College students and troubled boys—Assumptions, selection and design. *American Journal of Public Health,* 1967, **57,** 1772–1777.

Haley, J. *Strategies of psychotherapy.* New York: Grune and Stratton, 1963.

Hamilton, V. L. Who is responsible? Toward a social social psychology of responsibility attribution. *Social Psychology,* 1978, **41,** 316–328.

Hay, T. H. The Windigo psychosis: Psychodynamic, cultural, and social factors in aberrant behavior. *American Anthropologist,* 1971, **73**(1), 1–19.

Hay, T. H. A technique of formalizing and testing models of behavior: Two models of Ojibwa restraint. *American Anthropologist,* 1973, **75**(3), 708–730.

Heider, F. *The psychology of interpersonal relations.* New York: Wiley, 1958.

Hiroto, D. S., & Seligman, M. E. P. Generality of learned helplessness in man. *Journal of Personality and Social Psychology,* 1975, **31**, 311–327.

Janoff-Bulman, R. Characterological versus behavioral self-blame: Inquiries into depression and rape. *Journal of Personality and Social Psychology,* 1979, **37**(10), 1798–1809.

Janoff-Bulman, R., & Brickman, P. Expectations and what people learn from failure. In N. T. Feather (Ed.), *Expectancy, incentive, and action.* Hillsdale, New Jersey: Lawrence Erlbaum, 1981.

Kelley, H. H. Attribution theory in social psychology. In D. Levine (ed.), *Nebraska symposium on motivation* (Vol. 15). Lincoln, Nebraska: University of Nebraska Press, 1967.

Krebs, D. Altruism: An examination of the concept and a review of the literature. *Psychological Bulletin,* 1970, **73**, 258–302.

Ladieu, G., Hanfman, E., & Dembo, T. Studies in adjustment to visible injuries: Evaluation of help by the injured. *Journal of Abnormal and Social Psychology,* 1947, **42**, 169–192.

Langer, E. J., & Benevento, A. Self-induced dependence. *Journal of Personality and Social Psychology,* 1978, **36**, 866–893.

Langer, E. J., & Imber, L. When practice makes imperfect: Debilitating effects of overlearning. *Journal of Personality and Social Psychology,* 1979, **37**, 2014–2024.

Langer, E. J., & Rodin, J. The effects of choice and enhanced personal responsibility for the aged: A field experiment in an institutional setting. *Journal of Personality and Social Psychology,* 1976, **34**, 191–198.

Liberman, B. L. The role of mastery in psychotherapy: Maintenance of improvement and prescriptive change. In J. D. Frank, R. Hoehn-Saric, D. D. Imber, B. L. Liberman, & A. R. Stone (Eds.), *The effective ingredients of successful psychotherapy.* New York: Brunner/Mazel, 1978.

McCord, J. A thirty-year follow-up of treatment effects. *American Psychologist,* 1978, **33**, 284–289.

Morrison, J. K., Bushell, J. D., Hanson G. D., Fentiman, J. R., & Holdridge-Crane, S. Relationship between psychiatric patients' attitudes toward mental illness and attitudes of dependence. *Psychological Reports,* 1977, **41**, 1194.

Mullins, L. C. Locus of desired control and patient role among the elderly. *The Journal of Social Psychology,* 1982, **116**, 269–276.

Nadler, A., Altman, A., & Fisher J. D., Helping is not enough: Recipient's reaction to aid as a function of positive and negative self-regard. *Journal of Personality,* 1979, **47**, 615–628.

Nadler, A., Fisher, J. D., & Streufert, S. When helping hurts: The effects of donor–recipient self-esteem on reactions to aid. *Journal of Personality,* 1976, **44**, 392–409.

Nadler, A., & Porat, I. When names do not help: Effects of anonymity and locus of need attribution on help-seeking behavior. *Personality and Social Psychology Bulletin,* 1978, **4**, 624–626.

Nentwig, C. G. Attribution of cause and long-term effects of the modification of smoking behavior. *Behavioral Analysis and Modification,* 1978, **2**, 285–295.

Nunnally, J. C. *Psychometric theory.* New York: McGraw-Hill, 1967.

Overmier, J. B., & Seligman, M. E. P. Effects of inescapable shock upon subsequent escape and avoidance learning. *Journal of Comparative and Physiological Psychology,* 1967, **63**, 28–33.

Peterson, C., Schwartz, S. M., & Seligman, M. E. P. Self-blame and depressive symptoms. *Journal of Personality and Social Psychology,* 1981, **41**(2), 253–259.

Raps, C. S., Peterson, C., Jonas, M., & Seligman, M. E. P. Patient behavior in hospitals:

Helplessness, reactance or both? *Journal of Personality and Social Psychology,* 1982, **42**, 1036-1041.

Raskin, D. E., & Klein, Z. E. Losing a symptom through keeping it: A review of paradoxical treatment techniques and rationale. *Archives of General Psychiatry,* 1976, **33**, 548-555.

Renzaglia, G. J., & Coates, D. Participants' helping models and reactions to a learning skills program. Unpublished manuscript. University of Wisconsin-Madison, 1981.

Rodin, J. Managing the stress of aging: The role of control and coping. In S. Levine and H. Ursin (Eds.), *NATO conference on coping and health.* New York: Academic Press, 1980.

Rodin, J. & Langer, E. J. Long-term effects of a control-relevant intervention with the institutionalized aged. *Journal of Personality and Social Psychology,* 1977, **35**, 897-902.

Rosen, J. *Direct psychoanalysis.* New York: Grune and Stratton, 1953.

Ross, L., Rodin, J., & Zimbardo, P. G. Toward an attribution therapy: The reduction of fear through induced cognitive-emotional misattribution. *Journal of Personality and Social Psychology,* 1969, **12**, 279-288.

Schachter, S. Recidivism and self-cure of smoking and obesity. *American Psychologist,* 1982, **37**(4), 436-444.

Seligman, M. E. P. *Helplessness.* San Francisco, California: Freeman, 1975.

Seligman, M. E. P., & Maier, S. F. Failure to escape traumatic shock. *Journal of Experimental Psychology,* 1967, **74**, 1-9.

Skinner, B. F. The ethics of helping people. In L. Wispe (ed.), *Sympathy, altruism, and helping behavior.* New York: Academic Press, 1978.

Storms, M. D., Denney, D. R., McCaul, K. D., & Lowery, C. R. Treating insomnia. In I. H. Frieze, D. Bar-Tal, and J. S. Carroll (Eds.), *New approaches to social problems.* San Francisco, California: Jossey-Bass, 1979.

Storms, M. D., & Nisbett, R. E. Insomnia and the attribution process. *Journal of Personality and Social Psychology,* 1970, **16**(2), 319-328.

Taylor, S. E. Hospital patient behavior: Reactance, helplessness or control? *Journal of Social Issues,* 1979, **35**(1), 156-184.

Tessler, R. C., & Schwartz, S. H. Help-seeking, self-esteem, and achievement motivation: An attributional analysis. *Journal of Personality and Social Psychology,* 1972, **21**, 318-326.

Urban, H. B., & Ford, D. H. Some historical and conceptual and perspectives on psychotherapy and behavior change. In A. E. Bergin and S. L. Garfield (Eds.), *The handbook of psychotherapy and behavior change: An empirical analysis.* New York: Wiley, 1971.

Wack, J., & Rodin, J. Nursing homes for the aged: The human consequences of legislation-shaped environments. *Journal of Social Issues,* 1978, **34**(4), 6-21.

Weiner, B. (ed.) *Achievement motivation and attribution theory.* Morristown, New Jersey: General Learning Press, 1974.

Weiss, R. F., Boyer, J. L., Lombardo, J. P., & Stich, M. H. Altruistic drive and altruistic reinforcement. *Journal of Personality and Social Psychology,* 1973, **25**, 390-400.

Wortman, C. B., & Brehm, J. W. Responses to uncontrollable outcomes: An integration of reactance theory and the learned helplessness model. In L. Berkowitz (Ed.), *Advances in experimental social psychology,* (Vol. 8). New York: Academic Press, 1975.

Wortman, C. B., & Dintzer, L. Is an attributional analysis of the learned helplessness phenomenon viable?: A critique of the Abramson-Seligman-Teasdale reformulation. *Journal of Abnormal Psychology,* 1978, **87**(1), 75-90.

Wortman, C. B., & Dunkel-Schetter, C. Interpersonal relationships and cancer: A theoretical analysis. *Journal of Social Issues,* 1979, **35**(1), 120-155.

Zajonc, R. B., & Bargh, J. The confluence model: Parameter estimation for six divergent data sets on family factors and intelligence. *Intelligence,* 1980, **4**, 349-361.

Zajonc, R. B., Markus, H., & Markus, G. B. The birth order puzzle. *Journal of Personality and Social Psychology,* 1979, **37**, 1325-1341.

CHAPTER 11

Reactions to Aid in Communal and Exchange Relationships*

Margaret S. Clark

INTRODUCTION

It is easy to imagine having very different reactions to being offered precisely the same aid from people with whom we have different types of relationships. Receiving an offer to help paint your living room from a close friend may result in warm feelings toward the friend, an expression of appreciation, and acceptance of the offer. However, receipt of the same offer from a student in your class may elicit surprise, concern about whether the student desires a closer relationship with you than you desire or feel appropriate, or about just what the student expects from you in return. Such an offer is also likely to be turned down.

*Preparation of this chapter and a portion of the research reported were supported by National Institute of Mental Health Grant RO3MH35844-01. Some of the material in this chapter was first presented at a symposium on "Recipient Reactions to Aid" chaired by J. Fisher at the 1980 Meetings of the American Psychological Association in Montreal, Canada.

Or, imagine receiving an offer of aid right after you have aided another. Your close friend has been having car trouble. You happen to be a mechanic and you offer to look it over. It takes you quite a bit of time but you find the source of the problem and solve it. As soon as you finish, your friend says, "Say, I was going to wash and wax my car this afternoon. Bring yours over and I'll do yours too." In this case, your friend's offer of aid probably appears to be a payment and you might react by being surprised and perhaps even hurt. Furthermore, you would probably refuse the offer, believing it to be inappropriate. However, had the person been a customer whom you did not know personally, you would have *expected* payment, although, no doubt, you would prefer money to having your car washed and waxed.

In the first situation you react positively to being aided by someone who has one type of relationship with you, a relationship that might be characterized as "close," and negatively to receiving the same aid from someone with whom you have a different, more "formal" type of relationship. In the second, you react negatively to being aided by someone who is close to you, but you would have reacted positively to receiving a benefit from someone with whom you have a more formal relationship.

In this chapter a distinction between two types of relationships, communal and exchange, made by Clark and Mills (1979; Clark, 1981; Mills & Clark, 1982), is drawn. Then implications of this distinction for reactions to receiving aid in different types of relationships are described and supporting research is reviewed. In doing so, the reasons behind the varied reactions in the situations just described should become clear.

DISTINGUISHING COMMUNAL
AND EXCHANGE RELATIONSHIPS

We have many relationships with others and different names for the other people involved in those relationships—friends, relatives, romantic partners, co-workers, and clients. Some of the differences between those relationships are captured in a distinction between communal and exchange relationships (Clark & Mills, 1979; Mills & Clark, 1982).

The norms that govern behavior in communal and exchange relationships differ. For instance, in communal relationships, members have a special obligation to be responsive to one another's needs, whereas in exchange relationships they do not. This and other distinguishing characteristics of communal and exchange relationships are discussed subsequently. First, though, some comments are in order regarding the circumstances under which people tend to apply communal norms to a relationship and the circumstances under which they tend to apply exchange norms to a relationship.

Most people apply communal norms to relationships with members of their family. They may also choose to apply them to other relationships. Although this matter has received little research attention, the likelihood of a person choosing to apply communal norms to a relationship with another seems to depend on factors such as (1) the attractiveness of the other to the person, (2) the availability of the other for a communal relationship, and (3) the number of existing communal relationships in which the person is already involved. The more attractive and available the other seems to be and the fewer existing communal relationships a person already has relative to the number desired, the greater the likelihood that the person will apply communal norms to the relationship. The relationships we have with the people whom we call "friends" or "romantic partners" are typically communal relationships.

Most people apply exchange norms to relationships with people with whom they do business, and they may choose to apply exchange norms to other relationships as well. They seem more apt to apply exchange norms to another when that other can provide valuable benefits but the other is (1) not particularly attractive to them, (2) is unavailable for a communal relationship, and/or (3) to the extent that they have many already existing communal relationships relative to the number they desire. The relationships we have with people whom we call "acquaintances" or "clients" are typically exchange relationships.

Norms Governing the Giving of Benefits

In the following discussion, the term *benefit* is used to refer to anything of value that is intentionally given by one member of a relationship to the other.

In communal relationships a norm exists to give benefits when the other has a need for them. Benefits are also appropriately given when something can be provided that would be particularly pleasing to the other. As Suttles (1970) has noted, transfers of benefits in friendships "must take into consideration what are judged to be the other's particular tastes, preferences or needs" (p. 99). Thus we often do such things as drive our friends, relatives, or romantic partners to the airport to catch planes, help them shovel their stuck cars out of snowbanks, buy them birthday gifts that suit their preferences, comfort them when they are feeling down, or take them out to their favorite restaurant on a special occasion. People with whom we have communal relationships expect such benefits, and react positively to receiving them and negatively when they are not forthcoming. Adherence to the norm to be responsive to one another's needs in communal relationships provides members with a sense of security; they can count on each other.

The general obligation that members of communal relationships have to benefit one another when needs arise is not altered by receipt of a specific benefit (Mills & Clark, 1982). In other words, when one member of a communal relationship provides another with aid, the two people's obligations to be responsive to one another's needs are not altered.

In exchange relationships, benefits are given when one person owes the other for a benefit received from that other in the past, or they are given with the expectation of receiving a benefit of comparable value in return. In other words, recipients of benefits expect to repay the other for specific benefits, and know that the other expects to be repaid as well. If benefits are not repaid, negative feelings may result. Unlike members of communal relationships, members of exchange relationships do not have a special obligation to fulfill the other's needs.

Mills and Clark (1982) have noted that from the perspective of members of communal relationships, benefits given and received are not part of a specific exchange. On the other hand, members of exchange relationships *do* perceive benefits given and received to be part of an exchange. They keep track of these benefits to ensure that they are of comparable value.

As a result of the norms just outlined, members of exchange relationships may tend to give and receive comparable benefits. Returning a benefit that is comparable to a benefit received makes it clear that the debt created by that prior benefit has been eliminated. Members of exchange relationships may also return benefits (or promise to return benefits) very *soon* after having received a benefit. The sooner a debt is eliminated, the better. In contrast, members of communal relationships often give and receive noncomparable benefits. This may happen in part because they need not be concerned with fulfilling specific debts and in part because two people's needs and preferences are rarely the same. In addition, members of communal relationships may not give a benefit soon after receiving a benefit if the other has no need for the benefit or if a suitable occasion has not arisen (Mills & Clark, 1982).

Variability in Strength of and Certainty about Relationships

Communal relationships may vary in strength. A communal relationship with one's child may be stronger than a communal relationship with a friend. Therefore the needs of the child may take precedence over the needs of the friend. In contrast to communal relationships, exchange relationships do not vary in strength (Mills & Clark, 1982).

Peoples' certainty about having either kind of relationship with another may also vary (Mills & Clark, 1982). For instance, after going out on a first date with a woman to whom he is attracted and with whom he desires a communal relationship, a man may be uncertain about whether or not she will follow communal norms in their future interactions. Two years later, however, having continued in the relationship in which both members have consistently followed communal norms, the man will be far more certain about the nature of his relationship. Similarly, a set of parents may agree to an exchange relationship with another set of parents in which each will perform babysitting services for the other. After babysitting for the first time, that couple may experience some uncertainty about whether the other couple will "live up to the bargain." However, after some experience with the arrangement and/or after hearing from others about how responsible the other couple is, their certainty may rise.

Other Typical Differences

Communal and exchange relationships often differ in ways other than those outlined above, including how interdependent the members' outcomes are, whether or not the rewards derived from the relationship are intrinsic to the relationship, and in terms of the length of the relationship. These differences are discussed subsequently. However, it should be emphasized that these differences are unlike those discussed thus far in that they are conceptually distinct from the type of relationship.

Interdependence of Outcomes

A number of authors have noted that members of relationships may come to perceive themselves as a unit (e.g., Hatfield & Sprecher, 1983; Levinger, 1979; Walster, Walster, & Berscheid, 1978; Wegner & Giuliano, 1981). This often happens in communal relationships and, as it does, benefits that one member gives the other often provide the donor with positive outcomes as well. Thus, I may give my husband a camera for his birthday but, because we are a unit, I may derive positive outcomes from that gift. I may use it myself, I may enjoy looking at the photographs he takes, I may even derive pleasure from his enjoyment in using it. In short, it is difficult to separate our outcomes. Of course, benefits given in the context of communal relationships do not always produce joint positive outcomes. Parents may buy their child the sort of clothing that everyone in school is wearing even though the parents personally dislike it and are somewhat embarrassed to have the child wear it.

In contrast, members of exchange relationships seem not as likely to perceive themselves as a unit, and benefits given by one member to the other rarely provide positive outcomes for the donor as well. The person in business who repairs a leak in another person's roof receives a payment for that service, but the repair itself does not produce positive outcomes for the person. However, there are exceptions to this rule. For example, a person may produce a good or service that enhances his or her professional reputation even after it has been sold or exchanged. An architect's reputation may be enhanced when people view a building that is clearly associated with the architect's name even though the plans were sold long ago.

Intrinsic/Extrinsic Nature of Rewards

Many of the rewards and benefits derived from communal relationships are intrinsic to the relationship itself.[1] As Blau (1964) notes, "Friends find pleasure in associating with one another, and the enjoyment of whatever they do together—climbing a mountain, watching a football game—is enhanced by the gratification that *inheres* in the association itself. The mutual affection between lovers or family members has the same result" (p. 15); and a man's "association with the woman he loves is intrinsically rewarding and an end-in-itself for him" (p. 36). Existence of a particular relationship itself is often terribly important to members of communal relationships and they may benefit one another solely to demonstrate their affection and to maintain the relationship. Indeed, members of a communal relationship may derive a sense of identity from the relationship that is very important to them. In exchange relationships, in contrast, rewards derived are much less likely to be intrinsic to the relationship itself. As Blau (1964) notes, "The salesman's associations with customers are not intrinsically rewarding for him but means for making profitable sales" (p. 36). The sale could have been made to anyone.

Length of Relationship

Communal relationships usually involve an expectation of a long-term relationship, whereas exchange relationships need not be long term. However, as was the case with whether or not both members of a relationship derive positive outcomes from a benefit, and whether or not there are intrinsic rewards to be derived from a relationship, type of relationship and length of relationship are conceptually independent. Many exchange relationships last for a long time (Mills & Clark, 1982). For instance, parents may have a long-term exchange relationship with a particular babysitter.

---

[1]Here rewards are distinguished from benefits. A reward is something of value to a person which the other may *or may not* intentionally give to the person.

IMPLICATIONS OF THE COMMUNAL– EXCHANGE DISTINCTION FOR REACTIONS TO AID

Now that communal and exchange relationships have been distinguished, we can turn to a discussion of the implications of the distinction for reactions to receiving (or to not receiving) aid. First, though, it is necessary to define what is meant by the term *aid*. Aid is a benefit in that it is something of value to the recipient that the donor has *intentionally* given to that recipient. However, not *all* benefits may be considered to be aid. The term *aid* is usually reserved for benefits that are given with the intention of meeting a specific need on the part of the other. Thus, money given to a professional painter who has just painted your living room is a benefit, but it is not ordinarily called aid. It has not been given to fulfill a specific need but rather to fulfill a debt. Also, gifts purchased simply to please another or to celebrate a special occasion are usually not referred to as aid, as their primary purpose is not to fulfill a specific need.

In the remainder of this chapter, the implications of the communal–exchange distinction for reactions to aid under various circumstances are discussed. Some of the implications to be discussed have received empirical support and they are presented along with that support. Others have not received research attention. Thus, they must be considered tentative.

Implications of the Norms Regarding the Giving of Benefits

General Comments

How should people react to being aided in communal and exchange relationships? In a communal relationship the recipient should appreciate the aid, be grateful, take it as an indication of the other's affection or caring and perhaps perceive the relationship to be stronger. The person should not react by feeling specifically indebted to the other, nor by attempting immediately to benefit the other unless receiving the aid makes it obvious that the other has a need. The other was obligated to be responsive to the person's needs and as Heider (1958) has noted, a person will not feel obligated when he accepts a benefit if he thinks "that O ought to benefit him, that it was O's duty to benefit him" (p. 264). Feelings of gratefulness and a perceived increase in the strength of a communal relationship should be especially likely to occur when a person desires a communal relationship with another but feels uncertain about that relationship and/or when a person perceives the relationship to be relatively weak.[2]

Do we have evidence for these types of reactions in communal relationships? In one study to be described in greater detail later (Clark & Mills, 1979, Study 2), when the expectation of a communal relationship with another was created, receiving aid (with no request for repayment) did increase attraction for the other relative to receiving no aid. Other than that, in almost all research on reactions to aid, the donor and recipient have been strangers and there has been no reason to believe they would not remain strangers in the future. They probably perceived their relationships to be exchange relationships. Thus, the hypotheses that aid is likely to be taken as a sign of the other's affection in a communal relationship and that aid does not result in a feeling of specific indebtedness (although it might produce feelings of gratitude) in communal relationships remain to be tested in the future.

In exchange relationships, as in communal relationships, aid may be appreciated and the other may be liked for giving it. However, in contrast to communal relationships, aid in exchange relationships should be less likely to be taken as a sign of the donor's affection for the recipient. In addition, aid should arouse feelings of indebtedness and a desire to eliminate the resultant debt as soon as possible by giving a benefit of equivalent value. If the aid cannot be quickly repaid, it may result in negative feelings. If it is assumed that in most studies in which participants are strangers, those participants tend to consider their relationships with others to be exchange relationships, then there is much evidence for these propositions.

Tesser, Gatewood, and Driver (1968), for instance, have shown that the greater the amount of aid a subject receives, the more indebted to the other they feel. Furthermore, there is considerable evidence consistent with the idea that receipt of aid in such relationships arouses a desire to repay the other specifically. In several studies involving pairs of strangers, it has been reported that receipt of aid results in the return of aid or benefits of comparable value (e.g., Goranson & Berkowitz, 1966; Kahn & Tice, 1973; Pruitt, 1968; Stapleton, Nacci, & Tedeschi, 1973; Wilke & Lanzetta, 1970).

---

[2]There is one special situation, however, in which receiving aid that has clearly been given to fulfill one's needs may produce negative feelings in a communal relationship. This situation is most likely to arise in a strong communal relationship. In such a relationship, even when one person's needs become great, the other is obligated to be responsive to those needs. In meeting those needs, the other's *own* needs may be neglected. Consequently, the person whose needs are great may feel like a burden and experience some negative feelings (as well as gratitude) in reaction to receiving aid. This situation may occur when, for instance, one member of a communal relationship becomes chronically ill and the other takes care of that person.

Receiving Aid after Having Just Given Aid

Turning now to a consideration of how people react to receiving aid or an offer of aid under specified circumstances, first consider reactions to aid offered or given soon after one has been asked to aid or has aided the other. Such aid is likely to be perceived as a repayment for the aid the other has requested or received. As such, it should be welcomed and accepted in exchange relationships because it eliminates the other's debt. Furthermore, it should result in greater liking for the other than if no such aid was received. For example, if our neighbor, with whom we have an exchange relationship, asks us to babysit her child and immediately offers to provide the same service for us in return, we should welcome and accept her offer (assuming that we have agreed or intend to agree with her original request).

In contrast, aid received or offered after having aided the other may result in decreased attraction and a refusal (in the case of an offer) in communal relationships. As Clark and Mills (1979) have noted, a repayment or offer of repayment is inappropriate in a communal relationship. It may be taken as a sign that the other does not want a communal relationship or does not believe we desire a communal relationship. However, exceptions to negative reactions to receiving aid immediately after having given aid in communal relationships should occur when our need for that aid is compelling. For example, if we help shovel our friend's car out of a snow bank and we are in immediate need of the same service, it is perfectly appropriate for our friend to offer it to us. Such aid should not appear to be a repayment (Mills & Clark, 1982).

These differential reactions to being offered or given aid following prior aid have received empirical support in three studies (Clark & Mills, 1979, Study 1; Clark & Waddell, 1981, Studies 1 and 2). Each of these studies is now briefly described. In the Clark and Mills study, unmarried male subjects were recruited for a study on verbal skills. The subject and an attractive female, whom he could see on a television monitor, and who was supposedly in the next room, were to work on separate vocabulary tasks. The subject expected to have an opportunity to meet the woman later. Half the subjects were led to anticipate a communal relationship with the attractive female by implying that she was new at the university and was looking forward to meeting people. The remaining half were led to expect an exchange relationship. They were told the female was married, had a child, and lived off campus.

The vocabulary tasks that the subject and confederate worked on consisted of forming 10 words from some scrabblelike letters. They could share letters and each could earn points toward an extra credit by finishing quickly. The real subject finished first and the experimenter asked if he wished to give any letters to the woman. All subjects agreed and the experimenter took the letters to the other. The confederate could then be seen on the monitor accepting the letters, finishing her task using these letters, and writing a note. Soon thereafter the subject was given, presumably from the woman, a note thanking him and saying she wished to give him one of the points she had earned toward extra credit. Finally the subject filled out a measure of attraction for the female under the guise of a premeasure for a future task.

The results from this study are presented in Table 1. As predicted, in the exchange conditions, subjects liked the other better if she gave them the point following their aid than if she did not. In the communal conditions though, just the opposite occurred. The other was liked better when she did *not* than when she did give the subjects a point following their aid. Thus we have evidence that aid from another that follows aid voluntarily given to that other increases attraction in exchange relationships but decreases attraction in communal relationships.

In the study just described, subjects initiated an act of aid and then reacted positively to receiving aid in return soon afterward in exchange relationships, but reacted negatively to receiving aid soon afterward in communal relationships. Next consider a related question: Will the reactions to aid following prior aid fall in a similar pattern in communal and exchange relationships if subjects do not initiate the first act of aid but rather provide aid in response to a request for aid from the other? Once again, in exchange relationships people should expect repayment for aid. We assume that when others request our aid in an exchange relationship they intend to repay us as well. Therefore, receiving aid after having responded to a request for aid in an exchange relationship should serve a preventative function; it should prevent feelings of exploitation and a decrease in attraction.

In communal relationships, however, people are obligated to help an-

TABLE 1

Attraction toward Another as a Function of Relationship and Aid Received Following Aid Freely Given to the Other[a]

Relationship	Aid from the other	
	Present	Absent
Communal	177	194
Exchange	193	176

[a] The higher the score, the greater the attraction. Scores could range from 0 to 240. $N = 24$ per cell. Copyright (1979) by the American Psychological Association. Reprinted by permission of the publishers and authors.

other who asks for aid in order to fulfill a legitimate need. Thus, even after another has requested aid, receipt of aid in return should not be necessary to prevent feelings of exploitation and decreases in attraction in such relationships. Two studies by Clark and Waddell (1981) provide evidence supporting these ideas.

In the first study, female subjects were led to expect a communal or an exchange relationship with an attractive female confederate, whom, they believed, had left for a moment but would be back shortly. In the communal conditions, she was supposedly anxious to begin the study because she was looking forward to meeting people, whereas in the exchange conditions she was anxious to begin because her husband was picking her up after the session. Further, in the communal conditions the subject was told that she and the other would be discussing common interests later on, whereas in the exchange conditions they would be discussing differences in interests. (A separate study done solely to check on the effectiveness of these manipulations indicated that they were effective and is reported in detail in Clark and Waddell [1981]).

Following the manipulation of relationship type, the experimenter seated both subjects in a room, explained their tasks, and left them alone to work on those tasks. After they both finished, the confederate asked the subject to help her on a research methods project by filling out a lengthy questionnaire. All subjects agreed. Afterward, the confederate either did or did not say she would send the subject two dollars from class funds for filling out the questionnaire. Finally, under the guise of a first-impressions rating of the other for purposes of an upcoming part of the study, all subjects filled out a questionnaire in which they were asked questions to tap how exploitative they perceived the other to be, as well as how much they liked the other. The results on both measures are presented in Table 2.

TABLE 2

Feelings of Exploitation and of Attraction as a Function of Relationship and Benefit Received Following Receipt of Requested Aid[a]

Relationship	Measure	Benefit from the other	
		Present	Absent
Communal	Exploitation	11.5	14.1
	Attraction	152.0	152.0
Exchange	Exploitation	10.7	19.3
	Attraction	168.3	138.2

[a] The higher the scores, the greater the feelings of exploitation or of attraction. Exploitation scores could range from 0 to 42. Attraction scores could range from 0 to 121. $N = 10$ per cell.

As predicted, in the exchange conditions subjects liked the other more and felt less exploited by that other if she benefited them in return than if she did not. In contrast, the receipt of a benefit did not significantly affect liking or feelings of exploitation in the communal conditions.

It must be acknowledged that the benefit returned in this study does not fit the definition of aid given earlier. Even so, it might be argued on the basis of these results that an effect of receiving any benefit, including aid, following prior fulfillment of a request for aid from the other in an exchange relationship is a prevention of feelings of exploitation and decreases in attraction, whereas aid or a different benefit following prior aid is not necessary to prevent similar feelings in communal relationships.

Finally, it should be noted that the idea that in communal relationships others from whom we have requested and received aid will react negatively to receiving aid in return was not supported as it was in the first Clark and Mills (1979) study. There are at least three plausible explanations for this. First, in the repayment conditions of the Clark and Waddell study, the confederate implied that she repaid everyone who was willing to fill out her questionnaire. Thus the subjects may have thought of the payment as a standard procedure that did not reflect upon their relationship with the other. A second possibility is that members of communal relationships may not mind being repaid when repayment does not come directly from the other but rather from a third source, in this case class funds. Finally, because the subjects did not initiate giving aid to the other, they should not have interpreted the giving of a benefit in return as a rebuff of a gesture of friendliness as the subjects in Clark and Mills (1979) may have.

A second study by Clark and Waddell (1981) also investigated the conditions under which repayments for specific prior aid are important to prevent feelings of exploitation, this time by asking subjects questions about their existing communal and exchange relationships. Again, it was predicted that payments for aid received would be more important for preventing feelings of exploitation in exchange than in communal relationships.

In this study, subjects were simply asked to imagine themselves having been asked for help by another person. They imagined situations in which the other was a parent and in which the other was a romantic partner (communal conditions) as well as situations in which the other was a landlord and in which the other was a co-worker or fellow student with whom they were not friends (exchange conditions). (Manipulation checks, which are reported in detail in the Clark and Waddell [1981] paper, supported our assumptions that relationships with parents and romantic partners tend to be communal relationships, whereas relationships with landlords, coworkers, and fellow students tend to be exchange relationships.)

The other either asked to siphon some gas from the subject's car to the other's own, or asked for some charcoal for a barbecue. The subjects imagined they had responded to each request and reported how exploited and how hurt they would feel if the other failed to repay them. For comparison purposes, they also reported how exploited and how hurt they would feel if the other *did* repay them. Subjects' answers to these questions were summed to provide a measure of exploitation. The results of this study are presented in Table 3.

Although, on the average, for all relationships, subjects reported they would feel more exploited and hurt if they were not repaid than if they were repaid, the magnitude of this effect was much larger for the exchange than for the communal relationships.[3] Thus, once again, benefiting someone after having requested aid from that person proved to be more important to the prevention of feelings of exploitation in exchange than in communal relationships, and again we assume that this result would apply to the effects of aiding someone after having requested aid from them as well.

Reactions to Aid Given to Fulfill Clear Needs

In communal relationships, people expect their needs to be fulfilled by the other. Thus, in general, they should react positively whenever their needs are met and quite negatively whenever those needs are not met. Furthermore, when their needs are met, they should not anticipate having to repay the other.

TABLE 3

Feelings of Hurt and Exploitation as a Function of Relationship and the Other's Failure to Repay a Favor[a]

Relationship	Repayment		Increase in feelings of exploitation as a function of failure to repay
	Present	Absent	
Communal (parents and romantic partners)	−4.0	−2.8	+1.2
Exchange (co-workers, fellow students and landlords)	−4.2	+0.7	+4.9

[a]The higher the score, the greater the hurt plus exploitation score. Scores could range from −6 to +6. $N = 13$ per cell.

[3]The fact that failure to give repay produced some feelings of hurt and exploitation in the communal conditions is understandable if one takes into account the fact that our communal relationship manipulation was probably not perfect. It seems likely that some of our subjects did not have communal relationships with their parents and/or romantic partners.

On the other hand, in exchange relationships, people do not have a mutual agreement to be responsive to one another's needs. Therefore, how positive will be their reactions to receiving aid when they have a need should be dependent upon whether or not they can repay the other, or whether or not the other has a prior debt to them. Furthermore, not being aided when one has a need should produce less negative affect in an exchange than in a communal relationship (assuming the other in the exchange relationship is not in one's debt).

The second study by Clark and Waddell (1981) provides some support for one of these ideas, specifically the idea that receiving aid in response to one's needs is more important to the prevention of negative feelings toward the other in communal than in exchange relationships. Subjects in that study were asked to imagine not only situations in which they benefited another and were repaid or not but also situations in which they had a particular need that the other either met or did not meet. The situations were ones in which their car was out of gas or in which they were about to have a barbecue but had no charcoal. Again they pictured themselves in each situation with a parent and with a romantic partner (communal relationships) as well as with a landlord and a co-worker or fellow student with whom they were not friends (exchange relationships). The other always knew about their need and they rated how hurt and exploited they would feel if the other failed to and if the other *did* fulfill their need. Once again, the subjects' ratings of hurt and exploitation were added together to form a single measure of exploitation. The results of this study are presented in Table 4.

Although in all relationships subjects reported they would feel more

TABLE 4

Feelings of Hurt and Exploitation as a Function of Relationship and the Other's Failure to Fulfill a Need[a]

Relationship	Need fulfillment		Increase in feelings of exploitation as a function of failure to fulfill a need
	Present	Absent	
Communal (parents and romantic partners)	−5.1	+2.3	+6.4
Exchange (co-workers, fellow students and landlords)	−4.3	−1.5	+2.8

[a]The higher the score, the greater the hurt plus exploitation score. Scores could range from −6 to +6. $N = 13$ per cell.

exploited and hurt if their need was not fulfilled than if it was fulfilled, the magnitude of this effect was much greater for communal than for exchange relationships.[4] Thus we have evidence for the hypothesis that aiding someone when they have a need one knows about is more important to the prevention of feelings of exploitation in established communal than in exchange relationships. This result fits nicely with a finding reported by Bar-Tal, Bar-Zohar, Greenberg, and Hermon (1977). Those authors found that the closer a relationship, the stronger subjects' expectations that the other should offer help when it is needed and the greater the feelings of resentment they say they would experience if no help was forthcoming. In their study, *close* relationships were represented by relationships with parents, friends, and siblings—relationships we would characterize as communal. *Distant* relationships were represented by acquaintances and strangers—relationships we would characterize as exchange.

Effects of Opportunity to Repay on Reactions to Aid

The norms regarding when benefits should be given also imply that the impact of having an opportunity to repay aid on reactions to aid will depend upon type of relationship. People in exchange relationships should react positively, or at least neutrally, to aid given to fulfill needs so long as they have an opportunity to pay it back, but their reactions to aid should be less favorable if aid cannot be repaid. In contrast, having an opportunity to repay should be less important for reactions to aid in communal relationships. Indeed, members of communal relationships may be insulted or feel that the nature of their relationship is in jeopardy if they are required to pay aid back.

Two existing studies in which the relationship between the donor and the recipient of aid would seem to be an exchange relationship support the prediction for exchange relationships. First consider a study by Gergen, Maslach, Ellsworth, and Seipel (1975) in which the relationships studied seem to be exchange relationships. In that study, males who did not know one another to begin with, and had no reason to suspect they would get to know one another well in the future, served as subjects. While participating in a betting game, these subjects found themselves to be low on chips and in danger of being forced out of the game. At this point, subjects received aid from another in the form of additional chips along with a note from

[4]The fact that failure to give aid in response to a need produced some feelings of hurt and exploitation in the exchange conditions is understandable if one takes into account the fact that our exchange relationship manipulation was probably not perfect. It seems likely that some of our subjects had communal relationships with their landlords and/or co-workers/fellow-students.

the other. The note told a third of the subjects not to repay that other, that the other did not need the chips; a third were told to repay an equal amount when they had enough, and the final third were told to repay an equal amount when they had enough *and* that perhaps they could do an extra favor for the donor later on.

Later in the game subjects had a chance to rate their attraction for the other. Consistent with our hypotheses regarding exchange relationships, reactions to receiving aid were most positive when subjects were given an opportunity to repay the other with an equivalent amount of aid. When the other told the subject *not* to repay, *or* when the asked for a repayment larger than the original aid, liking was lower. Castro (1974) also reports evidence consistent with the idea that subjects who are strangers to one another like another who has aided them more if they have an opportunity soon afterwards to repay that other than if they do not have an opportunity to repay. Thus, these studies support the idea that aid will be reacted to more favorably in an exchange relationship if the recipient has an opportunity to repay.

The Gergen *et al.* and Castro studies, unfortunately, offer no evidence for the hypotheses that the ability to repay the other will not influence reactions to aid in communal relationships, or that actually being asked for repayment will result in negative feelings in a communal relationship. However, a second study by Clark and Mills (1979, Study 2) does offer some evidence for the second point, as well as some additional evidence for the idea that aid will be reacted to more favorably in an exchange relationship if the recipient can repay the donor than if the recipient cannot.

In this study, female college students worked on a vocabulary task requiring use of small letter tiles, while an attractive female worked on a similar but, the subject was told, easier task. Expectations of exchange relationships were created by telling subjects that the other was married, had a child, lived far from the university, and would be discussing differences in interests with the subject later. Expectations of a communal relationship were created by telling subjects the other was new at the university, did not know many people and that she and the subject would be discussing common interests later on.[5] The other finished her task first, received a point toward extra credit, and either gave aid, in the form of extra letter tiles, to the subject, or did not give aid. With (or without) this aid, the subject finished *her* task and received four points for finishing her supposedly more difficult task. The other female then either sent a note to the subject in which she requested a point or in which she explicitly indicated that she did

---

[5]The relationship manipulations used in this study were very similar to those used in the Clark and Waddell study, which, as noted earlier, a manipulation check revealed to be successful.

not want any points from the subject. Finally, the subject's liking for the other was assessed.

In the exchange conditions, we expected results that would fit well with the Gergen *et al.* (1975) and Castro (1974) findings. In other words, we predicted that subjects would like another who gave them aid more if she then asked for a point than if she explicitly informed them that she did not want anything in return. In contrast, we expected people in the communal conditions to like the other who gave them aid *less* if she then asked for a point in return than if she explicitly informed them that she did not want anything in return. The mean attraction ratings in all conditions are presented in Table 5. As can be seen, from the means in the conditions in which subjects received aid (those depicted on the left half of the table), the results supported both of these hypotheses.

Subjects in the exchange conditions did like the other who gave them aid more when that other subsequently requested than when the other did not request a point. Also as predicted, in the communal conditions subjects liked the other who gave them aid more when the aid was not followed by request for a point than when it was followed by a request for a point.

The addition of conditions in which no aid was given also allows us to make some other comparisons. First, in the exchange relationships, we can say that receiving aid, if it is not followed by a request for repayment, decreases attraction relative to receiving no communication from the other (i.e., no aid or request from the other). On the other hand, receiving aid from another if it is followed by a request for aid does not affect attraction toward the other relative to receiving no communication from the other. We can also say that, in the communal relationships, receiving aid, if there is no request for aid in return, results in higher attraction than receiving no communication (no aid and no request), but receiving aid *and* a request for repayment results in lower attraction than receiving no aid with no request.

Thus far, predictions derived from the communal–exchange distinction

TABLE 5

Attraction as a Function of Relationship Type and Request for Repayment Following Receipt of Aid from the Other[a]

Relationship	Aid given		Aid not given	
	Aid requested	Aid not requested	Aid requested	Aid not requested
Communal	156	191	179	177
Exchange	173	149	149	173

[a] The higher the score, the greater the liking. Scores could range from 0 to 240. $N = 10$ per cell. Copyright (1979) by the American Psychological Association. Reprinted by permission of the publisher and authors.

about peoples' reactions to aid have been presented along with evidence to back up those claims. The communal–exchange distinction allows several other predictions about reactions to aid for which little, if any, evidence has been collected. Some of these other implications are discussed in the remainder of the chapter, but they must be regarded as more speculative than those presented thus far.

Effects of Comparability of Aid to Prior Aid on Reactions to Aid

Clark (1981) has found that the more comparable two benefits that members of a relationship give each other, the more likely it is that the second benefit will be perceived as a repayment for the first, and the less likely it is that the two people will be perceived as being friends. This, together with the evidence presented above on how people react to being repaid for benefits or having to repay the other for benefits in communal and exchange relationships has some implications for reactions to aid.

For instance, one might predict that following the giving of aid in an exchange relationship, receiving comparable aid should be reacted to more favorably than receiving noncomparable aid. We want to be specifically repaid for aid we give the other in our exchange relationships, and it is clearer that the other's debt to us has been eliminated if the other gives us comparable aid than if the other gives us noncomparable aid.

On the other hand, in a communal relationship we presumably do *not* want to be specifically repaid for aid we give the other. Thus, following the giving of aid in a communal relationship, receiving aid that is clearly not comparable should be reacted to more favorably than receiving aid that is clearly comparable. As Schwartz (1967:6) has observed, "Returning 'tit for tat' transforms the relation into an economic one and expresses a refusal to play the role of grateful recipient. This offense represents a desire to end the relationship or at least define it on an impersonal, non-sentimental level."

Similarly, in an exchange relationship one may react more favorably to having received aid if one is subsequently asked for comparable aid than if one is subsequently asked for noncomparable aid. In contrast, in a communal relationship one may react more favorably to having received aid if one is subsequently asked for noncomparable aid than if one is subsequently asked for comparable aid.

Of course, as was noted earlier, even in a communal relationship receiving aid that is clearly comparable to aid previously given or being given aid followed by a request for comparable aid should not be reacted to negatively if there is a compelling need for the comparable aid that has been received or requested. In the former case, the aid received should not appear to be a repayment for prior aid but rather a response to one's need, and in the latter case the request for aid should not appear to be a request for repayment but rather a request to fulfill a legitimate need.

Implications of Variability in Strength of and Certainty about Relationships

Certainty about Relationships

As noted earlier, peoples' certainty about both their communal and exchange relationships may vary (Mills & Clark, 1982), and this may be an important determinant of their reactions to receiving aid. Consider communal relationships first.

First, if we desire but are uncertain about whether or not we have a communal relationship with another, we may be particularly grateful if the other aids us and makes it clear that he or she does not wish to be repaid. This may be a welcome sign that the other does desire a communal relationship with us.[6] We may not be as grateful for the aid we receive from someone with whom we are absolutely certain we have a communal relationship. Children, for instance, are very accustomed to being aided by their parents and are probably less likely to express gratitude for any given act of aid received in that relationship than for aid received from someone with whom they are just forming a friendship. Heider (1958, p. 264) has made a similar point.

Second, if we desire but are uncertain about whether or not we have a communal relationship with another, we may be especially upset if that other immediately aids us after we have aided the other, or if the other aids us and then asks for aid. As noted above, such behaviors may cast doubt on how communal our relationship with the other is. The more uncertain we are of the relationship, the more serious a threat to the relationship such behavior may seem to be.

Certainty about exchange relationships may also influence reactions to aid. If we desire but are relatively uncertain of having an exchange relationship with another, we should be particularly pleased and relieved when the other does aid us following aid we have given, or does request repayment

---

[6]If, however, we are very uncertain of our relationship with another and that other aids us and does not tell us whether to repay, we may react by being uncomfortable and not knowing what to do next.

after giving us aid relative to the feelings we would have had if we were certain of the exchange relationship.

Strength of Relationships

Variations in the strength of the communal relationships we have with others may place some important qualifications on reactions to receiving aid (or to not receiving aid) in those relationships. Consider reactions to *not* receiving aid first. Earlier it was noted that members of communal relationships expect to be aided and will experience negative feelings if their needs are not met. However, if our needs are not met by another with whom we have a communal relationship, either because that other had obligations to meet in a stronger relationship or because the other assumed we would be aided by someone with whom we had a stronger relationship, we should not experience those negative feelings. For instance, we may have a need that arises at the same time that our friend's child has a need of equal magnitude. If our friend fails to fulfill our need in order to fulfill her child's need, we will probably not be hurt. We realize our friend's obligation to her child takes precedence over her obligation to us. Or, if our friend does not aid us because he or she honestly expected that our spouse would do so, then we will not be hurt. The assumption was reasonable and lack of responsiveness to our need does not indicate a lack of concern for us.

The idea that communal relationships vary in strength may also have some implications for how favorably people will react when they *do* receive aid from others with whom they have communal relationships. If another unexpectedly chooses to help us in preference to helping a different person with whom the other also has a communal relationship, we may be especially grateful. It implies that the other feels our communal relationship is quite strong. Assuming that we *want* the relationship to be stronger, we should be happy and like the other more. If, however, we are satisfied with the existing hierarchy of our communal relationships, and to strengthen our relationship with the other would alter that hierarchy, we may actually be unhappy about receiving such aid.

Implications of the Nature of Aid

Earlier in this chapter it was noted that benefits given in the context of communal and exchange relationships may be of value to one or to both members of the relationship, and that rewards derived from the relationship may be intrinsic or extrinsic to the relationship. As noted previously, aid that is beneficial to both members of a relationship, or rewards that are intrinsic to a relationship, are relatively rare in exchange relationships but occur commonly in communal relationships. Communal relationships have received little research attention in general, and this may be why these variables have received little attention from researchers interested in reactions to aid. However, these variables do have implications for reactions to aid in both communal and exchange relationships and they may be especially important to study if we wish to understand reactions to aid in communal relationships. Furthermore, there may be some types of aid that are of value only in communal relationships. These issues are briefly addressed in the remainder of the chapter.

First, consider the fact that aid may or may not produce positive outcomes for the donor as well as for the recipient. In a communal relationship about which a person is uncertain, aid that produces positive outcomes only for the recipient may result in that recipient's feeling more secure in the relationship and in increasing the recipient's certainty about the relationship, whereas aid that produces positive outcomes for both parties may have less impact either on feelings of certainty or on feelings of security. This may occur because, in the latter case, the donor's motives for aiding the person are unclear. Thus, in a communal relationship it is possible, at least when there is uncertainty about the relationship, for aid that only benefits the recipient to be more valued than aid that benefits both the recipient and the donor. When there is more certainty about the relationship, however, aid that benefits both parties may be preferred.

In exchange relationships, regardless of certainty about the relationship, the rare instances in which aid produces positive outcomes for both the recipient and the donor may be reacted to more favorably by the recipient than instances in which aid benefits only the recipient. In an exchange relationship, aid presumably produces feelings of inequity (Hatfield & Sprecher, 1983) or indebtedness (Greenberg & Westcott, 1983) along with an obligation to repay, which may in turn be distressing. However, aid that benefits the donor as well as the recipient should be less likely to result in these feelings. Hatfield and Sprecher (1983) make a similar point in connection with "intimate" relationships, but here it is made only in connection with exchange relationships because the position taken in this chapter is that receipt of aid creates a specific debt only in exchange, not in communal relationships.

Next consider an implication of the point made above that the rewards members derive from communal relationships are often intrinsic to the relationship itself, although this tends not to be true for members of exchange relationships. For example, members of communal relationships may derive satisfaction just from being together. This implies that even if attempted aid fails in a communal relationship, it may still be reacted to positively; at least it provides an opportunity for the donor and recipient to interact and an indication that the donor is responsive to the recipient's needs. In contrast to communal relationships, attempted aid that fails should be less likely to lead to positive feelings in an exchange relationship. Indeed, such "aid" might create some distress on the part of the recipient because the recipient may wonder whether the donor is owed anything in return.

Finally, consider one type of aid that may be reacted to favorably only in communal relationships—aid from the resource class that the Foas label *love* (Foa, 1971; Foa & Foa, 1980). Aid from this resource class ordinarily consists in unconditional expressions of concern and caring for the other. To give this kind of aid is, by definition, to follow the communal norm to be responsive to the needs of the other without expecting repayment. Consequently, aid from this resource class should be reacted to favorably in existing communal relationships and in relationships we hope will become communal relationships, but ordinarily not in other relationships. Indeed, in exchange relationships, receipt of such aid may produce distress. The recipient may worry that the other wants something in return or that the other has a desire for a relationship that the person does not share.

CONCLUSION

In this chapter many specific implications of the distinction between communal and exchange relationships for reactions to aid have been spelled out and an argument has been made that taking into account the type of relationship existing or expected between a donor and a recipient of aid is crucial for understanding recipient reactions to aid. Heretofore, the variable of relationship type has received little research attention from psychologists interested in reactions to aid and, unfortunately, the relationships within the contexts of which people probably receive most aid, their communal relationships, have been almost entirely neglected. It is my hope that the variable of relationship type will receive more research attention in the future from investigators interested in reactions to aid. Not only may the distinction between communal and exchange relationships discussed in the present chapter prove to be useful in understanding these reactions, but examining additional types of relationships may prove to be useful as well.

REFERENCE NOTE

Clark, M. S., and Waddell, B. Feelings of exploitation in communal and exchange relationships. Unpublished manuscript, 1981.

REFERENCES

Bar-Tal, D., Bar-Zohar, Y. B., Greenberg, M. S., & Hermon, M. Reciprocity behavior in the relationship between donor and recipient and between harm-doer and victim. *Sociometry,* 1977, **40**, 293-298.

Blau, P. M. *Exchange and Power in Social Life.* New York: Wiley, 1964.

Castro, M. A. C. Reactions to receiving aid as a function of cost to donor and opportunity to aid. *Journal of Applied Social Psychology,* 1974, **4**, 194-209.

Clark, M. S. Noncomparability of benefits given and received: A cue to the existence of friendship. *Social Psychology Quarterly,* 1981, **44**, 375-381.

Clark, M. S., & Mills, J. Interpersonal attraction in exchange and communal relationships. *Journal of Personality and Social Psychology,* 1979, **37**, 12-24.

Deutsch, M. Equity, equality, and need: What determines which will be used as the basis of distributive justice? *Journal of Social Issues,* 1975, **31**, 137-149.

Foa, U. G. Interpersonal and economic resources. *Science,* 1971, **171**, 345-351.

Foa, E. B., & Foa, U. G. Resource theory: Interpersonal behavior as exchange. In K. J. Gergen, M. S. Greenberg, and R. H. Willis (Eds.), *Social exchange: Advances in theory and research.* New York: Plenum Press, 1980.

Gergen, K. J., Ellsworth, P., Maslach, C., & Seipel, M. Obligation, donor resources, and reactions to aid in three nations. *Journal of Personality and Social Psychology,* 1975, **3**, 396-400.

Goranson, R. E., & Berkowitz, L. Reciprocity and responsibility reactions to prior help. *Journal of Personality and Social Psychology,* 1966, **3**, 227-232.

Greenberg, M., & Westcott, D. R. Indebtedness as a mediator of reactions to aid. In J. Fisher, A. Nadler, & B. DePaulo (Eds.), *New directions in research on helping* (Vol. 1), *Recipient reactions to aid.* New York: Academic Press, 1983.

Hatfield, E., & Sprecher, S. Equity theory and recipient reactions to aid. In J. Fisher, A. Nadler, & B. DePaulo (Eds.), *New directions in research on helping* (Vol. 1), *Recipient reactions to aid.* New York: Academic Press, 1983.

Heider, F. *The Psychology of Interpersonal Relations.* New York: Wiley, 1958.

Kahn, A., & Tice, T. E. Returning a favor and retaliating harm: The effects of stated intentions and actual behavior. *Journal of Experimental Social Psychology,* 1973, **9**, 43-56.

Levinger, G. A social exchange view on the dissolution of pair relationships. In R. L. Burgess and T. L. Huston (Eds.), *Social exchange in developing relationships.* New York: Academic Press, 1979.

Mills, J., & Clark, M. S. Communal and exchange relationships. In L. Wheeler (Ed.) *Annual review of personality and social psychology.* Beverley Hills, California: Sage, 1982.

Pruitt, D. G. Methods for resolving differences of interest: A theoretical analysis. *Journal of Social Issues,* 1972, **28**, 133-154.

Suttles, G. D. Friendship as a social institution. In G. J. McCall (Ed.), *Social relationships.* Chicago, Illinois: Aldine, 1970.

Schwartz, B. The social psychology of the gift. *The American Journal of Sociology,* 1967, **73**, 1-11.

Stapleton, R. E., Nacci, P., & Tedeschi, J. T. Interpersonal attraction and the reciprocation of benefits. *Journal of Personality and Social Psychology,* 1973, **28**, 199-205.

Tesser, A., Gatewood, R., & Driver, M. Some determinants of gratitude. *Journal of Personality and Social Psychology,* 1968, **9**, 233-236.

Walster, E., Walster, G. W., and Berscheid, E. *Equity: Theory and research.* Boston, Massachusetts: Allyn and Bacon, 1978.

Wegner, D. M., & Giuliano, T. The forms of social awareness. In W. J. Ickes and E. S. Knowles (Eds.), *Personality, roles, and social behavior.* Berlin and New York: Springer-Verlag, 1981.

Wilke, H., & Lanzetta, J. T. The obligation to help: The effects of amounts of prior help on subsequent helping behavior. *Journal of Experimental Social Psychology,* 1970, **6,** 488–493.

CHAPTER 12

The Nature of the Help-Related Interchange as a Determinant of Person's Attitude toward Other*

Stanley J. Morse

This chapter is concerned with how the specifics of Person's help-related interchange with Other may shape Person's feelings toward Other. The first section discusses our epistemological viewpoint, defines *help,* proposes a framework for examining determinants of reactions to Other, and mentions limitations in existing research on the topic. The second analyzes

*I would like to thank David Amorena, Adelmar N. Alcantara, J. M. Innes, Cyrene Barretto-Morse, Philip L. Pearce, and the editors of this volume for their very helpful comments on an earlier draft of this chapter. As a Brazilian, an urban planner, and a former social worker, Dr. Barretto-Morse helped to broaden my view of help and of cross-cultural variations in attitudes toward help. By bringing to my attention his then unpublished work (with Smithson and Amato) on helping episodes, Dr. Pearce impressed upon me the narrowness of existing work in the field.

305

contextual or situational factors that might influence Person's evaluation of Other and reviews relevant literature. The third presents conclusions.

IMPORTANT PRELIMINARIES

Some Epistemological Considerations

General Points

Simply to summarize existing studies on response to a provider of help requires at least two assumptions: (1) that cataloging the myriad ways in which help has been operationalized is equivalent to defining the concept, and (2) that we can safely generalize from the laboratory to the real world. The pitfalls of this approach have been trenchantly discussed by Harré and Secord (1973), Moscovici (1972) and others. Harré and Secord stress the need to think conceptually about a phenomenon before empirically investigating it, and demonstrate the perils of concluding anything about behavior in the real world from experiments in which subjects interact with strangers on a one-shot basis in highly constrained settings. Moscovici emphasizes the usually overlooked fact that real interaction occurs against a backdrop of social structural and cultural inputs that give it content and meaning. It will thus pay to think conceptually about what help is and about larger social processes that may influence a recipient's response to a provider, as well as to approach existing empirical research cautiously.

Complexity in Helping Situations

Helping transactions are inherently complex. Some help may not in fact be very helpful. Whether actually helpful or not, Other may think he or she is helping Person but Person may perceive Other's actions otherwise. Person, finally, may think Other has been helpful whereas Other may really have had other intentions. The activities of the notorious Charles Sabhroj, who befriended tourists, secretly poisoned them, and nursed them back to health while at the same time swindling them, illustrate this last point (Neville & Clarke, 1979).

Although "help" may constitute a "fuzzy set" (Zadeh, Fu, Tanaka, & Shimara, 1975), it must nevertheless have a core. Despite clear differences (Pearce & Amato, 1980), varied instances of help must have *something* in common.

A Definition

Defining Help

Help is clearly some kind of benefit (or attempted benefit) provided by one person to another, although not all benefits constitute help. The benefit must ostensibly be aimed at fulfilling a specific, limited, goal-directed need on the part of the recipient and must not be provided as part of a contractual or ritualized exchange. A benefit provided by Other to Person constitutes *help* if it would appear (to Person, to Other, or to an outside observer, but not necessarily to all three) to be an attempt (whether successful or not) to facilitate the achievement by Person of a specific goal.

What Is Excluded

According to our definition, giving Person a Christmas present would not be help because the present cannot be seen as facilitating the achievement of a specific goal, and teaching Person to play the piano would not be help if Other were paid for doing so. A complication arises when we consider Person's interactions with someone whose job it is to provide help—a teacher or welfare worker for example. In such instances it might be best to say that Other helps Person only when the benefits Other appears to be attempting to provide are outside the bounds of clear role requirements.

Our emphasis on need fulfillment means, furthermore, that benefits that are enriching rather than need fulfilling cannot strictly be considered help. Two examples of such benefits are research grants awarded to especially meritorious applicants and special benefits provided to gifted children so that they may fully utilize their gifts. In the first case we must clearly distinguish between reward and help. The second is somewhat more complex. Here the main point seems to be that no very specific, short-term (or bounded) need is involved. Perhaps in this instance we should distinguish between aid and help, reserving the term *aid* for diffuse, long-term benefits geared to facilitate the attainment of equally diffuse long-term needs.

A Conceptual Scheme

Benefits and Costs

Having attempted to bound the phenomenon of help, we must consider how the nature of Person's interaction with Other may influence attraction toward Other. It seems useful to think of Person's response to Other in terms of the benefits and costs Person may experience in interaction with

Other or, more precisely, the subjective value to Person of these benefits and costs. Benefits are simply immediate or delayed consequences to Person of Other's actions that Person considers to be positive or rewarding, and costs are immediate or delayed consequences to Person of Other's actions that Person considers to be negative, aversive, or punishing. We assume that benefits and costs are additive and that the higher are Person's *net* benefits, the more positively Person should evaluate Other (Berscheid & Walster, 1978). The crucial task of course is to identify the specific benefits and costs that Person may experience in interacting with Other under different circumstances.

Task-oriented Benefits

Three components figure prominently in our definition of help: (1) Person's need, (2) Other's attempt to meet Person's need and (3) the extent to which Other's actions toward Person facilitate Person's need fulfillment. If Other's actions actually facilitate Person's goal attainment, Person experiences a benefit; otherwise Person does not. These relationships are shown in Figure 1. Person is pursuing a goal (G_1). Need arises because achievement of the goal is blocked in one way or another. Other takes an

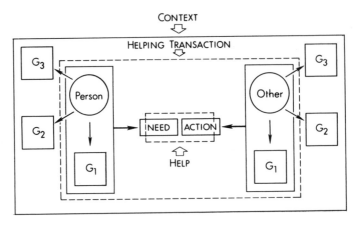

Figure 1 A model of a helping transaction considered as part of a larger context. Person's pursuit of a particular goal (G_1) generates a need. Other takes an action toward Person supposedly designed to facilitate Person's attainment of G_1. Help is the intersection of Person's need and Other's need-oriented action. If help facilitates Person's attainment of G_1, Person receives a task-oriented benefit. Both Person and Other may however be pursuing a number of goals simultaneously. The specific goal that prompted Other's action (G_1) may be unclear to Person, especially because Other may also be pursuing additional goals (G_2 and G_3). Although Person may achieve G_1, Other's actions may also influence other goals that Person has (G_2 and G_3).

action toward Person that is designed to facilitate Person's goal attainment (to remove or dissolve or bypass the block). The help itself is the intersection of Person's need and Other's need-oriented action toward Person, which may or may not result in facilitating the achievement by Person of G_1.

Conceptualized in this way, Person should clearly respond to Other on the basis of the extent to which Other's action facilitates Person's goal attainment. There are however two possible reasons for this. First of all, Person might respond to the fact that there appears to be a direct connection between Other's action and the benefit received. An additional possibility is that Person may respond positively to Other through a process of stimulus generalization (Lott & Lott, 1974) or spread of affect (Isen, 1970) simply because Other's presence is contiguous with the benefit received. We are, in any case, dealing in both instances with response to what might be called *task-oriented* benefits.

Self-oriented benefits.

Another type of benefit that needs to be considered might be called *self-oriented* benefits. Figure 1 also shows that Person may be pursuing a number of goals simultaneously. These additional goals are represented on the figure by G_1 and G_2. One goal is maintenance or reinforcement of self-esteem. Person may thus want to believe that Other cares about or is concerned with Person's welfare. Other's action on Person's behalf may serve as a signal of such caring or concern. Person may thus also respond positively to Other on the basis of this very different type of benefit.

An Experimental Illustration

That these different considerations may influence response to a provider of help is shown in an experiment by Morse and Marks (Note 3). Subjects worked to complete a jigsaw puzzle in the allotted time in order to win a monetary prize. They were allowed to complete 65, 80, or 95% of the puzzle, or the entire puzzle. Half of the subjects were led to believe they had reached these points thanks to extra time provided by the experimental assistant (Other), whereas half were led to believe that the amount of time they received was part of the standard experimental procedure. Subjects rated the assistant as more helpful when they finished the puzzle than when they did not, regardless of whether or not they received help on it. When the puzzle was completed, the assistant was in fact rated just as positively in the No Help condition as in the Help condition. This clearly indicates that feelings about a stimulus person are influenced at least in part by simple task reward or reinforcement. Collapsing across all task completion conditions, however, subjects also rated the assistant as more helpful when she helped them than when she did not, showing the importance also of considering Person's perceptions of Other's action on Person's behalf. The actual goal-facilitation properties of Other's help, finally, is likewise crucial. As long as the task was *not* completed, the assistant was not rated more highly as she provided more help.

Task-oriented Costs

The costs attached to receiving help can also be divided into task-oriented and self-oriented varieties. *Task-oriented costs* are those that decrease the benefit or reward Person receives for achieving G_1. On an immediate, short-term basis there may be some situations in which the actual reward Person receives when G_1 is reached decreases to the extent that Person employs help from Other in achieving the goal. This consideration seems, however, to be relatively unimportant, for if it is assumed that Person could not reach the goal unaided, reaching it with help still yields higher benefits than not reaching it at all. DePaulo and Fisher (1980) nevertheless report that more subjects sought help on a task when the penalty for doing so was less.

Of more interest is the longer-term, task-oriented cost of receiving help. This involves usually having to repay Other for help received, as discussed in this volume by Hatfield and Sprecher under the rubric of *equity* and by Greenberg and Wescott under that of *indebtedness*. How compelling this cost is remains unclear. In most instances, the cost of having to repay Other appears to be a cost imposed not by Other but by Person, based upon Person's notions of appropriate social behavior. Another distinct possibility is that Person is in fact not concerned with behaving properly for its own sake but with the consequences that not repaying help received may have upon Person's relationship with Other. Reciprocity may well be primarily a self-presentational strategy (Morse, Gruzen, & Reis, 1976) or a particularly American phenomenon (Gergen, Morse, & Gergen, 1980), at least when dealing with relative strangers. It is perhaps even questionable whether or not equity or indebtedness considerations in ongoing relationships should be considered as costs at all. Imbalance in social exchange is, after all, a primary social glue or bond (cf. Ekeh, 1974); repaying help may not necessarily be considered aversive by Person.

Self-oriented Costs

There are two especially salient aspects of *self-oriented costs,* one directly self-related and one Other-related. We can assume, as mentioned, that Person wants to hold himself or herself in high regard. This should be impeded by Person admitting to himself or herself that help is needed (DePaulo & Fisher, 1980; DePaulo, 1982). We can also assume that Person will usually strive to create a good impression upon others (Schlenker, 1980). Both appearing to need help and availing oneself of help may undercut the positivity of self-presentation.

Balance of Two Types of Benefits and Costs

It seems, at least over the short term, that the benefits of involvement in a help transaction relate primarily to the task at hand, whereas costs relate primarily to the self. In this regard, it will ultimately be necessary to consider different specific types of help that may condition judgments of each type of benefit and cost. Needed is a typology of help based upon a typology of needs because the fit between the two is crucial. Instead there are just typologies of prosocial behaviors (Wispé, 1972), helping behaviors (Lau & Blake, 1976) and helping episodes (Pearce & Amato, 1980; Smithson, Amato, & Pearce, 1983).

Not Easily Categorized Benefits and Costs

As Figure 1 shows, not only may Person be pursuing several goals simultaneously; Other may also be doing so. Person may or may not be aware of which precise goal (G_1), if there is only one such goal, prompted Other to provide help. To understand Other's likely actions and their likely consequences, Person must obviously make attributions about what Other is up to. Other may provide unsolicited help to belittle Person, to show solidarity with Person, or to make Person feel indebted (perhaps because Other is interested in seducing Person, the prospect of which Person may consider either a benefit or a cost). At least the long-term benefits and costs Person might incur may thus be problematic from Person's point of view.

Bias in Benefit–Cost Perspective

Implicit in this emphasis on benefits and costs is a rather hedonistic, self-centered view of social interaction as "behavior exchange" (Gergen, 1969). Although it serves usefully to limit our focus, we do not intend to imply that Person will respond to Other solely on the basis of what is in effect the "hedonic relevance" (Jones & Davis, 1965) to Person of Other's actions. Benefit–cost calculations may not always be relevant or be employed. In the Morse and Marks (Note 3) experiment, after all, subjects rated the assistant as more helpful when she helped them than when she did not, even when this help did not allow subjects to complete the puzzle. Although this could be interpreted as showing that self-oriented benefit for subjects in the Help condition were higher than in the No Help condition (the assistant had demonstrated concern and caring), this seems unlikely. Subjects who did not complete the puzzle may simply have evaluated the assistant impersonally, on the basis of her presumed orientation toward people in general.

Limitations in Existing Literature

Before trying to isolate important situational factors that may influence attitudes toward a help-giver and to assess their likely impact, we should consider several limitations inherent in existing literature in addition to those that characterize social psychological research in general.

Trivial Focus

People undoubtedly receive help all the time: as part of an ongoing relationship, in a context in which clear norms and expectations are involved, or when in great need. Do we then actually learn much about real-world helping interchanges by examining how one responds to receiving a Coke from a stranger (Brehm & Cole, 1966), to different repayment plans (Freeman, 1977), or to differential distributions of rewards (Leventhal, Allen, & Kemelgor, 1969)? Many of these situations may not in fact involve help at all. The "help" provided is in any case normally slight and not addressed to a pressing need (or any need for that matter).

Attention to three situational considerations is conspicuously absent: (1) to the rules and roles operative in a particular interchange, (2) to cross-cultural variations, and (3) to the intimacy and length of the relationship between Person and Other. These factors are components of the context within which Person's transaction with Other is embedded, signified in Figure 1 by the solid line surrounding the helping transaction.

Rules and Roles

Three of the nine dimensions or elements Argyle, Furnham, and Graham (1981) use to describe social situations seem especially pertinent to helping transactions: (1) goals, (2) rules and (3) roles. Goals have already been briefly considered. Argyle and his colleagues define *rules* as behaviors people believe should, should not, or may be performed in a given situation, and *roles* as the rules that apply to an occupant of a particular position. The crucial point about rules and roles is that the way in which Person perceives these situational components influences Person's expectations concerning Other, concerning how Person should respond to Other's actions, and concerning what actions are or are not appropriate.

Cross-cultural Variation

Because the rules and roles associated with a given social situation may well be culturally variable, one might expect marked variation in response to help based upon one's cultural background. Americans socialized within an ethic stressing independence and self-sufficiency may not normally expect help, may see help as prompted by ulterior motives, by negative evaluations, or by liking, and may believe that almost immediate reciprocity is required. Brazilians, who appear to consider the giving and receiving of help to be a much more legitimate and basically positive type of interchange, may respond quite differently, expecting help, attributing help to situational rules, and believing that reciprocity will work itself out in the long run.

Cultural differences in attitudes toward help are reflected in dictionary definitions of the term. Our conceptualization of help generally accords with that in *Webster's Seventh New Collegiate Dictionary* (1977), which says that, as a transitive verb, "help" means to supply what is needed to accomplish an end, with the strong implication of advance toward a goal. An English–Portuguese dictionary (Vallandro & Vallandro, 1970) also gives "to succor" *(socorrer)* and "to attach value to" *(valer)* as definitions of help, and a French dictionary (Burtin-Vinholes, 1950) adds "to protect" *(protegér)* and "to back up" or "to support" *(seconder).*

White (1978, 1980) examined personality descriptors used by A'ara speakers in the Solomon Islands and found no such term as "helpful." The closest approximations are *kokhoni di naikno,* which literally means "sorry for people," and *nahma,* which means "kind" or "loving." White (personal communication, 1982) indeed suggests that in "communal" societies (i.e. in most non-Western societies), cooperative activity is so much an expected, everyday occurrence that acts that could distinctly be labelled as help are rare. Lebra's (1976) discussion of the concepts of "obligation" and "reciprocity" among the Japanese, finally, clearly implies that the dynamics of providing and receiving help in Japan may be distinctly different from those in the United States.

Intimacy and Length of Relationship

In their attempt to map domains of help-giving, Smithson *et al.* (in press) convincingly show that work on prosocial behavior by social psychologists has almost entirely ignored helping within the context of close and longstanding relationships. Rubin (1973) in fact seems to suggest that helping is a central feature of love relationships. One would expect those involved in close relationships to expect to receive help when in need without having either to ask for it or to repay the helper except in so far as Person will help Other in turn when the opportunity arises.

DETERMINANTS OF REACTION TO OTHER

Nature of Section

Focus

We have defined help and identified two conceptually distinct sets of benefits and costs that should condition Person's response to Other. Now the task is to pinpoint specifics of Person's interaction with Other that may influence the benefits and costs incurred in receiving help.

Although we discuss all four types of benefits, for several reasons the primary focus is upon task-oriented benefits and self-oriented costs. First of all, the dilemma in which recipients of help often find themselves seems to center on the conflict between task-oriented benefits and self-oriented costs. Secondly, the main task-oriented cost seems to be the cost of repaying help received. This issue revolves around reciprocity considerations, which are discussed in other chapters. (Here we are not specifically concerned with reciprocity except insofar as a case can be made that felt need to reciprocate or the demand for repayment correlates with how Person is likely to evaluate Other.) Finally, we earlier observed that within a restricted time perspective task-oriented benefits seem to be more important than task-oriented costs, and self-oriented costs seem to be more important than self-oriented benefits. Self-oriented benefits indeed appear to be a rather long-range consideration. Within this wider time-frame they may merge with task-oriented benefits.

Literature Cited

Because of the general paucity of relevant literature, this section is often highly speculative. We specifically ignore studies dealing with inter-nation helping. Their applicability to interpersonal helping is problematic because of the different levels of analysis involved and because many such studies involve role playing. In the study by Morse and Gergen (1971) in which American college students "represented" nations with different levels of need applying for aid from a donor nation, did the students respond as if they personally had different levels of need, as they felt a representative would respond, or as they thought people in the country in question might respond?

We will often have to rely on studies that do not directly deal with atitudes toward a provider of help. Many of these studies examine either propensity to seek help or willingness to accept help. In citing such studies, we are forced to make the risky assumption that situational factors that increase willingness to seek or accept help should also increase liking for someone providing help. Results of studies on willingness to seek help may only be pertinent to situations in which Person must ask for Other's help, whereas results of studies on willingness to accept help may only be pertinent to situations in which Other provides unsolicited help. (Then again, such studies may be irrelevant altogether.)

Assumptions

Several key assumptions guide the analyses that follow:

1. The more valuable the goal (G_1) is to Person, the higher the task-oriented benefit that will accrue to Person upon reaching the goal. Receiving help in achieving a goal will not decrease the task-oriented benefit received. The first part of this assumption can be derived from a Lewinian perspective (Lewin, 1951).

2. The less able person believes himself or herself to be to reach the goal unaided, the higher the task-oriented benefit of reaching the goal will be. This can be derived from a Lewinian perspective (Lewin, 1951).

3. Task-oriented costs imposed by Other will be more aversive than task-oriented costs Person may self-impose. This can be derived from a reactance perspective (Brehm, 1966).

4. If Person's self-esteem is engaged in reaching the task-oriented goal—in other words, if a self-oriented goal is also operative—the more valuable the goal is to Person, the higher will be the self-oriented cost of receiving help to reach the goal. This and the next three assumptions can be loosely derived from self-esteem (Gergen, 1971) and self-presentational (Schlenker, 1980; Schlenker & Leary, 1982) considerations.

5. If Person's self-esteem is engaged, the self-oriented cost of receiving help to reach the goal will increase to the extent that Person's need and Person's receipt of help are visible to others.

6. Person will be concerned with why Other has provided help. If Person's self-esteem is engaged, the self-oriented cost of receiving help to reach the goal will increase to the extent that Person believes Other may have a negative view of Person. Attribution considerations are also involved here.

7. If Person's self-esteem is engaged, Person will be motivated to discount the help received or, if this cannot be done, to discount Person's need or the value of the goal.

8. Person will generally not like to admit needing help or that the need for such help reflects on Person's own abilities. To the extent that Person needs help (especially if Person's self-esteem is engaged), the self-oriented cost of receiving help will be less if Person believes task performance does not reflect ability and/or Person needs help for extrinsic (not self-related) reasons. This can also be derived from attribution considerations (cf. Shaver, 1975).

9. Person will be concerned with Other's ability to provide useful help, generally preferring help from someone perceived to be better able to provide help more likely to facilitate goal attainment. This can be derived from social exchange considerations (Homans, 1974).

10. Whether or not Person expects to receive help and expects to have to repay it will be a function of cultural norms, the nature of Person's relationship with Other, and the way Person defines the rules and roles operative in the social situation in which the helping interchange is embedded. This can be derived from general work in anthropology (cf. Bock, 1980) or on social situations (Argyle *et al.,* 1981).

11. When expectations, however derived, are disconfirmed, Person will respond in more extreme ways to Other than when they are confirmed. This can be derived from Thibaut and Kelley (1959).

CONCEPTUAL ANALYSES
AND EMPIRICAL RESEARCH

Organization of Section

Situational or contextual factors that may influence Person's response to Other are discussed below under two main headings: Noncontingent Relationships and Contingent Relationships. Under the first heading, we consider variables that are expected generally to increase or to decrease liking for Other. Other variables may well heighten or lessen the impact of noncontingent variables but are not expected to reverse their effects. Variables for which noncontingent relationships are posited are discussed in terms of the presumed temporal or logical ordering of their impacts, as indicated by arabic numerals. Factors grouped under the Noncontingent Relationships section are expected to show strong interaction effects; here the order in which variables are analyzed is more or less arbitrary. For both sets of variables, conceptual analyses precede reviews of relevant research.

Noncontingent Relationships I: Self-esteem

Analysis

Probably the most potent variable influencing the benefits and costs that may accrue to Person from a particular helping interchange is (1) whether or not Person's self-esteem is engaged. There are a number of reasons why the task itself may cause Person to focus on himself or herself. The most important factor is probably whether or not the task is thought to reflect ability or another valued personal quality. To the extent that Person thinks this, Person should respond negatively to receiving help. There are, however, some extenuating factors that should be considered. One is the reason Person feels he or she needs help. The task may reflect ability, but if it is especially difficult or if other people also usually need help on it, response to a helper should be less negative. Likewise, if the individual who will evaluate Person's performance on the task *will not* know if Person has received help, and if Person is motivated to create as good an impression as possible on this individual, or if this individual is in a position to dispense high task-oriented or self-oriented benefits, response to Other should be less negative. If the individual evaluating Person's performance, on the other hand, *will* know if Person has received help, reaction to a provider of help may be particularly negative. (These and other moderating variables are examined later.) It should be noted, in connection with these hypotheses, that Nadler, Shapira and Ben-Itzhak (1982) present a general discussion of self-presentational considerations in help-seeking, emphasizing such factors as Person's motivation to create a good impression upon Other as a function of Other's characteristics. Although relevant on a theoretical level to the present discussion, their work (on Other's physical attractiveness and on the sex of Person and Other) falls outside the scope of the present chapter.

Research on Self-relevance of Task Performance

In studies by Tessler and Schwartz (1972) and by Wallston (1976), subjects rated for neuroticism audio tapes of TAT dialogues. Subjects in the first study were told that task performance did or did not reflect one's intelligence and mental health and, in the second study, that the task was a "male" or "female" one. When the task was less central to subjects (i.e., when it did not reflect intelligence or was sex-inappropriate) more subjects sought help.

Morse (1972) actually assessed attitudes toward someone who provided help on a task that did or did not have implications for subject self-regard but found that this had no impact upon ratings of Other. On an opinion survey on which subjects could see Other's opinions, however, subjects who had received help on a task presented as an intelligence test showed more counter-conformity and less social influence attributable to Other's opinions than did subjects who had received help on the same task presented as a rather unimportant test of hand–eye coordination. This result suggests that receiving help on a task engaging one's self-esteem does indeed generate negative affect toward Other. More important, though, it casts doubt on the sensitivity with which ratings made by Person of Other can tap Person's feelings toward Other in what may be affect-charged circumstances.

Research on Attribution of Need

Calhoun, Dawes, and Lewis (1972) and Mikesell and Calhoun (Note 1) found that persons who saw their psychological problems as more severe were less favorably disposed toward seeking professional help. Although these results may be interpreted in a number of ways, one possibility is that persons who felt they had more severe problems were less able to attribute them to situational causes.

Believing that others also need help on a given task should itself allow difficulties to be more readily attributed to situational factors and thus encourage more help-seeking. This is shown in the study by Tessler and Schwartz (1972) already mentioned. More subjects sought help when they thought 65% as opposed to 10% of other subjects also needed help. Two other studies in which self-oriented costs may be presumed to be especially high indicate, however, that to lead subjects to believe that help-seeking is normative only increases help-seeking or acceptance of help when self-oriented costs can somehow be reduced or when compensatory task-oriented benefits are available. In this connection, Nadler and Porat (1978) found results similar to those reported by Tessler and Schwartz but only when subjects thought they would remain anonymous. Broll, Gross, and Piliavin (1974) used an extreme manipulation of normativeness, telling subjects that 98 or 30% of previous subjects had needed help on very difficult logic problems. Here, only if subjects were offered an incentive of three dollars for completing the task within a given time period was there a tendency for those in the normative condition to accept or to request more help than did those in the nonnormative condition. This was so despite the fact that the experimenter encouraged all subjects to utilize help.

Research on Evaluation of Task Performance

A study by Shapiro (1978) used the same task as employed by Tessler and Schwartz (1972) and by Wallston (1976). Subjects, who were led to believe they had performed poorly on the task, were encouraged to consult guidelines that would supposedly facilitate future performance. A confederate could or could not observe whether subjects actually consulted the guidelines. Subjects were also led to believe that their performance would be evaluated (by someone else) in a face-to-face encounter or anonymously. When they expected a face-to-face evaluation, subjects were more likely to consult the guidelines if the confederate would not observe their doing so than if the confederate would, whereas in the anonymous evaluation condition this manipulation had no effect. In this study we can assume that subjects were motivated to present themselves positively to both the evaluator and the confederate. Help-seeking would presumably be interpreted by the confederate as a sign of poor task-performance but would be unknown to the evaluator. Only subjects in the situation in which help-seeking would not be observed and performance would be evaluated in a face-to-face context were therefore in a position in which they might possibly impress both parties. That help-seeking was indeed greatest under these circumstances at least suggests the relevance of self-presentational considerations in situations in which task performance can be presumed to engage Person's self- esteem.

Noncontingent Relationships II: Need, Utility, Repayment

Analysis

Although self-esteem considerations might moderate these relationships, we can predict that Person will respond positively toward Other when Person receives help from Other if (2) Person feels he or she actually needs help, (3) the help received facilitates Person's goal attainment, (4) Other does not attach "strings" to the help received, (5) Person feels he or she needn't repay Other for the help received or, if repayment is felt to be necessary, (6) the payment is not considered aversive. Response to Other will be negative if, on the other hand, (2) Person doesn't feel he or she needs help, (3) Other provides help considered by Person to be either too much or too little, (4) Other attaches "strings" to the help provided or (5) Person feels he or she must repay Other and (6) the payment is considered aversive. All of these variables deal directly with the task-oriented benefits and costs that accrue to Person, except for when Person feels he or she doesn't need help and it is provided anyway; here self-oriented costs may also be operative.

Research on Goal Facilitation

We have already discussed the study by Morse and Marks (Note 3) that shows that Other is evaluated more positively when Other's help facilitates Person's goal attainment. This study also provides some evidence that Person will respond less positively toward Other when the amount of help received increases but is still insufficient to facilitate goal attainment. The experimental assistant was rated by subjects receiving help from her as significantly more attractive in the 65 and 100% completion conditions than in the intermediate 80 and 95% conditions. This was even more true of ratings made of the assistant's helpfulness. On a 10-point scale, helpfulness decreased from 8.1 in the 65% condition, to 7.6 in the 80% condition, to a low of 6.7 in the 95% condition, rising to 9.7 in the task-completion condition.

Research on Level of Need

Research shows that people who can be presumed to experience less need seek less help. DePaulo and Fisher (1980) employed a nonverbal cue recognition task and found that university students majoring in fields stressing interpersonal sensitivity sought slightly less help than did students majoring in other fields, and also that subjects sought more help on more difficult items. People who accept or recognize their need likewise seek more help than those who do not (Nadler, Sheinberg, & Jaffe, 1982), although the studies by Calhoun et al., (1972) and by Mikesell and Calhoun (Note 1) might be interpreted to the contrary.

The only study dealing directly with the influence of level of need upon feelings toward Other is, unfortunately, the inter-nation simulation experiment by Morse and Gergen (1971). In this study, which stimulated later work on expectations rather than on need, "representatives" of countries with less need for aid responded more positively toward an Other providing requested aid than did "representatives" of countries with greater need for aid. The authors explain that expectations may be created in institutionalized types of helping situations, with those in greater need simply coming to expect more help than those in less need.

Research on Repayment

The issue of repayment is covered more fully in other chapters. Freeman (1977) has shown that people prefer help that yields the greatest benefit at the lowest cost. Gergen, Ellsworth, Maslach, and Seipel (1975) indicate, in contrast, that people prefer situations in which benefits do not exceed costs. Perhaps the difference between the two studies is that, in Freeman's research, both benefits and costs were established by the experimenter. In the Gergen *et al.* study, subjects apparently imposed additional costs upon themselves.

Our prediction, however, was that Person will respond positively to Other when repayment is not demanded, when Person feels he need not repay the help, or when the repayment is not considered aversive. These are somewhat different issues. If "strings" are considered to be repayment that Person views as excessive, the Gergen *et al.* study provides supportive evidence. Subjects preferred a situation in which benefits matched costs to one in which costs exceeded benefits. A major problem is that we do not know under what precise conditions people feel they must repay help. It may be that people will feel they need not repay help when they do not expect by not doing so to suffer externally imposed consequences such as general social disapproval, hostility from Other, or inability to receive help from Other in the future. In this connection, a study by Morse, Gergen, and Reis (Note 2) shows that when an individual believes nobody will know whether he or she does requested work in return for a payment, little work is actually done. This issue is discussed by Reis (1981) within the context of distributive justice.

Contingent Relationships I: Task Importance

Analysis

If task completion is very important to Person (i.e., if the task-oriented reward to be obtained from completing the task is great and the task-oriented cost of not completing it is also great), this may have one of two somewhat paradoxical effects. A task considered to be very important should invest Other's actions toward Person with high "hedonic relevance" (Jones & Davis, 1965), augmenting how positively or negatively Person responds to Other on the basis of factors already discussed. If task completion is extremely important to Person, though, this might actually swamp all other effects. If it is not important at all to Person (especially if self-oriented benefits and costs are also not involved), what Other does may have no discernible impact upon Person's feeling toward Other. If it is not important in a task-oriented sense but self-oriented considerations are involved, finally, this may augment the salience of self-oriented considerations. In this case Person might well refuse offered help.

The most interesting situation, as mentioned, is that in which task completion is very important but completing the task with help will generate high self-oriented cost. Crucial here, of course, is Person's judgment of the relative value within short-term and long-term perspectives of the task-oriented benefits and self-oriented costs involved. It may be that when the task is considered very important and also engages Person's self-esteem—a classic approach–avoidance situation—some of the conflict implicit in this situation will be resolved through cognitive distortion. Person may, for example, come to believe that he or she did not really receive significant or very useful help from Other. To the extent that task performance is evaluated by someone who will not know whether or not Person has received help, it should be easier for Person to adjust self-perceptions in order to decrease self-oriented costs. Studies by Gergen, Morse and Bode (1974) and Morse *et al.* (1976) demonstrate how subjects may cognitively reassess task-linked benefits and costs.

Research on Task Importance

Surprisingly, the only study to vary the task-oriented importance to subjects of task completion is that by Broll *et al.* (1974) in which, as indicated, level of task reward had little impact. Self-oriented costs here were however apparently high whereas the incentive used (three dollars, or nothing) was minimal.

Contingent Relationships II: Expectations

Analysis

Person's expectations may have an augmenting influence similar to that for task importance. If Person expects help from Other and such help is provided, Person may respond to Other with indifference, whereas if Person expects help from Other and it is not forthcoming, Person may react with hostility. Unexpected help from Other may, in contrast, heighten positive affect based upon other considerations.

Research on Expectations in General

Morse (1972) led subjects to expect or not expect help from Other. When they unexpectedly received help they evaluated Other very positively, whereas when they unexpectedly failed to receive help they evaluated Other very negatively. Reactions to Other in the two parallel expectancy confirmation conditions were relatively neutral. The findings for the Expect–Do Not Receive and Expect–Receive conditions of this experiment are particularly interesting in suggesting that if Person expects to receive help, providing such help may not generate positive feeling toward Other; not providing help, on the other hand, may generate negative feelings.

For Person to respond more positively to Other when Other provides unexpected rather than expected help, the help must, however, not be perceived as situationally "inappropriate" because then someone who provides unexpected help is evaluated more negatively than is someone who provides expected help (Morse, Gergen, Peele, & van Ryneveld, 1977). Perhaps this is one reason why people respond more negatively to help from a "foe" than from a "friend" (Nadler, Fisher, & Streufert, 1974) or to help received in a competitive compared with a cooperative context (Worchel & Andreoli, 1974).

Research on Role Requirements

Expectations are influenced by perceived role requirements. When Other is commanded to provide help or when this is Other's job, Person should expect help from Other and thus respond less positively to Other than when such situational or role constraints are not operative. It is therefore not surprising that subjects who receive help that appears to be given voluntarily evaluate Other more positively than subjects who receive help that appears to be given upon instruction of the experimenter. This is demonstrated in studies done within an attribution framework such as those by Goranson and Berkowitz (1966), Greenberg and Frisch (1972), and Nemeth (1970).

Research on Person's Relationship with Other

Another general factor that we said should influence Person's expectations is the nature of the relationship between Person and Other. The closer and more communal the relationship, the more Person should expect to receive help when in need and the less Person should feel that immediate repayment is necessary. Bar-Tal, Bar-Zohar, Greenberg, and Hermon (1977) asked respondents to imagine requesting a ride from a parent, sibling, friend, acquaintance, or stranger. The closer the relationship, the more respondents felt they need not repay the help received. There is indeed evidence that the exchange between two people of benefits of essentially comparable value is actually perceived as a sign that the two do not have a close relationship (Clark, 1981). In line with this, Clark and Mills (1979) found that an offer of reciprocity is resented in a *communal* compared with an *exchange* relationship, and Nadler, Bar-Tal and Drukman (Note 4) report that students living in a high-rise dormitory felt more need to reciprocate help than those living in a low-rise dormitory, in which relations were presumably more intimate. In an experiment by Shapiro (1980), though, no difference was found in felt obligation to repay help from a friend compared with help from a stranger, although subjects thought that a friend would be more likely to provide help when asked. An implication of this experiment is that the presumed cost to Other of providing help deters one from seeking help from a stranger but not from a friend.

Contingent Relationships III: Other's Ability

Analysis

The expected impact upon Person's feelings toward Other of Other's presumed ability to provide help useful to Person is more difficult to map. We can, however, predict that if Other is seen as not being able to provide useful help this may heighten otherwise negative feelings toward Other and cancel what would normally be positive feelings. Complexity arises when we consider what happens when Person needs and wants help and the only available source of such help is someone who does not really have the ability to provide adequate help. If Other attempts to help anyway, especially if Other thereby incurs great cost, Person may actually feel very grateful to Other.

Research on Other's Ability

In terms of simple variation in Other's presumed ability to provide useful help, Druian and DePaulo (1977) found that university students sought more help on a spelling test from a 19-year-old than from a 10-year-old. The most interesting situations, though, may be precisely those in which Person must make trade-offs between task-relevant benefits and self-relevant costs, as mentioned earlier. There is evidence that when two potential helpers may be presumed to be equally able to facilitate Person's task performance, help from a nonthreatening Other—a nonpeer or non-"expert"—is preferred (Nadler & Fisher, Note 5; Nadler, Fisher, Klein, & Raviv, Note 6). It also appears that in a context in which help is unsolicited, help from someone with essentially the same amount of task-relevant experience as the subject causes subjects to rate themselves as less intelligent and self-confident that does help from someone with more such experience (Fisher, Harrison, & Nadler, 1978).

Contingent Relationships IV: Visibility of Need and of Help

Analysis

Also difficult to chart is the probable effect on Person's attitudes toward Other of the presence of third parties. Obviously crucial is precisely *what* is visible to these others and how Person is likely to interpret how they will evaluate him or her on the basis of their observations. Consider the issue of self-esteem. When the task context engages Person's self-esteem, Person should respond more negatively toward Other when Other's help is visible than when it is not, whereas when Person's self-esteem is not involved, the visibility of Other's help to outside observers may be irrelevant. A forced public request for help by Person when Person's self-esteem is involved may generate especially negative feelings toward Other. On the other hand, as previously mentioned, when only Person's performance is visible to others and Other's help allows improved performance, Person may respond positively to Other—particularly when Person's self-esteem *is* involved.

What about the visibility to Other of Person's need? This is a more straightforward issue. If Person's need is visible to Other, there are two possible reasons why Other might provide help: (1) because Other sees that Person actually needs help or (2) because Other simply believes that Person probably would need help on a task of this sort. If Person's need is not visible to Other, in contrast, providing help for Person can only be the result of the fact that Other presumes Person needs help (without any evidence of this), wants something in return from Person, or wants to demonstrate that Other is more competent than Person. To the extent that the task is more important and engages Person's self-esteem, help from an Other who *cannot* see Person's need should be especially resented.

Research on Visibility

A study by DePaulo, Brown, Ishii and Fisher (1981) can be interpreted to show that in order to elicit a positive response from Person, Other must indicate that the help provided is in response to, or recognizes, Person's need. Subjects in this study performed poorly on a task graded by someone who was supposedly another subject (Other). Later, subjects received or did not receive a suggestion from Other that would presumably facilitate future performance. At the same time, subjects in both the Help and No Help conditions received a note from Other saying either "Good luck on the next task," or "I guess this is hard for you," or received no note at all. DePaulo *et al.* interpret the "good luck" note as supportive and the "this is hard" note as threatening. The second note might actually appear to subjects as a sign that Other recognizes their need while no note at all (the Neutral condition in this experiment) and the first note might appear to indicate no such recognition. If our interpretation is correct we should expect Person to respond more positively to Other when Other helps Person *and* signals recognition of Person's need than when Other helps Person without doing so. We should also expect Person to respond more negatively to Other when Other does not help Person but nevertheless indicates awareness of Other's need than when Other does not help Person and also does not necessarily appear to be aware of Person's need. In line with this, Other was evaluated most positively in the Help–Threatening condition (i.e., in what we would consider to be the Help–Need Recognition condition) and least positively in the No Help–Threatening condition (i.e., in what we would consider to be the No Help–Need Recognition condition).

The study by Shapiro (1978) is also relevant to the issue of visibility, especially Shapiro's finding that subjects in the public help-seeking condition rated their performance on what were supposedly practice trials as worse than did subjects in the private help-seeking condition, even though all had received the same feedback. Unfortunately at what point subjects evaluated their practice performance is not clear. If the confederate was present at this time for subjects in the public help-seeking condition, these results may mean that believing that someone who is immediately visible might find out about one's performance or simply making the existence of others more salient may lead to a decrement in self-esteem.

Contingent Relationships V: Request versus Offer

Analysis

The impact of being offered help versus requesting it should depend upon a myriad of factors. If Person's self-esteem *is not* engaged and Person expects help from Other, Person may respond more favorably when Other offers help than when Person requests it, whereas when Person's self-esteem *is* engaged reactions may be reversed. We can probably say in general that when Person expects help, an offer will produce a more favorable reaction than a request, whereas when help from Other is somehow threatening, help that results from a request from Person will produce a more favorable reaction toward Other than will an unsolicited offer of help from Other. But we must also consider precisely why Person must request help and to what extent Person can turn down an offer of help. If Person must request help because Other is not in a position to know whether or not Person needs help, Person should respond more positively toward Other than if Person believes Other is aware of Person's need but is just not responding to it. Furthermore, if an offer of help can be rejected without hurting Other's feelings or jeopardizing the chance of receiving help in the future, Person may respond more positively to an offer of help than if the offer must instead simply be accepted, in which case Person may well prefer soliciting help to having it unilaterally imposed.

Research on Request versus Offer

Interpretive difficulty abounds because existing research considers neither the extent to which the task engages Person's self-esteem nor the other variables just mentioned. A number of unpublished experimental studies and that by Broll *et al.* (1974) are reviewed by Gross, Wallston, and Piliavin (1979). All used tasks that were probably perceived as very difficult and thus engaged subject self-esteem. They also all encouraged the use of help and made help available on a regular basis by offering or allowing subjects to request it. In the offer condition, help was not keyed to apparent need because Other did not monitor Person's performance. Contrary to the investigators' hypotheses, all of these experiments found that subjects liked the helper more (and obtained more help) in Offer than in Request conditions. This may be because asking for help places Person under more obligation toward Other than does merely accepting proferred help (Greenberg & Saxe, 1975).

To explore further these issues in a real-world context, research reported by Piliavin and Gross (1977) and by Gross *et al.* (1979) created two conditions for mothers receiving Aid to Families with Dependent Children. In one, the mothers were visited in their homes every 3 or 4 months and, in the other, they were encouraged to phone the agency social worker whenever they needed services. Mothers requested more new *nonfinancial* services when the social worker visited periodically than when they had to phone the social worker. This manipulation did not however influence requests for new *financial* services.

As far as attitudes toward Other are concerned, the article by Piliavin and Gross (1977) summarizes responses to a questionnaire completed when contact with the social service agency terminated. Although the agency was evaluated in essentially the same way by clients offered help as by those having to request it, those in the Request condition rated their worker as having been less helpful. These results unfortunately are difficult to interpret. Comparisons between Request and Offer conditions in this field experiment are in fact comparisons between two different types of request conditions: phone requests and face-to-face requests. We do not, furthermore, know what expectations clients had, to what extent they felt the worker could honor their requests, how useful the agency's services were perceived to be, or how clients felt about asking for help.

CONCLUSION

General Observations

Although the focus of this chapter has been deliberately modest, the conclusion seems inescapable that we in fact know very little about situational or contextual factors that may trigger differential response to Other.

The fit between the studies reviewed and the rather straightforward, perhaps simple-minded, hypotheses advanced in this chapter is dubious at best. Whether or not one concludes that "we in fact know very little," though, obviously depends upon what one actually wants to "know" (and additionally upon what is believed to constitute "knowledge"). From the vantage points of both social psychological theory and real-world relevance, it seem that the goal should be to understand naturally occurring social phenomena. This implies starting with the phenomenon itself: that is, obtaining a comprehensive picture of the phenomenon in order to pinpoint (1) problematic features, (2) what needs to be explained, (3) which aspects of the phenomenon may relate to existing, broader range theoretical concerns and (4) how the dynamics of the phenomenon may be most usefully conceptualized. For social psychologists the link with theory may be central. There are at least two interrelated issues here. Do the apparent dynamics of the phenomenon reinforce or do they cast doubt upon the generalizability of existing theories? Can existing theories help explain aspects of the phenomenon, therby extending the theories' range of applicability?

Considerable observational and conceptual work must be undertaken before key variables are isolated and subjected to empirical investigation. Such work simply does not seem to have been done as far as response to help is concerned. What appears to have happened is that, for some reason, a new topic of research materialized. Without stopping to ask what help is and what forms it may take, social psychologists cast about for existing theories that might be tested within this new domain. The seemingly unreflective application of abstract theories or paradigms to concrete interchanges has meant that what should be controlled or questioned has not been: Is help on a logic problem the same "thing," after all, as additional welfare benefits? Because of this, the cumulative nature and comprehensiveness of existing research is dubious.

Suggestions for Studies

Before proliferating more laboratory studies, at least two vital preliminary questions require answers. First of all, In what contexts do different types of helping transactions occur? And, second, What factors influence whether or not a given interchange between Other and Person will be considered "help"? Related to this second question, How appropriate do Person and Other consider various responses to Other on Person's part to be under different conditions? Both questions can only be answered through survey research.

To answer the first question, a representative sample of respondents might be asked to describe in detail all instances during the past week in which help was given and received. These respondents might also be asked what, if anything, these different instances of help have in common. What, in other words, makes them *help* rather than something else? And what else might they conceivably be? A pilot study can be used here to generate a list of major types of help. If a respondent thus fails to mention a particular type of help but further questioning reveals that the respondent has indeed been involved in similar types of interchanges during the past week, the respondent can be asked why he or she does not consider such interchanges to be help. A similar procedure could be used when instances of help are mentioned that do not match findings of the pilot study. Why do these interchanges fall under the rubric of help as far as the respondent is concerned? How do they differ, if at all, from other types of helping interactions? Through such procedures we can arrive at a commonsense definition of help.

The results of this first study can provide the raw data for a study designed to answer the second question. This time respondents would be asked to categorize a number of interactions as involving or not involving help and to tell how they feel people in general and they in particular would and should respond to each. The reasons for their perceptions of help-related norms and rules could also be explored.

Through the approach just outlined, the terrain in question can be mapped, the phenomenon bounded, and hypotheses generated. Hypotheses derived in this way can be supplemented by others based upon existing theories. This seems the appropriate point at which experimental work should begin. If nothing else, research on response to help approached from this real-world direction should be more sensitive to key variables (especially variables that do not relate to existing theories or conceptual models) and to issues of external validity.

REFERENCE NOTES

1. Mikesell, R. H., & Calhoun, L. G. *Attitudes toward seeking professional help as a function of causal attribution and severity of disturbance.* Paper presented at the meeting of the Southeastern Psychological Association, Miami, Florida, April, 1971.
2. Morse, S. J., Gergen, K. J., & Reis, H. T. *Communication and responses to pay.* Unpublished manuscript, New York University, 1974.
3. Morse, S. J., & Marks, A. *Amount and utility of help received as determinants of reactions to a stimulus person responsible or not responsible for such help.* Unpublished manuscript, Massachusetts Institute of Technology, 1981.
4. Nadler, A., Bar-Tal, D., & Drukman, O. *Density does not Help: Effects of residential*

density on help-giving, help-seeking, and reciprocity behaviors. Unpublished manuscript, Tel-Aviv University, 1978.
5. Nadler, A., & Fisher, J. D. *When giving does not pay: Recipient reactions to aid as a function of donor expertise.* Unpublished manuscript, Tel-Aviv University, 1978.
6. Nadler, A., Fisher, J. D., Klein, A., & Raviv, D. *Effects of peer tutoring in a field context.* Unpublished manuscript, Tel-Aviv University, 1978.
7. White, G. M. Personal communication, February 18, 1982.

REFERENCES

Argyle, M., Furnham, A., & Graham, J. A. *Social situations.* London and New York: Cambridge University Press, 1981.

Bar-Tal, D., Bar-Zohar, Y., Greenberg, M. S., & Hermon, M. Reciprocity in the relationship between donor and recipient and between harm-doer and victim. *Sociometry,* 1977, **40,** 293-298.

Berscheid, E., & Walster, E. H. *Interpersonal attraction* (2nd ed). Reading, Massachusetts: Addison-Wesley, 1978.

Bock, P. K. *Continuities in psychological anthropology: A historical introduction.* San Francisco, California: Freeman, 1980.

Brehm, J. W. *A theory of psychological reactance.* New York: Academic Press, 1966.

Brehm, J. W., & Cole, A. H. Effect of a favor which reduces freedom. *Journal of Personality and Social Psychology,* 1966, **3,** 420-426.

Broll, L., Gross, A. E., & Piliavin, I. Effects of offered and requested help on help-seeking and reactions to being helped. *Journal of Applied Social Psychology,* 1974, **4,** 244-258.

Burtin-Vinholes, S. *Dicionário Frances-Português Portugues-Francês.* Pôrto Alegre, Brazil: Editôra Globo, 1950.

Calhoun, L. G., Dawes, A. S., & Lewis, P. M. Correlates of attitudes toward help-seeking in outpatients. *Journal of Consulting and Clinical Psychology,* 1972, **38,** 153.

Clark, M. S. Noncomparability of benefits given and received: A cue to the existence of friendship. *Social Psychology Quarterly,* 1981, **44,** 375-381.

Clark, M. S., & Mills, J. Interpersonal attraction in exchange and communal relationships. *Journal of Personality and Social Psychology,* 1979, **37,** 12-24.

DePaulo, B. M. Social psychological processes in informal help-seeking. In T. A. Wills (Ed.), *Basic processes in helping relationships.* New York: Academic Press, 1982.

DePaulo, B. M., Brown, P. L., Ishii, S., & Fisher, J. D. Help that works: The effects of aid on subsequent task performance. *Journal of Personality and Social Psychology,* 1981, **41,** 478-487.

DePaulo, B. M., & Fisher, J. D. The cost of asking for help. *Basic and Applied Social Psychology,* 1980, **1,** 23-35.

Druian, P. R., & DePaulo, B. M. Asking a child for help. *Social Behavior and Personality,* 1977, **5,** 33-39.

Ekeh, P. *Social exchange theory: The two traditions.* London: Heinemann, 1974.

Fisher, J. D., Harrison, C., & Nadler, A. Exploring the generalizability of donor–recipient similarity effects. *Personality and Social Psychology Bulletin,* 1978, **4,** 627-630.

Freeman, H. R. Reward vs. reciprocity as related to attraction. *Journal of Applied Social Psychology,* 1977, **1,** 57-66

Gergen, K. J. *The psychology of behavior exchange.* Reading, Massachusetts: Addison-Wesley, 1969.

Gergen, K. J. *The concept of self.* New York: Holt, 1971.

Gergen, K. J., Ellsworth, P., Maslach, C., & Seipel, M. Obligation, donor resources, and reactions to aid in three nations. *Journal of Personality and Social Psychology,* 1975, **3,** 390–400.

Gergen, K. J., Morse, S. J., & Gergen, M. M. Behavior exchange in cross-cultural perspective. In H. C. Triandis & R. W. Brislin (Eds.), *Handbook of cross-cultural psychology* (Vol. 5). Boston, Massachusetts: Allyn & Bacon, 1980.

Goranson, R. E., & Berkowitz, L. Reciprocity and responsibility reactions to prior help. *Journal of Personality and Social Psychology,* 1966, **3,** 227–232.

Greenberg, M. S., & Frisch, D. M. Effect of intentionality on willingness to reciprocate a favor. *Journal of Experimental Social Psychology,* 1972, **8,** 99–111.

Greenberg, M. S., & Saxe, L. Importance of locus of help initiation and type of outcome as determinants of reactions to another's help attempt. *Social Behavior and Personality,* 1975, **3,** 101–110.

Gross, A. E., Wallston, B. S., & Piliavin, I. M. Reactance, attribution, equity, and the help recipient. *Journal of Applied Social Psychology,* 1979, **9,** 297–313.

Harré, H., & Secord, P. F. *The explanation of social behaviour.* Totowa, New Jersey: Littlefield, Adams, 1973.

Homans, G. C. *Social behavior: Its elementary forms* (rev. ed.). New York: Harcourt, 1974.

Isen, A. M. Success, failure, attention and reaction to others: The warm glow of success. *Journal of Personality and Social Psychology,* 1970, **15,** 294–301.

Jones, E. E., & Davis, K. E. From acts to dispositions. In L. Berkowitz (Ed.), *Advances in experimental social psychology* (Vol. 2). New York: Academic Press, 1965.

Lau, S., & Blake, B. F. Recent research on helping behavior: An overview and bibliography. *JSAS Catalog of Selected Documents in Psychology,* 1976, **6,** 69. (Ms. No. 1289)

Lebra, T. K. *Japanese patterns of behavior.* Honolulu, Hawaii: University Press of Hawaii, 1976.

Leventhal, G. S., Allen, J., & Kemelgor, B. Reducing inequity by reallocating rewards. *Psychonomic Science,* 1969, **14,** 295–296.

Lewin, K. *Field theory in social sciences.* New York: Harper, 1951.

Lott, A. J., & Lott, B. E. The role of reward in the formation of positive interpersonal attitudes. In T. L. Huston (Ed.), *Foundations of interpersonal attraction.* New York: Academic Press, 1974.

Morse, S. J. Help, likeability, and social influence. *Journal of Applied Social Psychology,* 1972, **2,** 34–46.

Morse, S. J., & Gergen, K. J. Material aid and social attraction. *Journal of Applied Social Psychology,* 1971, **1,** 150–162.

Morse, S. J., Gergen, K. J., Peele, S., & van Ryneveld, J. Reactions to receiving expected and unexpected help from a person who violates or does not violate a norm. *Journal of Experimental Social Psychology,* 1977, **13,** 397–402.

Morse, S. J., Gruzen, J., & Reis, H. T. The nature of equity-restoration: Some approval-seeking considerations. *Journal of Experimental Social Psychology,* 1976, **12,** 1–8.

Moscovici, S. Society and theory in social psychology. In J. Israel & H. Tajfel (Eds.), *The context of social psychology: A critical assessment.* New York: Academic Press, 1972.

Nadler, A., Fisher, J. D., & Streufert, S. The donor's dilemma: Recipient's reaction to aid from friend or foe. *Journal of Applied Social Psychology,* 1974, **4,** 275–285.

Nadler, A., & Porat, I. Names do not help: Effects of anonymity and locus of need attribution on help-seeking behavior. *Personality and Social Psychology Bulletin,* 1978, **4,** 624–626.

Nadler, A., Shapira, R., & Ben-Itzhak, S. Good looks may help: Effects of helper's physical attractiveness and sex of helper on males' and females' help-seeking behavior. *Journal of Personality and Social Psychology,* 1982, 42, 90–99.

Nadler, A., Sheinberg, L., & Jaffe, Y. Coping with others by help seeking: Help seeking and receiving behaviors in male paraplegics. In C. D. Spielberger, I. G. Saronson, & N. A. Milgram (Eds.), *Stress and anxiety* (Vol. 8). Washington, D.C.: Hemisphere Publishers, 1981, pp. 375–386.

Neineth, C. Effects of free versus constrained behavior on attraction between people. *Journal of Personality and Social Psychology*, 1970, **15**, 302–311.

Neville, R., & Clarke, J. *The life and crimes of Charles Sobhraj*. London: Pan, 1979.

Pearce, P. L., & Amato, P. R. A taxonomy of helping: A multidimensional scaling analysis. *Social Psychology Quarterly*, 1980, **43**, 363–371

Piliavin, I., & Gross, A. E. The effects of separation of services and income maintenance on AFDC recipients' perceptions and use of social services: Results of a field experiment. *Social Service Review*, 1977, **9**, 389–406.

Reis, H. T. Self-presentation and distributive justice. In J. T. Tedeschi (Ed.), *Impression management theory and social psychological research*. New York: Academic Press, 1981.

Rubin, Z. *Liking and loving: An invitation to social psychology*. New York: Holt, 1973.

Schlenker, B. R. *Impression management: The self-concept, social identity, and interpersonal relations*. Monterey, California: Brooks/Cole, 1980.

Schlenker, B. R., & Leary, M. R. Social anxiety and self-presentation: A conceptualization and model. *Psychological Bulletin*, 1982, 92, 641–669.

Shapiro, E. G. Help seeking: Effects of visibility of task performance and seeking help. *Journal of Applied Social Psychology*, 1978, **8**, 163–173.

Shapiro, E. G. Is seeking help from a friend like seeking help from a stranger? *Social Psychology Quarterly*, 1980, **43**, 259–263.

Shaver, K. G. *An introduction to attribution processes*. Cambridge, Massachusetts: Winthrop, 1975.

Smithson, M. J., Amato, P. R., & Pearce, P. L. *Dimensions of helping behaviour*. Oxford: Pergamon, 1983.

Tessler, R. C., & Schwartz, S. H. Help-seeking, self-esteem, and achievement motivation: An attributional analysis. *Journal of Personality and Social Psychology*, 1972, **21**, 318–326.

Thibaut, J. W., & Kelley, H. H. *The social psychology of groups*. New York: Wiley, 1959.

Vallandro, L., & Vallandro, L. *Dicionário Inglês-Português*. Pôrto Alegre, Brazil: Editôra Globo, 1970.

Wallston, B. S. The effects of sex-role ideology, self-esteem, and expected future interactions with an audience on male help-seeking. *Sex Roles*, 1976, **2**, 353–356.

Webster's seventh new collegiate dictionary. Springfield, Massachusetts: Merriam, 1977.

White, G. M. Ambiguity and ambivalence in A'ara personality descriptors. *American Ethnologist*, 1978, **5**, 334–360.

White, G. M. Conceptual universals in interpersonal language. *American Anthropologist*, 1980, **82**, 759–781.

Wispé, L. G. Positive forms of social behavior: An overview. *Journal of Social Issues*, 1972, **28**, 1–19.

Worchel, S., & Andreoli, V. A. Attribution of causality as a means of restoring behavioral freedom. *Journal of Personality and Social Psychology*, 1974, **29**, 237–245.

Zadeh, L. A., Fu, K. S., Tanaka, K., & Shimura, M. (Eds.). *Fuzzy sets and their applications to cognitive and decision processes*. New York: Academic Press, 1975.

PART V

Summary
and Implications

CHAPTER 13

Some Thoughts about Research on Reactions to Help

Leonard Berkowitz

Several of the chapters in this interesting collection have noted that the recipients of aid often suffer a loss of self-esteem. Running the risk of such a decline in my self-regard, I have to confess that I found many of the chapters to be quite beneficial; they called my attention to a growing literature that I somehow seem to have neglected, provided me with a good deal of information about the research findings in this specific area, and stimulated a considerable amount of thought. A number of the authors have also pointed out that help recipients frequently feel obligated to reciprocate for the benefits they have received. In this spirit I would like to offer a few thoughts to the writers and readers, an outsider's observations, that might provide some return for the rewards I have gotten from these articles by broadening the range of questions that are brought to bear on this intriguing reserarch.

THE POSSIBLE ROLE OF CULTURAL INFLUENCES

It is interesting to look at the research we are now considering from the vantage point of a historian of science. Social psychologists certainly are not immune to the cultural, economic, and historical processes that affect our society generally, and we might wonder what influences have governed at least the selection of this line of investigation. Such a question is particularly apt to arise if we consider the history of our discipline. There has long been a bipolarity in the field resulting in a rough fluctuation between two kinds of research problems. One end of the continuum, we might say, reflects an *independent-variable* orientation in which interest is centered largely on a few psychological processes that can lead to a great variety of outcomes. This orientation was manifested in the 1960s by the great attention given to cognitive dissonance, in the 1970s by the focus on attribution notions, and is revealed today by the interest in cognitive processes affecting judgments and decision making. The opposite extreme has more of a concern with *dependent variables,* particular outcomes or actions. As an example, social psychological research in certain problem areas such as conformity and attitude change or aggression and helpfulness has flourished more in some years than in others. Because the former, process-focused orientation has generally had greater status in our discipline, some special circumstances are probably necessary if there is to be a widespread interest in certain classes of behaviors as dependent variables. The social unrest of the late 1960s undoubtedly contributed greatly to the attention received by the research on aggression and may even have affected the popularity of the studies of help-giving. Indeed, one can only marvel at the sharp increase in the number of investigations of help-giving since the late 1950s and early 1960s. When I conducted my first experiments on the determinants of helpfulness (in 1958 and 1959), we could count on the fingers of one hand those social psychologists who were systematically exploring this problem. There was something suspect about the topic at the time; it did not seem to be "fundamental" enough and even smacked of an overly "goody-goody" preoccupation with moralistic matters. Attitudes had to change and concerns had to develop before the field as a whole could regard helpfulness as a topic worthy of investigation.

Even a cursory survey of the articles published in *Journal of Personality and Social Psychology* in the past several years indicates that we are now in the largely independent-variable phase of the cycle. Fewer and fewer studies of social interaction are appearing and there now seems to be much less research on aggression than there was a decade or so ago. Has there been a somewhat similar decline in interest in the determinants of helpfulness? But at any rate, the present volume has also led me to wonder why attention is now being given to the possibly injurious effects of receiving help. I am not casting any innuendos when I raise this question. There is a natural and easy progression from the determinants of helpfulness to the consequences of such behavior for the help recipient. I also suspect that most of the researchers represented in this volume were attracted to the problem more by theoretical questions than the social policy implications of their findings. And yet I can not help wondering if our socially conservative times are not somehow making it easier to suggest that helpfulness can be hurtful. Do not get me wrong. I truly accept the observations reported by a number of the authors regarding the deleterious consequences of some forms of aid. Yet, this notion seems to be more acceptable these days than it would have been, I think, in the 1960s.

Whether our present sociopolitical climate has affected this thinking or not, several chapters in this volume also highlight the role of cultural influences on our research. It might be helpful to consider how the concepts we employ, the theories we favor, and even the research procedures we use can be affected by the ideas that are now afloat in our cultural surroundings. Let me start with a relatively minor matter. In their provocative chapter in this book, and in other papers as well, Brickman, Kidder, and their associates spell out four different models (or conceptions) of helping, which are based on two dimensions: the help recipient's responsibility for being in need and this individual's responsibility for his or her state of affairs in the future. Although such a categorization is a useful way of organizing our discussion of helpfulness, as the authors demonstrate, I am somewhat dubious about the merits of at least one of the category names—the *moral model* in which the persons in difficulty are assumed to be responsible for both their present plight and their future conduct. Judging from the writers' comments about this conception in several of their chapters, it seems to me that this "morality" reflects more of a traditionally Protestant than an old-line Catholic approach to the world. A generation or more ago, at least, traditional Catholics were more apt to possess a passive and fatalistic view of human troubles than their Protestant counterparts (cf. Berkowitz, 1964, pp. 24–28). It is the morality of the Protestant ethic that sees people's calamities as being their own fault in some way and it is this way of thinking that then calls on them to solve their problems by themselves. As another example of the authors' cultural blinders, in some parts of the globe a fatalistic orientation toward helping (the low–low category) may be more characteristic of orthodox Buddhists than of doctors and patients, although Brickman and his colleagues term this category the *"medical model."*

It seems to me that cultural influences are especially important in determining the extent to which social interactions are affected by equity considerations. Anthropologists tell us that even the most homogeneous societies are likely to have more than one system of ideas as to what is right or just (Nader, 1975) and, of course, notions of justice are bound to become increasingly more complex as societies become ever more heterogeneous. Testifying to some of these complications in our own society, Leventhal (1976) has noted that a variety of principles govern what is regarded as the appropriate allocation of resources. For our purposes we can simplify the discussion by contrasting equitable allocations with equal ones. Let us also define the equity—or distributive justice—principle as calling for the distribution of resources according to certain specified inputs (such as effort, intelligence, or even social status), and say that egalitarian conceptions maintain that the resources should be divided equally among the group members. Our question, then, is whether the equity value is generally dominant over the equality ideal, as some equity enthusiasts appear to suggest.

Confining ourselves to western European history (again for ease of discussion), there can be little doubt that equity notions were predominant when society was clearly structured in terms of hereditary ranks, with a king and the nobility at the top of the social order and peasants at the bottom. Feudalism obviously operated along distributive justice lines. The peasants exchanged their labor, crops, and goods for the protection provided by the lord. However, the exchange was far from equal, at least as far as the distribution of material resources was concerned, for the lord and his relatives certainly enjoyed a far better life than did the lowly serfs. This inequality was generally seen as just (although it was occasionally disputed by working class leaders, especially during the working class rebellions of the time). The nobility's rank as well as military power gave them the right to the greatest share of society's resources. Here, in relatively pure form, is the essence of the equity idea of justice: rank has its privileges. Social status was an input legitimately requiring a considerable outcome.

The passage of time has seen a change in the specification of just what inputs are socially valued and deserving of special returns. Hereditary rank has declined in importance whereas merit and ability have gained in value. Nowadays some people grumble every once in a while but there is a widespread consensus that it is right (or at least not wrong) for physicians, movie stars, and professional basketball players to receive a substantial income. Generally speaking, those who perform well in areas that are important to the group are viewed as being entitled to extraordinary benefits. Related to this notion is the still widely accepted idea that hard work should be rewarded and is deserving of special outcomes. Such a conception is, of course, closely tied to the Protestant ethic and the associated beliefs comprising the spirit of capitalism. If fewer and fewer people hold to the value of hard work these days, as many conservatives now complain, this surely must represent a still further drop in adherence to the equity principle. Moreover, as Western society increasingly questioned the view that resources *ought* to be distributed unequally because of differences in quantity or kinds of inputs, it also began to place greater value on the ideal of social equality. Some writers believe this has come about in part because the developing middle class insisted on social and political rights consistent with its economic power (cf. Sampson, 1975). From the eighteenth century on, according to this analysis, the equity principle has been increasingly challenged by notions of equality, and there even are indications that the equality ideal is now dominant in many situations. We can see some of these signs in the experimental studies of how people allocate their group's resources (Deutsch, 1975; Leventhal, 1976; Sampson, 1975). The research findings in this area agree that many persons prefer equal rather than equitable distributions of resources when they want to achieve harmonious social relations with the others in their group. Surely, people would not believe that they could promote friendship in this manner if they did not think that equality was apt to be preferred over equity. But here, too, there is an ebb and flow to what is usually desired. Attitudes and values do not remain fixed as societies alter. The moral principles that are predominant at one time may give way to other ideals as circumstances change. In my estimation, the equity concept (which maintains that certain inputs deserve greater outcomes) is especially likely to be bound by historical and cultural conditions.

All of us are subject to cultural biases, of course, and this can be seen in the research methodologies we prefer as well as in our ideas of justice or the schemas we use to organize data. Consider how different is the article by Kenneth and Mary Gergen (on "the social construction of helping relationships") from the other chapters in this book. Whereas most of the other writers embrace a logical-positivistic approach to behavioral science, at least to a considerable degree, the Gergens argue against such a research orientation. They maintain that our emphasis on objectivity is illusory. "What has been accepted [by investigators] as an event in nature," they say, "[has] no existence independent of a meaning system." Research subjects construct their own particular realities out of the events they encounter so they may not interpret the experimental manipulations in the way the investigator intended. The action the experimenter regards as helpful may not be so viewed by the subjects themselves. Thus, according to the Gergens, most studies of help and its consequences do "not deliver as promised [the] assumption that investigators are testing hypotheses about the real-world conditions giving rise to helping behavior and the conditions under which various reactions to help occur seems wholly unwarranted." From this "social-constructivist" perspective (an orientation very close to Harré's [1980] "ethogenic" approach) we should not waste our time conducting carefully controlled laboratory experiments. Instead, it supposedly would be far more profitable to investigate the accounts that people establish to explain and justify their behavior.

My guess is that only a small proportion of American social psychologists with a psychological rather than sociological background will agree with the Gergens. Our disciplinary culture has provided us with a way of thinking about research that leads us to frown on highly subjective modes of inquiry. Let me add a footnote here. A number of Marxist-oriented sociologists have insisted that capitalism's dehumanizing view of people as only objects has shaped our discipline's preference for objective methodologies. What a vast oversimplification this is! Of the European social psychologists I have met, those who are most critical of American laboratory experimentation are from capitalistic countries such as England and France, whereas young Polish social psychologists, who grew up in a communist society, are likely to have a logical-positivist orientation similar to our own. But at any rate, our culture and our experience give us a number of easy answers to the Gergens, Harré, and other critics. For one, even though these critics—along with their symbolic-interactionist bretheren in sociology—typically believe that societal influences have a major role in the development of the individual's meaning systems, we are more apt than they to assume there is a substantial degree of commonality in people's interpretations of the research procedures because of their similar socialization. Our meaning systems, our ways of thinking about the social world, surely must have a good deal in common or else society could not function. This implies that any one subject's conception of what is taking place is not necessarily unique to this person but may well be shared by the other participants. Despite the doubting Thomases, we know that quite a few laboratory results have been replicated in other, more naturalistic settings (Berkowitz & Donnerstein, 1982), and this couldn't happen unless all of the people involved imparted much the same meaning to the situation they were in. But social psychologists do not always take this commonality of meaning for granted; we frequently question our subjects, in the form of manipulation checks and in other ways, to determine just how they understood the research procedures.

At this point I must insist that I am not being inconsistent. Here, I am arguing for the validity of experimental research, which typically looks into the effects of immediate, situational factors, but I have also noted the possibility of long-term historical and cultural influences on our thoughts and values. How can the former contention be reconciled with the latter idea? To answer such a question we have to keep in mind the investigation's fundamental aim. Kruglanski (1975) has differentiated universalistic and particularistic types of inquiry, noting that they do not seek the same kinds of generalizations. Particularistic research is highly restricted in scope and asks how people will react in certain specific situations usually of applied interest. For example, how do typical consumers respond to different packages? Universalistic research, on the other hand, tentatively claims an extremely broad and even universal generality for its findings so that the subjects and research setting are seen as arbitrary samples from the surrounding world. "This means the tentative denial of interactions between the [experimental] treatment and any of the background conditions of the research," such as the populations studied and the historical context (Kruglanski, 1975, p. 105). In sum, as theoreticians and researchers we must be alert to the possibility of historical and cultural boundaries to our findings, and it is important to consider whether our results might be restricted to a particular time and place. In keeping with this notion, I suggested that the equity conception of distributive justice is especially likely to regulate the allocation of resources when the people involved subscribe to the Protestant ethic and its associated ideas. However, we need not be paralyzed by the possibility of historico-cultural limitations. If we have universalistic intentions, we can employ the working assumption that the relationships we discover among the contructs of interest to us hold around the world. It is thus appropriate to hypothesize, as Hatfield and Sprecher do, that "people [everywhere] prefer gifts that can be repaid over those that cannot." Subsequent research can then either lend force to this assumption of universality or demonstrate how the initial results are limited to particular populations and/or situations.

The position I have taken here is pertinent to Gergen's (1973) claim that most social psychological theories are primarily reflections of contemporary history because they deal mainly with acquired dispositions and these learned characteristics are apt to be modified as the culture changes. I think Gergen is probably right, to a considerable degree anyway. However, rather than give up the search for universal theories, I suggest we continue our endeavors—with some changes—tentatively assuming that our hypotheses and conceptions are valid everywhere until research shows otherwise. Nevertheless, the Gergen argument has at least one implication that investigators might want to consider. Because our theoretical generalizations might be restricted to particular times and places, we would do well to favor those lines of thought that are most apt to be universalistic in nature. Analyses based on presumably fundamental cognitive processes or (if I may be pardoned the expression) on associationistic notions are particularly likely to hold everywhere, it seems to me, and thus might be more profitable in the long run than constructs such as equity and indebtedness.

THE MULIPLE DETERMINATION
OF SOCIAL BEHAVIOR

The assumption of universality I have just been discussing is relevant to the independent-variable orientation I mentioned at the start of this chapter. As was noted then, those who adopt this approach usually try to show that the particular psychological process of interest to them influences a wide range of apparently different behaviors. In my view, this is entirely appropriate; scientists ought to search for synthesis and should ask whether their theoretical formulations can be applied to a broad range of phenomena. The difficulty, of course, is that in generalizing their favored notions they might blind themselves to the influence of other processes. The approach I have termed the "dependent-variable" perspective in social psychology is probably less susceptible to such a flaw; by focusing on a mode of conduct, such as help-giving, or a particular phenomenon, such as reactions to being aided, the investigators may be more open to the multiplicity of factors that are often in operation. Human behavior is a multisplendored thing. Most of our socially significant actions, especially those that are fairly complex in nature, are governed by a variety of processes and we would do well to recognize this complexity.

Many of the chapters in the present collection have emphasized single determinants, as is their right, but one notable exception is the article by Brickman and Kidder. Perhaps more than any of the other chapters, this paper explicitly acknowledges the multiple determination of helping. Thus, the authors begin by noting that there is more than one type of help, and they differentiate impulsive from more deliberate forms of assistance. The research literature highlights the value of such a distinction. Several studies have shown, for example, that the likelihood that aid will be given in an emergency tends to decline with the passage of time (e.g., Fellner & Marshall, 1970; Latané & Darley, 1970). It is as if many people act quickly or not at all. But help can be given deliberately as well as impulsively. Clearly, under some conditions people can be affected by long-lasting influences so that they render aid even though considerable time has passed.

Having agreed with Brickman and Kidder in this important matter, I wonder if their subsequent discussion of the determinants of helpfulness is sufficiently complete, and I briefly mention here several factors that they appear to have neglected. (If this seems too much of a digression, my hunch is that these considerations could well be relevant to the topic of special concern to this volume, reactions to the receipt of help, and I will suggest some of the possible connections as I go along. I should also note, however, that the points to be raised have a bearing on a number of the articles; the

Brickman and Kidder chapter serves only as a starting point for these observations.)

To begin, the writers identify the bystanders' empathic reaction to the person in difficulty as the principal determinant of impulsive helping. Vicariously experiencing the dependent individual's distress, the bystanders are often motivated to come to his or her assistance (Aderman & Berkowitz, 1970; Aronfreed, 1970). Nonetheless, they conceivably might also have another emotional reaction to the emergency situation that is not mediated by empathy with the victim. The mere perception of the incident might arouse them emotionally, not because they actively imagine themselves as the person in trouble—which is empathy—but because of that incident's aversive meaning for them. I could become upset at the sight of an automobile accident simply because I associate such accidents with misery and without thinking of myself as one of the victims. This emotion arousal could then serve as a fairly quick spur to some helpful behavior (Gaertner & Dovidio, 1977).

Other feelings could also affect the potential helpers' willingness to render assistance. Their mood is especially significant. A truly impressive body of evidence indicates that people who feel good for almost any reason are particularly inclined to aid those in need (e.g., Berkowitz & Connor, 1966; Holloway, Tucker, & Hornstein, 1977; Isen, Shalker, Clark, & Karp, 1978; Veitch, DeWood, & Bosko, 1977). This mood-induced helpfulness might have facilitated at least some of the reciprocity noted by a number of the authors in the present volume. That is, the subjects could have helped someone after they themselves had received assistance because the aid they had gotten put them in a pleasant mood and not because they felt indebted to someone or sought to "restore equity with the world." Being in a good mood, they might not have resisted the explicit or implicit pressure on them to aid the dependent person (Berkowitz, 1973), or they might have had the thoughts that encouraged helpfulness (Isen *et al.,* 1978). This is not to say, of course, that we never believe we are obligated to reciprocate for the favors we have received. Furthermore, I also accept the observations (reported in several of the chapters) indicating that many of us—or at least those of us with high self-esteem—want to be able to pay our benefactors back. I am suggesting only that a mood-induced willingness to be helpful should be distinguished from the desire to return good for good received. To be on the safe side, investigators should obtain direct evidence of a specific inclination to reciprocate (or to restore equity or to lessen indebtedness) and should not merely assume the operation of such an instigation.

On the other side of the same coin, those who feel bad for some reason are often less inclined to aid others in need (Weyent, 1978). Here again, a reluctance to assist Person A after one was not helped by Person B might conceivably be due, in part at least, to the bad mood created by the unpleasant state of affairs and not to a definite striving to get even with the world in general.

The point in all this is that a variety of factors can affect people's reactions to the help given them. However much we might be attached to a particular theory, we obviously have to be open-minded enough to recognize the operation of influences not specified by that conception. I will go even further: If social psychologists were as open to different ideas as they ought to be, I think they would be less susceptible to the pitfall of word magic. By this term I mean the all-too-common tendency to believe one has explained a phenomenon by attaching a label to it. If a devotee of psychoanalytic theory sees an adult act in a childish fashion, he might say this is a case of regression, and then maintains that he has adequately explained the adult's conduct. I have the impression that at least some of the contemporary references to attributions are guilty of this oversimplified thinking. Quite a few of the chapters in the present volume have noted that an individual's reaction to the help given him can depend to a considerable extent on the attributions he makes regarding his benefactor's behavior. If this book had been published a generation earlier, the writers would have expressed much the same idea by saying the recipient's reaction depended on how he *interpreted* the favor given him. When social psychologists speak of attributions nowadays, do they necessarily have more in mind than just an interpretation of what is happening? Often yes, but sometimes no. Anyway, and more important, I have wondered at times whether researchers have really explained the behavior of interest to them when they have said the action was produced by attributions. One (and only one) example can be found in the way we say that responsibility attributions affect people's readiness to help those in need. Many of us have held that people are less inclined to aid those who are seen as the cause of their own difficulty. Such a statement is unsatisfactory for two reasons: (1) it neglects the role of the dependent person's supposed *control* over the cause of his difficulty (Meyer & Mulherin, 1980; Weiner, 1980), and, more relevant, (2) nothing is said about *why* this attribution has the effect it does. In uncritically accepting the general notion that attributions affect behavior, we have stopped short of a truly satisfactory explanation of this particular phenomenon. The concept is so popular that it has inhibited our thinking about the matters to which it is applied. Another illustration can be found in the Greenberg–Westcott interpretation of the lower level of indebtedness to a friend than to a stranger. According to them, people do not feel particularly obligated to repay a friend's favors because they attribute the friend's action to an external cause (the norm calling on friends to help each other). This may sound good, but if we go beyond the simple attribution idea and look at the explanation in common sense terms it becomes somewhat less satisfactory. I do not believe that we really attribute our friends' aid to us as being due to the external pressures they feel to give us help. And moreover, would not we be disappointed if we actually thought our friends helped us only because they thought they had to? It is time for social psychology to go beyond attributions.

REFERENCES
TO NORMATIVE INFLUENCES

Normative expectations are yet another class of determinants affecting both the willingness to aid someone in need and the reactions to being helped. Many of the writers in this volume invoke norms to explain their observations—but they do not always have the same ones in mind and may also be too quick to assume that the actions of interest to them are due to the operation of these social rules. For Brickman and Kidder, Hatfield and Sprecher, and Greenberg and Westcott, the moral prescriptions call for some form of fairness, whereas Clark's conception seems to exclude considerations of fairness in dealings with friends. The former appear to be thinking of a rule prescribing fairness in the distribution of resources, whereas Clark suggests that such a fairness norm is more applicable in the exchange relationships between people who do not care for each other and is less appropriate in the communal relationships between those who want to be friends. In this latter case, friends are presumably expected to be responsive to each other's needs without regard to input–outcome calculations. The consequence, Clark maintains, is that those involved in communal relationships do not feel obligated to repay the benefits they have received from each other; any help their friends gave them was supposedly prescribed by the rules of friendship and thus does not have to be reciprocated.

There is an important issue in the difference between the equity–indebtedness formulation on one hand and the exchange–communal relationship conception on the other. I will highlight this point in terms of the way Hatfield and Sprecher attempt to reconcile their approach with Clark's notions. Basically, the former suggest that the only real difference between the exchange and communal relationship norms has to do with the time limits within which repayment ought to be made; reciprocity is expected fairly soon in exchange relationships but can be achieved much later in the dealings between those seeking to be friends. Nonetheless, Hatfield and Sprecher hold, even friends are supposed to pay each other back—sooner or later.

I suspect that there is some validity to all of these views—and that both parties have a somewhat oversimplified conception of social relationships. Consider these different kinds of "favors" or "benefits": (1) the Adamses invite the Browns to a dinner party; (2) Joe is seriously ill and in need of a blood transfusion, but has a rare blood type. Jim has the same blood type and rushes to the hospital to provide the required blood; (3) Florence, a professor at Midwestern U., has received an attractive offer from another university. Her colleague, Susan, works hard to convince the Midwestern U. administration to offer Florence a substantial raise in pay if she would remain at Midwestern. In all three situations someone has benefited another, but are there the same expectations as to whether the favors are to be returned? My guess is that the beneficiaries in the first two examples would feel a greater obligation to pay the other back in some way, and within a reasonable time, if the benefactor were a casual acquaintance rather than a close friend. But would Professor Florence have the same greater inclination to reciprocate if Professor Susan were an acquaintance and not a close friend? For me, these three cases have a number of implications.

First of all, as far as I can tell, only Clark's formulation would suggest that the second situation, dealing with the blood donation, should be differentiated from the other two incidents. Someone was benefited in the first and third examples (and thus the Hatfield–Sprecher and Greenberg–Westcott analyses should apply), but *aid* was not given in Clark's sense of the term (i.e., meeting a specific need). It is not clear, then, what her line of reasoning would say about the incident mentioned last involving Susan's effort in behalf of Florence. (I doubt that Florence would feel especially indebted to her colleague because she probably would believe her raise was deserved under the circumstances.) At any rate, all of this is intended to show that the equity–indebtedness formulations and even Clark's analysis must offer distinctions that do not now exist; all benefits given to others are not alike. We can go even further and suggest that a comprehensive account of how people react to the receipt of aid has to determine just what kinds of norms are evoked in different types of situations. The rules regarding reciprocity in one class of situations may not be the same as the norms operating in other settings. In this regard, the investigators would do well to consider the research by Argyle, Harré, and others in England into situation-specific rules.

But now let me raise another question: Are we sure that all of the benefactors in the three examples acted because of social norms? Jim, the blood donor in the second example, might have felt obligated to help Joe, especially if he were a friend, but did Susan believe that she had the same kind of obligation to obtain a substantial and extraordinary raise for her friend Florence? I do not think so. She more simply might have wanted to avoid a personal loss—the loss of the pleasure her friend provided or a reduction in her department's professional prestige. For that matter, Jim's blood donation could also have been prompted by nonnormative concerns, such as empathy. We might be quicker to aid a friend than a stranger at times because we are more likely to empathize with the friend's distress and not because of the expectations we believe others have for us.

I am not questioning the existence or importance of social norms in raising these alternative possibilities (although I do believe, along with Schwartz [1977], that it may be better at times to think of norms as personal ideals rather than as society-wide expectations). Rather, I am trying to note only that we may be too ready to invoke this concept in explaining both helpfulness and reactions to aid and, thus, may be blinding ourselves to the operation of other influences. Latané and Darley (1970) probably went too far in challenging the role of social norms in the provision of help, but they made a valid point: We can almost always refer to some social ideal to justify or explain an action after the fact. It is easy to say a behavior was motivated by normative pressures, but it is harder—and better—to show that they actually did control the given action. Indeed, I sometimes suspect that behavioral scientists employ normative explanations of behavior because they want to maintain the rationality and purposiveness of human conduct and do not like to think of human behavior as governed by nonthoughtful, involuntary processes. We do reason and even frequently strive to do what is socially and morally proper. But we sometimes also act mindlessly, as Langer has recently discovered after decades of research by associationist theorists. These relatively involuntary reactions can affect our willingness to assist others and even our responses to the help given us. As I said before, a good many different processes regulate human behavior.

ON THE ROLE OF THE SELF-CONCEPT

Without backtracking at all on my contention that we must recognize the multiple determination of social behavior, I suspect that the interpretations of help reactions based on the self-concept will prove to have a greater generality over time and place than the other formulations summarized in this volume. My hunch in this regard is based partly on the supposition that humans everywhere possess a self-concept that they seek to protect or even to enhance (although their cultures may differ in the approved ways of doing this), and partly on suggestive research findings.

For one thing, the research results obtained by Fisher, Nadler, De-Paulo and others seem to me to be especially convincing. Taken together, they form a nice, coherent package pointing to the sometimes self-esteem-damaging consequences of the provision of help. None of the other formulations can do as well as this conception in accounting for the broad spectrum of observations reported by Fisher, Nadler, and DePaulo, or so it appears to me. But more than dealing nicely with these particular findings obtained in contemporary Western society, self-concept-oriented analyses might also apply to a wide variety of people around the world.

Cognitive dissonance research is suggestive here. Wicklund and Brehm have noted, in private conversations with me as well as in their writings (e.g., 1976), that a number of the phenomena initially documented by dissonance theorists in the United States have also been reported by researchers in other countries. If we view dissonance reactions as attempts to protect one's self-concept, as I prefer to do, this generality indicates that middle-class American university students are by no means the only people who try to preserve their pride. By extrapolation, then, we could guess that a good many persons, in the United States, Israel, and elsewhere, might be adversely affected by the receipt of help. Then too, some dissonance research even suggests that the desire to protect one's self-concept may develop fairly early in life before there is a considerable amount of cultural learning. Eisenberg's review in this book points to a somewhat later development than I am proposing; she believes that children younger than 7 or 8 years of age are unlikely to be bothered by the self-threatening aspects of aid. This may be, but I wonder if self-concerns do not arise in many youngsters well before 7 years of age. Recall the studies by Aronson and Carlsmith (1963) and Freedman (1965) dealing with nursery school children's self-justifications in response to external threats. The 4-year-olds in these experiments evidently tried to enhance their self-concepts by justifying their compliance to minimal threats. If children this young are concerned with their pride, they might also be affected by the threats to their self-esteem that are inherent in the assistance they receive from others.

I do not know how this particular issue will be resolved. However, I do firmly believe that the research summarized in this book deals with highly significant matters. It is obviously important for social psychologists, as well as everyone concerned with social policies, to understand the effects on people of the help they are given. But more than this, the research touches on a whole host of issues going well beyond this immediate topic. For example, there is little doubt in my mind that these investigations will teach us a great deal about the formation and operation of the self-concept. The social psychologists represented in this volume are to be congratulated for choosing this exciting, challenging, and important problem for study.

REFERENCES

Aderman, D., and Berkowitz, L. Observational set, empathy and helping. *Journal of Personality and Social Psychology,* 1970, **14,** 141–148.

Aronfreed, J. The socialization of altruistic and sympathetic behavior: Some theoretical and experimental analyses. In J. Macaulay and L. Berkowitz (Eds.), *Altruism and helping behavior.* New York: Academic Press, 1970. Pp. 103–126.

Aronson, E., and Carlsmith, J. M. The effect of the severity of threat on the devaluation of forbidden behavior. *Journal of Abnormal and Social Psychology,* 1963, **66,** 584–588.

Berkowitz, L. *The development of motives and values in the child.* New York: Basic Books, 1964.

Berkowitz, L. Reactance and the unwillingness to help. *Psychological Bulletin,* 1973, **79,** 310–317.

Berkowitz, L. and Connor, W. H. Success, failure and social responsibility. *Journal of Personality and Social Psychology,* 1966, **4,** 664–669.

Berkowitz, L., and Donnerstein, E. External validity is more than skin deep: Some answers to criticisms of laboratory experiments. *American Psychologist,* 1982, **37,** 245–257.

Deutsch, M. Equity, equality and need: What determines which value will be used as the basis of distributive justice? *Journal of Social Issues,* 1975, **31,** 137–150.

Fellner, C. H., and Marshall, J. R. Kidney donors. In J. Macaulay and L. Berkowitz (Eds.), *Altruism and helping behavior.* New York: Academic Press, 1970. Pp. 269–281.

Freedman, J. L. Long-term behavioral effects of cognitive dissonance. *Journal of Experimental Social Psychology,* 1965, **1,** 145–155.

Gaertner, S. L. and Dovidio, J. F. The subtlety of white racism, arousal and helping behavior. *Journal of Personality and Social Psychology,* 1977, **35,** 691–707.

Gergen, K. J. Social psychology as history. *Journal of Personality and Social Psychology,* 1973, **26,** 309–320.

Harré, R. Making social psychology scientific. In R. Gilmour and S. Duck (Eds.), *The development of social psychology.* New York: Academic Press, 1980.

Holloway, S., Tucker, L., and Hornstein, H. A. The effects of social and nonsocial information on interpersonal behavior of males: The news makes news. *Journal of Personality and Social Psychology,* 1977, **35,** 514–522.

Isen, A. M., Shalker, T. E., Clark, M., and Karp, L. Affect, accessibility of material in memory, and behavior: A cognitive loop? *Journal of Personality and Social Psychology,* 1978, **36,** 1–12.

Kruglanski, A. W. The human subject in the psychology experiments: Fact and artifact. In L. Berkowitz (Ed.), *Advances in experimental social psychology* (Vol. 8). New York: Academic Press, 1975. Pp. 101–147.

Latané, B., and Darley, J. M. *The unresponsive bystander: Why doesn't he help?* New York: Appleton, 1970.

Leventhal, G. S. The distribution of rewards and resources in groups and organizations. In L. Berkowitz and E. Walster (Eds.), *Advances in experimental social psychology* (Vol. 9): *Equity theory.* New York: Academic Press, 1976.

Meyer, J. P., and Mulherin, A. From attribution to helping: An analysis of the mediating effects of affect and expectancy. *Journal of Personality and Social Psychology,* 1980, **39,** 201–210.

Nader, L. Forums for justice: A cross-cultural perspective. *Journal of Social Issues,* 1975, **31,** 151–170.

Sampson, E. E. On justice as equality. *Journal of Social Issues,* 1975, **31,** 45–64.

Schwartz, S. H. Normative influences on altruism. In L. Berkowitz (Ed.), *Advances in Experimental Social Psychology* (Vol. 10). New York: Academic Press, 1977.

Veitch, R., DeWood, R., and Bosko, K. Radio news broadcasts: Their effects on interpersonal helping. *Sociometry,* 1977, **40,** 383–386.

Weimer, B. A cognitive (attribution)–emotion–action model of motivated behavior: An analysis of judgments of help-giving. *Journal of Personality and Social Psychology,* 1980, **39,** 186–200.

Weyant, J. M. Effects of mood states, costs, and benefits on helping. *Journal of Personality and Social Psychology,* 1978, **36,** 1169–1176.

Author Index

Numbers in italics show the page on which the complete reference is listed.

A

Abramson, L. Y., 252, 254, 260, 268, *276*
Adams, J. S., 8, *13,* 28, *44,* 52, 53, *80,* 115, 117, *135, 136*
Aderman, D., 343, *349*
Ainsworth, M. D. S., 200, *218*
Albrecht, S. L., 127, *136*
Alesseio, J. C., 115, *136*
Alinsky, S. D., 33, 42, *44*
Alkire, A. A., 258, *276*
Allen, J., 53, *83,* 312, *331*
Allen, V. L., 32, *44, 45,* 224, *247,* 275, *276*

Altman, A., 78, *83,* 144, *162,* 173, 174, 175, 183, *187,* 226, 242, *249,* 254, *278*
Amato, P. R., 306, 311, *332*
Ames, R., 231, 232, *248*
Anderson, R. B., 127, *140*
Andreas, C. R., 59, 61, 69, *80*
Andreoli, V. A., 57, 58, 61, 64, *84,* 100, *112,* 323, *332*
Anscombe, G. E. M., 146, *161*
Antaki, C., 147, *161*
Archer, R., 57, *84*
Argyle, M., 312, 316, *330*
Aronfreed, J., 127, *136,* 343, *349*

351

Subject Index